War and Conflict in the Middle East and North Africa

War and Conflict in the Middle East and North Africa

ARIEL I. AHRAM

polity

First published in 2020 by Polity Press

Polity Press
65 Bridge Street
Cambridge CB2 1UR, UK

Polity Press
101 Station Landing
Suite 300
Medford, MA 02155, USA

ISBN-13: 978-1-5095-3281-0
ISBN-13: 978-1-5095-3282-7 (pb)

A catalogue record for this book is available from the British Library.

Library of Congress Cataloging-in-Publication Data
Names: Ahram, Ariel I. (Ariel Ira), 1979- author.
Title: War and conflict in the Middle East and North Africa / Ariel I
    Ahram.
Description: Cambridge, UK ; Medford, MA : Polity, 2020. | Includes
    bibliographical references and index. | Summary: "A conceptually and
    empirically rich introduction to war and conflict in the MENA"–
    Provided by publisher.
Identifiers: LCCN 2020002545 (print) | LCCN 2020002546 (ebook) | ISBN
    9781509532810 (hardback) | ISBN 9781509532827 (paperback) | ISBN
    9781509532841 (epub)
Subjects: LCSH: Petroleum–Political aspects–Middle East. |
    Petroleum–Political aspects–Africa, North. | Geopolitics–Middle East.
    | Geopolitics–Africa, North. | Civil war–Middle East. | Civil
    war–Africa, North. | Peace-building–Middle East. |
    Peace-building–Africa, North. | Middle East–History–20th century. |
    Middle East–History–21st century. | Africa, North–History–20th
    century. | Africa, North–History–21st century. | Middle East–Ethnic
    relations. | Africa, North–Ethnic relations.
Classification: LCC DS62.8 .A375 2020 (print) | LCC DS62.8 (ebook) | DDC
    355/.033056–dc23
LC record available at https://lccn.loc.gov/2020002545
LC ebook record available at https://lccn.loc.gov/2020002546

Typeset in 10 on 13 pt Swift by
Servis Filmsetting Ltd, Stockport, Cheshire
Printed and bound in Great Britain by TJ International Limited

For further information on Polity, visit our website: politybooks.com

Contents

Tables and Figures

Tables

Figures

Abbreviations

AKP	Justice and Development Party
AQI	al-Qaeda in Iraq
CBL	Central Bank of Libya
FLN	National Liberation Front
FSA	Free Syrian Army
GNA	Government of National Accord
GNC	General National Council
GTD	Global Terrorism Database
HoR	House of Representatives
IBC	Iraqi Body Count
ICRC	International Committee of the Red Cross
IRGC	Islamic Revolutionary Guard Corps
IS	Islamic State
JAN	Jabhat al-Nusra
JCPOA	Joint Comprehensive Plan of Action
KRG	Kurdistan Regional Government
LNA	Libyan National Army
LNOC	Libyan National Oil Company
MENA	Middle East and North Africa
MNF	Multinational Force in Lebanon
MSF	Doctors without Borders
NDC	National Dialog Conference
NFZ	no-fly zone
OECD	Organization for Economic Cooperation and Development
OPEC	Organization of Petroleum Exporting Countries
P–A	principal–agent
PA	Palestinian Authority
PKK	Kurdistan Workers' Party
PLO	Palestine Liberation Organization
PMCs	private military contractors
PYD	Democratic Union Party
PRIO	Peace Research Institute Oslo
R2P	responsibility-to-protect
RMA	revolution in military affairs

SANG	Saudi Arabian National Guard
SDF	Syrian Democratic Forces
SNC	Syrian National Council
STC	Southern Transitional Council
TNC	Transitional National Council
UAE	United Arab Emirates
UCDP	Uppsala Conflict Data Program
UNEF	UN Emergency Force
UNFIL	UN Interim Force in Lebanon
UNTSO	UN Truce Supervision Organization
VDCS	Violations Documentation Center in Syria

Acknowledgments

There are, as always, too many people to thank. Louise Knight and Inès Boxman at Polity have been excellent stewards of the book since its inception. I benefited from the insights and critiques of my colleagues at the Virginia Tech School of Public and International Affairs, especially Joel Peters, Giselle Datz, Chad Levinson, Gerard Toal, and Mehrzad Boroujerdi. Bruce Pencek at the Virginia Tech library provided amazing support on issues of data collection and analysis. The Virginia Tech Statistical Application and Innovation Group helped with organizing quantitative data. I also received financial support from Virginia Tech's Institute for Society, Culture, and the Environment. My work was inspired and informed by a number of inquisitive and tenacious graduate students, including Greg Kruczek, Gabi Mitchell, Nada al-Wadi, Jeanette Ruiz, Sezaneh Seymour, Joe Kushner, Joe Karle, Sayyed Ghanem, Mamoun Sulfab, and Pishtiwan Jalal. Crucial advice came from Boaz Atzili, Nadwa al-Dawsari, Stacey Philbrick Yadav, Mara Revkin, Nabil al-Tikriti, Raslan Ibrahim, Jonathan Wyrtzen, Lisa Anderson, Ellen Lust, Avishalom Rubin, Gabe Rubin, Jalel Harchaoui, Mohammad Tabaar, Marc Lynch, Kenneth Pollack, David Patel, Dan Byman, Steve Heydemann, Alexandra Stark, Daniel Neep, Sara Goodman, and Wendy Pearlman. Much of the writing of this book overlapped with my collaboration with Ranj Alaaldin on the Proxy Wars Project, funded by the Carnegie Corporation of New York. From halfway around the globe, Ranj was an important sounding board for many of the ideas developed in this volume. I am grateful to Hillary Wiesner at Carnegie for her confidence and support. Rachel Templer assisted with editing. Hers were often the first pair of eyes to read the manuscript. I would never have begun – much less finished – this book if not for my fortuitous friendship with Paul D. Williams and our grim mutual interests.

Finally, I thank my family for their love and care. My mother, Judi, was a constant source of support. My wife, Marni, and daughters, Matilda and Leonie, all played a role they will never know. I hope, as always, that this book contributes to a good they can inherit.

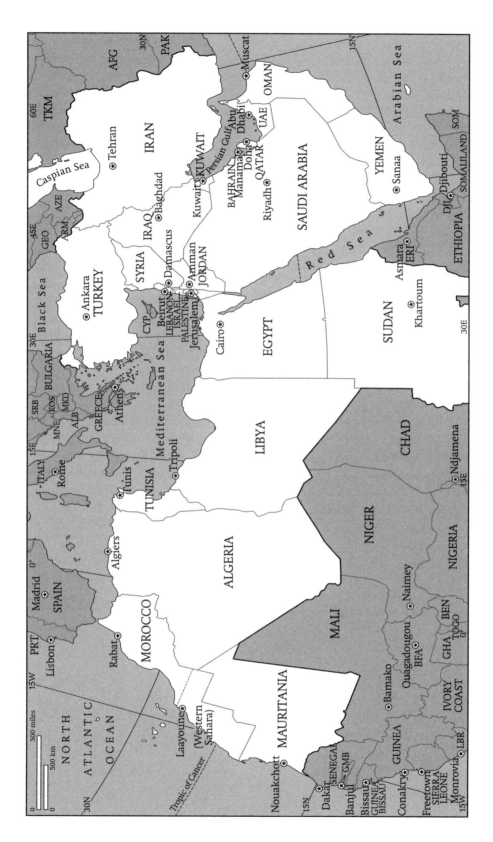

Introduction

Iraq. Palestine. Libya. Yemen. Syria. Today these words denote not just countries, but also brutal, interminable, or recurrent wars. News reports of massacres, bombings, assassinations, and airstrikes in the Middle East and North Africa (MENA) have become so frequent that some are desensitized to the bloodshed. But this violence is not far away. Weapons and troops dispatched from the West are deeply involved in the fighting. At the same time, the threat of foreign terrorism unleashed in cities like New York, London, Brussels, Paris, or elsewhere has become a major security concern.

Beyond the moral and political problems, war and violence in MENA pose an analytic puzzle. Scholars of international relations have described a general decline in war and lethal violence, although the causes and even moment of the beginning of the decline remain in some dispute.[1] MENA stands out as the anomalous outlier. The researchers at the Stockholm International Peace Research Institute diagnose MENA as suffering "chronic insecurity and persistent susceptibility to armed conflict" at the heart of contemporary global security concerns.[2] A former senior US official finds MENA "more combustible than ever."[3]

This exception has elicited a number of exceptional explanations. Some focus on geopolitics and the destabilizing impact of outside powers. This approach, typically anchored in realist theories of international relations, argues that the balances of power and threat amongst countries is the primary determinant of war. Outside interventions create regional instability and precipitate conflict. This approach has proven useful in explaining the region's interstate rivalries and conflicts, including the Arab–Israeli wars. Yet geopolitical explanations tend to falter when it comes to the region's myriad internal wars. They are also mute as to the larger questions of war's social ramifications and the ability of regional actors to make their own political and military designs.

Some analyses focus on the region's natural resources, particularly oil. Economics – or, more crassly, greed – drives war. The region's surfeit of oil and gas is a kind of attractive nuisance. This abundance of wealth elicits outside intervention that creates further destabilization. It also empowers autocratic regimes to repress internal enemies and combat external ones. Again, this type of explanation has purchase on certain cases, but leaves

1

important questions unanswered. It says little about the Arab–Israeli wars, fought mainly by energy-poor countries. It also misses some of the important mechanisms by which oil affects regional politics and indirectly contributes to the propensities for violence.

A third common and problematic strand of explanation focuses on the clashes between the region's ethno-sectarian communities. Identity is undeniably important in MENA's politics, but no more so than in politics in any other region. Emphasizing specific proclivities for violence among ethno-sectarian groups verges on cultural determinism or outright racism. Worse yet, such arguments are empirically dubious. If identities are static and hard-wired, conflict should be constant and perpetual, not fluctuating. While there are many conflicts in the region, much of the violence occurs within ethno-sectarian groups, rather than between them. Moreover, while political violence is common, it is by no means incessant. To explain ethnic war, we must also be able to account for periods of peace and cooperation. In sum, while identities matter for conflicts, specific social and political conditions must also be present to activate and guide violence. The enactment of violence often solidifies identities, not the other way around.

This book takes a socio-political approach to the causes and consequences of war. The core premise is that war is socially constructed and socially constrained. As sociologists Miguel Centeno and Elaine Enriquez put it, war is a behavior that reflects "who we are, what we believe in, and how we live together."[4] War differs from other kinds of violence in scale and complexity. It requires unique and intensive organization and institutions. There are no armies of one. So-called "lone wolves" are a myth. Wars are fought by relatively large and distinguishable groups for political ends. But war also transforms the institutions and groups that it touches. Increasingly, the field of security studies seeks to consider and measure the destructive impact of war. Wars, especially civil wars, are often deemed a kind of development in reverse, with long-lasting and dire effects on life expectancy, educational levels, and economic performance.[5] But war has had constructive social effects as well. It shapes culture, alters economic relationships, and spurs technological and commercial innovations. One of the most important impacts, and a key theme of the book, is how war changes states and societies. In some accounts, the very creation of states and their positioning as cornerstones of politi-cal order comes as an ancillary externality or side-effect of the conduct of warfare.[6]

The first aim of the book is to probe the notion that MENA is exception-ally violent. To do this, it disaggregates the war in the region by frequency, form, and magnitude. Interstate wars, civil wars, and insurgencies are each conducted and organized differently. The intervention of outside powers com-plicates the picture further. Taking a cue from theories of human security, this book concentrates on two questions that are often overlooked: *who fights and who dies?* The modes of conflict have shifted through the region's history. Looking more closely and self-consciously at episodes of violence dispels the widely held view that MENA suffers a singular predilection for war. The violence in MENA departs from global trends in certain characteristics and dimensions, while in other respects it follows or even sets patterns that have become the worldwide norm.

Secondly, the book traces the connection between the progress of warfighting and processes of state formation in MENA, thus emphasizing the transformative role of war and conflict. The state, as German sociologist Max Weber famously put it in 1919, is a political entity that "successfully claims the monopoly over the legitimate use of force within a given territory." States are in a unique and paradoxical position when it comes to war and conflict. On the one hand, well-functioning states are important guarantors of human security and world peace. On the other hand, states are also the main instigators and organizers of war.[7] States face challengers within and outside their territory. Michael Mann, in a contemporary gloss on Weber, points out that most historical states "have not possessed a monopoly of organized military force and many have not even claimed it."[8] Economist Douglass North and his collaborators point out that states have a "comparative advantage in violence" – but states do not exclusively control force.[9] The contest between states and their challengers is a critical social process that defines the frequency, form, and magnitude of war and conflict. Periods of state breakdown are often associated with intense and expansive violence.

Thirdly, the book aims to elucidate specific "conflict traps" in MENA. Conflict traps are social, economic, and political conditions that make war and conflict enduring features of regional politics. Understanding conflict in this way entails revisiting some of the oft-cited causes of conflict. Geopolitics, resources, and identity conflict affect the process of state formation and become channels for consolidating political and economic inequalities. These inequalities, in turn, help embed war and violence as a recurrent feature in regional affairs. This understanding also helps further explain the persistence of certain forms of conflict as well as zones of peace.

Which MENA?

In an influential critique of scholarship about the Eastern (i.e., Oriental) world, literary scholar Edward Said noted how "[f]rom the beginning of Western speculation about the Orient, the one thing the Orient could not do was to represent itself. Evidence of the Orient was credible only after it had passed through and been made firm by the refining fire of the Orientalist's work."[10] Scholarship resorted to binary distinctions between the East and West, which explicitly and implicitly overlaid normative categories of normal versus exotic, free versus subordinate, "us" versus "them." This cultural tendency reinforced the drive for political and economic domination.

Heeding this warning, it is important to stress that the terms "Middle East" and "MENA" are neither indigenous nor inevitable. Rather, they are exonyms, terms applied by foreigners to describe an area they found strange and distant. Understanding the origins of this terminology is important for grasping some of the biggest drivers of political development and conflict. British and American officials coined the term "Middle East" around the turn of the twentieth century. It roughly denoted the lands between the Mediterranean Sea and Indian Ocean, comprised of the Levant, Arabian Peninsula, Iran, and Central Asia. Middle East replaced the older term "Near East," which was often used to describe Christian missionary activities in and around the Holy Land. Most of the Middle East was under the rule of the Ottoman and Iranian empires, two of the great Muslim empires of the early modern era. This was a space that European powers saw as a target for subordination. North Africa, at this time, was a different story. Morocco, Algeria, Tunisia, Libya, and Egypt were already being transformed into European colonies by the end of the 1800s. European powers thus treated this area, referred to as the Maghreb ("the west") in Arabic, as a separate region. Only in the mid-twentieth century did the unwieldy conjunction "Middle East and North Africa" became common.[11]

In its most basic sense, then, the term "MENA" reflects an imperial outlook that the people of the region do not share. Those living in Rabat, Cairo, or Tehran do not naturally think of themselves as "east" of anything; their politics and their territories deserve center stage. Although today the terms "Middle East" and its adjuncts are common in regional discourse, other conceptual terminology is available.[12] Indigenous terms like "Arab world" (al-'alam al-'arabi) or "Domain of Islam" (dar al-Islam) suggest different ideas about the origins of regional unity and shared regional destiny. Historian Nikki Keddie pointed out that the idea of "the Muslim world is too unwieldy a unit for most ordinary mortal scholars to deal with."[13] Nonetheless, she stressed, it must be remembered that this is the unit with which many inhabitants of the Middle East historically self-identified. Invocations of Islamic unity continue to the present day. On the other hand, when politicians or pundits in the region describe their country as "Western," they are often asserting their superiority over otherwise "eastern" neighbors. Regional terminology comes laden with particular historical and normative connotations.[14]

For the purposes of this book, MENA stretches roughly from the Atlantic coast and the Atlas mountains eastward across the southern edge of the Mediterranean to the Levant, the Arabian Peninsula, and the Persian Gulf littoral region. It includes the following countries: Algeria, Bahrain, Egypt, Iran, Iraq, Israel, Jordan, Kuwait, Lebanon, Libya, Mauritania, Morocco, Oman, Palestine, Qatar, Saudi Arabia, Syria, Tunisia, the United Arab Emirates (UAE), and Yemen. This agglomeration of countries more or less mirrors the administrative arrangement used in the regional directorates of the United Nation and World Bank. Like many regional delineations, this is a plainly imperfect sense of geographic, historical, and cultural proximity and homogeneity.[15]

About 436 million people inhabit the twenty MENA countries, comprising a little more than five percent of the world's population. Most of these people are Arabic-speakers and Sunni Muslim, although with a variety of dialects and forms of religious practices. Iran, one of the most populous MENA countries, by contrast, is overwhelmingly Shi'ite Muslim and Persian-speaking. Israel has a Jewish majority. Although small in population, Israel plays an outsized military and political role in the region. There are sizable Christian minorities in Egypt, Syria, Palestine, Iraq, and especially Lebanon, which have played significant roles in regional politics as well.

The region is also economically diverse. The most populous MENA countries, namely Iran, Egypt, Algeria, Iraq, Syria, and Tunisia, all fit within the broad bracket of the world's middle-income states. They are, in this sense, not nearly as well off as those of Western Europe or the United States, but significantly richer than some of the poorest regions of the world, like sub-Saharan Africa. In contrast, Qatar, Kuwait, Saudi Arabia, Bahrain, and the UAE have some of the highest per capita wealth in the world. These economies and the political systems that emerged from them are famously dependent on oil and gas revenues. Israel, a member of the Organization for Economic Cooperation and Development (OECD), is rich for another reason: it has an advanced industrial and service economy derived from high tech. At the other end of the spectrum, Yemen is among the world's poorest countries. According to World Bank estimates, in 2005 nearly 10 percent of Yemenis lived below the international poverty line (roughly $1.90 per day). The situation has gotten much worse through the wars of the 2010s. We shall see later on how these cultural and economic features influence war and conflict in the region.

Why MENA?

War occupies a peculiar place in both popular and scholarly discussions of MENA. Certainly, wars are often and repeatedly remarked upon. There are hundreds of texts written about individual wars or enduring conflicts such as the Arab–Israeli wars. There is a burgeoning literature on the more recent civil wars and regional conflicts featuring, among others, the United States, Russia, Iran, Saudi Arabia, the UAE, Turkey, Libya, Yemen, Iraq, Syria, and a host of non-state belligerents.[16] Despite this specificity, though, war as a general phenomenon remains an under-explored and under-theorized feature of MENA's politics. War stands as the elephant in the room in major textbooks on MENA's international relations. They skirt the burning question of why

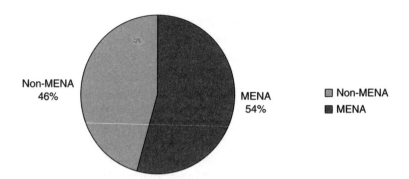

Figure 0.1 MENA's share of global battle deaths in 2017
Source: Peace Research Institute Oslo/Uppsala Conflict Data Project, data available at *https://www.prio.org/Data/Armed-Conflict/UCDP-PRIO/*; Nils Petter Gleditsch et al., "Armed Conflict 1946–2001: A New Dataset," *Journal of Peace Research* 39, no. 5 (2002): 615–37.

violent conflict is such a prominent and durable feature in MENA's regional affairs and how such violence affects the region socially and politically.[17]

There are a number of reasons why students and scholars should approach the question of conflict and war in MENA. One of the main reasons – and the primary purpose of this book – is analytical. MENA seems to be outside the norm of global peace and stability. We can make this case, albeit anecdotally, by looking at one recent year as an example. According to researchers at the Peace Research Institute Oslo (PRIO) and Uppsala University's Conflict Data Program (UCDP), premier organizations involved in collecting data on armed conflict, there were forty-nine wars going on around the world in 2017 which claimed a total of about 69,000 lives through battle deaths (battle deaths included both civilians and fighters killed as a result of direct combat). Of these, nine of the wars and 37,500 of the battle deaths occurred in MENA, a region which comprises only one-twentieth of the world's population, as shown in Figure 0.1. Armed with these figures, it is perhaps natural to presume that MENA suffers a unique pathology, a proclivity to war that spares other, more fortunate, regions.

This book is skeptical about the proposition that there is a unique conflict proneness in MENA, but takes seriously the charge of explaining the factors that seem to make war so frequent in the region. Overall, the book applies the same techniques and approaches to explain conflict in MENA as used in any other part of the world. As discussed later on, a "snapshot" look at cross-national statistics like these can be misleading. Data accuracy is always challenging. Moreover, a focus on battle deaths alone leaves out the impact of war on civilian infrastructure, such as the destruction of hospitals and water treatment facilities, which can lead to further deaths from disease or starvation.[18]

A second reason to examine war and conflict in MENA is to consider their effects. These statistics on battle deaths and war frequency also do not account for the "long tail" of conflict, its impact on political and economic development. On one hand, MENA's wars have brought down governments, ruined economies, fractured families, and killed people. On the other hand, wars have also spurred political and economic innovation, catalyzed social transformation, and fostered new senses of national belonging.[19] Addressing both the destructive and productive aspects of war in MENA is critical. The sheer variety and profligacy of violence in MENA can yield important insights into the nature of war, conflict, and political order. Twenty years ago, political scientist Steven Heydemann put forth an ambitious agenda to study the interaction between war and social change in the region:

> [W]e know relatively little about how states and societies in the Middle East have been shaped and reshaped by their intensive and prolonged exposure to and participation in war making and war preparation, often conducted by regimes that have embraced militarization as an everyday tool of governance as much as (if not more than) a means to ensure national security.[20]

A number of specialized and country-specific studies have answered this call.[21] Still, most generalized accounts of the region neglect war's role as a catalyst of social change.

A third reason to study conflict and war in MENA is normative. Social science cannot be morally disinterested; it is at its best when it aims to improve the condition of the world.[22] The scale of human suffering in MENA demands at least the effort to understand what perpetuates and intensifies these conflicts. Western powers often view MENA as vital to their strategic and economic interests. These powers have had a considerable impact on the war and conflict in MENA, sometimes for peace, sometimes for further war. Citizens of the United States, European countries, or other Western powers have specific responsibilities to examine the policies of their governments.

Still, the book does not offer policy prescriptions or lay blame on any specific actor. It is not inherently pacifist in nature. Yet it attempts to explain outcomes in a way that shows what might – and might not – be possible to avert or mitigate future war.

How to Read This Book

This book is intended for students of security studies and Middle East area studies. It explores key thematic issues of war and conflict in MENA using a number of comparative strategies. It is not a comprehensive military history of the region. Certain conflicts get more attention than others. The conflict in Western Sahara, for instance, is mentioned only a few times. The choice to focus on particular episodes of conflict and war is intended to illustrate themes and concepts using historical references that are likely to be familiar to most readers. They are not intended to downplay the importance of any particular conflict. For sourcing, the book largely relies on secondary materials published in English. This is deliberate, in the hopes of encouraging students to use the notes and bibliography for further research. In addition to this narrative element, at numerous points in the book there are graphs and tables that present longitudinal or cross-case comparative information. Again, this is deliberate, intended to demonstrate the value of examining cases of war and violence both intra-regionally within MENA and as part of larger worldwide trends.

Part I of the book sketches the context of conflict and war in the region, testing out the proposition that MENA is exceptionally prone to war. Chapter 1 analyzes different attempts to count and measure the frequency, type, and magnitude of wars in MENA over the last century. It highlights the way MENA diverges from certain global trends and follows others. It highlights the diverse forms of conflict within the region. Chapter 2 provides a conceptual and historical sketch of how the progress of state formation interacted with war-fighting. It describes how states and their rivals organized violence differently at different times during the last century. These differences in organization in turn had different ramifications for human security.

Part II examines the elements of the conflict traps that affect MENA. These are not intended as an exhaustive list of war triggers or immediate causes of specific conflicts. Rather, they explore the general conditions that singularly or in combination make war a recurrent and important feature in MENA's regional affairs. Chapter 3 examines the role of oil in war. It shows that states fighting to control oil markets is relatively rare. However, oil contributes to war and violence largely by affecting the ways states manage and respond to internal opposition and challengers. Chapter 4 examines the role of ethnicity or "ancient hatreds" in regional wars. Finding a common sense of national identity is a crucial component of state-building. But instilling and reproducing this identity often spurs violent resistance. Chapter 5 examines the role of geopolitics and outside intervention in conflict. It shows how outside powers have always played a major role in regional politics, but their ability to spur or restrain conflict has been equivocal. One of the most important elements of geopolitics is not the direct commission of war, but enabling states (and non-state actors) to conduct war on a larger scale.

Chapter 6 offers an extended case study of the last decade of MENA history as a protracted and multi-level regional war. It shows how the civil wars in Libya, Syria, Iraq, and Yemen, often treated as discrete conflicts, became interconnected as theaters in a larger regional and global contest. This contest involved the United States and Russia as the main extra-regional players, but most crucially Iran, Saudi Arabia, Turkey, the UAE, and others as regional actors asserting supremacy. Operating transnationally, the conflict traps escalate war to the point where initial objectives and interests no longer matter.

The seventh and final chapter of the book shifts the focus to peace and peacemaking. There have been innumerable diplomatic plans and efforts to end wars in MENA. Only a fraction have made much impact. Many of these initiatives came from extra-regional powers or their close regional allies. At the same time, "bottom-up" efforts to achieve local conciliation and peace also have a mixed record. This chapter evaluates how different approaches to conflict resolution and mitigation address the potential "traps" of oil, identity, and geopolitics. In many cases, "solving" one trap only exacerbates the problems of the other, creating a Gordian knot that cannot easily be untied. Nevertheless, attention to those places where peace has gained a footing is important for understanding how conflicts in MENA might end.

PART I
CONTEXT

1

Accounting for War in the Middle East and North Africa

War and conflict are common leitmotifs in descriptions of the Middle East and North Africa. Media coverage depicts the region as marred by constant crises, atrocities, and bloodlettings, a veritable breeding ground for violence. But how much war is there in MENA? How are these wars fought? How bad are they? These questions relate, respectively, to the frequency, the form, and the magnitude of armed conflict. Answering them requires an approach that compares MENA to other areas of the world and looks within the region for internal variation. This chapter examines the patterns of war and organized violence in MENA quantitatively. There are three main axes of comparison. First is the comparison between MENA and other regions, particularly in the developing world. Second is the comparison between MENA countries. Third is the comparison over time from the beginnings of the modern state system through mid-twentieth-century decolonization to the twenty-first century. MENA on the whole has followed global modes in most important respects. However, some countries within the region have been especially war prone. Moreover, the magnitude and impact of war have increased dramatically in MENA since the turn of the twenty-first century.

Measuring war is not easy. War is as complicated an activity as a social or behavioral scientist can study. It entails enormous feats of organization, coordination, and discipline. In 1971, sociologist Fred Charles Iklé, later a senior US defense official, described the challenges of amalgamating "the most diverse indicators: reports from the battlefield, statistics on potential military resources, and impressionistic predictions of how friend and foe will bear the cost and suffering of further fighting."[1] Accessing, collating, and assessing this data is always hard. Prevailing insecurity on the ground might obstruct the gathering of information. Belligerents wishing to promote specific narratives about who instigated violence or its impact sometimes deny access to information from conflict-affected areas or even fabricate events for the purposes of public relations. The obfuscation extends even to the words used to describe a particular conflict. War comes with attendant organizational, normative, and legal standards about how combatants (and civilians) should behave. Yet belligerents often try to upgrade or downgrade specific instances of conflict in order to control narratives of conflict. To call an adversary a terrorist or criminal, rather than a soldier, is both to elevate your standing and to denigrate the opponent.[2] These descriptions can have major implications for the conduct of conflict.

The question "What is war?" is simultaneously ontological, conceptual, and methodological. Many analyses revert axiomatically to German military theorist Carl von Clausewitz's dictum that war is the continuation of politics by other means. But that only begs the question of what political ends war extends. Historian Jeremy Black parses between functional and cultural/ideological elements in the definition of war. "Functionally, [war] is organized large-scale violence. Culturally and ideologically, it is the consequence of bellicosity."[3] In each of these domains there can be considerable variation, but the results are the same.

Roughly coinciding with Iklé's lament, social scientists in the 1970s launched the Correlates of War (CoW) project. Their aim was to remove the study of war from the sole purview of war-fighters and to address the study of war from a scientific perspective. Housed at the University of Michigan, researchers cataloged data on instances of conflict worldwide extending back to 1816. This was not an arbitrary cut-off point. The end of the Napoleonic wars is often cited as the beginning of the modern European state system. This fundamentally Euro-centric periodization was closely tied to the way the CoW researchers conceived of war itself. CoW was a product of the Cold War. Many of its researchers saw their role as finding ways to address US–Soviet tensions. The CoW definition favored large-scale war (with over 1,000 battle deaths) mostly conducted by the standing armies of powerful states. It was not that CoW researchers were unaware of internal (civil) conflicts. It was that they regarded these wars as less consequential to the global calculus of peace and conflict between the United States and the Soviet Union.[4]

In the 1990s, there was a push to expand definitions of what war was, why it happened, and what its effects were. Some argued that war had assumed entirely new features, with different kinds of antagonisms and involving different – often non-state – antagonists. Political scientist Mary Kaldor, for one, suggested that these "new wars" did not involve a contest of combatants' political wills, as Clausewitz had suggested. Instead, the combatants treated war as an opportunity for commercial expansion, not political victory. As a result, war is self-perpetuating as actors reproduce political identity and seek to further narrow economic interests.[5] For some analysts, these characteristics suggested that these contests were not war at all, but something different and apart. For others, though, there was little novel in these supposedly "new wars," as profit and power had commingled in war for centuries.[6]

The advent of human security dovetailed with this broadening concept of war. Traditionally, the academic field of security studies focused on explain military victory in the pursuit of national security. Accordingly, when measuring the impact of war, this approach focused on ascertaining damage inflicted by and upon professional armies. The human security approach, though, insisted on considering harms civilians suffer as equally worthy objects of inquiry. If war was indeed a social process, then the civilian experience had to be regarded as a salient explicandum.[7] The emphasis on human security inspired new efforts to catalog and categorize wars. Scandinavian researchers associated with the Peace Research Institute Oslo (PRIO) and Uppsala University's Conflict Data Program (UCDP) created what is now the most comprehensive database on conflict in the post-1945 era. Again, this periodization matters. The year 1945 is often cited as a critical juncture, with the beginnings of decolonization and independence for countries of the developing world. These countries had been (and probably still are) systematically underrepresented in traditional security studies approaches, even though they contain the bulk of the world's population and the bulk of its conflicts. The types of war in these regions differed from what CoW had aimed to measure. As the PRIO/UCDP effort showed, after 1945 most wars were fought not between countries, but within them. These wars overwhelmingly occurred in the developing world.

In terms of organizational bases, such internal wars are highly variegated. Some internal wars involve two (or more) sides fielding more or less conventional military structures of roughly equal stature waging battles to control clearly demarcated territories. Some are more asymmetrical, with conventional and centralized state armies fighting against irregular forces that are loosely organized and militarily weak. These opposition forces are variously dubbed guerrillas, insurgents, or militias, or, less sympathetically, bandits and criminals. They rarely control much territory but wage a low-level campaign to disturb state control. Finally, in some circumstances both state forces and rebels are relatively weak or decentralized. The distinction between rebel fighter and state forces becomes less distinct, comporting with the "new wars" hypothesis about apolitical war.[8] Additionally, internal wars often attract outside intervention, leading to distinctly "internationalized" dynamics in which foreign powers provide belligerents with economic, political, and military support.

Terrorism is closely tied to internal wars. Terrorism is almost necessarily a pejorative term. No one self-defines as a terrorist or deems their actions as terrorism. Security scholars Tarek Barkawi and Mark Laffey described the use of the term as a categorical error which delegitimizes resistance to Northern domination by non-state actors.[9] Other specialists have developed more workable and perhaps useful definitions of the concept of terrorism, but acknowledge that the designation is problematic.[10] Nevertheless, the specter of terrorism holds unique valence in the Middle East, especially when conjoined with concerns about "resurgent" or "radical" Islam.[11] The US invasions of Afghanistan in 2001 and Iraq in 2003 were couched in a discourse about a "global" war on terror. The unquestionable focus of the campaign, however, was predominantly Muslim regions of MENA and nearby Central Asia. This phrasing was counterproductive from an analytic or strategic perspective. It did, however, have the discursive advantage of simultaneously ennobling the United States' actions while denigrating its opponents as illegal combatants who were not entitled to the kinds of protections stipulated in international laws of war.[12] Such discourse continues today. An American think-tank report, for instance, opines that "radical Islamist terrorism in its many forms remains the most immediate global threat to the safety and security of US citizens at home and abroad, and most of the actors posing terrorist threats originate in the greater Middle East."[13]

Over the last seven decades, MENA offers examples of interstate wars, internal wars, and internationalized civil wars. But not all of these types of conflicts were evident the whole of this time. They appeared in different times and places. Examining these intra-regional differences and comparing MENA to global trends is a useful entry point to assessing the peculiarities of violence in the region.

First Cut: Frequency of War

The first cut at an answer about whether MENA is particularly conflict prone comes by comparing the number of conflicts within the region to the rest of the world. Figure 1.1 uses the PRIO/UCDP data to tally every type of

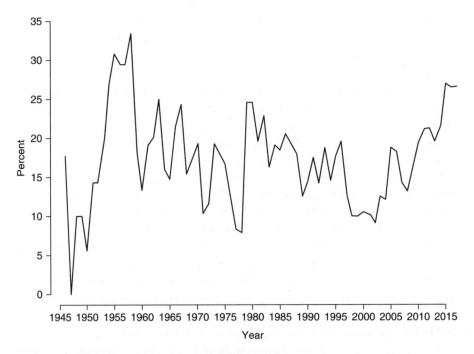

Figure 1.1 Percentage of conflict in MENA countries
Source: Peace Research Institute, Oslo/Uppsala Conflict Data Project, data available at *https://www. prio.org/Data/Armed-Conflict/UCDP-PRIO/*; Nils Petter Gleditsch et al., "Armed Conflict 1946–2001: A New Dataset," *Journal of Peace Research* 39, no. 5 (2002): 615–37.

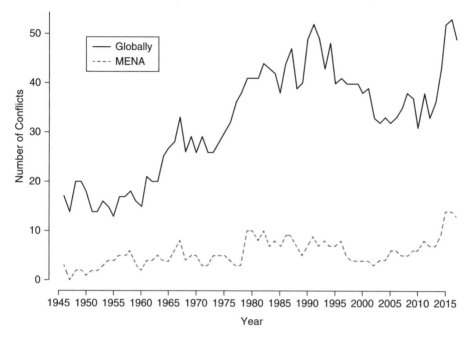

Figure 1.2 Number of conflicts by year
Source: Peace Research Institute, Oslo/Uppsala Conflict Data Project, data available at *https://www. prio.org/Data/Armed-Conflict/UCDP-PRIO/;* Gleditsch et al., "Armed Conflict 1946–2001: A New Dataset."

conflict that occurred each year between 1945 and 2016. Figure 1.2 calculates the number of wars in MENA annually as a percentage of the global total.

The results show that while MENA has had decadal spikes in conflict episodes, there have also been years in which the region has been comparatively peaceful. From 1980 until 2000, war in MENA declined both in absolute number and in global proportion. Put another way, the rest of the world experienced more conflicts, but MENA remained stable or declined. Looking at the conflict frequency statistics from 1960 to 2003, PRIO researchers concluded that Asia and Africa were just as conflict prone as MENA or even more so.[14]

At the same time, it is worth noting that since around 2003 the number of conflicts worldwide has increased dramatically. This increase is driven at least in part by the spike in conflict within MENA itself.

Zooming in on the regional perspective produces an interesting insight into how these wars and conflicts are distributed across the region (Figure 1.3). Certain countries, like Israel and Iraq, have been in continual war over the last seven decades. By contrast, countries like Oman, Tunisia, Kuwait, and Saudi

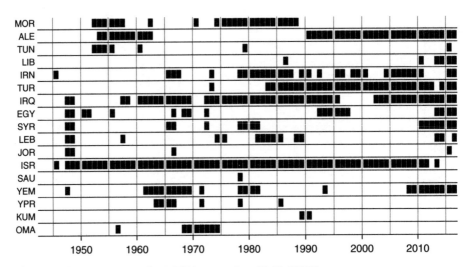

Figure 1.3 Years at war for MENA countries, 1945–2017
Source: Peace Research Institute, Oslo/Uppsala Conflict Data Project, data available at *https://www. prio.org/Data/Armed-Conflict/UCDP-PRIO/*; Gleditsch et al., "Armed Conflict 1946–2001: A New Dataset."

Arabia have seen relatively infrequent and short-lived conflicts (at least until recently). This is not to say that these states were wholly pacific. Rather, it is to suggest that the impact of war-making and its ancillary effects on state and society vary within the region.

Second Cut: Conflict Types

Another step in interrogating claims of regional exceptionalism is to examine the types of war fought within MENA. Figure 1.4 presents the data on interstate war regionally and globally. Interstate war is clearly the least common form of warfare globally. Inter-state war is nearly entirely absent from Latin America and Europe. Some analysts deem interstate war so rare as to be obsolete or extinct.[15] Yet MENA consistently accounts for a significant portion of interstate conflicts globally. Much of this comes from the persistence of conflicts between Israel and its neighbors, a topic to which we shall return later on. But there are other cases to consider as well, such as the Iran–Iraq War and the Iraqi war against Kuwait in 1990 and 1991. The fact that MENA seems to be uniquely prone to interstate conflict adds an important caveat to the global-level analysis favored by both CoW and PRIO/UCDP projects. It suggests that regional security complexes, not just world systems, have a significant part in shaping conflict.

Figures 1.5 and 1.6 present the data on internal (civil) wars and

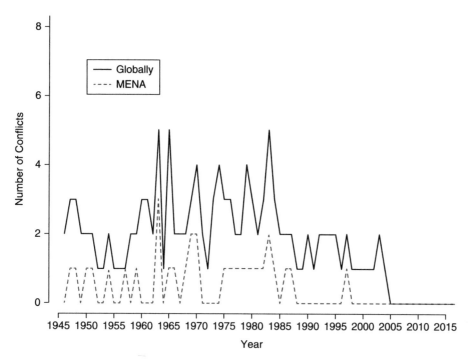

Figure 1.4 Interstate conflicts, MENA v. the world
Source: Peace Research Institute, Oslo/Uppsala Conflict Data Project, data available at *https://www. prio.org/Data/Armed-Conflict/UCDP-PRIO/*; Gleditsch et al., "Armed Conflict 1946–2001: A New Dataset."

internationalized internal wars. In examining trends in internal war, MENA is much less remarkable.

The global trend in internal wars began increasing in the 1960s and peaked in the mid-1990s, with MENA's trajectory basically following this global course. Internationalized internal wars rose dramatically in the mid-1990s globally, with MENA following course through the 2000s and 2010s.

Third Cut: Conflict Magnitude

Beside the frequency and form of war is the question of war's magnitude. Here, again, social scientists have run into substantial issues related to conceptualization and data collection. It requires a definition of war – which is difficult enough. It also requires an idea of the mechanisms by which war causes destruction. The human security approach, as discussed above, insists on accounting for not just the damage inflicted by and upon armies, but also the suffering borne by civilians. Indeed, it points out that over the twentieth century, civilians, not soldiers, experienced by far the most deaths during

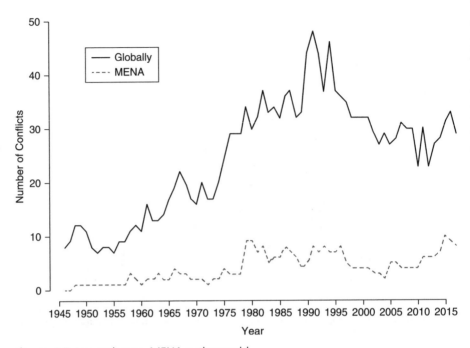

Figure 1.5 Internal wars, MENA v. the world
Source: Peace Research Institute, Oslo/Uppsala Conflict Data Project, data available at *https://www. prio.org/Data/Armed-Conflict/UCDP-PRIO/*; Gleditsch et al., "Armed Conflict 1946–2001: A New Dataset."

war.[16] Statisticians of war use the term *battle deaths* to denote all deaths, whether of civilians or combatants, attributable to direct military action. Battle deaths therefore include deliberate attacks as well as inadvertent (i.e., collateral) damage.

While the idea of battle deaths is somewhat intuitive, collecting accurate data is practically very difficult. Armies often keep track of their own casualties and try to monitor the strengthening or weakening of their adversaries. However, these data are often classified, censored, or subject to political bias. There is a tendency to undercount or ignore civilian deaths, either by denying they occur at all or by reclassifying the dead as combatants. This legitimates them as targets for violence. Reflecting on the experience of the Syrian civil war, novelist Khaled Khalifa observed that "during war, a body loses all meaning."[17]

But there is a countermove against this as well. International organizations have sought to collate reports of deaths from among combatant countries. A growing network of civil society organizations have developed techniques to cull data through local media reports about violent incidents. They have also begun using techniques for "crowdsourcing" casualties through social media.[18] This approach, though, has its limitations. As highlighted by Megan

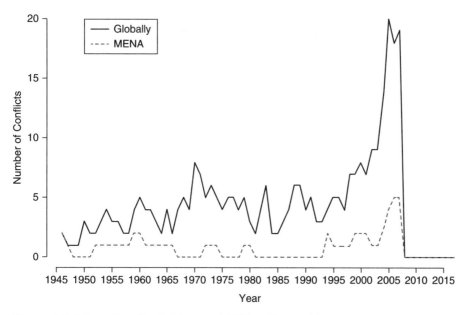

Figure 1.6 Internationalized civil wars, MENA v. the world
Source: Peace Research Institute, Oslo/Uppsala Conflict Data Project, data available at *https://www. prio.org/Data/Armed-Conflict/UCDP-PRIO/*; Gleditsch et al., "Armed Conflict 1946–2001: A New Dataset."

Price, Anita Gohdes, and Patrick Ball of the Human Rights Data Analysis group, "the chaos and fear that surround conflict mean that killings often go unreported and consequently remain hidden from view."[19] Reliable data become the scarcest in the areas most afflicted by violence. Moreover, because these techniques rely on third-party reporting via media or crowdsourcing, they tend to highlight violence in more densely populated urban settings while undercounting violence committed in remote rural areas.[20] While there are more data than ever on battle deaths, these data are often disparate and contradictory.

The Iraq War was a case in point. The United States refused to release data on civilian deaths in Iraq, and it is unclear whether it even collected such information. American and British military officials declared that they "don't do body counts."[21] President George W. Bush stated that "30,000 [Iraqi civilians], more or less, have died as a result of the initial incursion and the ongoing violence." Aides later clarified that this was not an official statistic, but an estimate based on published news accounts. Other organizations offered substantially different figures. In August 2006, the NGO Iraqi Body Count (IBC) estimated that number at between 47,016 and 52,142. The Brookings Institution, a US think tank, estimated the number at 62,000.[22]

But wars do not kill just by guns and bombs. They also damage the institutions necessary to assure access to basic needs like food, healthcare, and sanitation. They level economies and impel displaced populations and refugees.[23] During World War I, for example, combat largely spared Lebanon and Syria. Nevertheless, Ottoman military and labor conscription and their requisitioning of crops, timber, and fuels led to severe shortages for the civilians in the area and left millions vulnerable to hunger. Historians estimate that between 100,000 and 200,000 may have succumbed to starvation or disease and tens of thousands were displaced.[24]

The Yemeni civil war of the 2010s offers a more recent example. Blockades and direct strikes on food distribution centers, sanitation facilities, and hospitals have contributed to mass hunger and precipitous declines in public health, including a massive cholera outbreak.[25] UN officials called this "the worst humanitarian crisis of our time." An estimated three-quarters of the Yemeni population require food assistance and 1.8 million children suffer from acute malnourishment.[26]

Theories of human security insist on accounting for these indirect effects, even though collecting data on them is practically very daunting. During the Iraq War, the British medical journal *The Lancet* published a series of studies conducted by epidemiologists between 2003 and 2006. Deploying techniques commonly used to estimate death tolls from earthquakes and other natural disasters, investigators randomly sampled neighborhoods to conduct door-to-door surveys. They asked residents about anyone who had died in the previous year and the cause of death. The researchers then extrapolated to calculate how many Iraqis had died between 2003 and 2006 and compared that result to the period prior to the invasion. They concluded that Iraq's mortality rate had shot up from 5.5 deaths per 1,000 people annually before the invasion to 13.3 per 1,000 people after. Thus, they attributed 654,965 additional Iraqi deaths to the war, including 601,027 deaths due to violence (mostly by gunfire).[27] But the studies faced immediate criticism and accusation of political bias. In 2016 and 2017, Iraqi researchers used a sampling method that was similar to but more comprehensive than *The Lancet* studies. They calculated battle deaths at 155,000, higher but still in line with the previous IBC and Brookings studies. On the most substantive issue, they concurred with *The Lancet*, finding that overall mortality had nearly doubled during the war.[28] The disparities in calculating the magnitude of war in part reflect differences in methodology and in the rigor of application. They also represent varying understandings of the mechanisms by which wars cause harm.

Thinking in terms of magnitude adds an important dimension to the comparative study of war in MENA. The Arab–Israeli wars, for instance, stand out as a relatively uncommon case of interstate war in the developing world. The United States and other great powers granted these wars a great deal of attention. Nobel Peace Prizes were awarded to those who sought to end the conflict.

However, in terms of magnitude of violence, the Arab–Israeli wars have been comparatively modest.

In contrast, the Iran–Iraq War had by far the most battle deaths of any of MENA's wars, at over 644,000. Indeed, according to political scientists Bethany Lacina and Nils Petter Gleditsch's global study of battle deaths, it ranks just behind the Vietnam War, Korean wars, and the Chinese civil war as the bloodiest war since 1945.[29] The Iran–Iraq War illustrates the overlap and intersection between the ways wars are organized and their magnitude. It is commonly dubbed the largest interstate war fought between Third World countries. Contemporary commentators marveled at how the Iraqi and Iranian militaries were organized in conventional military formats and adopted modern weaponry supplied from Europe and the United States. The size of their armies was truly staggering. Iran began the war with about 270,000 soldiers in seven divisions. By war's end, it had 850,000 men, mostly conscripts, in 48 divisions. Iraq began the war with 12 divisions and 250,000 men under arms, an already remarkable 1.9 percent of its total population. By war's end, it had 51 divisions and an astounding 800,000 troops.[30] Some features of the Iran–Iraq War were reminiscent of World War I, such as the extensive use of trench warfare along the southern front and the resort to chemical weapons. Others aspects harkened to World War II, including massive bombardment of cities. Internal struggle between regimes and oppositions, particularly Kurdish opposition forces in both Iran and Iraq, was also an important dimension of this conflagration. While conventional fighting occurred along the southern and central Iraqi–Iranian frontier, northern Iraq was the stage for a protracted counterinsurgency campaign. At the end of the war, Baghdad sought to scotch the Kurdish threat definitively. Iraqi forces and locally raised militias massacred Kurdish civilians and destroyed their villages in order to root out the insurgents. The Iraqi army began using chemical weapons against Kurdish villages to finish off the work of ethnic cleansing. This campaign, which the Iraqi military code-named the Anfal, claimed at least 50,000 lives.[31]

Since the late twentieth century, MENA has had the unfortunate distinction of being a region where high-magnitude violence is increasing. PRIO/UCDP researchers have calculated the number of fatalities in war since 1989. Four MENA countries – Iraq, Syria, Sudan, and Yemen – were among the top twenty countries, as shown in Table 1.1. The magnitude of these conflicts is even clearer when fatalities are standardized by total population size. Note that even these figures, though, neglect the practically difficult issue of indirect deaths, which can be orders of magnitude higher.[32]

The UCDP data also provide a way to analyze the form of violence by distinguishing between three types of conflicts:

Table 1.1 Conflict-affected countries by fatalities, top twenty countries, 1989–2017

Country	Total fatalities	Magnitude (dead per 1,000 pop.)
Rwanda	520,639	62.51
Syria	313,418	18.69
Afghanistan	200,552	9.57
Ethiopia	177,449	2.59
Iraq	119,001	4.91
Congo, D.R.	107,773	2.23
Sudan	92,248	3.30
Sri Lanka	65,373	3.46
India	55,073	0.05
Nigeria	51,272	0.41
Somalia	45,408	4.89
Pakistan	41,073	0.29
Angola	33,178	1.95
Turkey	27,751	0.43
Colombia	27,462	0.67
Bosnia-Herzegovina	26,333	6.98
Russia (Soviet Union)	25,480	0.17
Liberia	23,244	7.77
Algeria	21,138	0.67
Yemen	20,863	1.13

Source: Therése Pettersson and Kristine Eck, "Organized Violence, 1989–2017," *Journal of Peace Research* 55, no. 4 (July 2018): 535–47.

- state-based conflict, where at least one of the parties is the government of a state, that is, violence between two states and violence between the government and a rebel group;
- non-state conflict, which involves two organized groups, such as rebel groups or ethnic groups, neither of which is the government of a state; and
- one-sided violence, where the government of a state or a formally organized group commits violence against unarmed civilians.

Table 1.2 breaks down the violence of MENA by type. In Syria, Iraq, Sudan, and Yemen, the vast majority of the violence has involved state actors as perpetrators or targets. The violence of non-state conflicts – where states are absent – is certainly present but pales in comparison.

It is useful at this point to step back to consider the role of terrorism in MENA's wars. Terrorism is, by definition, a non-state activity. The Global Terrorism Database (GTD), developed by the National Consortium for the Study of Terrorism and Response to Terrorism at the University of Maryland,

Table 1.2 State, non-state, and one-sided violence in MENA, 1989–2017

Country	State-based conflict	Non-state conflicts	One-sided violence
Syria	281,588	23,366	8,464
Iraq	98,009	2,985	18,007
Sudan	51,531	21,062	19,655
Yemen	18,993	1,687	183

Source: Pettersson and Eck, "Organized Violence, 1989–2017."

offers perhaps the most rigorous method for defining terrorist events.[33] The GTD defines acts of terrorism as acts involving "the threatened or actual use of illegal force and violence by a non-state actor to attain a political, economic, religious, or social goal through fear, coercion, or intimidation." Terrorist acts must be intentional, entail violence or the immediate threat of violence, and the perpetrators must be non-state actors.[34] Several points become clear in analyzing the GTD data. Since the 1970s, terrorism has been a global phenomenon in no way limited to MENA. Within MENA, Algeria, Egypt, Yemen, Israel/Palestine, Iraq, and Syria have especially high levels of terrorist influence. But there are many other hotspots outside the region, including in Colombia, Peru, Central America, Afghanistan, India, Pakistan, Somalia, Nigeria, and the Philippines. Moreover, when considered by fatalities, terrorist acts account for only a small scale of the overall violence in MENA. The data from 2018, for instance, list Iraq as having the second highest number of terrorist attacks, as shown in Table 1.3. But this is only a small portion of Iraq's total battle deaths.

Terrorism is closely correlated with asymmetrical internal wars, but it is far from the most consequential form of violence. While much of the United States and other world powers exhibit concern about terrorist attacks emanating from the Middle East, terrorism is hardly a peculiar characteristic of the region.

Internal war and terrorism often stem from states' inability to control violence effectively. This is not the same, though, as to say that states are somehow exempt from or uninvolved in such violence. In his study of war and conflict in Africa, Paul Williams argues that a state-centric perspective on Africa's conflicts would be inadequate and inappropriate "because many of the continent's armed conflicts take place on the peripheries of, or outside, the African society of states and do not involve government soldiers."[35] In MENA, by contrast, the exact opposite prevails. Even when violence is conducted by non-state actors, it is largely oriented toward winning control over states or establishing alternative political structures, that is, new states.

Table 1.3 Ten countries with the most terrorist events in 2018

Country	No. of events (% of global total)
Afghanistan	1,776 (18)
Iraq	1,362 (14)
India	888 (9)
Nigeria	645 (7)
Philippines	601 (6)
Somalia	527 (5)
Pakistan	480 (5)
Yemen	325 (5)
Cameroon	235 (2)
Syria	232 (2)

Source: Global Terrorism Database, available at *https://www.start.umd.edu/data-tools/global-terrorism-database-gtd*.

Conclusion

Counting armed conflicts, battle deaths, and indirect deaths is frustratingly inexact. The exercise depends on disputed concepts that, in turn, link to deeper normative concerns about what types of violence are legitimate versus illegitimate. Terms like "soldier," "terrorist," "civilian," "victim," or "casualty" connote different statuses within organizations devoted to fighting. Even if these theoretical and moral issues are resolved, the techniques used to collect data about war themselves face severe practical limitations.

Nevertheless, grappling with these conceptual, normative, and methodological issues, however contingently, is essential for elucidating patterns and trends and to define the field of inquiry for war and conflict in MENA. The data show several notable things. When viewed over the duration of the post-World War II era, the patterns of conflict in MENA are mostly unexceptional. MENA largely tracked with global trends in the frequency and form of war. War became rarer in MENA at roughly the same time as it became rare globally. War became more prevalent in MENA when it became more prevalent globally. The epidemic of internal wars in MENA roughly coincided with the global turn toward internal wars. As in other regions, war is not evenly distributed within MENA itself. Some countries, like Israel and Iraq, have experienced nearly perpetual war. Other countries in the region have seen only sporadic warfare. This suggests a need to consider the issue of war from both a global system and regional sub-system perspective.

In terms of magnitude of conflict, the data are far grimmer. For much of the second half of the twentieth century, it was wars in eastern Asia that claimed the most lives. However, since the turn of the twenty-first century, conflicts in

MENA have been proliferating and intensifying. Most of the recent violence in MENA is broadly attributable to episodes of internal (civil) war and state failure. Yet states in many ways remain at the fulcrum of violence. The next chapter explores how contestation over statehood generates different forms of violence.

2

The MENA Security Predicament

In frequency and form, MENA's conflicts accorded with many of the trends in other developing regions for much of the twentieth century. War in the region has varied spatially and temporally, experienced differently in different countries and at different times. From the 1950s to the turn of the millennium, there was little evidence of any unique proclivities for violence in MENA. Since the turn of the twenty-first century, however, the region has seen dramatic increases in the magnitude of conflict. Yemen, Iraq, Syria, and Libya have been most gravely affected. Chapter 1 highlighted the primacy of states in the conduct of war. This is especially obvious in interstate wars. But even in internal wars, states remained the focal point of violence despite their frequent inability to maintain exclusive control over violence. Violence is not exclusively controlled by states, but it is usually *about* states.

States are surrounded by actors and institutions that constrain or empower their efforts to control violence. On the one hand, all of MENA's wars involved extra-regional powers like the United States, Russia, and European states to some extent. War intertwined with the circulation of capital, ideas, and people to constitute its own form of globalization.[1] On the other hand, a state's abilities to mobilize for war also depends on its domestic constituencies, and the relationship between state and society. Violence induces innovations that restructure and reorder social, economic, and political life.[2] The processes of transformation and reconstitution are a function of what sociologists call state strength or capacity. Capacity is distinct from raw coercive power. State strength means the ability to make binding rules and organize society through bureaucratic measures. It also entails a measure of legitimacy through popular acceptance of those rules. State capacity thus partially determines how violence is organized and implemented.

This chapter explains how weak states facing societal resistance are most prone to make drastic, even disastrous, use of violence. This seemingly paradoxical combination reflects what security studies scholars call the Third World "security predicament."[3] Traditional security studies focuses on how states respond to threats that emanate from beyond their borders. War is thus a response to perceived external dangers. The Third World security predicament retains the emphasis on states, but argues that threat is mostly found within the state's boundaries. As political scientist Mohammed Ayoob put it, "external threats quite often augment the problems of insecurity that exist within state boundaries and, in many cases, would be quite ineffective if internal threats and domestic fissures did not exist within Third World societies."[4] This situation leads to forms of conflict and violence mobilization that differ from those typical of the developed world. External threats augment and compound this abiding internal insecurity.

To understand the security predicament in MENA, it is necessary to consider the relationships of states and societies as they co-evolved within the global system and international society. The state, as political scientist Alex Bellamy puts it, is "simultaneously the most awesome warmaker and the most effective peacemaker ever devised."[5] The first part of this chapter explains differences in the levels of analysis and explanation – global, regional, and national – that can account for the connections between the processes of state formation and war. These levels are not analytically exclusive. Rather, they operate simultaneously and interactively. The second part of the chapter offers a historical sociology of war and state formation, shifting from variation in spatial scale to variations of timing and tempo. MENA states are the product of two different historical processes. The first was the long-term and slow-going process of cultural contact and evolution in the region. The second was the abrupt implantation of European economic and political systems in the late nineteenth and early twentieth century.[6] This linkage and interplay of these two process helps explain how MENA states are collectively at once weak and fierce. Finally, the chapter concludes by considering a less state-centered conceptualization of security. Following the lead of the Beirut School of Critical Security Studies, it asks what happens when individuals and communities become the primary referents of security. The results deepen the paradox of security in MENA, as the state is at once its greatest potential champion and greatest menace.

MENA's Wars and Levels-of-Analysis Problems

One of the key debates in the field of security studies and international relations relates to the appropriate level of analysis and explanation. Levels of analysis can be analogized to scales, images, registers, or degrees of magnification. Three distinct levels are relevant: the global, the regional, and the national. Advocates for different levels of analysis combine analytical and etiological claims about where the prime mover or first cause in security relationships might be located. This in turn defines where scholars look for explanations about the causes and consequences of war. Much of this debate, though, has proceeded deductively, without regard for the empirical or historical record under examination.[7] Trying to alight on a single level of analysis for inquiry and explanation is akin to searching for a single master variable.

Such parsimony is theoretically alluring but usually found empirically wanting. Wars take multiple manifestations across different scales. Often the most
fruitful points of analysis comes from toggling between scales, registers, and
dimensions.[8]

Global/Strategic Level

The highest order of aggregation is *global-* or *strategic-level analysis*. This
approach attempts to account for war and conflict in MENA by reference to
the features of a global system, particularly the global balances of power.
Power can derive from military might, as in neorealist theory, economic
power, as in dependency theory, or a combination of both.[9] The common
denominator is that the United States and Europe had power and MENA did
not. In this respect, MENA's position is typical of other parts of the Global
South. MENA's peculiarities are largely the result of accidents of geography (namely the historical relations between Christian and Islamic leaders
across the Mediterranean domains) and geology (namely the presence of
sub-soil natural gas and oil). Global-level actors thus singularly determined
the generation and perpetuation of statehood in MENA (and for the rest
of the developing world).[10] In global-level analysis, the wars and conflicts
within MENA are caused by intrusive greater powers and their drive to assert
hegemony from the outside.[11] Regional powers, both states and non-state
actors, had little choice but to follow the lead of superior external actors.
A global-level analysis focuses on the way these external powers shaped
regional powers, from the era of colonialism, through the Cold War, and into
the period of American primacy.[12]

Such a top-down view can be extremely constraining. Even at the height of
the Cold War, no external power could exercise effective control over regional
states in a way comparable to the Soviet Union's control over its Eastern
European satellites. Ultimately, the superpowers mostly regarded MENA as
a sideshow, not the main stage. Their primary concern in the region wasn't
to assert their own supremacy but to avoid being dragged into escalating
conflicts by proxy powers within the region.[13]

Regional Level

Regional-level analysis, in contrast to global/strategic analysis, privileges the
rivalry among MENA states themselves. Perturbations within the regional
balance and the enactment of rivalries drive war and conflict, not exogenous
shocks from intervening outsiders. Regional-level analyses treat MENA not
just as a theater for larger conflicts initiated by other states but also as a
territorially bounded sub-system possessing distinctive geopolitical and internal features. This means that MENA's internal forces are consequential for

regional politics even as the region is subordinated within the global system and experiences the penetration of global powers.[14]

Among the most important destabilizing factors within the region is the inability of any single state to dominate its neighbors and assume the role of regional hegemon. MENA is stubbornly multipolar. Examining the cross-hatching between regional- and strategic-level analyses, political scientist Ian Lustick points out that "international norms and great power policies have been responsible for blocking the emergence of a great power in the Middle East by deterring or preventing state-building wars from being fought to successful conclusions across existing Middle Eastern boundaries."[15] Extra-regional powers blocked would-be regional hegemons, such as Egypt under Mehmet Ali in the nineteenth century and Gamal Abd al-Nasser in the mid-twentieth century or Iraq under Saddam Hussein in the late twentieth century.

Another key element of regional-level analysis is the unique normative, cultural, and ideological landscape in which regional interstate rivalries play out.[16] Many analyses of MENA politics note the tensions between pan-Arab nationalism (*qawmiyya*) and more localized state-based forms of identity (*wataniyya*).[17] The former promised the possibility of pan-Arab unification and gestured toward notions of self-determination that had inspired decolonization efforts since World War I. The latter provided for the continuity and territorial integrity of individual states consistent with emerging norms of sovereignty.[18] But these were not the only contested identities in MENA. Minorities, such as Kurds, Jews, and Berbers, offered their own nationalist visions that transcended state borders. Pan-Islamists, meanwhile, envisioned unification along religious, rather than ethno-linguistic, lines.[19]

This normative dissonance helps explain several contradictory tendencies within the region. On the one hand, there was the repeated rise of challengers who promised to rectify colonial-era mistakes, dissolve existing state structures, and achieve political unification. On the other hand, the same dissonance also explains the durability of the regional state system, despite its congenital defects. There were few successful efforts to change borders, much less agglomerate territory by military means. States rarely died. Arab states in particular hardly ever engaged in direct military conflict with each other.[20] Indeed, despite repeated upheavals, MENA's interstate borders have been remarkably static, enduring longer than many of the borders in Europe and East Asia during the twentieth century.[21] But there were still avenues for regional states to subvert, intervene in, or otherwise intrude on their fellow states, especially when they succumbed to civil war. Internationalized internal wars seemed to substitute for traditional modes of interstate conflict.

Non-Arab states, like Israel and Iran, were key actors within the region. Indeed, each of these played major roles in the region's wars. Yet neither enjoys full integration into the region's regular networks of diplomatic or political exchange. Israel, which has the most substantial military in the region, including a nuclear arsenal, is also the most ostracized.[22] This, again, reinforces the region's tendency toward multipolarity.

State Level

Both global- and regional-level analyses tend to see states as metaphorical billiard balls, differentiated primarily by their relative positions in the regional and global arenas. State-level analysis, in contrast, posits that domestic political configurations matter for regional security-building.[23] The struggles within the political elite (regime) and between regimes and their populations are therefore intrinsic to war and conflict. State elites and citizenry in MENA often lack fundamental agreements about the content and composition of political order. Even the territorial dimensions of the state – where exactly the state should rule – remain in dispute, as indicated by the persistence of various supra- and sub-state identities. Counter-elites repeatedly mobilize and contest state supremacy. They often invoke alternative notions of political legitimacy, including alternative ideas of community derived from sub- or supra-national identities. As a result, MENA states generally lack the capacity to impose administrative order or win popular acceptance and legitimacy. In this view, the formal apparatus of statehood in many parts of MENA is a false front, façade, or simulacrum.

Without the simultaneous empowerment and constraint that comes with state strength, MENA leaders have tended to confront challengers with the only means at their disposal: brute violence. In his influential study of Arab statehood, Nazih Ayubi describes states as having "large bureaucracies, mighty armies and harsh prisons, [but] they are lamentably feeble when it comes to collecting taxes, winning wars or forging a really 'hegemonic' power bloc or an ideology that can carry the state beyond the coercive."[24] States are thus seldom strong in terms of capacity, but often hard and fierce. Coercion and raw force are the only ways states can cope with societal resistance. Similar conclusions can be drawn to some extent about Israel and Iran as well. More broadly, cross-national research has shown a strong correlation between weak administrative capacity and the tendency toward violent repression.[25]

Limited state capacity is central to the security predicament and the persistence and intermingling of domestic and foreign threats. Domestic instability makes states more vulnerable to outside intervention. The difference between preserving the state and preserving the regime becomes blurred. States are permeable, interconnected, and perpetually susceptible to transnational appeals.[26] State rulers oscillate between internal and external threats, a practice known as omnibalancing.[27] Instead of providing for the representation and provision of the citizens broadly and equally, state institutions reward and punish citizens according to their presumed political reliability and loyalty.

Omnibalancing takes different forms in different types of regimes. Monarchies, such as those of the Persian Gulf, Morocco, and Jordan, by definition rely on hereditary principles to allocate political prerogatives of rule. Close kin exclusively staff top positions. A similar situation prevails in the regimes of many authoritarian republics where so-called "presidents for life" reign. Such regimes rely on patrimonialism and cronyism to staff the most important decision-making positions.[28] In both instances, the vast majority of citizens are denied access to full political participation.

Debates about political identity, often tied to ethno-sectarian cleavages, amplify the tendency toward exclusion. Certain groups receive privileged access to jobs, education, land, and other subsidies from the state. Meanwhile, other groups of citizens endure government coercion, including tax collection and conscription, while receiving fewer benefits. From 1921 until 2003, a nearly unbroken string of Sunni Arabs ruled Iraq. As early as the 1930s, Shi'i politicians noted that "taxes and death are for the Shi'i while [government and military] posts are for the Sunni."[29] Even when Iraqi rulers abjured the logic of ethno-sectarian hierarchies or tried to transcend them, the security predicament compelled them toward exclusionary modes. Saddam Hussein and his cadres from the Ba'ath Party, for example, may not have conceived of their regime in sectarian terms. They tried hard to cultivate a unified Iraqi identity. Nevertheless, because of concerns about the reliability and stability of their own population, they made sure that Sunni Arab tribes from Saddam's home region of Tikrit filled top military and political posts. As violence emerged as the dominant mode of governance in MENA, specialists in violence steadily gained prominence within the ruling elite. Service in the military became a preferred path to social advancement for groups and individuals. Paradoxically, those closest to the regime's power centers are also the best positioned to seize power themselves. Military coups became a recurrent feature of the regional politics of the 1950s and 1960s.

MENA states deploy a number of techniques to prevent military officers from seizing power. They select senior officers based on political loyalty rather than professional competency. This often coincides with broader patrimonialism and ethno-sectarian hierarchies or divisions of labor. Another coup-proofing technique is to establish duplicate security and intelligence services. As a rule, the more redundancy and fragmentation, the greater the level of mutual suspicions. Some security services are praetorian guards or shock troops specially selected and trained to protect the regime. There are also special intelligence branches (*mukhabarat*) tasked with monitoring the regime elite and the general public. Some regimes also recruit semi-professional militias or private mercenaries. Coup-proofing measures have hampered preparedness for interstate wars, since they divert resources from the task of combat with other armies.[30]

Overall, analysis anchored in the state level suggests that the security predicament makes war and conflict endogenous and self-perpetuating. Societal
resistance ineluctably induces state repression. But repression in turn incites
further alienation and resistance. This means that MENA states maintain a
delicate but negative equilibrium in which everyone is worse off. Wars erupt
when normal repression breaks down and societal actors become unfettered
or emboldened. Outside interference intensifies what are originally struggles
for control over states.

A Historical Sociology of War and Conflict in MENA

Any adequate understanding of war and conflict in MENA requires a grasp
of both general global conditions and the peculiar contours of the region
and its constituent elements. The specific and variegated history of MENA
becomes more important with each step down in level of analysis. Shifting
from the relatively static levels-of-analysis approach to a historical sociological
approach can help further illustrate how specific states managed the security
predicament. In MENA, as in other regions, efforts to address security concerns and establish the state's monopoly over the use of force connected with
efforts to obtain political legitimacy and strategies of economic development.

The evolution of the security predicament and its ensuing conflicts can
be divided into three historical eras. The first was the era of colonial wars,
which took place through the nineteenth century until roughly the middle
of the twentieth century and involved contests which pitted imperial states
against non-state resistance. The second was the era of wars among independent states, which predominated from the mid-twentieth century until around
the 1990s. Statehood seemed to take firm hold in the region as state armies
became the predominant purveyors of violence to the exclusion of non-state
armed actors. Finally, the turn of the millennium witnessed what some pes-
simistically call the region's "forever wars."[31] These saw a broad breakdown
of states, the reassertion of militia actors, and intensified regional and global
competition within MENA.

Colonial Wars

Many studies date the beginnings of MENA's security predicament to the era
of colonialism. In this narrative, European imperialists "invented" MENA's
states, rendering them artificial, illegitimate, and unable to respond to the
needs and aspirations of their own populations, setting up the tension between
weak states and social resistance. As in so many caricatures, this one has an
element of truth, but is also an oversimplification. One often-overlooked issue
is the specific impact of warfare during the colonial era. Colonial wars molded

institutions and governance and shaped the struggle over political inclusion. They involved the exercise of imperial power, but also granted indigenous actors the agency to shape states.[32]

The Ottomans were the most important Islamic dynasty of the early modern era. In the early 1700s, the Ottoman empire ruled much of the Balkans and southeastern Europe, Anatolia (Turkey), the Levant, the Arabian Peninsula, Egypt, and North Africa. Ottoman rulers claimed both political powers as sultans and spiritual authority as caliphs, successors to the Prophet Muhammad and leaders of the world's Islamic community. Christian and Jewish communities had religious autonomy within the empire as long as they accepted Islamic rule. These religious minorities played prominent roles in imperial politics. Trying to match the technological and military progress of the European powers, the Ottomans embarked on a series of military, education, and administrative reforms through the 1800s. Constitutional changes sought to promote a new sense of civic Ottoman identity among subjects of all religious faiths. Decline was not abated, however, as the European powers continued to pick apart the Ottoman territories. By the turn of the twentieth century, nearly all the empire's European territories were lost. Furthermore, France held Tunisia, Algeria, and Morocco. France also had a special sphere of influence over Lebanon as guarantor of the safety of the indigenous Christian community. Britain dominated Egypt, Aden, and the Persian Gulf. Italy plotted to expand into the African coast.[33]

Importantly, these early European imperialist incursions did not so much foist new political entities on the Ottoman territories as subsume and encapsulate already existing ones. The Europeans mostly preferred to work with and through existing elites. The Persian Gulf princedoms, the beys of Algiers and Tunisia, and the Khedive of Egypt already enjoyed considerable political autonomy and territorial differentiation. There was also some sense of local patriotism that distinguished these areas within the Ottoman domain. As political scientist Iliya Harik noted, by detaching these polities from the empire, the European presence "enforc[ed] the particular notion of the one-country one-state idea and provid[ed] the state with a more accomplished formal character."[34] The Europeans also accelerated processes of legal and economic change. In efforts to spur economic productivity, they replaced systems of communal village or tribal property with individual proprietorships. Large landowners as a result agglomerated massive estates that supplied cereals, cotton, and other commodities for the global economy. These landed magnates were often natural partners for the European powers.

But the colonial project also faced indigenous resistance. Through the 1800s, a string of rebellions adopted the slogan of Islamic jihad (holy war). The repeated Wahhabi uprisings in Arabia, the millenarian Mahdi movement in Sudan (1881–99), and the Abd al-Qadir revolt in Algeria (1830–42) each claimed to defend Islam from foreign infidels and domestic heretics.[35] The

Urabi rebellion in Egypt (1879–82) gestured toward a more local sense of patriotism, but also sought the restitution of Ottoman sovereignty.[36] Imperial powers, including the Ottomans, used a combination of advanced technologies and local partners to put down the rebellion. Gatling guns and naval bombardment were key force-multipliers against rebel forces that were often massive, but were also under-trained and ill equipped. Beside these major events were innumerable smaller acts of rebellion. Ottoman administrators and European colonial officers dealt with problems of sabotage, banditry, tax evasion, and other forms of criminality. These minor disturbances often involved peasants, tribesmen, and laborers aggrieved over lost economic and political privileges. Colonial police and armies were continually occupied with deterring or repressing such activities.[37]

Colonial wars expanded and intensified through World War I and its aftermath. The 1920s and 1930s in MENA were rife with disturbance and revolts. These included the Alawite and Aleppo uprisings in Syria, the Iraqi Revolt (1920), the Rif rebellion in Morocco (1920–7), the Tripolitanian republic rebellion (1918–23), numerous revolts in Iraqi and Turkish Kurdistan (1920s–1930s), the Great Syrian Revolt (1925–7), the French campaigns in the Atlas and Sahara (1927–34), the Italian–Senussi war in eastern Libya (1927–32), and the Arab revolt in Palestine (1936–9). These wars involved hundreds of thousands of fighters and tens of thousands of deaths.[38]

World War I and its aftermath left MENA transformed. The war completed the dismemberment of the Ottoman empire. Britain and France occupied the Levant and Mesopotamia. But the global conflagration opened opportunities for indigenous actors to pursue their agendas as well. President Woodrow Wilson's pronouncements on national self-determination emboldened many indigenous actors. Leaders from MENA, like their compatriots from India, Asia, and Africa, hoped that America might back their bid for independence.[39]

Colonial warfare of the 1920s and 1930s reflected the unsettled colonial control, the impetus to create new states, and the still inchoate sense of national identities, community, and boundaries. These tensions were especially acute in the Levant and Mesopotamia. Diplomatic pressures and continued military resistance prevented Britain and France from simply divvying up these territories in a grand strategic bargain. The territories comprising Syria, Iraq, Lebanon, Palestine, and Jordan were subject to a novel juridical formula, the League of Nations mandate. This meant that they were not colonies but provisional states representing fledgling nations. Britain and France were tasked (mandated) to help them build institutions, including armies, in preparation for independence. In reality, the imperial powers tried to avoid the cost of day-to-day administration while keeping these countries under the imperial thumb. As in other colonial ventures, they sought to install pliant state elites and to recruit supporters from the larger landowners and others whose economic and political interests aligned with empire. This put the mandatory state leaders in a unique position in the annals of colonialism. They had no hope of gaining sovereignty without the approval of the colonial power. But formal independence would be meaningless without the backing of their own populations. The situation in the mandate territories was especially complicated because of the absence of pre-existing administrative infrastructure or national identities from which these new states could derive benefit and allegiances. Prior to the European conquest, the terms "Palestine," "Syria," and "Iraq" loosely denoted geographic regions. Unlike in Tunisia or Egypt, there was no clear administrative delineation of where these countries began and ended territorially. Moreover, indigenous communities sometimes lacked a strong sense of local nationalism attached to these states.[40] Consequently, political disputes often combined questions about political power with challenges to the existence of the state itself.

Iraq, again, is an illustrative example of how colonial warfare under the mandate shaped state formation. In 1920, Iraqi tribes launched a massive insurrection against the British occupation. The uprising crossed sectarian lines, involving both Sunni and Shi'i leadership and fighters. The revolt seemed to occasion a sudden moment of national unification. A senior Shi'i jurist issued a religious edict declaring it "the duty of the Iraqis to demand their rights."[41] Britain turned to aerial bombardment of villages to put down the rebellion. They also sought to entice rebellious tribal leaders to quit the fight, offering incentives of financial subsidies and land. Ultimately, an estimated 2,000 to 4,000 civilians were killed. Convinced of the futility of direct rule, the British redoubled their efforts to entice the Sunni tribal elite to work with the colonial authority. Tribal sheikhs gained land holdings and virtually unfettered authority in their territories. Britain invited Faisal bin Hussein, scion of the aristocratic Hashemite dynasty of the Hejaz, to serve as king of the newly created kingdom of Iraq. Faisal's family had backed the British during World War I on the promise of British support to create an Arab kingdom spanning the Hejaz and Levant. After France crushed his effort to establish a state in Syria, Britain awarded Iraq as a kind of consolation prize. But the position of the monarchy and the state was always precarious. As Faisal himself would note, "there is still – and I say this with a heart full of sorrow – no Iraqi people but unimaginable masses of human beings devoid of any patriotic idea." Moreover, the Iraqi state was still "far and away weaker than the people . . . [the people have] more than 100,000 rifles whereas the government possesses only 15,000." Iraq faced myriad challengers. In the south, Shi'i sharecroppers complained of their political and economic marginalization. Conscription was a particular source of concern and contention with Iraqi Shi'i leaders (as well as other minorities). Iraq's Shi'i leaders demanded political influence commensurate with their demographic majority. In the north, Kurdish tribal leaders demanded the right to form their own Kurdish state commensurate with the promises of Wilsonianism. The government responded by renewing its partnership with large landowners and redoubling its reliance on coercion. Between 1921 and 1932, the British bombers were called upon 130 times to help put down these disturbances.[42] Similar patterns were visible across the region. States, in alliance both with the colonial powers and with indigenous elites, struggled to deter or repel the advances of counter-elites.

Nowhere were questions of identity more intertwined with colonial violence than in Palestine. The League of Nations mandate specified that Britain was to prepare Palestine to serve as the national home for Jews. Jewish nationalists, called Zionists, organized immigration and settlement of Jews to what they claimed as their ancestral homeland. They set up institutions of self-governance, including their own militias. Muslims and Christian Arabs overwhelmingly rejected the mandate as an infringement on what they claimed were their indigenous rights. They were particularly aggrieved as Zionists purchased land for Jewish settlements that effectively dispossessed Arab inhabitants. The British favored Zionism out of both moral conviction and an abiding anti-Semitic paranoia, but could not afford to alienate the Arab and Muslim world. In 1936, Palestinians launched a nation-wide strike in protest against Jewish immigration and land purchases. Violence targeted British outposts and expanded to Jewish settlements and eventually the Arab elite, who were seen as complicit in land dispossession. The British resorted to collective punishment, curfew, and other harsh measures. The Zionists accelerated the build-up of their self-defense militias as part of their state-building project. While most Zionist leaders tried to partner with the British, radicals launched a military campaign to intimidate both Arabs and the British. Ultimately, the revolt left the Zionists stronger whereas the Palestinian Arabs were exhausted and divided.[43]

The era of colonial wars helped define the institutional endowment that MENA states would inherit upon gaining independence. By and large, the armies of MENA were trained, equipped, and molded by their European counterparts. They relied on European technologies and techniques to enact violence. As with colonial armies, pacification and internal suppression became key parts of their mission. In 1933, less than a year after Britain formally ended its mandate, the Iraqi army used aerial bombardment and ground assaults to crush a rebellion by Assyrian Christians. The Assyrians had been a key component of the British colonial forces. With the cessation of the mandate, Assyrian political leaders demanded their own statehood. The Iraqi army responded to this internal challenge with exactly the same technologically enhanced violence that the British had routinely used in the previous decade. Iraqi politicians of all stripes regarded it as a vital confirmation of Iraqi sovereignty.[44]

Colonial wars were formative experiences that helped establish the parameters of violence in MENA. The experience in these wars delineated what kinds of violence could be used, by whom, and against which targets. Foreign powers often deliberately staffed the colonial armies with minority groups to counter any titular majority from gaining too much power. In Syria, for example, the French relied on marginalized minorities like the Alawites, Kurds, and Druze to staff colonial security forces in the belief that they would counter the largely Sunni Arab contingent that dominated Damascus.[45] These designs prefigured later manifestations such as omnibalancing and coup-proofing.

Colonial wars also shaped notions of national identity and community. Nationalist thinkers often pointed to the anti-colonial revolts as proof of national solidarity and cohesion. Certainly, in some cases revolts helped galvanize senses of national identity in resistance to outside encroachment. The belated Algerian anti-colonial revolution of the 1960s fits this description. But often these events are embellished in retrospect. Colonial wars were also internecine wars. Some 120,000 Algerians served in the pro-colonial militias during the war.[46] Just as individuals and groups made the calculation to oppose colonial rule, others hitched their political and economic fate to the colonial powers. Collaborating, either opportunistically or ideologically, discredited a generation of state elites and left them vulnerable to new challengers upon ascension to independence.

Wars of States

The end of colonialism and the advent of the global Cold War brought new dynamics to war and conflict in MENA. It inaugurated a period of regional interstate rivalries and precipitated new kinds of interstate wars. In this evolving regional arena, states vied to gain access to either US or Soviet material, economic, or diplomatic support. States gained new means of penetrating society and marginalizing internal opposition. This, however, did not neutralize internal threats as much as change the terrain of conflict. MENA's regional security predicament came into full effect in this era as the need to confront external threats complicated and interlinked with persistent challenges from domestic challengers and armed non-state actors.

The region's first interstate war occurred in Palestine. The first Arab–Israeli war was a kind of inflection point in which the status of new states and the tenets of Arab solidarity were tested. The war began in autumn 1947, following the pattern of previous colonial wars. With Britain announcing its intention to quit Palestine, the UN outlined a plan to partition the mandatory territory into separate Jewish and Arab states. Inter-communal violence erupted almost immediately. The Palestinian Arab majority still labored under a deficit of political institutions and resources and relied mostly on irregular guerrilla bands. The Zionists, in contrast, had already established many of the trappings of statehood, including a sizable and relatively well-trained military that was often able to overwhelm Arab-inhabited areas and expel residents. The war changed when the UN formally announced partition. The

Zionist leadership declared Israel's independence in May 1948. Egypt, Iraq, Syria, and Jordan invaded the following day, intending to snuff out the Jewish state. Although the Arab armies collectively enjoyed superior weaponry and professional training, there was little coordination or cooperation among the Arab armies. Each state pursued its narrow state interests. Palestinian irregulars were sidelined. What Israelis celebrated as their War of Independence (*milkhemet ha'atzmaut*), Arabs commemorated as the Disaster (*an-nakba*). Some 100,000 Palestinians became refugees or internally displaced. At the armistice of 1949, Israel expanded territorially into the Negev, the Galilee, and western Jerusalem, which had been designated as an international city. Egypt took over Gaza and Jordan took East Jerusalem and the West Bank.[47]

The Palestine conflict exhibited two overlapping dimensions of security in the coming decades. On the one hand, it was a conflict between Israel and its neighbors over territory and strategic superiority. Israel, Egypt, Jordan, Syria, and other regional states vied to gain political, economic, and military support from the United States and Soviet Union, turning MENA into a front in a larger global conflict. As in Iraq, conscription and military service were crucial factors in Israel's development. Instead of an impediment to national cohesion, though, military service was more an engine of nation- and state-building. The Israeli state also possessed considerable institutional infrastructure. Israel pushed its organizational and technological advantage in the military domain, including the acquisition of nuclear weapons in the late 1960s. Major wars erupted in 1956, 1967, and 1973, interspersed with numerous skirmishes and militarized disputes. The 1967 Six Day War saw Israel capture Gaza and the Sinai Peninsula from Egypt, the Golan Heights from Syria, and East Jerusalem and the West Bank from Jordan. Israel eventually returned Sinai as part of its 1979 peace treaty with Egypt, but the rest of the territories remain under occupation fifty years later.

On the other hand, the Israeli–Arab conflict also retained much of its colonial-era characteristics as a struggle for internal supremacy and control within the state. Israel was emphatically a Jewish state legally and politically. Following the 1947–9 War, Jews made up about 80 percent of the population. Although Arabs resident within the territorial boundaries had citizenship, the Israeli democratic system systematically advantaged Jews over Arabs. Arab communities in Israel lived under martial law until 1966 and were generally treated as a potential fifth column. Most Arab citizens of Israel were excluded from military service.[48] The acquisition of the occupied territories in 1967 increased the number of Arabs under Israel's authority, while Israel denied Arabs living in the West Bank and Gaza citizenship rights. Meanwhile, Palestinian refugees organized their own non-state forces to carry on the fight against Israel from Jordan, Lebanon, and Syria. Initially, countries like Egypt and Syria supported these groups as low-cost proxy forces to keep pressure on Israel. After 1967, especially, however, Palestinian nationalists demanded more autonomy from their Arab sponsors. They exploited episodes of state fragility, especially in Jordan and Lebanon, to turn refugee camps into veritable states-within-states. They used these platforms to launch attacks into Israel. Israel responded by attacking Palestinian outposts. It also sought to punish the countries that allowed Palestinian fighters to operate, holding Jordan and Lebanon responsible for attacks originating in their territory. This complicated trilateral deterrence efforts, though, often compounding the underlying problems of state weakness.[49] Within the occupied territories of the West Bank and Gaza, the Israeli army served in a manner reminiscent of a colonial garrison. Its technological superiority served to maintain surveillance and deterrence of Palestinian nationalist ambitions.[50]

It is important to view the Arab–Israeli conflicts in the context of wider regional rivalries emergent with MENA's decolonization. Intra-Arab conflicts played out slightly differently. Israel was regarded in the region as an imperialist intrusion and thus a legitimate target for attack. In contrast, norms of intra-Arab amity precluded such direct confrontation among fellow Arab states. The Arab League, founded in 1945, gestured toward Arab unification but actually simply reinforced norms of territorial integrity and mutual respect among sovereign states. The UN further provided a kind of guarantee for the endurance of all post-colonial states. The leaders of independent Arab states tended to guard their sovereignty and independence jealously, rebuffing calls from the dogmatic pan-Arabists about unification. There would be no territorial aggrandizement at the expense of other Arab states.[51]

But the failure of Arab leaders to defeat Israel and their more general complicity with imperialism brought discredit and public antipathy. In 1952, Nasser led a military coup that deposed the Egyptian monarchy and declared Egypt to be henceforth a republic. The Free Officers, as they were known, touted slogans of anti-imperialism, socialism, and Arab nationalism. Acolytes launched similar coups, succeeding in overthrowing the old ruling elite in Iraq, Syria, and Libya. Algeria and South Yemen, the only two Arab countries where anti-colonial uprisings succeeded, joined the radical ranks in the 1960s. New regimes sought to launch social revolutions from above, hastening modernization, nationalizing industries, accelerating land reform and redistributions, and broadening social welfare systems. They tried to build political alliances that incorporated workers, peasants, and the new middle classes. Still, political decision-making remained tightly controlled. In fact, repression became more common as the new regimes realized that their own citizens might work with a foreign power to subvert them. In foreign policy, the Arab republican regimes adopted stances of non-alignment or sought Soviet support directly. The relationship between the Soviets and so-called Arab "radical" camp was often dictated more by strategic interests than ideological rapport. Likewise, alliances among radical Arab regimes proved fleeting. Efforts to deploy pan-Arabism often reflected the need of leaders for protection from internal challenges. Iraqi Sunni Arab leaders adopted pan-Arabism as a way to deny legitimacy to Shi'i and Kurdish actors who envisioned a more localized Iraq-centered nationalism. Pan-Arabism was not just an offensive tool for intervention, but also helped to defend beleaguered rulers. The inability of ruling elites to consolidate their hold on power pushed them to consider pan-Arabism as an alternative source of legitimacy and support.[52]

So-called "moderate" or "traditional" regimes, in contrast, continued to rely on tenets of obedience and Islam to justify their rule. Coercion, of course, was still present. No regime offered citizens a true political voice. However, for those like Saudi Arabia and the Gulf states, the coincidence of large oil deposits and small populations allowed them to provide citizens with lavish subsidies that assuaged some popular disaffection. Their authoritarian bargains were perhaps more generous but no less restrictive on substantive political actions. Richer conservative regimes often used economic means to prop up allies. They generally sought to align with the United States, Britain's obvious successor. Again, however, there was no natural ideological kinship among these regimes or with their sponsors. The United States largely positioned itself as an offshore balancer, relying on regional allies, first Iran and then Saudi Arabia, to maintain regional order and ensure the stability of the global oil supply.

Intra-Arab rivalries played out less through direct conflict over territory than through proxy wars and semi-covert interventions. Outside actors backed rival armed factions whenever states proved unable to control opposition. The civil war between monarchists and republicans in Yemen in the 1960s became a testing ground in the contest between US-allied Saudi Arabia and Soviet-aligned Egypt. Oman's civil war (1962–76) and Moroccan campaigns in Western Sahara (1970–present) similarly involved regional interventions that warped Cold War geopolitics. The Lebanese civil war (1975–91) became a regional mêlée. Sectarian militias fought each other for control over the Lebanese state. Syrian troops invaded in 1976 in a futile effort to enforce peace. Other states, including Iraq and Iran, gave financial and military support to various sides. Militias did not fight just for political advantage, but also for control over key economic resources, such as smuggling routes and ports. They often extorted "tax" revenues from populations that they claimed to protect. In 1982, Israel invaded Lebanon in an effort to root out Palestinian forces. Israel partnered with Christian militias, trying to install a friendly government in Beirut. The invasion, however, only deepened the conflict. Hezbollah, a Shi'i militia backed by Syria and Iran, waged a protracted struggle against Israeli forces. By the late 1980s, Israel controlled southern Lebanon with support from Christian militias, and Syria enforced its hegemony over the Lebanese state through Hezbollah and other proxies. The war thus left Lebanon unable to control violence within its territory, yet still enjoying nominal sovereignty and standing in the international community.

The Iran–Iraq War (1980–8) in many ways epitomized how the MENA security predicament defined war and conflict by the late twentieth century. As already discussed, the war was the bloodiest in the region's modern history. It evinced the linkage between internal and external threats and the overlapping of global and regional security concerns. Iraq and Iran had inherited territorial disputes from the Ottoman era. Through the 1970s, each had meddled in the other's affairs, often by supporting rebel groups. In 1979, the Islamic Revolution in Iran intensified the conflict. Iraq's Sunni Arab leadership saw the revolutionary chaos as an opportunity to push their military advantage, particularly in claiming oil-rich and predominantly Arabic-speaking areas along the Shatt al-Arab river. But Iraq's leadership also feared that Iran's revolution would infect Iraq's Shi'i majority. Indeed, Iran's leaders sought to incite Shi'is in Iraq and the Persian Gulf to rise up against secular, Sunni leadership. In September 1980, Iraq invaded Iran. Demonstrating the fluidity of alliances, Saudi Arabia and most of the Gulf monarchies backed Iraq, once among the vanguard of the radical Arab bloc. Iran, meanwhile, allied with Syria, another radical regime, against its neighbor. The United States tilted steadily toward Iraq as the risk of oil disruption grew more severe. US naval intervention in the Persian Gulf was one of the factors that compelled Iran to accept peace in 1988. The war precipitated profound changes in domestic institutions for both Iraq and Iran. Both regimes appealed to religion, ethnicity, and patriotism to mobilize and motivate their citizens to fight. They launched initiatives to satisfy demands for housing, education, and food. But they responded to perceived disloyalty with greater brutality, as illustrated by the genocide of Iraqi Kurds at the end of the war. At the same time, the wars spurred intra-elite competition. Saddam was able to consolidate power and dominance over the Ba'ath Party in the course of the war. In Iran, factions from the elite Islamic Revolutionary Guard outmaneuvered their rivals and asserted supremacy.[53]

War and conflict played a complex role in the formation of MENA's states after independence. New international norms and dynamics solidified borders and assured states of continuity. Yet states still faced internal challenges from armed non-state actors. Moreover, independence inaugurated more intense regional rivalries that challenged states in new ways, making the security predicament more pronounced. A handful of MENA countries managed to skirt the most intensive experience of war and conflict by settling under the protection of external powers. Behind the aegis of American power, Saudi Arabia, the UAE, and other smaller Gulf states avoided any substantive military build-up. When Iraq invaded and annexed Kuwait in 1990, these countries had little choice but to plead with the United States to intervene for their defense.

Some campaigns against external rivals helped states build their domestic institutional capacity. In Israel, Iran, Iraq, Egypt, and other countries, wars allowed states to impress themselves upon their populations. The mass conscription which war necessitated was also accompanied by nationalist indoctrination and broader forms of economic redistribution. Material and diplomatic support from superpowers often hastened this transition, as states put the resource rents from abroad to purposes of establishing domestic stability.[54]

But interstate competition could also prove debilitating. Unable to solve the internal dimensions of the security predicament and impose political order within, regional interventions effectively left states like Lebanon as hollow shells. Armed non-state actors retained their own foreign patronage, controlling territory and embedding themselves into the national economy. Statehood remained intact, but only in the most nominal, juridical form. Most non-state actors still defined themselves as working on behalf of national interests, seeking to correct the state, not to break away. As the twenty-first century approached, MENA states had not resolved the underlying security predicament, but had devised various ways to cope with it.

"Forever Wars"

The wars of the twenty-first century deflated any notion that the states of MENA were moving, however falteringly, toward consolidation. These wars, beginning with the war in Iraq in 2003 and continuing through wars in Libya, Syria, and Yemen in the 2010s, all saw armed non-state actors regain prominence. Some militia groups supplanted crippled states, others collaborated with beleaguered state forces, creating a kind of parallel state that buttressed the legitimate state authority. Outside intervention, both as direct military action and as indirect use of proxy wars, intensified the violence and further undercut state control.

A concatenation of factors operating across the state, regional, and global levels drove these conflicts. The beginnings of the crisis, though, came from within the domestic political arena. By the turn of the millennium, ruling coalitions in many MENA states struggled to uphold their ends of the authoritarian bargain. Political opposition began adopting the slogans and doctrine of political Islam, blaming economic stagnation on secular politics that offered inauthentic and immoral forms of rule. But the impetus for reform and political opening seemed risky when viewed through the prism of the security predicament and the necessities for stability. After the Islamic Salvation Front won Algeria's first free and fair election in 1991, the Algerian army annulled the results and seized power for itself. Algeria's Islamists splintered, with radical branches waging a decade-long war against the military regime.

Changes in the global environment affected inter-regional dynamics. The United States was the world's sole superpower after the Soviet Union collapsed. Moreover, with the 1990–1 Gulf War, it was no longer an offshore balancer. Rather, American forces stood at the geopolitical epicenter. Using advanced technologies, such as GPS-guided missiles and other "smart" weaponry, they easily dispatched the Iraqi army, then considered the most formidable in the region. The United States subsequently retained bases in Saudi Arabia, the Persian Gulf, and Turkey, which it used to contain both Iraq and Iran.[55] Iran held out in what could be called the rejectionist bloc. Isolated regionally, it tried to build influence with Shi'i groups and others who resented American hegemony.

With the Soviet counterweight gone, the United States pushed neoliberal economic reforms and political opening on the region. These, however, were often ill conceived and half-hearted. They undermined the authoritarian bargain but offered no positive path forward for economic prosperity and political participation. This, in turn, exacerbated underlying problems of the security predicament. The populist authoritarian regimes that had guaranteed socio-economic security in the 1960s mutated into various forms of crony capitalisms. The bulk of the population saw their safety net evaporate. Countries like Egypt, Tunisia, Morocco, Jordan, and Kuwait oscillated between brief political opening and renewed repression.

Most Islamist opposition groups worked within the bounds that regimes imposed. They stood in elections they knew were rigged against them. They criticized corrupt ministers, but rarely the ruler himself. (It was, invariably, a "he" who ruled.) Opposition groups focused on building connections within a civil society that had been battered by regime repression and economic shortfalls. A handful of Islamist groups, though, took a more radical and violent approach. They aimed to demonstrate the impotence of rulers and regimes through attacks on civilians and military targets. Al-Qaeda, established by Osama bin Laden and other Saudi dissidents immediately after the 1990–1 Gulf War, launched an even more intensive campaign. Al-Qaeda and its ilk were not content to combat corrupt and repressive regional governments like the Saudi regime. Rather, they targeted the United States, the far enemy, as the bulwark of the entire regional system.[56] Attacks on civilians dramatized the asymmetries between the United States as a global superpower, its state allies within the region, and the still loose network of Islamist radicals that operated in fringe territories. From a strategic perspective, however, they were largely inconsequential.

Al-Qaeda's attacks in New York and Washington in 2001 brought the United States into MENA affairs as never before. While US leaders described their intentions as counter-terrorism, this often appeared a pretext to a much wider objective of transforming the nature of statehood in the region. A complete discussion of the US invasion and occupation of Iraq is beyond the scope of this book. It suffices to say that the US plan simultaneously occasioned a moment of expanded political participation and contention with the effective dissolution of the Iraqi army and accompanying state institutions. The United States struggled to balance between newly empowered Shi'is and Kurdish groups and the once-dominant Sunnis. The US occupation force proved too small to preserve order, despite increasing reliance on advanced technologies like aerial surveillance. Iraqis were thrown back to rely on a bevy of armed non-state actors for protection. Some of these militias were associated with political parties, tribes, or religious communities. Some were little more than racketeers. Criminal and political violence escalated. The measures that one community took for self-defense provoked other communities to take up arms to counter them. Sunnis and Shi'is each accused the other of seeking their elimination.[57] Importantly, though, most Iraqis did not see these sub-national identities as superseding their commitment to Iraq (with the notable exception of the Kurds). Rather, they defined their actions as necessary to assert their belonging in Iraq, not to negate it.[58]

The outside powers that took advantage of Iraq's collapse, however, had no similar compunction. Al-Qaeda and other radical Islamist groups infiltrated Iraqi territory, attacking both the United States and most any Iraqi who refused to adhere to their doctrine of global jihad. Al-Qaeda's Iraqi affiliates sought to stoke a full-on ethno-sectarian war between Sunnis and Shi'is as part of a global conflagration. Iran, for its part, backed Iraqi Shi'i groups, some of which were US partners, while others maintained their own armed resistance. Neighboring Sunni states, principally Saudi Arabia and Jordan, supported Sunni groups, even when those groups were implicated in terrorist violence. The Saudi–Iranian regional competition, at once political and sectarian, spilled over into Lebanon in 2005 and 2006. Riyadh sought to block Hezbollah, a pro-Iranian militia, from dominating the weak national government in Beirut. A brief but intense period of fighting ensued, including the assassination of a senior pro-Saudi politician. The following year, Israel launched its own military campaign against Hezbollah, seeking to destroy the militia's strongholds along the Lebanese–Israeli border. Despite marked advantages in technology and equipment, Israel proved unable to dislodge Hezbollah.

The pattern of state collapse and civil war coupled with outside intervention continued through the string of uprisings that began in 2011. The first demonstrations in Tunisia began with relatively modest demands for jobs, pay hikes, and an end to endemic corruption. Opposition activists across the region grew bolder as satellite television and social media spread the images and messages of protest. The opposition converged on a repertoire of non-violent tactics. Following the playbook from similar protests in Belgrade and Kiev earlier in the 2000s, they occupied key public spaces, urban squares, and intersections.[59] They confronted autocratic regimes at a common weak point of their armed mediocrity: their facile claims to embody sovereignty as national self-determination and popular will. Opposition leaders emphasized national unity and patriotism instead of divisive issues like Islamic government or sectarianism. The ubiquitous slogan of protest, "the people want the downfall of the regime," struck at the pillars of regime legitimacy.

Meanwhile, perhaps even more significant events were happening in barracks, officers' clubs, and the closed corridors of the interior and defense ministries. National armies and police were typically reluctant to attack protests draped in the national flag. Moreover, security services had their own institutional agendas at stake. Through the 1990s, rulers Zine al-Abidine Ben Ali (Tunisia), Hosni Mubarak (Egypt), Hafez al-Assad (Syria), and Ali Abdullah Saleh (Yemen) had centralized authority and funneled political and economic benefits to cronies and close kin while excluding other important regime partners. When Hafez al-Assad died in 2000, transferring power to his son Bashar, the old Ba'ath elite and military circle could only offer mumbled complaints, asking how a proudly republican regime had morphed into a hereditary dynasty. Now the street protesters demanded the ouster of kleptocratic rulers. Many even hoped for the military to serve as saviors in a transitional government. Indeed, some military leaders were willing to jettison "presidents for life" for the chance to preserve or even enhance their own institutional or personal fortunes. Breakdown in the security services, either through elite defections or mass dissension, was critical for deciding the fate of regimes.[60]

But the results of the uprising varied across contexts. The Tunisian military refused to attack fellow citizens, effectively dooming President Ben Ali. In Egypt, the army leadership orchestrated the ouster of Mubarak and entered into an uneasy alliance with the opposition. The Muslim Brotherhood won Egypt's first free and fair election in 2012. In 2013, however, the military turned on its erstwhile allies, blaming the new regime of Mohammed Morsi for economic malaise and complicity in Islamist terrorism. In July, the military deposed the elected president and brutally put down pro-Brotherhood street protests.

Where security services themselves were especially riven by patrimonial ties, such as in Libya, Yemen, and Syria, individual garrison and battalion commanders' defections led to even more profound fragmentation and disorder. While initial protests were generally peaceful, rebels began to set up their own insurgency. Military units became effectively free agents. Armed actors took over large swaths of territory. They embedded themselves in local economies, alternatively protecting or preying on civilians in their midst. They competed for valuable oil and gas fields, smuggling routes, and transit points. They administered justice, collected taxes, and ran schools. Even as they undercut state efforts to preserve exclusive control over the use of force, many of these armed non-state actors sought to associate with the state at the symbolic level. Most dubbed themselves revolutionary councils, self-defense forces, or armies of national liberation or salvation. In Syria, the Bashar al-Assad regime tried to deputize tribal and sectarian militias into pro-government militias. In Iraq, the government chose to induct or disarm locally raised armed groups based on political loyalty and control. In Libya, armed groups pledged nominal support to the revolutionary government even as they jealously guarded their political autonomy and blocked plans to bring them under the control of the central government. Even in the absence of actual power, existing states continued to hold symbolic valence, at least to some.

But with the breakdown of so many regional states at once, other armed actors came forward with different ideas of political community. Many of these ideas returned MENA to original questions about political borders left unresolved from the colonial era. Separatists in Iraq and Syrian Kurdistan, Southern Yemen, and eastern Libya sought to reclaim sovereign entities that had been lost or overtaken during the twentieth century. Though they made tactical alliances with central governments, they hoped to transform their zones of control into new national borders. The Islamic State (IS), a splinter group from al-Qaeda's Iraq franchise, had an even more expansive agenda. After seizing control over an immense territory on both sides of the Iraqi and Syrian border, IS proclaimed itself a caliphate, the rightful successor of medieval Islamic polities. It deemed the entire notion of national statehood an apostasy and demanded total loyalty from all Muslims. IS brutally attacked anything associated with unbelief, including Shi'is and other heterodox minorities. It even attacked fellow radical Islamist groups, such as al-Qaeda, for lacking revolutionary zeal.

Again, the MENA regional environment impinged upon these domestic struggles. For its part, the United States vacillated between seeking democratic reforms and concern for political stability, and especially concern about the expansion of radical Islamist groups. After the disaster of Iraq, it was reluctant to commit its own forces in the region.[61] This situation allowed other foreign states to come to the fore, including regional actors, as well as France, Russia, and other European states. Most outside intervention involved financial, diplomatic, political, or military support to belligerents. There were certainly some elements of opportunism in these interventions. However, in many cases there was also a considerable sense of vulnerability stemming from fear that violence would spill over across porous and insecure borders. Iran's Supreme Leader claimed that if its expeditionary forces did not confront IS in Damascus and Mosul, they would soon be fighting in Tehran. Saudi Arabia similarly feared that political unrest in Yemen or Iraq would reach its territory. In Yemen, Saudi Arabia and the UAE launched a direct military intervention to counter the Houthis, whom they viewed as an Iranian proxy force. The region became a bewildering crisscross of alliances and partnerships, complicating any effort to negotiate ceasefires or end the violence.

But while war crippled Yemen, Syria, and Libya in the 2010s, other states emerged more powerful. In response to the increasing military threat, Qatar, UAE, and Kuwait, long free-riders on the security provisions of the United States, announced plans to introduce conscription.[62] The UAE in particular launched its own program of military development and overseas expeditions. In Iran, the Revolutionary Guard Corps, which had orchestrated the expeditionary mission to support allies in Lebanon, Syria, Iraq, and Yemen, gained more political influence. Wars, then, had a double role in making and breaking statehood in MENA.

Conclusion: A View from Beirut

The idea of the security predicament, first introduced in the 1980s, revolutionized the study of Third World security. Highlighting the interaction between domestic and international threat helped to explain the volatility and violence of MENA politics, both the proclivity toward civil wars and the persistence of regional rivalries. The security predicament also helped explain why so many moments of nascent regime transition ended in state breakdowns and civil wars. As violence has worsened through the 2010s and into the 2020s, however, there are new approaches to understanding security that seek an even more radical break with traditional approaches to security. The Beirut School focuses not on the centrality of states but on the lived experiences of people as they endure insecurity. The location was not incidental. In the 1970s and 1980s, Lebanon's experience of an internationalized civil war and proliferation of armed militias had seemed exceptionally horrific. Now, with civil wars, mass protests, and coups rampant across the region, the Lebanese experience appears more typical and thus instructive. Lebanon's was, in some respects, the first of the forever wars.

The view from Beirut is very different from those from Tehran or Riyadh, much less Washington or Moscow. As Lebanese political scientist Waleed Hazbun puts it,

> Taking seriously the experience of such so-called weak and insecure states points to an approach toward understanding the geopolitics of the Arab world that recognizes the heterogeneous nature of the security environment composed of diverse state, non-state, and transnational actors that serve as agents of both security and insecurity. The security calculations of these actors also must be understood as embedded in transnational security relationships.[63]

The Beirut School, borrowing ideas from human security, interrogated the process by which ideas of threat and security materialized. The security predicament is not innate or inevitable. What a ruler defined as a security concern did not necessarily accord with the experience of citizens as they endured war and conflict. Individual and communal survival must be at the core of the political calculus, not the stability of states or regime endurance. Yet even within this corrective, states are far from irrelevant. Rather, they play a complicated and often problematic role in ensuring human survival. It is not enough to label MENA states as "weak" or "failed." For better or worse, Lebanese sociologist Jamil Mouawad claims, the state in the Arab world remains central to the accumulation of resources and as a site of contestation. Most importantly, the state is alive in people's imaginary and [they] are longing for it as a "source of justice.". . . How people experience the state – and how this generates demands for a Weberian state – need to be central to our understanding.[64]

Ultimately, the Beirut School offers a reminder that war's costs are inherently disproportionate and unequal. Questions about who fights and who dies are often distinct from who wins and who loses. This is an important injunction as we proceed in the coming chapters to examine the causes and consequences of MENA's wars.

PART II

CONFLICT TRAPS

Accounting for the patterns of war and conflict in MENA is a daunting task. Chapter 1 has discussed key conceptual and empirical challenges. It is difficult to find a definition of what should count when counting wars. Different conceptual approaches emphasize different aspects of conflict and can leave different impressions about how frequent war and conflict really are. Even if there is conceptual agreement, gathering empirical data about war and conflict is difficult owing to the challenges of accessing war zones. Calculating body counts is hard enough. Estimating war's broader economic and social ramifications is even more challenging. There is a growing interest in how – or whether – researchers can study conflict zones, a question that has unique pertinence for work in MENA.[1]

Another challenge is explaining the causes and impact of conflict and war. Indeed, there is disagreement about what the idea of a "cause" would mean for explaining war.[2] For most historians, wars are caused by specific human action, primarily (although not always) decisions of political leaders. Each war is *sui generis* because the circumstances of these actions, including the leaders making them, are different. Debate about the causes of World War I, for example, hinges on the reading of diplomatic cables, diaries, and recollections to identify specific motives and consequent actions that set the gears of war in motion.[3] It is often difficult to isolate a single event or actions as a singular cause, as there is always an immediate and prior causal condition to consider.[4]

Social scientists, in contrast, tend to look for causes of war in a more general form. Some offer systemic analyses, which consider war as an outcome of balances of power operating across the state, regional, or global levels.[5] Others consider war a fundamentally biological and evolutionary phenomenon that shapes how human socialize.[6] But war is such a vast and variant type of event that it is difficult to fit it under a single theoretical and conceptual rubric. Are interstate wars different than civil wars? Has war changed over the long span of human history? Do the causes of World War I apply equally to the causes of the Anglo-Zulu wars, the Peloponnesian War, or today's war in Yemen? Without anticipating these questions, social scientists risk attributing causal impact to variables that are stretched into amorphous platitudes.

This book charts a middle course between the specificity of the historian's case-by-case approach and the social scientific search for generalized theory. It aims at middle-range theories that are broad enough to accommodate a number of cases, but specific enough to capture with accuracy the diversity of historical experiences within MENA. With that in mind, it is useful to consider more deeply what we mean when we talk about the causes of war. International relations scholar Hidemi Suganami details three interrelated but distinct queries:

1. The first relates to the conditions necessary or permissive for war. What are the conditions which must be present for wars to occur?

2. The second considers the factors that raise or lower the probability or likelihood of war. Under what sorts of circumstances have wars occurred more frequently?
3. The third asks about triggers or events involved a specific instance of war. How did this particular war come about?[7]

Specific triggers (i.e., Question 3) are largely the domain of historians and other ideographically inclined researchers seeking an explanation for specific outcomes and cases of war. But Questions 1 and 2 are closer to the ambit of social scientific inquiry. One of the key themes of this book, as discussed in Chapter 2, focuses on statehood as a permissive and necessary condition for war in MENA. War as we know it is virtually inconceivable without states. The formation of states itself was closely linked to the progress of warfare. MENA's states developed through internal and external wars. The regional security predicament reflected the twin pressures of defending states from internal challengers and international rivals.

The coming chapters look more closely at Question 2: the factors that have made war more prominent, frequent, and impactful in MENA, either individually or in some combination. I call these elements conflict "traps" to distinguish them from the more conventional metaphor of conflict "triggers." The idea of a conflict trap emerged in the 2000s in a series of studies of civil wars conducted by researchers at the World Bank. These studies concluded that countries that had experienced one civil war are at far greater risk of succumbing to war again.[8] Economic changes wrought during war create conditions whereby leaders have an incentive to continue fighting indefinitely or return to fighting. As economist Paul Collier and his collaborators put it:

> Once a country stumbles into civil wars, its risk of further conflict soars. Conflict weakens the economy and leaves a legacy of atrocities. It also creates leaders and organizations that have invested in skills and equipment that are only useful for violence. Disturbingly, while the overwhelming majority of the population in a country affected by civil war suffers from it, the leaders of military organizations that are actually perpetrating the violence often do well out of it. The prospect of financial gain is seldom the primary motivation for rebellion, but for some it can become a satisfactory way of life.[9]

Post-war arrangements that exclude portions of the population tend to feed future grievances.[10] Thus, countries are trapped in conditions that make war and conflict more likely. The literature on interstate wars expresses a similar idea in its discussion of enduring rivalries. Wars between states tend to erupt among dyads of states that have long-standing and embedded rivalries. These rivalries often stem from prior experiences of war and conflict.[11] War begets war, both internationally and domestically.

Thinking in terms of the conflict trap is comparable in some sense to the epidemiological approach to diseases. Microbiologists know the processes associated with transmission and symptomology of diseases like cholera or malaria in individual patients. But epidemiologists and public health specialists know that conditions of poverty, poor sanitation, and weak infrastructure make infections more likely to afflict a general population. Moreover, the experience of disease itself causes economic and social problems which leave an entire population further susceptible to disease.[12]

What follows is not an exhaustive list of the factors that contribute to MENA's conflicts. Rather, the aim is to explore and interrogate some of the factors that are commonly cited as root causes for wars in the region. Chapter 3 examines the role of oil in war. Fighting over oil fields is relatively uncommon. However, oil affects the ways states manage and respond to internal opposition and challengers and thereby contributes to war and violence. Chapter 4 examines the role of ethnicity or "ancient hatreds" in regional wars. While a common national identity is an important part of state-building, instilling and reproducing this identity can often spur violence. Chapter 5 examines the role of geopolitics and outside intervention in conflict. Outside powers have always played a major role in regional politics, but often see their ability to manage conflicts surprisingly limited. Geopolitical interventions provided states (and non-state actors) with the ability to conduct war independently and on a larger scale. Examining these factors in individual chapters should not give the impression that they are analytically distinct or separable. On the contrary, these factors often compound each other and interact at the state, regional, and global/strategic levels. Chapter 6 examines the turbulence of the 2010s in MENA. It shows how this decade witnessed a kind of "perfect storm" of factors that contributed to the bloodiest period in MENA's modern history. Chapter 7, finally, evaluates ways that actors inside and outside the region have tried to escape the conflict trap and discusses the potential for peace in a region too often marred by violence.

3

Oil as Conflict Trap

At first glance, the Middle East and North Africa appear uniquely blessed with oil, a commodity so valuable that historian Daniel Yergin simply called it "the prize."[1] In the late 1980s, nearly two-thirds of the global oil supply originated in MENA. Even today, a period of increasing diversity in world energy supplies, MENA accounts for more than half of the world's oil, as shown in Figure 3.1.

Oil (and gas) has bestowed enormous wealth on MENA, but the impact has been uneven. On a per capita basis, there is a significant difference between the scale of petroleum wealth in Qatar or Kuwait and in more populous Iran or Iraq, as shown in Figure 3.2. Countries with little or no oil, like Tunisia or Jordan, often benefit from it indirectly through labor remittances and subsidies from oil-rich neighbors.

Oil has raised expectations in MENA about social and political transformation commensurate with economic abundance, but rarely delivered on them. Social scientists often describe oil as less a blessing than a curse, or, rather, a series of curses. Oil-producing countries "suffer authoritarian rule, violent conflict, and economic disarray *because* they produce oil – and because consumers in oil-importing states buy it from them," political scientist Michael Ross finds.[2]

The connections between oil and war are obvious to some. "No war for oil" was a popular refrain criticizing the US invasion of Iraq in 2003. Osama bin Laden, the founding leader of al-Qaeda, urged his supporters to attack oil installations in Saudi Arabia, Iraq, and elsewhere. "The biggest reason for our enemies' control over our lands," he stated, "is to steal our oil."[3] More than a decade later, President Donald Trump still suggested that the United States should expropriate Iraqi oil as "compensation" for the cost of the invasion and occupation and seemed obsessed with maintaining physical control over oil facilities in MENA.[4]

But the connections between oil and conflict in MENA are more complicated than just stealing or seizing it. Oil has profoundly affected the evolution of states in MENA and their propensities to wage war both on their neighbors and on their own populations. It is thus difficult to isolate the impact of oil from other factors propelling regional state formation. Oil has complicated regional geopolitics, as outside powers have intervened in the region

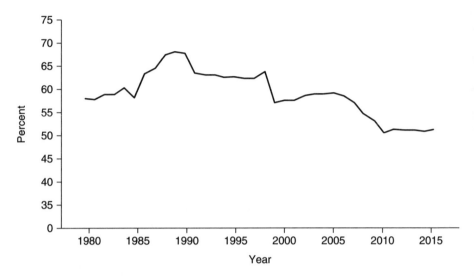

Figure 3.1 MENA share of global oil production
Source: BP Statistical Review of World Energy, available at *https://www.bp.com/en/global/corporate/energy-economics/statistical-review-of-world-energy.html.*

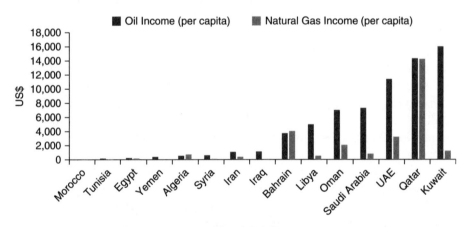

Figure 3.2 Oil and gas income per capita (2005)
Source: Stephen Haber and Victor Menaldo, "Do Natural Resources Fuel Authoritarianism? A Reappraisal of the Resource Curse," *American Political Science Review* 105, no. 1 (2011): 1–26, appendix data.

in order to assure the free flow of this vital resource. States within the region have also competed to dominate the global oil market. Furthermore, oil-rich states have been able to invest heavily in building up the military capacity to attack other states and repress internal opposition. In the domestic arena, oil has simultaneously empowered internal repression while also engendering stronger societal resistance. It has been a symbolic and material resource for rebel mobilization, especially when populations have felt that they have been denied fair access to the benefits of oil. In some circumstances, however, oil may help facilitate cooperation and dampen the incentives that lead to violence. More generally, though, oil has exacerbated the pinch of the MENA security predicament, collapsing the distinction between internal and external domains of security. In such conditions, states and regimes adopt aggressive postures that make violence more likely.

A Social History of MENA's Oil Curse

The resource curse is a result not of oil's physical or chemical properties but rather of the economic and social forces surrounding the modern oil industry. Oil has been known in MENA since antiquity, but only in the late 1800s did it become a valuable economic commodity. With far greater potential energy than coal, oil was a superior fuel for heating, shipping, railroads, and automobiles. Industrial powers immediately took notice. Britain, which had relied on indigenous coal for much of its industrialization, shifted to oil, which was only available outside its borders. By the turn of the twentieth century, oil was an increasing imperial priority. The Anglo-Iranian Oil Company (forerunner to British Petroleum) and other quasi-private firms received subsidies from the British government to develop MENA's oil resources. British colonial administrators also tried to block competitors from other countries. Across the region, colonial powers used force to defend oil fields and pipelines from insurgent attacks and installed harsh labor regimes within oil installations.[5]

Oil always had unique political and social valence, especially in MENA. Nationalist leaders railed against the dominance of Western firms from the inception of the oil industry. It was certainly true that the global oil economy favored consumers over producers in the first half of the twentieth century. Regional governments received a set percentage of oil revenues and sometimes tax revenues from oil company profits. But states often could not conduct audits to determine fair compensation from oil companies, much less set the sale prices for oil. In nationalist discourse, the impunity of these foreign oil companies violated national sovereignty. Post-colonial leaders steadily pushed for greater shares of oil wealth. In 1951, Prime Minister Mohammed Mossadeq of Iran unilaterally nationalized Iran's oil assets and established a national oil company. Britain and the United States conspired with Iranian army officers to oust Mossadeq, whom they labeled a communist sympathizer. Iran's democratic parliament was neutralized and the pro-Western Pahlavi monarchy was reinstated. Yet the wave of oil nationalization in MENA continued. In the countries under radical regimes such as Iraq, Egypt, and Libya, leaders touted expropriation as a blow against colonialism and a step toward returning the national patrimony to the people. Even Western-aligned governments, like Kuwait and Saudi Arabia, eventually assumed full ownership of their oil fields.

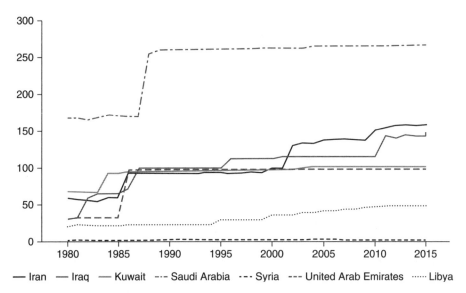

Figure 3.3 Top MENA oil producers (millions of barrels)
Source: BP Statistical Review of World Energy, available at *https://www.bp.com/en/global/corporate/*
energy-economics/statistical-review-of-world-energy.html.

Today the global oil trade is larger than that of all other commodities combined. State-owned national oil companies typically contract with private multinational oil companies (many the descendants of the foreign firms that had pioneered oil development early in the twentieth century). Still, producing countries have rarely been able to control global pricing. This is largely a function of the diversity of oil suppliers and the problems of coordinating supply. To ensure cooperation on supply production and pricing, Iran, Iraq, Kuwait, Saudi Arabia, and Venezuela founded the Organization of Petroleum Exporting Countries (OPEC) in 1960. OPEC has since grown to include nine other countries. But collusion among oil producers has been mostly short-lived and unsuccessful. Figure 3.3 shows the production among the largest MENA oil states. Saudi Arabia, by far the largest oil producer in the world, is probably the only country with enough spare capacity to affect global prices. Even then, its impact is likely fleeting.

Politically, oil economies reinforce hierarchical relationships between rulers and the ruled. Large-scale oil producers with small populations, such as Saudi Arabia and the other Arab Gulf states, can generally afford to subsidize citizens directly. They provide a generous basket of housing, education, energy, and healthcare at nominal costs, along with government jobs. More populous Iraq, Iran, and Algeria must divide their oil wealth more parsimoniously, but they still employ massive public sector payrolls and provide indirect subsidies on energy and other basics. Overall, the oil resources in state hands place citizens in the role of government dependants and reinforce the strength of the authoritarian bargain. Given these heightened expectations, though, even modest austerity measures meet with vociferous objection. Opposition figures complain of the squandering of the national patrimony. Indeed, national oil companies tend to have bloated payrolls and inept management.[6] Unsurprisingly, allegations of corruption and cronyism surround many of these state-owned enterprises. Rather than serving as the foundation for economic and political stability, state-owned oil actually undermines notions of political voice and reciprocity. This is the essence of what political scientist Terry Lynn Karl calls "the paradox of plenty": the gap between the promise and attainment of oil wealth.[7]

But as MENA suffers the unmet expectations of oil abundance, Western countries are perpetually concerned about oil scarcity. Few commodities are more vital to Western economies than oil and associated petrochemicals. Oil was essential to the entire structure of twentieth-century Western societies – what political economist Timothy Mitchell calls the era of "carbon democracy." Any restriction or shortfall in supply threatened the entire edifice of these socio-economic arrangements.[8] During the 1973 Arab–Israeli war, for example, Saudi Arabia and other Arab states boycotted the United States and Western powers in retaliation for their support for Israel. Cutting oil production drove up global prices and crippled the global economy. Western states, including the United States, have surreptitiously considered seizing oil installations to prevent shortfalls in anticipation of such actions. Anxiety about oil scarcity, like the paradox of plenty, is as much a product of ideology as of economics. In hindsight, the global economic slump of the 1970s appears the result not of economic blackmail on the part of oil producers but of global business cycles exacerbated by poor economic management on the part of consumers. OPEC enjoys even less global market share today than it did in the 1970s, making producer collusion even less efficacious. Moreover, technological advancements have led to new oil discoveries, the emergence of alternative fuels, and greater energy efficiency, further lessening the power of MENA oil producers.[9] The oil market is stubbornly global in composition, and producers rarely succeed in discriminating among oil buyers. Consequently, the cost of seizing oil almost certainly exceeds any economic benefit.[10] Nevertheless, the tensions between the mindsets of oil plenty and oil scarcity generate strife at multiple levels.

Oil and International Wars

International relations scholars and pundits have long commented on the possibilities of war for oil. Working at the geopolitical and regional level of analysis, MENA is an obvious place for petro-aggression to occur. Jeffrey Colgan, a political scientist, details multiple pathways and mechanisms by which oil contributes to interstate war. The first and most intuitive is "resource war," when states try to acquire oil reserves by force. Unquestionably, colonial powers waged war to gain control over rich territories in MENA. They subsequently used force to maintain friendly regimes that could assure them of access. The pattern carried over into the era of independence. In both the Iran–Iraq War (1980–8) and the first Gulf War (1990–1), Iraq tried to seize oil-rich territories of a rival state.

Oil-rich states finance military build-ups and interventions abroad with oil revenues instead of taxes. Petro-revolutionary states, such as Iraq and Iran, are especially prone to aggression and miscalculation.[11] There is no doubt that Iraq and Iran financed their military build-up in the 1970s and 1980s with oil revenues. But it is difficult to trace any particular miscalculation to oil surfeit as opposed to other causes. Iraqi President Saddam Hussein and Iranian Supreme Leader Ayatollah Khomeini certainly had moments of wild overconfidence, but these were tempered with a profound sense of vulnerability. Both leaders went to war in the belief that their foreign and domestic enemies were colluding against them – the classic symptom of the MENA security predicament.

A broader look at MENA's regional politics shows that direct interstate strife over oil has been relatively rare. Against the tally of aggressive petro-revolutionaries like Iran and Iraq, we must weigh the likes of Algeria and the People's Democratic Republic of Yemen, petro-revolutionaries that have mostly avoided foreign wars, or have had wars thrust upon them. Additionally, oil-producing countries like Saudi Arabia and most of the Persian Gulf states have, until recently, dodged foreign military entanglements – a topic addressed below. Equally importantly, none of the major belligerents in the Arab–Israeli wars were oil-rich.

In some circumstances, oil has even dampened the incentive for regional conflict. Oil requires a trans-national infrastructure. Pipelines crisscross national boundaries and effectively knit together a system of export terminals, refineries, and production fields that span the region and the globe. The sunk cost of this infrastructure inclines users toward long-term cooperation, although states have at times threatened to shut down or blockade these networks. The 1979 Egypt–Israel peace treaty involved return of the Sinai Peninsula to Egypt while granting Israel a long-term supply of oil and gas from Egyptian fields. The Israel–Egypt pipeline has since been extended to Jordan.[12] Iran and Qatar agreed in the 1980s to develop the maritime oil and gas fields jointly. The partnership in hydrocarbons is an important part of a pragmatic and amiable bilateral relationship.[13]

There is a third important pathway from oil to international conflict: MENA's oil resources might induce or entice military interventions from states outside the region. Oil-importing states might undertake military action in response to perceived economic threats to the oil market. This motivation is distinct from resource wars involving a state's efforts to seize oil reserves for itself.[14] For their part, leaders within MENA have long accused outside powers of coveting the region's oil and trying to take it by force. Iraqi President Saddam Hussein warned a year before he invaded and annexed Kuwait that

> if the people of the Gulf, as well as all Arabs, are not careful, they will all be under American control and command. In addition, if they remain weak, the situation might evolve to the extent that the US can set standards for the amount of oil allowed to be produced for each Gulf country, and who it [is] allowed to sell it to in the world, as well as determining the price of oil based on US interests, not anyone else's. This effectively means that peace in the Middle East is not actually desired based on the US point of view.[15]

The United States generally has avoided taking direct control over oil-producing territories. This does not mean, however, that it is uninterested in dominating the global oil market. On the contrary, the United States has made sure that oil trade is conducted in dollars, effectively placing the entire global market under US purview. It has used its forward military position in MENA to prevent any actor from obstructing the global oil market. This has simultaneously ensured the global energy supply and confirmed US geostrategic dominance. "Capturing oil and oil fields and establishing direct or imperial control over oil," historian Toby Craig Jones notes, "has not been part of the United States' strategic logic for war. But protecting oil, oil producers, and the flow of oil has been."[16]

The oil-rich Persian Gulf illustrates this logic. Beginning with the Iran–Iraq War, the United States sought to prevent any actor from blocking the Gulf. It reflagged Kuwaiti oil tankers to prevent Iranian attacks. After repelling the Iraqi invasion of Kuwait, the United States tried to contain both Iran and Iraq using a military threat and economic sanctions. But when it did invade and occupy Iraq in 2003, it did not expropriate or even privatize Iraqi oil. On the contrary, it opened Iraq's oil field to foreign investors, including Russia and Iran. Most of Iraq's oil exports in fact were bound for Asia. US military engagements are *about* oil, but not *for* oil.

But while US policy may have brought war to the northern littoral of the Gulf, it arguably helped secure peace for Saudi Arabia and the states on the southern side of the Gulf. The US–Saudi alliance dates to the 1930s, when Saudi rulers chose to partner with a US-backed private oil consortium (led by the predecessors to Chevron and Exxon) as a counterweight to British Petroleum. The alliance was more than just commercial. The Saudi monarchy shared the United States' antipathy to communism and backed US ventures to combat communist influence in Afghanistan and Pakistan during the Cold War. With the Iranian Revolution of 1979 and the Iran–Iraq War in 1980, Saudi Arabia became the default leader of the Arab Gulf states. In 1981, Saudi Arabia,

Bahrain, the UAE, Kuwait, Qatar, and Oman formed the Gulf Cooperation Council (GCC).[17] By allowing the United States operational bases in their territory, the GCC members avoided the need to fight battles of their own. Saudi Arabia and others spent heavily on US military hardware, but without the expectation of actually using it.[18] Saudi units that joined the US-led Gulf War coalition were well equipped but woefully trained and roundly ineffective in 1991. The centerpiece of the Saudi security services was the Saudi Arabia National Guard (SANG) – praetorian units tasked with preventing coups and insurrections, not combating foreign adversaries. In the larger sense, though, the US military umbrella may have allowed GCC member states to avoid military confrontation despite historical enmities, ideological rivalries, and latent territorial disputes.[19]

But American hegemony, enticed by oil, is neither inevitable nor perpetual. At almost the exact time when US forces became mired in the quagmire of the Iraqi occupation, US dependence on oil imports began to decline. By the 2010s, many actors in the region doubted the United States' resolve to back its allies. Saudi Arabia and the UAE undertook dramatic military build-ups in the 2010s. Saudi Arabia saw Iran as fomenting crisis within the Arab world generally by inciting Arab Shi'i communities in Lebanon, Yemen, Bahrain, Iraq, and Saudi Arabia itself. The Saudis sent troops to Bahrain and launched an expeditionary war in Yemen, with the UAE as a junior partner. Riyadh and Abu Dhabi also initiated a military dispute with neighboring Qatar, which the Saudis considered the instigator of internal subversion and Islamist terrorism. In 2014, Saudi Arabia blockaded Qatar, another US ally and the site of a major US military base. US efforts to resolve the conflict failed. Saudi Arabia and the UAE also provided military and financial support to militias and other non-state actors in Libya and Syria in order to counter Qatar and Iran. US predominance, motivated in part by oil, arguably stabilized some conflicts and exacerbated others.[20] The US presence, though, heightened the anxiety of regimes that viewed internal and external threats as interchangeable and interlocking.

Still, for many MENA states, oil is simply too valuable to fight over. In 2018 and 2019, a direct confrontation between Iran and Saudi Arabia seemed almost inevitable. There were escalating tit-for-tat attacks between Iran, Saudi Arabia, and its Emirati partner. Iranian forces damaged Saudi and Emirate vessels in the Persian Gulf. Saudi Arabia and the United States seized Iranian vessels in the Red Sea and the Gulf. Iranian-backed militias in Yemen and Iraq launched missile and drone attacks on Saudi territory, including major cities, military bases, and oil installations. In September 2019, a drone attack, launched either from Iraq or Yemeni territory by Iranian-backed forces, inflicted substantial damage on a Saudi oil terminal. The attack temporarily cut off 60 percent of Saudi production, around 5 percent of the global oil supply. Yet the long-awaited counterattack never came. Neither side could afford an escalation that would further endanger oil exports. The United States, which had broadly allied with Riyadh and touted its mantra of applying maximum pressure on Tehran, demurred. Ultimately, quiet diplomacy prevailed and conflict was averted, largely for the sake of maintaining oil sales.[21]

The Oil Price Cycle and MENA's Regional Conflict

Patterns of conflict in MENA sometimes coincide with cyclical fluctuations in oil prices. MENA's regional economy is tethered to oil's perpetual boom-and-bust price cycle. This cycle is largely the result of normal supply-and-demand dynamics. As oil prices rise owing to limited supply, it becomes profitable to invest in extracting oil from more costly oil fields. The marginal cost of production – the amount of money it takes to extract one more barrel of oil from a field – reflects the outlays of capital and labor needed to lift oil from the ground, plus the costs of transportation, taxes, and administrative and royalty fees necessary to bring it to market and ultimately a buyer. Oil investors keep the marginal cost of each field a closely guarded secret. By almost every estimate, MENA countries have some of the lowest estimated marginal costs in the world, as depicted in Table 3.1. With low marginal costs, countries like Saudi Arabia, Iran, and Iraq can sell oil relatively profitably even while prices are low. By comparison, oil fields in the United States, the United Kingdom, and Canada have a relatively high marginal cost owing to geology and other factors. These producers only come online once global prices already reach higher levels and there is a considerable shortage of oil relative to demand. The more expensive producers enter the market too late to make up the shortfalls. But almost exactly when high energy prices seem to stifle global economic growth, demand falls. Additionally, high energy costs spur investment in wind, solar, nuclear, and other alternative energy sources, which are normally not price-competitive when oil is cheap. Supply eventually but inevitably overshoots demands. Prices fall and the higher-cost fields shut down. The cyclical downturn can have an especially heavy impact on MENA countries where a large part of the economy depends on oil revenue. One of OPEC's prime historical concerns has been to sustain oil prices at a high enough level to generate profit but without smothering global growth.

The oil price cycle involves more than just the economics of supply and demand. Cullen Hendrix, a political scientist, shows that oil-rich states are most likely to initiate military disputes with their neighbors when oil prices are high. During these periods, they have the money to stockpile weaponry and confidence to use it.[22] Going a step further, economist Mahmoud el-Gamal and oil expert Amy Myers Jaffe use a sophisticated mathematical formula to track the correlation between oil price fluctuations and moments of wars,

Table 3.1 Marginal cost to produce one barrel of oil (or gas equivalent) in US dollars (2016)

United Kingdom	44.33
Brazil	34.99
Canada	26.64
US shale	23.35
US non-shale	20.99
Russia	19.21
Iraq	10.57
Iran	9.08
Saudi Arabia	8.98

Source: "Cost of Producing a Barrel of Oil and Gas," *Wall Street Journal*, April 15, 2016, available at *http:// graphics.wsj.com/oil-barrel-breakdown/*.

military confrontations, and other kinds of geopolitical risk. They argue that military provocations within MENA drive up lagging oil prices beyond basic market forces. Consumers pay a security premium to insure against possible disruptions of the future oil supply. The inevitable price downturn, though, sparks compounding domestic and regional crises. Thus, Saudi Arabia's aggressive military posture since 2011 reflects a combination of strategic and economic thinking. The blockade of Qatar, war in Yemen, and diplomatic efforts to curb Iranian oil exports created an artificial price shock that boosted otherwise lagging oil prices.[23]

Another aspect of the oil price cycle is the opportunity for large-scale producers to block out higher-cost producers. Oil prices themselves are susceptible to manipulation, at least in the short term. Wealthy producers can treat their spare capacity as a strategic weapon, flooding the market to keep prices artificially low while preventing a strategic rival from gaining revenues.[24] This is a different "oil weapon" than the typical image of a sales boycott. Instead, the target is other oil producers. With higher production costs and fewer reserves, they may not be able to bear the pain of a protracted oil price slump. Saudi Arabia especially can afford to undercut its rivals in order to retain customers in Asia that might otherwise buy from Iran and Russia, at least in the short term. This allows Riyadh to capture the benefits of the artificial risk premium while denying revenues to its rivals. Still, such economic coercion tactics require Saudi Arabia to sacrifice some of its domestic revenue. It is unclear how sustainable the policy of price competition is over the long term.

In the wider sense, the close correlation between the oil price cycle and MENA's political risk crisis is evidence of the compounding impact that oil has on the underlying security predicament in the region. Economic changes contribute to military aggression in MENA, but military aggression precipitates economic perturbations as well. Riding a fiscal rollercoaster of booms and busts, regimes take riskier positions when oil prices are high and fear the potentially catastrophic impact of downturns.

Oil and Internal Wars

The impact of oil in MENA's internal wars is as complex and equivocal as it is in international conflicts. Much of the current analysis of oil and civil war uses cross-national statistical techniques that look for the average effects of the oil variable globally. Findings have been ambiguous. While useful for certain purposes, this quantitative approach necessarily excises context and makes it more difficult to consider complex causal patterns. To understand the role of oil in MENA's internal wars, it is important to trace its effect in the prevailing regional security predicament and in the balance of power between regimes and opposition.

Intuitively, oil should advantage states to overawe internal opposition, thus resolving at least one element of the MENA security predicament. This trump card works through two distinct mechanisms. First, possessing large oil wealth enables states to buy off or appease would-be challengers. The richest oil states, like Saudi Arabia, Qatar, and the UAE, avoided the difficult negotiation over taxes and other forms of extraction from their own society. The satiation of citizens makes rebellion unnecessary. Secondly, the fear of losing access to oil wealth can also daunt a would-be rebellion. As Libya's popular uprising erupted in the spring of 2011, Saif al-Islam Qaddafi, the son and heir-apparent of Muammar Qaddafi, recorded a YouTube video describing the "rivers of blood" that would come if the rebellion continued. Saif specifically mentioned the crippling of the oil industry: "You will emigrate from Libya, because the oil will cease to flow, and the foreign companies will leave Libya tomorrow. The oil companies will leave Libya. The oil ministry will cease to function, and tomorrow, there will be no oil and no money."[25] But Saif's warning went unheeded. The people of Libya *did* rise up. Oil-rich Algeria and Iraq have seen repeated bouts of political instability and civil war. Saudi Arabia, the largest oil producer in the world, spawned the radical opposition of al-Qaeda. The greatest political revolution in the late twentieth century occurred in Iran in 1979 in the midst of an unprecedented oil bonanza. These episodes of conflicts in countries seemingly blessed by oil wealth underscore the paradoxical effects of such bounty.

Oil revenues often yield a particularly brittle form of state capacity. States with no need to tax populations often forgo opportunities to build effective bodies for political representation. When times are good and budgets seem inexhaustible, competence, efficiency, and responsiveness in administration are low priorities. But when oil prices dip, these deficits contribute to compounding economic and political crises. Notably, not every crisis has led to civil war. Different institutional structures derived from the legacies of pre-oil stages of state formation have also constrained how countries like Libya, Saudi Arabia, Iraq, Iran, and the Gulf states have responded to oil's booms and busts and helped determine state resilience. The impact of oil on state capacity has thus been historically variegated and context-dependent.[26]

A second and more consistent mechanism by which oil empowers states is by granting them the means for brute coercion. The sheer scale of the military build-up might discourage most opposition and crush the few who do challenge the state. Again, this mechanism highlights the abiding logic of the security predicament, in which internal and external security fields are indistinguishable. All MENA regimes are concerned about internal security. Most have adopted some form of coup-proofing, including creating praetorian guards or parallel forces. Oil states have the resources to pursue this strategy most fully.[27] In Saudi Arabia, the SANG recruits heavily from tribes of the Najd region, which have strong familial and dynastic ties to the ruling family. It receives better weaponry and training than other security branches. Along with the other favored military branches, SANG even has dedicated housing arrangements and hospitals for service members and their families. Iran's Islamic Revolutionary Guard Corps (IRGC) similarly originated as a force to protect the revolutionary regime from internal subversion after 1979. Although the IRGC adopted a more conventional military role during the Iran–Iraq War, it is still regarded as more ideologically trustworthy than the regular Iranian army and receives a larger budget. The IRGC also began to play a prominent role in Iran's oil sector through parastatal construction and business companies.[28]

Oil wealth can also make a state a more attractive partner for international alliances. American hegemony in the Persian Gulf was not just about protecting client states from external aggression, but also about ensuring the endurance of reliable regime partners. It was the United States, after all, who equipped and trained the Saudi security services, for example. Foreign backers can also help shield regimes from outside scrutiny on human rights issues. Human rights advocates have long pointed out a double standard when it came to Saudi Arabia, which seemed exempted from the US democracy promotion efforts. American officials have been far more reluctant to speak publicly about Saudi Arabia's human rights record than about those of other regional states.[29] The US–Saudi strategic partnership, then, has effectively lowered the cost of domestic repression.

Oil-rich regimes also enjoy the means to hire private contractors to train and support their armies and intelligence agencies. The Omani and Bahraini military have long relied on foreign mercenaries, including former British special forces as well as Jordanian and Pakistani nationals.[30] Rulers hope that mercenaries, unlike domestically raised forces, will have no allegiances beside their paymaster. They also often offer loyal foreign servants a chance to gain citizenship. The UAE has hired American private military contractors to set up a mercenary force comprised of ex-Colombian, South African, British, French, and American soldiers.[31] Private Western security firms have helped Saudi Arabia and the UAE to set up sophisticated programs to censor social media and spy on their populations and foreign adversaries. Furthermore, US arms manufacturers have helped to scuttle legislation that would have curtailed US assistance for the Saudi war in Yemen.[32]

But just as oil empowers states, it also emboldens and energizes internal opposition. It is easy for the opposition to blame the rulers of oil-rich states for squandering the national patrimony, especially during times of economic hardship. Challengers take the regime's misuse of oil revenues as a theme in their criticisms of regimes. Bin Laden accused the Saudi monarchy of trying to appease the US by underpricing oil revenue, thereby cheating the Saudi people. The US military presence in Saudi Arabia after 1990, which bin Laden claimed was an affront to Islam, stemmed directly from the kingdom's oil wealth.

Oil grievances tend to have a specific sub-national geography. Centers of oil production, like Benghazi, Kirkuk, Kuwait City, Dhahran, and Ahwaz, have witnessed unheralded population growth over the last century. The arrival of foreign capital made them some of the wealthiest parts of their countries almost overnight. But the uneven impact of the oil boom is always apparent in the way these cities expanded. Saudi novelist Abdul Rahman Munif's magisterial *Cities of Salt* trilogy explores the kinds of social dislocation oil discovery occasioned.[33] New urban developments accommodated trained technicians, administrators, and other government officials. Foreigners were housed in special enclaves. Industrial laborers, meanwhile, remained in squalid work camps on the outer rim or squeezed into urban shanties. The contrast was often fodder for social criticism. Journalists in Kuwait noted how hovels sprung up in the shadow of the newly built Sheraton Hotel in Kuwait City's burgeoning shopping district in the 1960s.[34] The pattern of uneven growth persists even today. A resident of a shantytown near Wasit in east-central Iraq noted, "We see oil around us in all directions. . . . But we don't benefit from any of the oil. We only inhale the smoke and fumes and fear the diseases they bring."[35]

Not surprisingly, oil workers were often the vanguard of the proletariat across the late developing world. Through the 1960s, left-wing opposition parties made inroads among oil workers in Iraq, Saudi Arabia, Iran, Sudan, and elsewhere, mobilizing laborers to seek better wages and living conditions. MENA's oil fields and adjacent infrastructure were epicenters of labor militancy. To counteract the potential of radicalization within the industrial ranks, many of the Gulf countries recruited industrial labor from South Asia. These workers can easily be expelled if they show an inclination to organizing.

The tension within the oil cities represents a microcosm of the larger national-level contestation of the rights to oil revenues.[36]

Restiveness is especially pronounced in oil-producing regions that suffer political and economic marginalization. Oil heightens disparities of political and economic opportunity and highlights cleavages within these states. Many of these are the historical legacies of state formation that brought conquest and subordination.[37] The case of al-Hasa, Saudi Arabia's main oil-producing region, is illustrative. Saudi Arabia conquered and annexed the predominantly Shi'i region only in 1913. The US consortium that developed the eastern fields recruited local Shi'is as a major part of its labor force. Some Shi'is were even able to move into managerial tracks. However, a combination of factors blocked their path for advancement. First, the US firms installed a system of racial segregation modeled explicitly on the Jim Crow South. Saudi nationals were paid less, given sub-standard housing and healthcare, and excluded from the "whites only" compounds reserved for American and European staff.[38] Compounding this localized socio-economic exclusion, Shi'is in general were marginalized within Saudi politics. The Saudi government was constantly concerned with "troublemakers" in the oil fields and used security services to root out the influence of communism and Arab nationalism. There was a major uprising in al-Hasa in 1979 after the Islamic revolution in Iran, inspired and perhaps instigated by followers of Ayatollah Khomeini. The region saw another uprising in the 2011 Arab spring rebellions, coinciding with a similar uprising in neighboring Bahrain. Residents demanded, among other things, a fair share of the wealth originating from their soil.[39] In other cases, outright secessionist or separatist movements claim oil as part of their national patrimony. The Southern Movement in Yemen and the Cyrenaican autonomy movement in Libya similarly complained the oil from their soil was being funneled to the coffers of the central government (see below). They spoke nostalgically about a previous era of autonomy and independence. The loss of oil symbolized the denial of sovereignty.

Although oil is typically a resource for the state, it can also serve to finance rebel activities. When state control over violence falters, oil becomes an outright object for greed. Insurgents commonly attack oil installations and pipelines, trying to throttle an important source of state revenue. Insurgents have repeatedly attacked the Egypt–Israel–Jordan pipeline. As the insurgency accelerated in Iraq through 2004 and 2005, there were attacks on pipelines and other installations more than twice per week.[40] But insurgents also try to siphon oil revenue to their own uses. Through the 2000s, Iraqi insurgents were notorious for smuggling state-subsidized gasoline and other refined products to Syria and Jordan. Emerging in the early 2010s, the Islamic State (IS) took over trafficking routes between Syria, Iraq, and Turkey and began extorting refineries and other oil production points. As the militaries of Syria and then Iraq buckled and collapsed between 2011 and 2014, IS conquered a handful of oil wells and refineries. IS moved from oil smuggling to oil production, using its revenues to fund its fighters. Some estimates hold that IS was able to generate $380 million daily from its oil sales. It used these revenues to finance a veritable rebel state that included a rudimentary welfare state meant to surpass that offered by Syria or Iraq.[41]

Besides physical control over oil facilities, rebels also vie to control the channels to the international oil market. Oil is not as easily looted or smuggled as diamonds or other "conflict resources." Without a national oil company and central bank that can access dollar-denominated international oil markets, rebels may not be able to gain full market price. During the 2011 uprisings, Yemeni, Libyan, and Syrian opposition leaders lobbied the international community to freeze the funds of the national oil company and the central bank. These moneys belonged to the people, they reasoned, not the repressive regime. The United States and its allies did consider granting the provisional rebel governments and governments-in-exile access to the funds and did impose economic sanctions on recalcitrant regimes. Rebels promised to reward foreign backers with preferential access to oil once they were firmly in command. Such "future booty," as Michael Ross calls it, certainly emboldened oppositions in launching rebellions and probably helped entice external sponsors.[42]

Oil has also been a considerable factor in Kurdish drives for autonomy and independence in Iraq. Kurdish rebels have fought for self-rule since the creation of Iraq in 1921. The discovery of oil in the vicinity of Kirkuk in 1927 added impetus to this secessionist movement. Kurdish leaders maintained that Kirkuk, which had been the seat of the medieval Kurdish principality, was their national capital. They demanded control over the city and access to its oil resources. The government tried to dilute Kurdish predominance in Kirkuk, gerrymandering administrative districts and recruiting Arab migrants to work in the oil sector.[43] Kurdish militants attacked and sabotaged pipelines. At the same time, Kurdish leaders tried to use access to the oil to entice outside support. In 1973, Mulla Mustafa Barzani, head of the Kurdish Democratic Party, openly offered future booty to the US in return for military support: "[W]e are ready to act according to US policy if the US will protect us from the wolves. In the event of sufficient support we should be able to control Kirkuk oilfields and confer exploitation rights on an American company."[44] Indeed, US, Iranian, and Israeli military support enabled Kurdish rebels to push the Iraqi government to offer an autonomy plan. Ultimately, though, the rebellion crumbled when the foreign backers withdrew. This basic stratagem was repeated in the 2000s and 2010s by the Kurdistan Regional Government (KRG) in Iraq. Under Iraq's 2005 constitution, Kurdistan had special status as a federal region within Iraq and received 17 percent of Iraq's total oil revenue (in proportion to its share of Iraq's total population). KRG forces tried to infiltrate into Kirkuk, which remained under central government control. They sought to reinstate displaced Kurds and pressure recent migrants to the city to leave. Iraqi Kurdish leaders insisted that Baghdad and the Iraqi National Oil Company were mishandling the funds and shortchanging the Kurds. Moreover, they asserted that the oil in Kurdistan rightfully belonged to the people of Kurdistan and should be disposed at their discretion. Accordingly, the KRG bypassed Baghdad's control by building pipelines to Turkey. The KRG's push to sell oil without Baghdad's approval precipitated a constitutional crisis, as the central government threatened to cut off allocation of funds if the KRG insisted on selling oil independently. The rise of IS in 2014 compounded this crisis. As Iraqi security forces crumbled, the KRG moved to take Kirkuk and its adjacent oil fields. The KRG talked more openly about outright secession. Hoping to bargain access to oil for international support, it appealed to Russian, American, Turkish, and Iranian oil firms. Yet few companies were willing to take such a gamble. The KRG furtively sold some oil through the Turkish pipeline at a discount. But as the KRG leadership pushed more explicitly for independence, it found the oil incentive less useful. Turkey and Iran had been willing to trade with the autonomous Kurdish region, but would not countenance Kurdish independence. The United States rejected the Kurdish claim to own the oil. Kurdish oil diplomacy raised expectations, but failed to deliver results.[45]

Case Study: Oil and War in Libya

The civil war in Libya is an especially useful case to consider oil's multivalent impact on conflict. Libya is the quintessence of an oil-dependent state. Oil accounts for almost all of the country's exports by value and at least half of its GDP. Successive Libyan regimes have tried to use oil revenue as a catalyst for social and economic development, as well as a tool to maintain authoritarian control. Muammar Qaddafi used oil to reward loyal constituents and maintain a robust police state to ensure political stability.[46] Confirming Colgan's argument about petro-revolutionary states, oil revenue allowed Qaddafi to undertake a series of provocative and rash foreign policy gambits, including sponsorship of terrorist organizations, the invasion of Chad, and an ill-fated confrontation with the United States in the 1980s. By the 2000s, though, he had tried to use oil to entice international investment and solidify alliances with Europe.[47]

But the lackluster economic performance, corruption, and political repression that oil engendered were also key factors inciting societal resistance. The 2011 uprising began in Cyrenaica, the site of Libya's largest oil fields. The contest to gain physical control over oil production and export was closely linked to the effort to assert legal title, the right to dispose of oil and receive the proceeds from its sale. Qaddafi tried to call in favors from countries interested in maintaining access to Libyan oil. He warned of dire consequences should oil cease to flow. At the same time, the Transitional National Council (TNC), the leading opposition organ that had formed in rebel-held Benghazi, lobbied for a freeze on Libya's oil sales, sovereign wealth fund, and other assets. The UN Security Council embargoed Libyan state assets. Upon gaining international recognition, the TNC assumed authority over the state-owned Libyan National Oil Company (LNOC) and the Central Bank of Libya (CBL). Still, many of the disparate revolutionary committees and militias operating across the country offered the TNC only nominal allegiance. Libya's sovereignty ruptured, with neither Qaddafi nor the rebel government actually able to exert control on the ground.[48]

Even after the capture and execution of Qaddafi in October 2011, the TNC and its successor interim government struggled to maintain physical control over oil fields, pipelines, refineries, and export terminals. The government assigned former revolutionary militias to paramilitary duties in lieu of the inchoate national army. These forces operated without effective oversight from central authorities. In July 2013, Ibrahim Jadhran, a commander of a paramilitary group from Ajdabiyya, seized the export terminals in the oil crescent region near Sidra. Jadhran appeared to some as another criminal seeking to profit from smuggling and extortion over oil. However, he asserted that he intended to claim the oil on behalf of the people of Cyrenaica. As early as 2012, tribal leaders in eastern Libya had expressed frustration with the Tripoli government and pushed to assert regional autonomy. They specifically demanded a reversion to Libya's original constitution of 1951, which had granted the region control over its own mineral wealth and its own security forces. Jadhran insisted that his actions were constitutionally sanctioned as part of Cyrenaica's rightful claim.[49] He announced the formation of a 20,000-man Cyrenaican army, comprised of paramilitary troops and tribal fighters. He hired lobbyists to reach out to Moscow and Washington, hoping to gain their favor with promises of oil. There were rumors of shady foreign buyers. The UN and the Libyan government warned that any oil exported from the captured port would be regarded as stolen Libyan state property. Yet the Tripoli government lacked the military means to retake the facilities. Libya lost an estimated $30 billion in export revenue. The United States intercepted a tanker sailing from Sidra in March 2014, quashing hopes to sell the contraband on the international market. Jadhran eventually agreed to relinquish the port in return for dismissal of pending arrest warrants, payment of back salaries, and a promise to begin relocating the LNOC headquarters to the east.[50]

The physical and symbolic contest over oil intensified through the 2014 election and the subsequent second civil war. The newly elected House of Representatives (HoR) relocated to the east, with the parliament seated in Tobruk. The holdover of the interim legislature remained in Tripoli. Both claimed to be Libya's sole legitimate government and both asserted authority over the national oil company and central bank. The situation became even more complicated with the rise of General Khalifa Haftar and his alliance with the HoR. Haftar denounced the Tripoli government for harboring the "radical" Muslim Brotherhood and fostering instability and lawlessness. He aimed to storm Tripoli, oust the purported Islamists, and establish a strong, centralized, and unitary Libyan state. Russia, Saudi Arabia, the UAE, and Egypt supported him in order to counter Qatar and Turkey, which backed factions originating in Misrata and Tripoli. Haftar's self-styled Libyan National Army (LNA) and associated militias fought to control eastern Libya, including the largest oil installations of the east, and attacked Tripoli.

The international community initially recognized the HoR as Libya's legitimate government, but insisted on working with the established CBL and LNOC technocrats based in Tripoli. In late 2015, the UN negotiated the installation of the Government of National Accord (GNA) in Tripoli in the hopes of reconciling the eastern and western factions. The HoR government, backed by Haftar, refused to stand down. One of the ways it challenged Tripoli was by launching its own central bank and national oil company, creating the simulacra of legal authority. The eastern oil company branch repeatedly tried to sell oil to foreign customers under its own authority through eastern ports and terminals. In 2016, it issued a directive on official stationery instructing that payments for Libyan oil should be submitted to a bank in Jordan. For the most part, though, international interventions stymied these efforts by insisting the proceeds of all sales be routed to the main CBL accounts. Some smuggling continued, but quasi-legal sales of Libyan oil through the eastern oil company and eastern bank were blocked. With backing from Russia, the UAE, Saudi Arabia, and Egypt, the HoR continued to issue debt and even printed banknotes. This was essential for financing the military struggle. The Tripoli government warned that the HoR-authorized debt was illegal, its tender counterfeit.[51] The LNOC and CBL, both based in Tripoli, paid salaries to civil servants across the country and secreted proceeds from oil sales to both warring factions. The IMF, the World Bank, and the UN hoped that assuring all parties access to oil wealth would create incentives for political reconciliation and avert a humanitarian catastrophe. Oil was too valuable to destroy outright.[52]

But Haftar and the eastern rebels continued to vie to gain a legal authority to match their physical control on the ground. In June 2018, LNA forces seized oil facilities around Sidra and immediately announced the transfer of their control to the eastern oil company. This Benghazi-based oil company issued a general memorandum on an LNOC letterhead announcing that it was now the sole representative of the Libyan national oil company. The letter deftly cited Libyan law and UN resolutions to designate itself as the sole owner of Libyan oil and petroleum-related products. The Tripoli government again accused the eastern oil company of fraud. The Tripoli-based LNOC declared force majeure in affected fields, effectively annulling any property claims over the captured oil. Haftar backed down after a fortnight, but the incident underscored the impotence of the Libyan state in physically defending its most valuable assets.

Oil played a complicated role in Libya's civil war. It motivated and enabled violent actions, but also held out the promise of conciliation and shared prosperity. Ultimately, while some belligerents clearly benefited from their access to oil, the Libyan people as a whole suffered. Oil production has yet to reach pre-2011 levels. Tens of billions of dollars have been lost due to interrupted production, corruption, smuggling, theft, and extortion of the oil fields. These losses add to Libya's downward economic momentum. When only those with guns can thrive, the conflict trap becomes all the more gripping.

Conclusion

Fighting for physical control over oil assets is only a small part of how oil leads to war. Oil's impact is mediated by the regional security predicament and the fundamental insecurity of regimes in relation to both regional challengers and domestic opposition. This impact has less to do with oil's chemical properties or economic value than with its unique socio-political valence. Oil raised expectations about economic transformation and political liberation in MENA. The gap between promise and reality contributed to popular disaffection and hamstrung state capacity. It also emboldened and motivated actors that might seize control over oil for themselves.

Equally important, oil-consuming countries, including the major Western powers, suffered irrational and exaggerated fears of scarcity that spurred them to military interventions in MENA. The alighting of outside powers to MENA, drawn in by oil, often heightened the tensions of the security dilemma and linked concerns about internal and external security even more tightly. Oil-rich states rely on external support during their foreign adventures and use their assets to secure foreign backing in their domestic repression. Rebels experience a mirrored effect. They also hope to finance their actions through oil rents, although here the structures of the international financial system create a bias against them. They try to barter access to oil for external support in waging their insurrections.

There is some speculation about what a "post-oil" future for MENA would look like. With the progress of newer, cleaner energy sources and the push to reduce carbon emissions, oil would be less important in the global economy. This could precipitate a geopolitical realignment and dampen the impetus for outside intervention in the region. However, reducing the value and allure of oil may not substantially change the prospects for war and conflict. Oil wealth at times serves as a disincentive to conflict and may even facilitate cooperation. This is most evident in cases of interstate cooperation in pipeline management, export agreements, and similar types of commercial ties. But oil-rich states also have unique means to buy off or otherwise satisfy popular opposition – at least when times are good. In this respect, oil ameliorates conflict. Finally, foreign engagement in the region often motivated by oil can help uphold stability, rather than just wreck it. A decline in oil's value could erode the very incentives that keep civil and international war at bay.

Oil is rarely a singular cause of war in MENA. All MENA states suffer from some form of the security predicament. States and non-state actors engage constantly in omnibalancing between internal and external threats. Oil provides unique resources to deal with these challenges but also introduces unique vulnerabilities. Seeking out an outside backer is a common tactical response to this challenge. It can, in some circumstances, lead to conflict and war. The differences among oil-rich states is less a matter of kind than of degree. Saudi Arabia and Iran have both used oil to finance military build-ups. They have both perceived an interlinking of foreign and domestic threats and turned to risky foreign military adventures abroad. But they still adhered to the basic rules of the game in regional conflict dynamics. They mostly eschewed direct military confrontations in favor of proxy wars in Syria, Yemen, and elsewhere. They made no efforts at territorial aggrandizement, focusing instead on extending informal spheres of influence. Oil is not the root of MENA's security predicament, but it does amplify the predicament's effects, making war and violence more prominent and flagrant.

4

Identity as Conflict Trap

MENA is often described as a "mosaic" of ethno-sectarian identity groups.[1] The region is especially volatile because allegiance to these deep-seated group identities supersedes loyalty to the state. The result is a "volcanic eruption of ancient feuds," as commentator Fred Kaplan put it.[2] Journalist Richard Engel offers another well-worn cliché in stating that "there is no distinction between modern and ancient history in the Middle East. No region is more obsessed with its own past."[3] In this view, communities of Jews, Muslims, and Christians, Sunnis and Shi'is, Kurds, Arabs, and Persians and others long predate the contemporary states. They have fought for centuries. Their claims to shared sacred spaces and homelands are mutually incompatible, making clashes inevitable and perpetual. If oil traps MENA in war through greed, by this view group identity dooms the region because of atavistic hatred and pride.

There is no gainsaying the complexity or diversity of group identities witnessed in the region. In his seminal study of Arab politics, Michael Hudson describes how the division of the region into multiple states riddled with minority groups and conflicting communal identities thwarted the impetus for unity in the Arab core.[4] The All Minorities at Risk (AMAR) project at the University of Maryland seems to confirm this assessment. Table 4.1 catalogs the multiple politically relevant ethnic groups in MENA states.

Internal heterogeneity becomes even starker when viewed quantitatively. In the 1990s, a group of economists used a simple arithmetical equation to calculate fractionalization, the odds that two randomly selected individuals in a country would hail from different ethnic, linguistic, or religious communities. As shown in Figure 4.1, with the possible exceptions of Tunisia and perhaps Egypt, almost every MENA state has significant cultural cleavage. The issue becomes further complicated when considering the number of groups whose territorial homelands are cleaved by state borders. The imbalance between state and nation is even more profound for stateless ethnic groups, like Kurds or Berbers, as well as tribes and clans that span international boundaries. This misfit between identity groups and state boundaries produces a constant and profound lack of legitimacy.

Still, we should not address ethnic conflict in MENA as somehow *sui generis* or exempt from the kinds of explanations applied to the rest of the world.

Table 4.1 Minority groups in MENA

Morocco	Arabs, Berbers, Saharawis
Algeria	Arabs, Berbers, Saharawis
Tunisia	Arabs, Berbers, Europeans
Libya	Arabs, Berbers
Iran	Arabs, Azeris, Baha'is, Bakhtiaris, Baluchis, Christians (Armenians), Christians (Assyrians), Christians (Chaldeans), Gilakis/Mazandaranis, Gypsies (Romanis/Domaris/Ghorbatis/Nawaris), Kurds, Lurs, Persians, Qashaqais, Talyshis, Turkmen
Turkey	Arabs, Kurds, Turks
Iraq	Arab Shi'a, Christians (Armenians), Christians (Assyrians), Christians (Chaldeans), Kurds, Persians, Sunni Arabs, Turkmen/Azeris
Egypt	Arab Egyptians, Bedouins, Coptic Egyptians, Gypsies/Domaris, Nubians
Syria	Alawis, Christians (Armenians), Christians (Assyrians), Christians (Chaldeans), Druze, Kurds, Palestinians, Sunni Arabs
Lebanon	Alawis, Armenians, Druze, Greek Catholics, Greek Orthodox, Kurds, Maronites, Palestinians, Shi'is, Sunni Muslims
Jordan	Armenians, Christians, Circassians, Iraqis, Palestinians, Transjordan Arabs
Israel	Bedouins, Druze, Ethiopian Jews, Israeli Arabs, Jews, Palestinians, Russians (Jewish)
Saudi Arabia	Bangladeshis, Egyptians, Filipinos, Indians, Indonesians, Jordanians/Palestinians, Nepalis, Pakistanis, Shi'is, Sri Lankans, Sudanese, Sunni Arabs, Syrians, Yemenis
Yemen	Akhdam, Shi'i Arabs, Somalis, South Asians, Sunni Arabs
Kuwait	Bangladeshis, Egyptians, Filipinos, Indians, Iranians, Jordanians/Palestinians, Kuwaitis, Pakistanis, Sri Lankans, Syrians
Bahrain	Egyptians, Filipinos, Indians, Iranians/Persians/Ajams, Jordanians/Palestinians, Pakistanis, Shi'a Bahrainis/Baharmas, Sunni Bahrainis
UAE	Bangladeshis, Egyptians, Emiris, Filipinos, Indians, Iranians, Jordanians/Palestinians, Pakistanis, Sri Lankans, Yemenis
Oman	Bangladeshis, Egyptians, Ibadhi Muslims, Indians, Pakistanis, Sri Lankans, Sunnis

Source: Jóhanna K. Birnir et al. "Introducing the AMAR (All Minorities at Risk) Data," *Journal of Conflict Resolution* 62, no. 1 (2018): 203–26.

Milton Esman, a specialist on ethnic conflict, concluded that in the degree of scope of violence "there is nothing unique about the Middle East." As he put it:

> All the states of the Middle East are pluralistic; but no more so than most Third World countries. The tensions are not any more severe than in Uganda or Vietnam, where ethnic minorities have been summarily and brutally despoiled and expelled, or in Burundi and East Timor . . . which have witnessed genocide on a terrifying scale, or in Burma and Ethiopia, where costly but indecisive ethnic insurrections have been waged for more than a generation.[5]

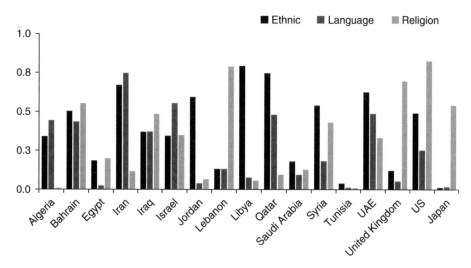

Figure 4.1 Fractionalization in selected MENA countries
Source: Alberto Alesina et al., "Fractionalization," *Journal of Economic Growth* 8, no. 2 (2003): 155–94.

This point is brought home in Figure 4.1 with the comparison of MENA to the United States and Japan, the former highly fractionalized across categories of measurement, the latter among the most homogeneous in ethnicity and language, but very diverse in religion.

This chapter argues that the most important mechanisms linking identity to war in MENA operate through and by states and elites. The crucial issue is not the content or valence of ethnic group identities. Rather, the configurations of ethnic identities relative to state power and the attitudes of elites toward those states play the most important role in determining the course of violence. The processes of imperial breakdown and modern state formation discussed in Chapter 2 yielded problematic incongruities between group identity and state territory. The lack of common identity and the persistence of ethnic cleavages retarded political reforms that might have led to more coherent nation-states. Instead, this situation fed into MENA's regional security predicament. Marginalized groups demanded access to resources and political power, either through an existing state or in states of their own. The persistence and ubiquity of cross-border ties, however, meant that there was often a diaspora of kin ready to provide support in times of crisis.

The incongruence between identity and territory in MENA, argues political scientist Raymond Hinnebusch, "explains the revisionism and irredentism that has precipitated frequent wars, two war-prone states (Iraq, Israel), and multiple enduring sites of civil war, either originating in artificial states (Lebanon, Sudan) or frustrated nations (Kurdistan, Palestine)."[6] In such

conditions, it was difficult to distinguish between internal and external challengers. States were more vulnerable to pressures and more likely to resort to
repressive responses.

But identities alone do not cause war. Elite actors play a critical role in
turning conditions of ethnic multiplicity into ethnic war. Identity wars
erupt when elites try to mobilize groups in pursuit of political and economic
agendas, either by enlisting or by defying the state. Struggles within groups
over strategy and power, in such circumstances, are as consequential as
struggles between groups. Most group leaders, whether of states or ethnic
groups, favor strategies of cooperation and coexistence with other groups.
These arrangements are generally peaceable, although not always equitable. After all, coexistence is the best way to ensure prosperity and status
for the group collectively and its members individually. A number of dis-
ruptive factors, however, can spur elites to take more risky and provocative
strategies.

This chapter proceeds in several sections. The first section discusses the
concept of group and ethnic identity and the role of states in shaping and
defining notions of belonging. It illustrates how modern elites constructed
definitions of ethnic groups in MENA. The second section examines the idea
of ethnic peace. While ethnic violence is spectacular and eye-catching, it is
also extremely rare. Most people most of the time comport themselves non-
violently with other ethnic groups. To understand why ethnic wars occur, we
must first understand the idea of an equilibrium that permits and promotes
cooperation between groups. The third section lays out the structural and
proximate causes of ethnic wars. While some conditions make war more
likely, it takes active decision-making on the part of elites to push toward
outright violence. Finally, the chapter offers a case study of ethnic civil war in
Syria in the 2010s, showing how communal leaders used ethnic identification
to mobilize violence.

Group Identities and States in the Middle East

What is an ethnic group? Ethnicity implies an idea of common origin, based
largely on notions of kinship. It also involves an inventory of supposedly
unique cultural traits that accompany that shared kinship.[7] These commonalities manifest in outward practices, such as customs and rituals,
language, dress, and (sometimes) physical attributes. Ethnic identity works
as a kind of social radar, allowing people to see where they stand in relationship to others, and also as a kind of social script, prescribing which
actions they take. Nationalism is the ideology advocating the unification
of ethnic identity and statehood. Ultimately, nationalism aims to create a
nation-state, a political body that exists symbiotically with an ethnic group

to serve as the vehicle for the group's political and cultural protection and aspirations.

It is easy to take ethnic group leaders at their word and assume that their communities originate in a distant primordial past. This makes group identity ancient and immutable. Primordialism is a common default assumption when it comes to MENA. This may be because so many narratives of ethnic origins in the region draw on a familiar historical corpus of ancient texts of the Torah, the Bible, and the Qur'an. Familiarity with these stories can lead Western audiences to be credulous when leaders claim to be carrying on a fight of biblical antecedents. The tendency to presume that every ethnic conflict in the region originates ultimately in an ancient struggle, then, fits Orientalist stereotypes of MENA as somehow frozen in time.

Most social scientists doubt this primordial premise, however. Although some groups' lineages may be more ancient than others, their identities are still constructed and socially conditioned. Ibn Khaldun, a fourteenth-century Tunisian scholar often credited as the founder of sociology, discussed the waxing and waning of group solidarity and cohesion ('*asabiyya*). His analysis described how tribes from the hinterland were able to conquer urban territories because they enjoyed stronger cohesion and loyalty. Through '*asabiyya*, every member of the group felt themselves bound to a common family-like structure, operating as a single fearsome unit. Once in power in the urban center, however, individual group members and their descendants became more interested in commercial pursuits. These undercut '*asabiyya* and drew individuals away from the group. Their affective ties to one another weakened, making it harder for them to maintain military readiness. Eventually, another hinterland group with greater '*asabiyya* emerged to conquer the city and dispersed the previous rulers.[8]

A combination of passive socialization and active engagement between individuals and the group generates group identity. Young people are often told who they are – and who they aren't. They are instructed at a very early age about how to adopt the outward trappings of their group: how to dress, how to speak, what rituals to perform, and with whom to associate.

There are several key analytical categories to consider when examining ethnic identity. First, ethnic identities are *inter-subjective*. They are defined through social action. Although individuals may try to assert or reinterpret their role within a group in a particular way, the group is often the final arbiter of what will or will not pass. Secondly, ethnic identities are *relational* in that they exist relative to other groups. Part of learning how to be a member of one group is learning how to spot members of another group. Finally, ethnic identities are never monolithic but rather *factionalized*, especially at the elite level. Elites often disagree about what types of strategies to pursue and how to construe claims of homeland and statehood. These strategies necessarily operate in relation to other groups. Moderates are willing to accommodate, conciliate, or coexist with rival ethnic groups. Maximalists, in contrast, take a more strident stance toward rival groups and on the agenda of state-building. These intra-elite disputes inevitably conflate group interests with the personal objectives of prestige, positions, and paychecks.

Modern states play a critical role in certifying and recognizing the existence of national and ethnic groups.[9] This is most apparent when it comes to citizenship, a core concept of modern political life. States selectively designate particular categories of the population as citizens and deny others. Instruments of statehood can reinforce or even generate collective senses of belonging. Historian Eugen Weber describes how French schools, military conscription, and mass media helped assimilate a heterogeneous population comprised of Catholics, Protestants, and Jews, speakers of Breton, Occitan, and other regional languages, in addition to immigrants from elsewhere in Europe. The French state, in this analysis, molded its citizenry into a single state-sanctioned ethnic category.[10]

It is important here to note the reciprocal process at work. Peasants didn't become Frenchmen simply because the government demanded they do so. Rather, they responded to the inducements offered by a certain set of government officials. They expected the benefit of gaining access to state resources and avoiding recriminations to outweigh the cost. In the course of socializing into a group, individuals derive a feeling of belonging, affection, and community. They also find out how to gain material rewards from the group, including physical protection and economic opportunity. The overlay of statehood and ethnic identity in nation-states increases both the demands of the state and its ability to induce compliance. Few individuals cling to group identities that will garner discrimination for themselves or their children. If states make access to education, jobs, or other means of social progress conditional on adopting specific clothing, diet, language, or creed, many people will accede individually. Repression can make this accretion even more rapid, giving people an offer they can't refuse.[11]

But states seldom demand a singular and undifferentiated loyalty from their citizenry. They often accommodate or tolerate specific markers of ethnic difference within their population. Expressions of ethnic identity thus operate within the channels the state provides. Instruments like the census or other official documents can prompt individuals to adopt certain group affiliations, giving a prefixed menu of choices to describe identity. The Ottoman empire, where multiple nationalist demands eventually flummoxed the political elite, offers a kind of negative counterpoint to the French example. In its heyday, the Ottoman state recognized imperial subjects based on their affiliation with sanctioned faith communities (*millets*): Muslim, Christian, and Jewish. Commonalities of language or region were (at most) of secondary import. This meant, at least theoretically, that a Turkish-speaking Muslim in Istanbul was deemed different and apart from her Christian neighbor, even if she spoke the same language, shared a business or factory together, but similar to an Arabic-speaking Muslim in faraway Yemen. The *millet* system was centered on the clerical elite. The Sultan was simultaneously the political and ecclesiastical head of the Muslim *millet* (although in practice he delegated religious oversight to highly trained clerics). Prelates represented the other *millet* communities in court. To recognize a *millet* meant necessarily to certify and elevate its leaders.[12]

The rise of nationalist movements in the nineteenth century pushed against the organizational principles of the *millet* system and posed a profound ideological challenge to the empire. The first nationalist movements were led by Christians, challenging the tenets of Muslim supremacy. Nationalist intellectuals within the empire drew inspiration from European nationalism. Europe's Christian powers directly supported many of the rebellions in the Ottoman domain. The Ottomans struggled to respond. Some Ottoman leaders adopted liberalism or accommodated ethno-nationalist demands with autonomy schemes. They tried to reform legal codes and re-tool the schools and military to promote a more ecumenical imperial citizenship open to people of all faiths and languages. In contrast, Sultan Abd al-Hamid pushed to renew a sense of pan-Islamic unity and supremacy and, asserting his leadership over all Muslims, confronted European Christian imperialism. At the turn of the twentieth century, a group known as the Young Turks tried to redefine the empire as a Turkish-speaking nation-state. Facing the choice of assimilation or subordination, non-Turkish peoples became even more adamant in their nationalist agendas.[13]

Imperial redefinition could not arrest the Ottomans' geopolitical freefall, though. Territorial losses continued. By World War I, the Ottoman empire was reduced to Anatolia, the Levant, and Iraq, with a rump territory in Europe. The Young Turks saw Germany as a useful geopolitical counterbalance to Britain and Russia and a role model in the nation-building process. At the same time, leaders of peripheral nationalist movements – Armenian, Arab, and Zionist, among others – also mobilized and sought outside allies. Britain engaged these non-Turkish groups as proxies to help destabilize the Ottomans.

Many historical analyses of MENA's transition from empire to statehood focus on the relationship between the outside powers and the nationalist movements, particularly Arab nationalism. Colonial designs undercut aspirations for a large, unified Arab state. Britain reneged on promises to create such a state and encouraged the Zionist project in Palestine, disregarding the wishes of the Arabic majority. Furthermore, the creation of separate colonial mandates for Syria, Lebanon, Iraq, and Palestine bisected the Arab homeland into separate states. Smaller groups, such as the Kurds, were split up as minorities in Syria, Iraq, Turkey, and Iran. Christians were forced to live under Muslims in Syria and Muslims forced to live under Christians in Lebanon. At the micro-level, tribes saw their territories bisected by state boundaries.

But elite instrumentalism and infighting had a major impact in creating

MENA's seemingly unworkable ethnic mosaic. As elites sought to claim state resources in the name of ethnic groups, the stakes for elite leadership became especially high. Achieving nation-statehood would essentially make the state and the ethnic elite interchangeable and contiguous. Ethno-nationalist leaders serve as a kind of cultural entrepreneur with unique cultural and political capital. They skillfully deploy the resources of the state – schools, the military, bureaucracies, and adjacent civil society institutions – to elevate both their personal status and their ethnic group. They can manipulate symbols of ethnic identity to build bases of support and power.[14]

Elite defection was therefore a critical element in the Ottomans' downfall. Nearly every leader of the nationalist movements that succeeded the Ottoman empire hailed from the Ottoman elite. Although these men (they were almost all men) hailed from disparate parts of the empire, their biographies converge in the experiences of training at prestigious Ottoman colleges and academies. They spoke various mother tongues at home, but were also fluent in Ottoman Turkish. As the empire broke up, these men devoted their training and expertise to divergent political projects of state-building. Many remained with the empire until the end of World War I before aligning with the one-time Ottoman general Mustafa Kemal (Atatürk). Kemal led the military campaign that ousted the Allies from Anatolia. Only later did he and other disaffected Ottoman officers move to abolish the empire, outlaw Ottoman Turkish, and found the Republic of Turkey. Another faction of ex-Ottoman officers joined the Arab revolt, spearheaded by Sharif Hussein and his son Faisal of the august Hashemite dynasty. The Hashemites were themselves disgruntled members of the Ottoman nobility from the Hejaz region of western Arabia. Faisal and his brothers trained at the imperial academies in Istanbul. Responding to the Young Turks' centralization policies, they sought out British support to establish an Arab kingdom. Faisal led the Arab revolt, declared Arab independence in Syria, represented the Arabs at the Paris peace negotiations, and eventually assumed the throne of Iraq. Ex-Ottoman officials following in his train became the first ministers of state, parliamentarians, generals, journalists, and academicians in the newly established Arab states of Iraq, Syria, Lebanon, and Jordan in the 1920s. Even David Ben Gurion, Israel's first prime minister, attended law school in Istanbul.

There was constant infighting among these aspiring nationalist elites, mixing personal career ambitions and ideological agendas. Many of the Hashemites' own courtiers criticized Faisal's political hesitancy and willingness to compromise with the Zionists and the British. They complained the Hashemites prioritized dynastic ambitions over the imperative to redeem and unite the Arab people. Ex-Ottoman officers repeatedly tried to prod or cajole Faisal to take a more aggressive stand for Arab independence, sometimes by provoking military confrontation with imperial powers. By the same token, though, many of these more strident Arab nationalists were willing to accept sinecures from the Iraqi state.[15] Factionalization would figure as a major force driving groups into violent conflict.

Ethnic Groups and the Equilibrium of Cooperation

One of the most challenging things about understanding ethnic violence is grasping how exceptionally rare it is. People belonging to different ethnic groups cooperate almost all the time, despite the vast opportunities and occasions when ethnic violence might occur.[16] Even in places that seem to be ground zero for ethnic conflict – Jerusalem, Beirut, Baghdad, or Kirkuk – most people comport themselves peaceably. They work and raise families alongside members of other groups. Some even socialize together. There are still competitions, rivalries, or antagonisms between members of different ethnic groups. However, these competitions are nested in a wider context that allows groups to cooperate sufficiently to avoid potentially disastrous bloodshed.

To explain ethnic war, then, we need to begin by examining the factors that uphold the equilibrium of non-violence. MENA states have deployed a wide range of strategies to manage ethnic diversity. These strategies can be grouped into three main clusters: assimilation, consociation, and domination. States often deploy them selectively and in combination, depending on circumstances and the identity of groups at play.

Assimilation Strategies

The presumption that ethnic identities in MENA are primordial and therefore have greater salience than artificial or imposed state identities ignores how common and significant assimilative strategies have been. MENA states have tried to reshape mass identity through assimilation strategies. Assimilation reduces the possibility of ethnic violence by eliding or eliminating ethnic differences themselves. It essentially aims to shape polities into a unitary and cohesive nation-state.

The most successful examples of assimilative strategies in MENA come from Israel and Iran. They, alongside Turkey, are the closest approximations to the nation-state ideal in the region. Both states have a single core and dominant ethnic group: Hebrew-speaking Jews in Israel, Persian-speaking Shi'is in Iran. Both states claim to represent – or, rather, resurrect – ancient civilizations. In this sense, the state elite and the ethnic elite are one and the same. Yet both Israel and Iran are very much the product of modern state- and nation-building efforts. Iran, once a peer of the polyglot Ottoman empire, probably followed the peasants-into-Frenchmen model most closely. Beginning in the 1920s, the Pahlavi dynasty launched an aggressive campaign to assimilate a previously disparate population into a common Iranian identity. This was part of a larger project of social modernization and political centralization that saw the state exert unprecedented control over peripheral territories. Kurdish, Arabic, Azeri, Turkish, and other predominantly rural languages were pushed from public life. Tribal groups lost their autonomy. Schools, museums, other media propounded Iran's illustrious history and ancient glories. Standard Persian, at once modernized and stripped of foreign loan words, was mandated at schools and in the army. The Islamic Republic of Iran has more or less continued this policy while also stressing the intrinsic linkage between Iranian nationalism and Islam.[17]

Israel's emergence as a Jewish state combines the elements of state-molded identities and mass migration. Even before the establishment of the state in 1948, Jews came to Palestine through the twentieth century. They hailed from dozens of countries, spoke different languages, and held dramatically different customs. While many Jews viewed Palestine as an ancestral homeland, or at least place of succor after the Holocaust, others were indifferent to Zionist claims about a building a Jewish nation-state. But the Israeli state persisted and insisted. Israel's Law of Return (1950) granted citizenship to anyone with a single Jewish grandparent. Through mandatory attendance at Hebrew school, conscription into the Israeli army, and living in a milieu saturated by Hebrew media, Israeli identity took a strong hold over Jewish citizens. As in Iran, social advancement depended on adopting the outward modes of identity the Israeli state prescribed. To be Jewish in Israel is essentially an unmarked category, the assumed default position. Some have labeled the Israeli experience a process of being immersed in an immigrant "melting pot."[18] The Israeli Arab minority, on the other hand, held Israeli citizenship but were roundly deemed poor candidates for assimilation. Despite holding civil and electoral rights, Arabs were not granted the same chances to join the Israeli national community or derive equal benefits from the Israeli state.[19]

The experiences of the twenty-odd Arab states with assimilation policies varied. Belying the prejudiced beliefs about so-called "artificial" states, Egypt, Yemen, Tunisia, Morocco, Oman, Saudi Arabia, and other Arab states could boast august political histories anchored in the Arab and Islamic past or even further back. Egyptians took pride in their Pharaonic heritage, Tunisians in their Carthaginian ancestry, Saudis in their role in Islamic history. More novel state creations, such as Iraq or Syria, tried to identify similarly august ancient political lineages. Sometimes there were disputes about where exactly "national" history began. Berbers (Amazigh) claimed to be the original and indigenous inhabitants of the land in North Africa. Yet the overwhelmingly Arab nationalist elites in the post-independence region regarded Berberism as a rural relic. They focused on cultivating

> a homogeneous national identity, based on a common Sunni Islamic
> faith and praxis according to the Maliki school; giving primacy to the

Arabic language, thanks to both its status as the sacred written language of the Qur'an and the need for a unifying, standardized idiom for building a modern society and political community; and fashioning an official legacy of the struggle for independence. . . . [V]ictorious nationalist elites were confident that upon achieving independence, they would successfully complete the task of national integration and state-building, and relegate the Berbers to folklore status.[20]

More important than just imagining communities, states across MENA did a good deal to implant themselves in the identity of their populations. Through a mixture of inducement and coercion, implied or explicit, these states, too, made social advancement contingent on compliance.

Perhaps the best indicator of how firmly entrenched notions of citizenship are comes from the Arab Barometer's surveys. Its 2012–14 and 2016–17 surveys show that country of origin is often the primary point of identification and affiliation, ahead of religion, Arab nationalism, tribe, or local community.[21] Impressionistic but still substantial evidence comes from observing how frequently MENA citizens wave national flags, sing national anthems, and cheer for national soccer teams.

Expressions of state identity in MENA often abut cults of personality surrounding individual rulers. Images of rulers dominate public space, including government offices, billboards, and so on. These could easily be described as tools to remind populations of the role of public surveillance.[22] But people also, more or less voluntarily, display pictures of their ruler in homes, businesses, and car windows. In fascinating studies of Syria and Yemen, political scientist Lisa Wedeen shows how these images have an almost totemic value. By signaling compliance with state demands for patriotism and reverence, their bearers hope to ward off unwanted attention from state security services. Of course, this may be feigned obedience that hides secret disaffection and resistance. Even so, such banal displays also obviate the need for separate ethnic identities or ethnic leaders to act as intermediaries between the citizen and the state. Bearing a portrait of President Assad or King Salman symbolically asserts standing as a member of the national community entitled to unmediated access to the state and its leadership.[23]

Consociational Strategies

If assimilative policies focus on eliding and eventually erasing some of the differences between citizens in favor of a unified whole, then consociational strategies take the opposite approach. Consociational approaches manage ethnic competition by granting groups recognition and relative autonomy to manage their own affairs. They assure each group access to power and resources from the state. Lebanese political scientist Iliya Harik describes consociationalism as a kind of "vertical" integration as opposed to "horizontal" assimilation:

the creation and promotion of political mechanisms connecting a community directly with the national government such that each community which is conscious of its ethnic distinctiveness may see in the national government a place for itself, recognition of its political and other rights, and responsiveness on the part of the government to the community's needs. The emphasis in vertical integration is on adjustment of community life to the central government; making demands on the political system and at the same time accepting constraints essential for the system's endurance and viability.[24]

Lebanon is often cited as the epitome of such consociational arrangements. Lebanon's confessional pact, struck between Sunni and Christian Maronite leaders in the 1940s, essentially divvied up state resources according to a rough estimate of communal demographics. The pact reserved the presidency for a Christian and the prime ministership for a Sunni. Later amendments adjusted the relative authorities and responsibilities of these posts and designated the parliamentary speakership for Shi'is, but kept the basic form intact. This power-sharing flows down through the Lebanese parliament, ministries, and government agencies. Every group was assured some measure of power and resources through the state. Much like in the Ottoman *millet* system, individual Lebanese citizens are categorized as members of preset sectarian groups: Sunni or Shi'i Muslims; one of several other Christian rites (Maronite, Greek Orthodox, Armenian, etc.); Druze; and Jews. These ethnic identities are emblazoned on government-issued identity cards. The electoral system hinges on balloting within one of these groups, reinforcing the power of affiliation through these identities. Citizens have few options but to rely on sectarian leaders to serve as conduits for state largesse, including access to education, housing, welfare, and even security.[25]

Assimilative and consociational approaches, though seemingly antithetical, are often complementary. The key question is which cultural and social markers are deemed legitimate and tolerable and which must be suppressed. Iran generally strives to assimilate linguistic minorities, but also reserves parliamentary seats for representatives of the specifically recognized religious minorities that are regarded as indigenously and intrinsically Iranian. These communities are allowed to maintain separate schools and religious institutions.[26]

The denial of recognition to a certain group is just as important as the decision to recognize it. The Iranian state regards Baha'ism as an aberrant and heretical cult, not a religious community entitled to equivalent protections to Islam, Christianity, Zoroastrianism, or Judaism, and Baha'is suffer discrimination and active persecution at the hands of the state.[27] Berbers in North Africa have similarly seen their cultural demands ignored, if not denigrated, by the state. Berber activists have, in turn, sought to have their language placed on the same legal footing as Arabic and to have Berber taught at universities and used in the mass media.[28]

In Iraq, different communities have had different levels of success in gaining recognition. Under Ba'ath rule (1968–2003), state policies explicitly recognized the Kurds as a national group. This recognition often meant more in theory than in practice, but in the late 1970s it did yield a separate Kurdish school system and parliament in the north. At the same time, though, the Iraqi state seemed intent on ignoring any differentiation of the Muslim majority based on sect. Iraqi Shi'is – the demographic majority – were officially invisible as a group. Identity cards identified Iraqi citizens as Arabs or Kurds, never as Sunnis or Shi'is. Archival documents and taped conversation from within Saddam Hussein's inner circle show they avoided using the word "Shi'i" aloud. Instead, Saddam's confidants, overwhelmingly Sunni Arabs, used euphemisms like "residents of the south" or "underdeveloped areas" to denote Shi'is. At some points, the term "Iranian" was applied to southern Shi'is, suggestive of national disloyalty. This both reflected and reinforced the Ba'ath's assumption that Shi'is could be assimilated into a common Arab–Iraqi national identity (while Kurds could not).[29] Following the overthrow of Saddam, however, Iraq's new elite had very different ideas. The 2005 constitution renounced sectarianism in one line, and then moved to inscribe and recognize specific groups in the next, "invoking the pains of sectarian oppression inflicted by the autocratic clique and inspired by the tragedies of Iraq's martyrs, Shiite and Sunni, Arabs and Kurds and Turkomen and from all other components of the people."[30] Iraq's politics since then has revolved around shifting but still more or less explicit ethno-sectarian pacts.

Consociational arrangements require sub-national ethnic elites to represent specific constituent communities. Elites set up clientelistic relationships with followers, serving as brokers between the general population and the state. This is illustrated at the micro-scale when examining how modern MENA states deal with nomadic and semi-nomadic tribes. Tribes are often depicted as the antithesis of modern MENA states, possessing a kind of organic legitimacy that states lack. However, anthropological research has shown how tribal groups and identities evolved symbiotically with modern states. States not only recognize specific tribal groups but also elevate members of the tribe to serve as sheikhs. These sheikhs represent the community to the national government and negotiate to bring benefits back to their constituencies. This pattern of consociational recognition, certification, and patronage goes beyond tribes and is replicated at every level and in multiple venues. Intergroup cooperation is orchestrated at the elite level and flows from the top down. In Beirut, for instance, urban planner Hiba Bou Bakr describes how ethnic leaders, municipal officials, and land developers vied to preserve or extend their ethnically exclusive neighborhoods by manipulating building codes, zoning rules, and various "gentlemen's agreements."[31] Ultimately, elites have a mutual interest in cooperation because conflict can be so costly. Elites are accountable to the state and to each other for their community's behavior. If communal leaders fail to police their followers and ensure that they stay within acceptable bounds, the state might remove them. On the other hand, if leaders fail to ensure their community's protection and status, their own flock might desert them in favor of other leaders.

Critics of consociationalism in general and Lebanese confessionalism in particular depict the system as an arbitrary contrivance. Vertical integration treats socially constructed identities as if they were primordial, ingrained, and unchanging. At the individual level, this traps people into association with a sub-national group that they might reject. At the societal level, it hinders the development of consciousness around class or more ecumenical forms of citizenship.[32]

But this does not mean that consociationalism necessarily causes people to favor the interests of their ethnic group over the good of the country at large. It does not preclude a strong sense of national identity, as evident from the strong sense of national affiliation in Lebanon itself. Effective vertical integrative strategies yoke sub-national and state-centered identity together. Rather than conflicting, they are concurrent and mutually productive. A Lebanese Shi'i who votes for Hezbollah or a Maronite who votes for a similar sectarian party, for instance, sees her support as the enactment of her vision of Lebanese nationalism.[33] This is not the ideal solution proposed by nationalism, but it can be an effective strategy when assimilation proves impossible.

Domination Strategies

Consociational and assimilation strategies aim for equality at the group and individual level, respectively. Yet both often mask tendencies for domination. State decisions to certify and recognize particular markers of identity are inextricable from policies that enforce group hierarchies. In this sense, assimilation merges seamlessly into the enactment of hegemony and dominance, demanding accretion from lesser groups. Likewise, consociation becomes cooptation, seeking ways to disarm a group by offering benefits to a select few. These forms of domination compound authoritarian systems and exclusion. Some groups are reduced to powerlessness and irrelevance, or face active discrimination.

Ethnic power relations can take a variety of forms. Sociologists Andreas Wimmer, Lars-Erik Cederman, and Brian Min offer a typology of institutional configurations and inter-group relationships.[34] In nation-states, a single group and associated set of ethnic leaders hold a monopoly or near monopoly over power. Because ethnic and state elites are interchangeable, the state serves the interest of that titular group. No MENA states, though, resemble this idealized description. Even Israel and Iran, the two countries closest to nation-state status, have significant minorities in their midst. A second type of ethnic power relation makes the distinction between the lesser, merely legal, forms of citizenship and the fuller notion of citizenship through membership in a nation. These kinds of arrays are visible across MENA. Alongside this is a third type, the matter of the *bidoun* ("without") – denizens of countries who are denied any official paperwork, much less citizenship. Estimates of these numbers are rough at best. Over 140,000 Syrian-born Kurds were denied official documentation stemming from an extraordinary 1962 census that seemed intended to dilute Kurdish demographic weight in the northeastern region. Until the Syrian government took some steps to rectify the position of these residents in the mid-2000s, many Syrian Kurds had no right to property, passports, or legal marriage. Similarly, several Gulf states have *bidoun* communities, mostly nomadic tribes that were excluded from the official census and recognition for reasons of demographic engineering.[35]

Ethnic power relations in most MENA states involve power-sharing bargains among ethnic elites. Some groups are senior or junior partners in coalitions, while others are excluded outsiders. Syria offers a useful example of this type of ethnic stacking. Over the last half-century it has become commonplace to describe Syria as "dominated" by the Alawis, a heterodox and historically marginalized Shi'i minority from the Latakiya highlands region. In the 1960s, a group of Alawi military officers aligned with the Arab Ba'ath party seized power. By 1972, Hafez al-Assad had emerged as the leading figure in the regime. Assad made sure to surround himself with his closest Alawi kinsmen in the most sensitive positions in the state. Following Hafez's death in 2000, his son Bashar al-Assad assumed the presidency, carrying on the tradition of Alawi dominance.

But within these decades of ethnic stacking there was considerable shifting. In the first decade of Ba'ath rule, a number of figures from other minority communities also had major roles in the regime. It is unlikely that these individuals conceived of themselves in sectarian terms. Yet they shared a common resentment of Syria's old ruling elite. This old elite hailed from the Ottoman aristocracy, owning massive rural estates and lavish city dwellings. They were, incidentally, overwhelmingly Sunni Muslim. When Syria gained independence, these were the class that presumed to rule. The new Ba'ath regime proclaimed their intention to bring unity, Arab nationalism, and socialism to Syria. It espoused ecumenisms, if not outright secularism. Sectarianism was taboo, just as in Saddam's Iraq. Nevertheless, the land and wealth redistribution policies of the 1960s and 1970s necessarily benefited poorer rural minorities at the expense of the great Sunni magnates.[36] By the late 1980s, however, the regime shifted to embrace neoliberal policies. This brought about something of a reconciliation between the regime and old landed elites. The sons of senior Alawi officers began marrying the daughters of Sunni magnates and business ties between the Ba'athi elite and Sunni landed elites became more prominent. This elite-level ethnic partnership benefited a much narrower set of cronies than the state socialism of the 1960s. Syrians of all stripes saw themselves left out of political and economic opportunity and alienated by the perceived corruption and aloofness of the regime.[37] As will be discussed below, the uprising of 2011 severely tested the mettle of the relationship between Sunni magnates and regime elites.

Electoral democracies can temper majoritarian domination in some respects but can also make these hierarchies more pronounced and entrenched. Israeli geographer Oren Yiftachel argues that Israel's electoral system has evolved into an "ethnocracy" whereby the Israeli state does not serve its entire citizenry but rather favors members of the Jewish ethnic group above others. The situation becomes especially complicated because nearly half of the world's Jewish population lives in the diaspora outside of Israel. Israeli Arabs enjoy some measures of protection through consociational arrangements, but this is as much a ceiling on social advancement as a floor of minimal and unequal inclusion.[38] In Iraq since 2005, successive popular elections have yielded a nearly unbroken string of parliamentary coalitions featuring Shi'i sectarian groups and Kurdish ethno-nationalist parties. The agendas of these two groups are hardly concordant. Iraqi Shi'i leaders consider themselves to be Iraq's rightful and natural governors by dint of their demographic majority. In this view, the deposition of Saddam Hussein in 2003 led to a rectification, delivering power to its rightful holder. Their version of state-building is strongly majoritarian, presuming that what is good for the Shi'is is necessarily good for Iraq.[39] The Kurdish leadership, by contrast, regard the Iraqi state largely as a vehicle to preserve or extend their own ethno-nationalist agenda. From 2005 onward, Kurdish leaders voted with the Shi'i-led coalition on condition of respect for Kurdish federal autonomy. This power-sharing arrangement largely excludes Sunni Arabs, who had harbored their own vision of "owning" Iraq stemming from the foundations of the state in the 1920s. This dynamic precluded the possibility of a true non-sectarian electoral option. In 2010, the Iraqiyya bloc won a slim parliamentary plurality. Led by a secular Shi'i politician, Iraqiyya won the bulk of its votes in Sunni areas in western and north-central Iraq. But the party could not find coalition partners and eventually had to yield in favor of another Shi'a–Kurdish grand alliance. In 2018, another non-sectarian electoral bloc, the Saairun (Forward), won the mandate. Campaigning on anti-corruption slogans and led by a Shi'i cleric known for his trenchant criticism of Iraq's political elite, Saairun won supporters across Iraqi sectarian lines. To form a government, however, Saairun had to compromise with the leading Shi'i sectarian and Kurdish ethno-nationalist parties, blunting any impetus to reform and de-ethnicize Iraqi politics.

Omnibalance, the tendency to shift or play off between internal and external threats to regime security, plays a crucial part in the construction of ethnic partnerships and alliances as well as domination. Dominant actors try to play their rivals off against each other through divide-and-rule strategies.

In this vein, successive governments in Baghdad responded to Kurdish ethno-nationalist demands by reaching out to smaller ethnic communities in northern Iraq, such as Turkomen, Yezidis, Shabaks, and Assyrian Christians. These second-order minority groups saw alignment with the central government as their counterbalance to falling under the domination of Kurdish ethno-nationalists.[40]

Smaller ethno-nationalist groups are more vulnerable to manipulation and often seek specific socio-political niches to avoid complete marginalization. Libya's population is overwhelmingly Arabic-speaking and concentrated in the northern coastal cities. In the far south along the borders of Chad, Niger, and Sudan, however, are some substantial pockets of the Tebu, who speak a Nilo-Saharan language. Estimates of their population are around 500,000 in Libya. King Idris of Libya (r. 1951–69) recruited Tebus into his personal bodyguard, confident in their loyalty because they lacked any attachment to Libya's larger Arabic society. At the same time, many Tebu were *bidoun* – denied Libyan identity papers or citizenship. In the 1970s, Qaddafi inducted Tebus into the Libyan army to fight in Chad. At the same time, though, he declared Libya an Arab state and effectively de-nationalized thousands who had resided within Libyan territory. General racial prejudices and active state discrimination blocked many Tebu from schooling, housing, or employment. Many Tebu were relegated to smuggling, mercenary service, menial labor, or other black market activities. Tebu community leaders sent missives to the Transitional National Council (TNC) during the 2011 uprising, seeking recognition of Tebu national rights and integration within the Libyan state. Various Libyan factions have tried to recruit Tebu militias to support their effort to gain control over Kufra and the Fezzan region.[41]

Overall, domination strategies maintain peace by threatening defectors. Higher status groups that benefit disproportionately from access to state resources obviously have no reason to risk changing the status quo. Disadvantaged groups might resent their diminution, but see few alternatives. They operate within state-approved norms for fear of losing the little they already have. No individual or collective has an incentive to deviate from its prescribed role.

Why Ethnic War?

What destabilizes this equilibrium of cooperation underpinning ethnic peace? Why do strategies of assimilation, consociation, and domination give way? It is useful to distinguish between the slow-changing structural conditions that make equilibrium more vulnerable to perturbations and the more immediate, agentive decisions that precipitate violence directly. This distinction between structural and agentive causes is important because it allows us to account for the episodic yet recurrent element of ethnic violence, how violence both surges and abates.

A wide range of structural factors, often overlapping and complementary, make ethnic violence more likely. One of the most commonly cited structural factors is ethnic geography: MENA's imbalance between state and nation; borders that bisect ethnic communities and create diasporic pockets. They offer multiple focal points for allegiance and affiliation that hamstring efforts to create nation-states. The promise of Arab integration or pan-Islamic unity also undercuts allegiances to states. Diasporic groups encourage actors in their homeland to take more aggressive postures, in part because diaspora members are not as susceptible to the risks that come from the breakdown of ethnic cooperation. Diasporic funding plays a highly visible role in support for Jewish settlement activity in the West Bank, including support for groups that attack Palestinian civilians. By the same token, the Palestinian diaspora has also provided support to militant groups seeking to escalate violence against Jews.[42] Diasporas were also important in supporting the emergence of Kurdish and Berber resistance. The issue of ethnic geography, especially when it comes to cross-national linkages, connects directly to MENA's regional security predicament and confluence of domestic with international threats.

The expansion of communication complicated the broader issues of MENA's borders and human geography. The rise of satellite television and social media in the region has made it possible to circumvent the state's monopoly over communication and to spread ideas and information across borders. Qatari-owned satellite station Al-Jazeera, Twitter, and Facebook helped spread the contagion of political protests during the uprisings of 2011, for example.

Economic factors also affect patterns of ethnic cooperation. Dramatic economic declines or shocks hasten competition among groups for a potentially smaller set of public goods. The cyclical downturn in oil markets can cause groups to become more assertive to get their piece of the proverbial pie. Economic development and modernization can destabilize ethnic equilibria also. Rural-to-urban migration, a persistent demographic feature in the region, complicated arrangements of ethnic domination and hierarchy. In the 1950s and 1960s, Beirut emerged as MENA's regional banking and commercial hub. The economic boom attracted migrants, particularly from impoverished Shi'i areas in the south of Lebanon and the Beqaa valley. Shi'is joined the urban labor force and settled new suburbs in southern Beirut. Although the Lebanese state refused to conduct a census, it was clear that the Shi'is' demographic growth was outpacing that of other communities. This further unsettled the balance of Lebanon's consociational pact. Shi'i leaders began to invest further in education and industrialization and to demand political representation commensurate with their demographic weight.[43]

Oil booms can have similarly drastic economic effects. We have discussed how the oil boom in eastern Saudi Arabia exacerbated tensions between Sunnis and Shi'is and the role of oil in spurring Kurdish nationalist demands. But the impact of oil booms can also hasten the construction and solidification of ethnic categories. Kirkuk in northern Iraq is today considered an ethnic tinderbox, coveted by Kurdish nationalists for both its symbolic and its economic value but still under the control of Baghdad. Examining the history of the city from the early twentieth century, however, historian Arabella Bet Shlimon shows how categories of ethnic identity in the past were fluid and nebulous. Befitting the old Ottoman aristocracy, Kirkuk's urban elite spoke Turkish, regardless of whether they hailed from Kurdish, Arab, Christian, or Turkish ancestry. The use of Kurdish was predominantly a marker of rural origins, not ethnic categorization. The advent of the oil industry in the 1920s, though, transformed the city's socio-economic life and hardened ethnic barriers. Labor migrants, both from the countryside and from elsewhere in Iraq, drastically changed the city's demographics. In addition, British and Iraqi officials from Baghdad and foreign nationals attached to the international oil companies alighted on the city. Local powerbrokers increasingly turned to these outsiders for patronage and support in their local disputes over city governance, land usage, and commercial affairs. Kurdish ethno-nationalists claimed Kirkuk as their capital and tried to recruit local Kurdish-speakers to their cause. The formidable Iraqi Communist Party, whose Kirkuk branches were led by Kurds, also drew support from industrial laborers and peasants. Turkomen leaders, in contrast, made alliances with the Sunni Arab-dominated government in Baghdad, which integrated the city (and its oil) within the Iraqi state. The city witnessed waves of violence between Turkomen and Kurdish factions following the military coup of 1958. Each faction tried to enlist support from one of the leading factions contending for control in Baghdad. In the 1960s and 1970s, the Ba'ath Party and its allies launched a campaign to resettle Arabs into Kirkuk and to otherwise dilute or drive out the areas of Kurdish population. The 1957 census of the Kirkuk province showed Kurdish-speakers to be a near majority at 187,593 people, although Turkish was the most commonly spoken language inside the city itself. By 1977, however, Arabic-speakers outnumbered Kurdish-speakers. The census of 1997 estimated that 72 percent of the province was Arabic-speaking, with Kurdish- and Turkish-speaking populations declining both in absolute number and in proportion.[44]

Finally, structural conditions of state incapacity make the turn to violence more likely because the state's ability to reward compliance becomes doubtful. Perceived incapacity, incompetence, and fecklessness suggest that the state cannot – or will not – uphold its end of the bargain for accommodation. Opportunities for employment or promotion become scarce, even with the requisite skills and acculturation. Many young Berbers found states unable to deliver adequate levels of employment. They became increasingly alienated from the official version of nationalism anchored in an assimilated

Islamic–Arab unity. In its place they adopted a resurgent Berber ethnic identification.[45] Defection and cheating become more attractive when the state's response is less assured.

While structural factors increase the chances for a breakdown in ethnic cooperation, many low-capacity states limp along with little to no violence for years or even decades.[46] Individuals and groups can find ways to self-regulate this coexistence in the absence of an effective state. It takes specific actions to initiate the course to ethnic violence. These actions may not be intended to spark violence, but they initiate and reinforce the processes of escalation that lead to war:

- *Pursuit of domination.* Some elites pursue hegemony and domination. The state's manifest shortcomings offer an opportunity to empower their group. They demand greater status, resources, and territory. Hegemony is the logical culmination of the unification of the nation and state in nationalism. Leaders become more aggressive toward rival groups, seeking to marginalize, remove, or even obliterate them. At the elite level, projects for hegemony seek a greater share of state resources – more positions and more authority – to the exclusion of others. This can come by taking control over an existing state or by seceding to establish a new state. At the mass level, hegemonic ambitions take the form of plundering the homes and property of local rivals.
- *Security dilemmas.* For others, the structural crisis is less a matter of opportunity than of risk and danger. When the state can no longer ensure the security of and accommodation to ethnic groups, leaders initiate measures for self-help and self-defense. They establish private security forces (militias) and fortify their physical positions. Such presumably defensive measures, though, look indistinguishable from offensive (hegemonic) initiatives and lock in the "ethnic security dilemma."[47] In this dilemma, each step a group takes for self-defense provokes rivals to do the same. Elites begin to use force against other ethnic groups and to regulate their own group's behavior to deter defection. Mutual retaliations accelerate the spiral of violence and compel individuals to cling more closely to the group for protection. Groups that might have been initially reluctant to adopt violence or relied on the state protection find they have no other choice than to mobilize as well.
- *Ethnic infighting.* In periods of crisis, factions within the ethnic group compete for the authority to speak and act on behalf of the group. Ethnic identities provide a kind of script through which to make the assertions. Competing elites rely on pre-existing knowledge to define what the group is and who its enemies are. Moderate leaders, by definition, stake their position on adhering to normative protocols of ethnic cooperation. They promise followers continued stability and opportunity if they abide by the state's

demands. Maximalists, in contrast, try to outbid the moderates by showing that the benefits of peaceful coexistence are no longer assured. They pillory the old elite as weak, naïve, compromising, and even traitorous. Radical action, they argue, is necessary. Maximalists try to ostracize or eliminate contending voices for conciliation. Without support from the state, moderates get neutralized or converted.[48]

- *Elite manipulation.* Elites are adept at combining both elements of offensive opportunities and defensive threats to frame crisis situations. At once utopian and apocalyptic, they promise both the incredible potential of group redemption and the grave dangers of group destruction. It is easy to understand how members of small and marginalized groups might fear for security and undertake defensive violence. But leaders might also convince them that the opportunity to achieve supremacy has arrived. Conversely, large and seemingly dominant groups might be concerned that the break-up of the state will bring about group annihilation. In this circumstance, they will try to deploy the full apparatus of the state security forces to crush the perceived threat. The combination of ethnic fear and state power can have devastating, even genocidal, consequences.

- *Outside intervention.* Finally, maximalist ethnic leaders are often aided and abetted by bad neighbors in MENA. This is more than the product of complicated ethnic geography. Rather, it stems from the way regional state leaders use ethnic relationships to justify interventions in neighboring states.[49] Iraq's invasion of Iran in the 1980s and Kuwait in 1990, for instance, rested on the pretext of backing indigenous movements for Arab liberation and unification. Iran currently provides support for fellow Shi'is in Iraq, Syria, Lebanon, and Yemen, while Saudi Arabia claims to defend Sunnism. Though couched as expressions of ethnic fraternity, these interventions often involve outbidding in the larger international arena. Saudi Arabia is not just targeting Iran, but also trying to outflank Qatar and Turkey, which were also positioned to champion the Sunni cause. Similarly, Iran's support for Shi'i groups involves efforts to prevent alternative centers of Shi'i theological authority from emerging.[50] For their part, Western powers, including the United States, have often involved themselves in the region as the protectors of MENA's Christians, Jews, and other non-Muslim minorities. All of these interventions embolden domestic ethnic elites to be more aggressive, confident – even cocksure – that foreign powers will grant them support.[51]

Case Study: Making Ethnic War in Syria

The Syrian civil war has been the most lethal of MENA's twenty-first-century conflicts. It is often depicted as ethnic or sectarian in nature, with the main belligerents described as Assad's Alawi-dominated regime and Sunni rebels.[52]

Syria checks most of the structural boxes for ethnic conflict. It has a problematic ethnic geography with incongruences between state boundaries and ethnic identities. It has a repressive but also ineffectual state bent on maintaining ethnic domination. Its economic growth has been sporadic and uneven. Yet before 2011 Syria had largely been at peace for over two decades. The last episode of war was in the early 1980s, when a radical Sunni Islamist insurgency confronted brutal state repression. To label Syria's conflict as an ethnic war, though, grasps only some of the mechanisms that led to this catastrophe and misses some of the most important dynamics involved in sparking and perpetuating violence. It took a special combination of bad leaders and bad neighbors to pit ethno-sectarian groups against each other. These alignments were never stable and consistent. Inter-ethnic coalitions were as significant as inter-ethnic rivalries. Moreover, maximalists had to commit violence against their own ethnic communities to maintain their dominance and the trajectory of conflict.

The trigger for the civil war was the popular protests against the Assad regime in 2011. There was little evidence of ethno-sectarian content or framing in these protests. Demonstrations began in the small Sunni city of Dara'a and soon spread countrywide. The protests were broadly peaceful, mimicking the tactics and slogans seen in Tunisia and Egypt. Many demonstrators complained about corruption, poor economic management, and the lack of representation. The regime responded harshly, firing on peaceful protesters and arresting and torturing organizers. Some elements within the army and police defected, handing over garrisons and arms stores to the opposition. State control ceased in some locations, creating a condition of contested sovereignty. Local committees organized protests and took up governance responsibility. The opposition in exile tried to stand up steering committees to coordinate the uprising from afar and represent the Syrian people abroad.

But as the Syrian state slid into failure, more and more of the mechanisms of ethnic dominance, insecurity, manipulation, and intervention became visible. The Assad government tried to maintain its outward image as a secular, non-sectarian regime while blaming the violence on foreign Sunni radicals and terrorists. To keep its base of support, it had to convince otherwise neutral or even disaffected citizens that the rebellion would not only endanger the regime elite, but also lead to a much larger catastrophe. Drawing on memories from the 1980s civil war, government propagandists claimed the rebellion would not stop with removing Assad, but only with the complete annihilation of the Alawis, Christians, secularists of all stripes, and anyone else even remotely tied to the regime. The regime thus manufactured an acute sense of group vulnerability that contributed to security dilemma dynamics. Regime moderates who advocated reform or a less repressive response were ousted from positions of authority. While there were some prominent defectors from within the elite, many Alawis hesitated because they feared they would not be accepted within rebel ranks. At the same time, Christians and other minority sects clung closely to the state for protection. As the security services receded, the regime promoted semi-independent pro-government militias recruited from local civilians. Many of these espoused explicitly sectarian agendas as part of their defense of Syria. The government continued its campaign with maximum force, including torture, mass killings, and indiscriminate bombardment of suspected rebel hideouts. In every phase of the war, the government's violence surpassed that of the rebels. While peripheral areas in the east and north slipped out of the government's hands, the state reinforced its control over Damascus and the Alawi heartland along the western coastal strip, where tens of thousands of Syrians of all ethnicities fled to find security. Noting the discrepancies in levels of mobilization by ethnicity, political scientist Kevin Mazur points out the contradictory processes that led to ethnic mobilization in Syria. Sunnis indeed dominated the opposition. But at the same time,

> members of non-Sunni ethnic groups participated only as individuals or small collectives, traveling to Sunni towns or the centers of Sunni-majority cities to protest. On the other hand, many Sunni towns did not engage in contention, and many Sunnis even turned out on the street to show their support for the regime. In other words, grievances held dispro-portionately by Sunnis generated mobilization, but they did so unevenly across the individuals and local communities of this ethnic identity. The primary factor differentiating Sunnis who engaged in challenge from those who counter-mobilized to support the regime or simply remained on the sidelines was inclusion in the regime's networks.[53]

Iran, the Assad regime's foremost foreign backer, helped accelerate the sectarian turn. Iran's relationship with the Assad regime was decades-long, but had mostly focused on common regional interests. Unlike Hezbollah in Lebanon, Assad showed no affinity for Iran's theocratic model of govern-ance. Fearing the loss of a key ally and the linchpin of its relationship with Hezbollah in Lebanon, Iran redoubled its military, economic, and diplomatic support to the regime. Under Iranian guidance, Hezbollah and Iranian Shi'i militias arrived to bolster the regime and to train militias, further inflecting sectarian attitudes into the fighting.

The rebels, too, initially took pains to portray themselves as representing an organic and multicultural Syria. They tried to induce defection from among the regime elite and encouraged civilians to join the uprising. But local organizers and national opposition figures struggled to cooperate among themselves. Some opposition leaders tried to adhere to non-violent tactics. Others advocated limiting attacks to the state security services. Responding in part to the regime's own violence, radicals took a more expansive view of who their enemy was and how to deal with them. Still other groups turned preda-tory, using the rebellion as cover for criminal extortion and expropriation.[54]

The influx of foreign financial and military aid to the rebels worsened this fragmentation. Qatar and Saudi Arabia particularly encouraged rebels to adopt increasingly strident sectarian rhetoric. Insurgents competed with each other to demonstrate their commitment to the Sunni cause. Feeding into Assad's narrative about genocidal intent, they also massacred Alawis, Christians, and other civilians, and assassinated Sunni leaders who continued to side with Assad.

The arrival of the Islamic State (IS) accelerated this outbidding process. Originating in the mid-2000s as al-Qaeda in Iraq (AQI), the group had taken a deliberately provocative and extreme position against Shi'is, deeming them inveterate heretics. In correspondence with the al-Qaeda leadership, AQI founder Abu Musab al-Zarqawi deemed Shi'is "the insurmountable obstacle, the lurking snake, the crafty and malicious scorpion, the spying enemy, and the penetrating venom . . . a sect of treachery and betrayal throughout history and throughout the ages. It is a creed that aims to combat the Sunnis."[55] He laid out a plan to attack Shi'is, the United States, plus any Sunni group that refused to participate in this campaign. His strategy was to spark a regional sectarian war that would draw in all Sunnis together to destroy the Shi'is and their American allies. Even the al-Qaeda leadership recognized this plan as extreme in nature and warned against measures that would alienate potential sympathizers and allies, but to no avail.

The war in Syria offered the IS leadership a chance to expand their territorial foothold. Most of IS's gains came at the expense of other rebel groups. IS avoided direct military confrontation with Syrian state forces. Some rebels chose to integrate under IS's banner, giving the group access to weaponry and funds secreted from the outside powers. Others, though, were massacred. By 2014, IS had taken control over a vast territory across the Iraqi–Syrian frontier, an area of 39,000 square miles (100,000 square kilometers) with an estimated population of between 2.8 and 8 million people. In July 2014, IS spiritual leader Abu Bakr Baghdadi declared himself caliph. The ceremony, which took place in Mosul's most august mosque, was widely disseminated on social media. Senior scholars and tribal leaders in Syria and Iraq offered their oath of allegiance to Baghdadi, validating IS's claim to spiritual and religious supremacy. IS ideologues deemed Iraqi and Syrian nationhood as artificial notions meant to divide Muslims. They portrayed IS's military triumph as heralding a new messianic era. Although estimates are fuzzy, tens of thousands of foreign fighters from dozens of countries traveled to Syria and Iraq to join the revolution. Some of these were veteran jihadists. Others were adventurers, thugs, and the recently radicalized.[56] Still, many Syrian rebel forces refused to accede to IS's leadership. Al-Qaeda disavowed the group and several senior IS figures broke off to form Jabhat al-Nusra (JAN), al-Qaeda's new designated affiliate. JAN allied with other Syrian rebel groups and both repelled the IS expansion and fought the Syrian state simultaneously.

Within its domain, IS imposed a harsh and brutal rule roughly modeled on the regime's understanding of Prophet Muhammad's practices. Disobedience was tantamount to heresy; corporal and capital punishment were common. Christians were provided protection conforming to the model of the Ottoman *millet* system. They were, at best, second-class citizens, their properties and homes conspicuously marked with a "*nun*" in Arabic, denoting Nazarene. Their protection depended on their good behavior. They could not build churches and, in some circumstances, saw properties expropriated by IS. More heterodox minorities, such as Yezidis, were totally denied any protection. They became targets for especially systematic and grotesque violence, with Yezidi women sold into sexual slavery. The progeny of Muslim men and Yezidi slaves were considered Muslims, demographic fodder for the Islamic State.[57] Such grotesque violence reflected not just ideology, but also IS's political aim for total control. It sought to reconfigure social relations through violence and thus constitute the very Islamic community which IS ideologues posited already existed.[58]

Moreover, IS was similar to many other rebel groups operating in Syria in that it tried to supplant the state as a military body and a service provider.[59] IS operatives attended to prosaic functions of statehood and governance: promulgating laws, levying taxes, managing oil refineries, agricultural cooperatives, and schools. IS paid technicians to keep the electrical system intact and IS jurists intervened in tribal land disputes. Many civilians who lived under IS saw value in the relative stability and orderliness of life compared to the corruption and crime of the previous years.[60]

The ultimate military defeat of IS between 2016 and 2018 was largely a function of geopolitical intervention. The intervention involved a tacit but still potent alliance that crossed geopolitical and sectarian lines. Both Moscow and Washington regarded IS as a significant threat, although for very different reasons. The United States had provided financial support and weaponry to the Syrian rebels, but grew increasingly concerned about the drift toward maximalism. Washington provided air support and logistical backing to Iraqi Kurdish and Iraqi forces fighting IS. Saudi Arabia, the UAE, and Jordan joined the anti-IS campaign. The United States also established direct support to the Democratic Union Party (PYD), an offshoot of the Turkish Kurdistan Workers' Party (PKK) and the leading political faction among Syrian Kurds. PYD leaders had reached a kind of bargain with the Assad regime at the beginning of the war. PYD forces took over territories in the northeast and north as government troops evacuated. Although the PYD leadership insisted on their loyalty to the Syrian state and the Assad regime, they unilaterally declared their territories a self-governing, autonomous region of Rojava (Western Kurdistan). In contrast, Russia was a long-standing ally of Assad. Russia equated the entire rebellion with radical Sunni Islamist groups like IS. In September 2015, Moscow launched its own aerial campaign to back the Syrian- and Iranian-aligned forces that attacked rebel positions across Syria, not just those held by IS. By the autumn of 2016, the ungainly coalition had reduced IS to a small foothold along the Euphrates river. Assad pressed his advantage, using Russian and Iranian backing to liquidate rebel strongholds around Aleppo and Idlib through 2017 and 2018.

In sum, while it is impossible to tell the story of Syria's civil war without reference to ethno-sectarian groups and categories, it is equally important to appreciate how these categories emerged. As international relations specialist Christopher Phillips put it, the importance of ethno-sectarianism in the war varied over space and time. Moreover, ethno-sectarianism was hardly the only factor motivating the fighting.[61] At the outset of the war, ethnic boundaries were only loosely set. The breakdown of the state provided an opportunity for elites to begin outbidding each other. International interventions intensified this impetus, providing an incentive for Syrian leaders to reinforce boundaries of ethnic belonging. But there was a major disjuncture between the way elites adopted ethnic framing and the way the masses responded. An estimated 11 million Syrians – about half of the country's population – lost their homes during the war, becoming either internally displaced or refugees in Turkey, Lebanon, or other countries. This massive evacuation suggests that the overriding concern for everyday Syrians was security. In a remarkable set of interviews with Syrian refugees, political scientist Wendy Pearlman shows how Syrian civilians clung to a broad sense of Syrian patriotism and disregarded purported ethnic threats, even when they confronted regime or rebel forces.[62] In this respect, the elites' ethnic war represented the betrayal of the Syrian people themselves.

Conclusion

War is an inherently group activity. Every group conflict necessarily involves a concept of identity differentiating ours from theirs, us from them. Many analyses point to ethnic geography, the incongruence between identities and political boundaries, as the root cause of MENA's conflict. Territorial boundaries are either too big, incorporating too many antagonistic groups in one space, or too small, breaking up the organic unity of larger groups. On this view, MENA's ancient ethnic groups and their atavistic hatreds are incompatible with modern statehood.

This chapter challenges the assumption that MENA's conflicts are driven by an insatiable urge for group supremacy by considering the interaction between ethnic groups and states. Belying claims to ancient provenance, ethnic groups have coevolved with modern states. Ethnic identities have been fluid, and ethnic groups are never monolithic in attitude and orientation. States have shifted and shaped citizens' notions of group belonging. MENA states have mixed approaches of assimilation, consociation, and domination to maintain a modicum of ethnic cooperation and channel group competition in peaceful ways. These approaches have, for the most part, succeeded in making violence prohibitively costly; cooperation is overwhelmingly the norm.

But MENA states do face structural conditions that render this equilibrium precarious. These factors are not unique to the region, but are broadly visible across the developing world in general. Ethnic geography compounds the challenges of the regional security predicament, linking up internal and external challengers to the state. Uneven and halting economic development and repressive but feckless states further lower the certainty that cooperation pays.

Still, elites' responses to these structural conditions critically determine when war and violence will occur. Elites turn the content of ethnic identities and awareness of ethnic scripts into plans of attack. Because ethnic identities are fluid and ethnic groups themselves factionalized, intra-group violence inevitably accompanies inter-ethnic war. While moderates stake their position on caution and abiding by the old rules of cooperation, maximalists frame situations by combining a sense of collective vulnerability with the opportunity for group redemption and hegemony. They use private and parochial conflicts between neighbors and families to catalyze larger group mobilization.

Ethnic wars occur when moderates lose out. While elites manipulate symbols of ethnic identity instrumentally, most people look for the best ways to protect themselves and their families. In some cases this might mean falling in line with maximalists. But in many other cases it just involves retreat and withdrawal to safety. Ethnic animosity alone is never the driver of ethnic war. The case study of Syria shows how geopolitical concerns created incentives for outbidding and drove a realignment of ethnic alliances. The tactical, even instrumentalist, nature of these maneuvers further undercuts the too-easy assumption that irrational or atavistic hatreds drive regional war.

5

Geopolitics as Conflict Trap

Discussions of MENA's past and current wars almost invariably mention the role of great powers from outside the region and the impact of geopolitics. Within the region, conspiracy theories often point to outside actors and secret intrigues as the roots of regional turmoil. Philosopher Sadik al-Azm describes returning to Damascus from a trip to Japan after the September 11, 2001 attacks

> to immerse myself in the immense and intense debates going on about September 11 and to listen to and take account of all the conspiracy theories circulating wildly not only locally but all over the Arab World and beyond. The point of the whole commotion was to distance the Arabs, Islam and Muslims from what happened to the World Trade Center and the Pentagon by blaming it all on the usual candidates: the Mossad, the CIA, the Pentagon itself, the Jewish-Zionist-imperialist plot, globalization's super plotters and schemers, the American military-industrial complex and so on.[1]

Attributing violence to outside actors simultaneously expresses and reinforces popular mistrust of all forms of institutionalized power.[2] Scholarly accounts sometimes lend credence to the suspicion that a good deal of MENA's conflict trap is imposed from without. The conflict and strife that seem to mar MENA stem from the encroachment of outside powers, beginning with European colonialism and extending through the twentieth-century Cold War and the subsequent era of US involvement. "Western powers have tried to impose an order on the Middle East beneficial to their own narrow strategic, economic, and ideological imperatives. These efforts of Western domination have always ended in failure and at enormous human costs," political scientist Stephen Zunes finds.[3] MENA's war and conflict, on this view, are the product of machinations initiated by external actors for their own geopolitical ends. The real causes of war operate on the strategic or geopolitical level, above and beyond the region itself.

This chapter offers a critical perspective on the geopolitical conflict trap. The previous chapters touched on how extra-regional actors affected the process of state formation in MENA and insinuated themselves into conflicts over oil and ethnicity. This chapter retraces and retreads some of this material but focuses on it more intently to demonstrate the myriad ways geopolitics and outside powers contributed to war and conflict in the region. The chapter argues that extra-regional powers' influence in MENA was significant but far from absolute. Depending on the shifting global balance of power and the changing ideas that animated geopolitical practices, outside interventions could constrain or enable state and non-state actors. Overall, geopolitical factors alternately reinforced and retarded the escalation of violence. Geopolitics is thus less a singular determinant than one of many elements affecting war and conflict in MENA.

Geopolitics as Practice and Discourse

Policy-makers and pundits talk about geopolitics a lot but seldom explain what they mean by the term. In colloquial usage, geopolitics amounts to the ways major powers take positions on the global scale. Scholars of global strategy and international relations offer a more refined but still conventional definition. Geopolitics, according to international relations expert Aharon Klieman, is

> what Great Powers engage in, what they practice and what they are best at. Variables originating in physical geography, including topography, climate and demography, still translate into assets and liabilities, openings or constraints, for rising, resident, and receding great powers just as they did in the Age of Empire. . . . Lastly, geopolitics provides the context – the landscape, the backdrop, the arena – in which great power contests take place at any given moment.[4]

These ideas harken back to the works of the late nineteenth- and early twentieth-century forefathers of geopolitics. Such studies were in some respects critiques of realist international relations theory. For this conception, instead of seeing global politics played out on a metaphorical planar billiard table, space matters. The physical configurations of oceans and landmasses, shipping lanes and air routes, ultimately determine how states interact. In other crucial ways, though, classical geopolitics comports with realism. The competitive interaction of global powers is the crucial determinant of war and peace.[5] Developing regions, like MENA, are as affected by geography as any other. But they do not figure weightily in the global balance of power or have much global political reach. Geopolitics is something enforced or imported from without. Some of the key factors driving war and conflict in MENA and the rest of the developing world are not intrinsic to the region or individual state. Rather, states higher in the global pecking order foster these conditions as part of their own geopolitical maneuvering.

Outsiders' geopolitical maneuvers can affect war in the developing world both direct and indirectly. The most obvious impact of geopolitics is by direct *initiation* of war, attacking countries in the developing world. Invasions of the developing world were common throughout the era of colonialism. Although frequently outnumbered in manpower, colonial armies tended to enjoy profound advantages in technologies of warfare that allowed them to overawe opponents. Initiation of war, therefore, was a kind of "punching down" in the global order. With the progress of decolonization, direct confrontations between great powers and states in the developing world have become rare. The Vietnam War, for instance, was often denounced as an illegitimate colonial campaign. So, too, was Britain and France's attack on Egypt in 1956, the Soviet Union's invasion of Afghanistan in 1979, and the United States' attack on Iraq in 2003. These incidents highlight the continued role of hierarchy in the international system and the discrepancies in geopolitical power that still affect developing regions like MENA.

Even as the most blatant forms of colonial aggression decreased, greater powers still exerted influence through alliances with less powerful states and, occasionally, armed non-state actors. These alliances created patron–client relationships that allowed outside powers to encourage or commission allies to initiate war against a common enemy. Israel was a crucial ally in Britain and France's 1956 invasion of Egypt, for example. Commissioning war is something very distinct from direct invasion. It situates the burden of war back into the regional sphere, allowing geopolitical actors less control and oversight over the course of the conflict.

Less direct, but in some ways even more important, is the way great powers enable the use of violence. Clients can launch wars at their own volition with the provision of economic, diplomatic, and military aid from great powers. In this dynamic, client proxies can use the resources provided by sponsors to adopt confrontational paths. These types of confrontations may – or may not – occur with the approval of the sponsor. This principal–agent problem shows up repeatedly in MENA's politics. Finally, and most diffusely, great powers had an inordinate role in shaping the international system, creating and enforcing the rules by which all other actors had to abide. Outside powers thus wove the causes of war into the fabric of the international and regional system. For example, many complain that MENA's economic, ethnic, and political challenges stem from the very borders which foreign powers inscribed during the course of colonialism. Violence, both between and within states, occurred as actors inevitably tried to rectify colonial-era malfunctions and malformations. Geopolitics structured the violence of MENA, even without directly initiating, commissioning, or enabling it.

Beside the classical geopolitical approach, though, is a more critical view. Critical theories of geopolitics are less interested in physical geography as a binding constraint and more focused on the political and ideological processes that contribute to particular discourses of geopolitics. The foundational concepts of geopolitics are themselves articulations and enactments of political powers through knowledge. Actors construe geopolitical relationships through narratives emphasizing binary distinctions between "us" and "them." In his seminal studies of Western depictions of the Arab and Islamic world, Edward Said focuses on the way academic specialists, the mass media, and popular stereotypes in the United States and Europe built a basically sinister imagining of MENA societies. The East, in this discourse, was riddled with obscurant Islam, misogyny, and terrorism. This depiction simultaneously produced "the West" as a countervailing power – a realm of toleration, peace, civilization, and Christianity. In this sense, MENA and the West are spatially and culturally distant and also destined to clash.[6] These presumptions were deeply engrained into the structure of the international system. Violence committed by certain actors was necessarily deemed as legitimate while others were classed as merely criminal or barbaric.

Orientalist renderings of geopolitical discourse, like any hegemonic project, generate their own counter-narrative, a subaltern response to domination. Mirroring Western discourse that defines MENA as an enemy other, discourse within MENA defines the West as an intractable foe. Such "Occidentalism" turns Orientalism on its head by denigrating and denouncing the West. Conspiracy theories relating to terrorism hint at this kind of retaliation as if through parody. In the case of the September 11th conspiracy theories, there is an assumption that Westerners are capable of depraved mass murder, while Arabs and Muslims are innocent victims wrongly accused.[7] At the same time, the most radical groups tout their resistance to the West by cultivating the very negative traits that Orientalism attributes to them. Such discourse, as al-Azm puts it,

> insists that what you, the West, and your local stooges call our backwardness is our authenticity, what you term our primitiveness is our identity, what you denounce as our brutality is our sacred tradition, what you describe as our superstitions is our holy religion, and what you despise as our illiteracy is our ancient custom, and we are going to insist on their superiority to all that you have to offer, no matter what you say and no matter what you do.[8]

By selectively reading scriptures and sacred texts, such discourse construes its own vision of a geopolitical chasm between Islam and the West. Approached critically, geopolitics is a kind of self-fulfilling prophecy. Ultimately, both the physical characteristics of space and power and the ideational notions of justification and legitimacy play an important part in explaining how outside powers have affected MENA.[9]

The Geopolitics of Colonialism

Much of the vocabulary used to describe MENA draws inextricably from imperial geopolitical imaginations. British colonial officers first coined the phrase

"Middle East" in the mid-1800s, supplementing the more familiar "Near East." American naval strategist Alfred Mahan popularized it at the turn of the century in a widely read treatise. For imperial geopolitical thinkers like Mahan and others, the idea of the Middle East emphasized the area's geographic centrality in the eastern hemisphere landmass.[10]

Such a neologism, though, was probably not needed to remind people of the long historical linkages between Europe and MENA. Geography defined MENA as Europe's near neighbor, but it did not preordain European domination. Through antiquity to the Middle Ages, while Europe lagged economically, culturally, and politically, the societies and states of MENA were generally oriented to commerce with the great civilizations of India and China.[11] Contrary to the assumption of a civilizational chasm between Christian Europe and Muslim MENA, it was competition over a common cultural legacy that proved the driver of war and conflict. The objective of the Crusades was to gain control over the holy sites in Jerusalem that were venerated by both Christians and Muslims. Upon conquering Constantinople in 1453, the Ottomans proclaimed themselves successors to the Roman emperors (*Sultan-i Rum*), challenging the pretensions of the Habsburg Holy Roman Emperors and the Tsars of Russia, the "new Rome."[12] The Ottomans dominated the Mediterranean, Black Sea, and southeastern Europe from the fourteenth to the sixteenth century. Muslim control of the overland trade routes to Asia spurred European efforts both to explore Muslim-ruled territories and to bypass them by sea during the age of exploration. Indeed, the decline of those trade routes and the influx of New World silver likely contributed to the Ottomans' fiscal and military decline. Even so, the Ottoman empire was a considerable military force and an important player in the concert of Europe.

Compared to the scramble for influence in Asia, the Americas, or, later, Africa, nineteenth-century European imperial incursions in MENA were muted and belated. The European powers shared the assumption that the Islamic empires, along with China and Japan, were inherently inferior, at best "semi-civilized."[13] Many European powers positioned themselves as the humanitarian protectors of the Ottomans' indigenous Christian communities. Britain's engagement in MENA largely reflected classic geopolitical calculations: protecting the passages to India. In the Persian Gulf and Aden, colonial officers offered local potentates subsidies and protection from the Ottomans in return for suppression of piracy and exclusion of any other foreign powers. Egypt, with its narrow Suez isthmus linking the Mediterranean and the Indian Ocean, was another geopolitical focal point. Britain encouraged Mehmet Ali, the Khedive (viceroy) of Egypt, to detach from Ottoman control and establish his own dynasty (although Egypt remained legally under Ottoman suzerainty). Britain funded the construction of the Suez Canal. After Egypt defaulted on its foreign loans in 1882, Britain forced the Khedive to accept colonial oversight. Still, only a handful of British colonial officers were stationed in the region and there was a general policy of working through indigenous elites.

France took a more intensive and intrusive approach in constructing its trans-Mediterranean empire. It invaded Algeria in 1830, waging a brutal war against opposition forces. By 1834, Algeria was formally annexed. Tens of thousands of French citizens settled in Algeria, making it one of the few parts of the region subject to colonization from the metropole. The conquest of Tunisia in 1881 and Morocco's capitulation in 1912 further consolidated France's hold in the western Mediterranean. France also forced the Ottomans to create a special Christian autonomous zone in Lebanon following intercommunal violence in the 1860s. Russia took Ottoman territories in the Caucasus and positioned itself as defender of the empire's Armenians and Orthodox Christians. Austria and the Balkan states jostled to grab the Ottomans' dwindling European territory. Italy invaded and annexed Ottoman Libya in 1911–12. Germany, meanwhile, sought to balance against Russia, France, and Britain by actively courting the Ottomans. Kaiser Wilhelm II touted himself as the champion of the world's beleaguered Muslims. The Ottomans made a secret treaty with Germany in 1914 and joined the Central Powers during World War I.

Imperialist encroachment in MENA accelerated with World War I and the break-up of the Ottoman empire. British officials made contradictory pledges to support Arab and Jewish nationalist agendas in return for support against the Ottomans. But Britain never intended to relinquish power. In 1916, it secretly negotiated the Sykes–Picot agreement, divvying up the rump Ottoman domain between Britain and France. As memorialized in a brief memorandum and a hand-drawn map, Britain would control oil-rich Baghdad, Basra, and Kuwait at the mouth of the Persian Gulf. France would rule the coastline of Anatolia and the northern Levant, including Mount Lebanon. From Iraq to Haifa on the Mediterranean would be a zone of indirect British influence, while inland Syria and Mosul would be under indirect French control. Upon the Ottoman defeat in 1919, Britain and France moved to enact their plan. They crushed popular resistance and betrayed their erstwhile indigenous allies. They divided and then ruled the newly created states of Lebanon, Syria, Iraq, Palestine, and Jordan.

The Sykes–Picot agreement has become a popular metonym for nefarious colonial dealings in MENA. Western analysts frequently cite the agreement as the origin of MENA's artificial states, malformed borders, and unworkable ethnic geography. The colonial powers subdivided Arab territories into multiple states. The Zionist state-building project in Palestine jabbed like a splinter into the Arab core. The influx of hundreds of thousands of Jewish migrants, many of them refugees from eastern Europe, confirmed Britain's imperialist aims to dispossess and neutralize Arab nationalism. The new states lumped together groups with grave historical enmities. Some minority groups, like the Kurds, saw their ethno-nationalist ambitions completely ignored. Within MENA itself, leaders often weave Sykes–Picot into discussions of foreign conspiracies. Osama bin Laden blamed the agreement for "the dissection of the Islamic world into fragments" and pronounced the American campaign against Iraq in 2003 "a new Sykes–Picot agreement [aimed at the] destroying and looting of our beloved Prophet's *umma* [people]."[14] As his country descended into civil war in 2012, Syrian President Bashar al-Assad declared the popular uprising to be part of the "dream of partition [that] is still haunting the grandchildren of Sykes–Picot."[15] The Islamic State promised to demolish the illegitimate "Sykes–Picot borders" in 2014. The governor of Erbil province in Iraq's autonomous Kurdistan Region told an American journalist that "hundreds of thousands have been killed because of Sykes–-Picot and all the problems it created."[16]

The geopolitical narrative of Sykes–Picot, however, glosses over a complicated historical record. First, it is notable that this agreement had no bearing on Egypt and North Africa, where the imperial hold of Britain and France had been long-standing and far more intrusive, or on the Arabian Peninsula, where Britain retained a light imperial footprint. Secondly, the process of demarcating and assigning territorial boundaries in the former Ottoman domains continued through the post-war Paris Peace Conference (1919), the San Remo agreement (1920), the Treaty of Sèvres (1920), the Cairo Conference (1921), and the Lausanne Conference (1922–3). On close examination, the resulting states and borders diverged substantially from what Sykes and Picot had agreed upon in early 1916. Thirdly, the League of Nations' mandate structure for MENA differed institutionally and legally from any prior forms of colonial rule. The mandates – and the League more generally – reflected new configurations of global power and new norms of geopolitical engagement. Upon entering the war in 1918, American President Woodrow Wilson championed the doctrine of self-determination as an antidote to a European imperialism that was willing to barter away peoples and territories like chattel. He even dispatched a special commission to the Levant to sound out popular sentiments. The League of Nations took up the Wilsonian mantle, despite the misgivings and naysaying of Britain, France, and other imperial powers. Wilson's pronouncement and the US ascent emboldened indigenous actors in their campaigns for statehood. Arabs, Jews, Kurds, and other nationalist groups specifically cited Wilsonian doctrine in their mobilizations. Arab nationalists quoted liberally from Wilson's Fourteen Points in their Damascus Declaration of 1919. Arabs, they asserted, were no less mature and worthy of statehood than "Bulgarians, Serbians, Greeks, and Romans [Romanians] at the beginning of their independence."[17]

Of course, the practice of mandatory rule in MENA often veered from its legal theory. The League still held to an essentially racist hierarchy of which peoples were eligible for self-rule. The ex-Ottoman subjects – Muslims, Christians, and

Jews – were found lacking in this criterion, at least initially. (Africans and Pacific islanders were rated even lower.) Furthermore, even if the program of self-determination were pursued in earnest, there was no practical way to sort out conflicting claims to territories. As nationalists mobilized in response to the arrival of the great powers, their conflicting agendas for cities like Kirkuk and Jerusalem became more salient. The League's own ambivalence abetted Britain's and France's prevarication when it came to the mandates. Both often treated their charges as conventional colonies. Both resorted to massive violence to uphold their rule. Any signs of opposition or public disturbance was regarded as akin to brigandage. Aerial bombardment, increasingly regarded as too inhumane to use against fellow Europeans, was frequently deployed in the mandate territories and across MENA.[18] Such novel technologies of repression were essential to allowing the exhausted empires to reduce their manpower commitments overseas.

Yet the mandates were transformative in unforeseen ways. The League insisted that former Ottoman territories were not imperial appendages, crown colonies, or traditional dependencies. Rather, Britain and France held the mandates in "sacred trust" to prepare the inhabitants for independence. The mandates granted indigenous leaders unprecedented standing in the international community as representatives of provisional states and fledgling nations.[19] Britain and France had no choice but to find indigenous leaders who would work with them, pliant enough to do their bidding but credible enough to maintain a measure of local legitimacy. These local actors often stymied European efforts to draw borders and divide territories.[20] Diplomatic discussions were often less about great power horse trading than about ratifying the facts on the ground that indigenous actors had initiated. Britain and France enjoyed unquestionable economic and military advantages, but they could not shape MENA unilaterally. They had to commission indigenous actors to commit violence instead of enacting it directly. This often involved relying on networks of informants and spies and using divide-and-rule strategies that deepened internecine conflicts. In North Africa, for example, France pitted Berbers against Arab nationalist factions.[21] In Palestine, British policy oscillated between backing the Zionists and placating the Arab opposition. At the same time, both colonial powers needed to extract resources, including military service, from their colonial possessions. Moroccan, Tunisian, and Algerian troops all served with the French army during the world wars. Some North African troops even served elsewhere in the colonial empire, including Syria and Indochina. Britain similarly relied on the Indian army to garrison Iraq and elsewhere. In desperation during World War II, Britain also considered ways to use the Egyptian and Iraqi armies, as well as the burgeoning Zionist forces, to protect the far-flung empire.[22]

But these colonial strategies intended to assure geopolitical dominance inadvertently enabled indigenous actors to make war for their own ends. With the exception of Algeria's National Liberation Front (FLN), all of the armies of MENA originated as colonial forces. The first Arab–Israeli war of 1948 was fought by forces at least partially trained by Britain or France. The Jordanian army was even commanded by a British officer. Yet Britain was a mostly hapless bystander during the war. Despite strong relationships, it could do little but stand aside and try to limit the damage to its imperial interests.[23]

Iraq was the most territorially contrived Arab state but also the first to gain formal independence, in 1932. Its efforts to pursue independent foreign and military policies exemplify how geopolitics enabled both war and state formation.[24] The Iraqi state leadership immediately put to use their British military equipment to repress their own population, starting with the Assyrians (as discussed in Chapter 2). By the mid-1930s, the Royal Iraqi Air Force was routinely bombing rebellious tribes in the north and south, even as some British counselors advised a more conciliatory approach. Iraqi politicians sought to circumvent Britain's continued diplomatic dominance. Britain, meanwhile, refused to remit sterling in order to block Iraqi efforts to buy armaments from Italy.[25] In 1941, after a group of Iraqi politicians seized power and tried to make contact with Germany, Britain was forced to re-invade and occupy Iraq in order to preserve its air bridge to India.

Ultimately, the key decisions about war slipped from the grasp of the colonial powers. Joost Hiltermann, a long-time Middle East observer and researcher for the International Crisis Group, observes that former colonies and mandates

> gradually lost their creators' defining imprint. It would be wrong today to blame these societies' many ills on the governing structures they originally received. They assumed lives of their own, with their own internal struggles over ideology, politics and resource allocation. Yet these lives were also shaped in constant interaction with an outside world that was economically and militarily much stronger.[26]

Cold War Geopolitics and America's Ascent

The Cold War changed the basic geopolitical tenets of the previous colonial era. The most obvious change was the rise of the superpower United States and Soviet Union. For the United States, buffered by the Atlantic and Pacific oceans, the distant MENA was hardly an essential zone of geopolitical competition. Through the duration of the Cold War, as shown in Figure 5.1, there were far more American troops deployed to Europe than to MENA. With its wars in Korea and Vietnam, the Asia-Pacific zone was far more consequential to the United States geopolitically.

In MENA, the United States enjoyed more latitude to pick and choose its engagement than the previous European imperial powers had. Two priorities

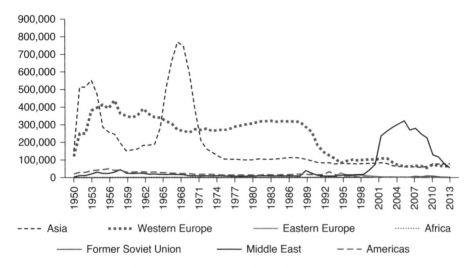

Figure 5.1 US troop deployment by region, 1950–2013
Source: Tim Kane, "Global US Troop Deployment, 1950–2003" *Heritage Foundation*, October 27, 2004, *https://www.heritage.org/defense/report/global-us-troop-deployment-1950-2003*. Additional data provided by Tim Kane.

emerged. First, the United States sought to preserve and protect the global oil supply. The ideology of oil scarcity, as discussed in Chapter 3, was an important component of US geopolitical imagination. Importantly, the United States at this time possessed enough oil for its own domestic consumption and could easily import from the Western hemisphere. Key allies in Europe and Asia, however, depended on MENA for industrial fuels, and the United States as a superpower endeavored to make those economic assurances. The United States cultivated close strategic relationships with MENA's largest oil-producing states, mainly Saudi Arabia, but also Iran, in the 1960s and 1970s. It sought not just to uphold their external defense but also to ensure the longevity of regimes and individual rulers. This inserted the United States into domestic contestations for power within MENA, often favoring the perceived stability of authoritarian rule over the uncertainty of political change. The second US priority was Israel. Initial US support for Israel was mainly moral: the US public was broadly sympathetic to the plight of Jews after the Holocaust, and US politicians tried to win support from Jewish voters. The "special relationship" between Israel and the United States, as John F. Kennedy called it, was strengthened through common cultural connections, antipathy to communism, and democratic values (at least when it came to the Jewish majority). By the 1960s, Israel clearly had the region's most formidable military and was a key US strategic asset. However, it was also a drag on the US ability to navigate within the wider Arab world. Many Arabs regarded Israel as an illegitimate colonial outpost.[27] Balancing these regional priorities with a

Table 5.1 Soviet and Eastern European military technicians in late developing countries

	1965	1970	1975	1979	Total	% of total
North Africa	605	1,020	1,005	2,835	5,465	14
Sub-Saharan Africa	400	965	1,580	3,990	6,935	18
East Asia	520	0	0	0	520	1
Latin America	0	0	35	110	145	0
Middle East	1,500	7,820	4,900	4,780	19,000	50
South Asia	610	320	700	4,150	5,780	15

Source: Central Intelligence Agency, "Communist Aid Activities in Non-Communist Less Developed Countries, 1979 and 1954–1979," October 1980, *https://www.cia.gov/library/readingroom/docs/DOC_0000499891.pdf.*

global agenda to contain or even roll back the Soviet advance preoccupied US policy throughout the Cold War era.

The USSR had more immediate interests at stake in MENA. The Soviets had long-standing geopolitical ambitions for the Black Sea and Mediterranean, a significant Muslim population, and shared a border with Iran, Turkey, and Afghanistan. The Soviets, too, had backed the creation of Israel in 1948, in order to weaken Britain. But the USSR had few natural allies in the region. Although there were significant communist movements in countries like Iran, Iraq, and South Yemen, the Soviets focused on building alliances with so-called "progressive" nationalists, typically military men, who rejected the dominance of the old elite that had been compromised by their cooperation with Britain and France.[28] While the US geostrategic planners spent most of the Cold War focused on Europe and East Asia, many Soviet planners regarded MENA as secondary only to Eastern Europe. Between 1955 and 1979, nearly half of Soviet economic aid toward non-communist developing countries was directed to MENA. Over 70 percent of the military technicians and advisors the Soviets and their allies dispatched to the developing world between 1965 and 1979 were bound for the region, as shown in Table 5.1.

Beyond the new bipolar alignment of global power, new norms and beliefs also animated the international system. Following World War I, the mandates seemed to be tentative and experimental steps toward decolonization. After World War II, decolonization was the rule, not the exception. The stakes were highest in Algeria, which the French regarded as integrally connected to the metropole. After over a decade of fighting, including massive violence against Algerian civilians and terrorist attacks within France itself, President Charles de Gaulle finally maneuvered France out of Algeria in 1962. Indicative of the patterns of colonial violence, some 90,000 Algerians who had served in the colonial constabulary force relocated to France after the war. An untold number of so-called "French collaborators" who remained in Algeria were assassinated or lynched.[29] Even after quitting India in 1948, Britain tried in vain to suppress the national liberation movement in South Yemen. It finally evacuated the Persian Gulf princedoms in the early 1970s.[30] In different ways and for different reasons both the United States and the USSR pressured the old European powers to relinquish their colonial possessions. The new rules of the international system, codified through the UN and enforced by the new superpowers, granted newly independent states unprecedented protection from foreign aggression and assurances of territorial integrity.

For their part, the United States and the USSR offered the post-colonial states alternative roadmaps for modernization along with competing packages of economic and military aid to woo states to their camp. The system was still hierarchical, but premised on a new dichotomy between the free and unfree, the developed and the underdeveloped.[31] State-building leaders found new opportunities to maneuver in the bipolar geopolitical configuration and under the new norms of international power. In some cases, they could even play superpower patrons off against each other to maximize leverage. The provision of diplomatic and material aid allowed MENA states to wage war against internal challengers as well as neighboring states.

The new rules of the game became visible in MENA in the first post-war decade. In 1946, the United States pressured the Soviets to cease their support for Azeri and Kurdish separatist movements. For the United States, this was a matter of containing communism. For the UN, however, it was a question of restoring Iran's territorial sovereignty in the face of foreign occupation. Upon the Soviets' withdrawal, the rebellions quickly collapsed. The Iranian army, though unable to deal with the Soviet threat, could now easily liquidate the separatist strongholds and restore central control over the periphery.[32] The United States came to regard Iran as a potential regional powerhouse by virtue of its size and relative development compared to other countries of the Gulf. Washington funneled military aid and development assistance to the country. In 1952, a new domestic crisis emerged in Iran when Mohammed Mossadeq became prime minister. Mossadeq hailed from an old Iranian aristocratic family and had trained in international law in Switzerland. He decried the Pahlavi monarchy's willingness to subordinate Iranian national interests to foreign powers. He criticized the deals the monarchy had struck that effectively ceded control over Iran's oil production and marketing to British Petroleum. Mossadeq unilaterally declared oil to be Iranian state property, while offering to compensate the British. Britain and the United States were alarmed at what they deemed Mossadeq's leftist leanings and his political alliance with the Iranian communist party. In 1953, British and US intelligence conspired with right-wing Iranian military officers and clerics to oust him. Mohammed Reza Shah Pahlavi was restored to full autocratic rule, while the Iranian parliament was effectively neutralized.[33] The US–Iran alliance would remain one of the centerpieces of US regional strategy until the Shah was deposed during the Iranian Revolution of 1979.

A similar crisis appeared almost concurrently in Egypt, but with very different results. Egypt, like Iran, was a prospective regional powerhouse. The Egyptian monarchy was part of the bulwark of Western-aligned regional states. It was not incidental that Mohammed Reza Shah's first marriage was to the daughter of the Egyptian king (they divorced in 1948). In July 1952, in the midst of the nationalization crisis in Iran, Colonel Gamal Abd al-Nasser deposed the Egyptian monarchy and declared Egypt a republic. In contrast to the genteel septuagenarian Mossadeq, Nasser and his so-called "Free Officer Movement" represented a new and younger nationalist sentiment. Nasser and his cadre were unwilling to accommodate the old imperial structures. They criticized Britain and France for their support of Israel and continued control over the Suez Canal. At the same time, they played the United States and the USSR off against each other. Many Egyptians saw the Aswan High Dam project, which had been funded by the United States and Britain, as a development panacea. As in Iran, though, development assistance and military aid were closely linked. The United States hesitated to provide Egypt with weapons that might be turned on Israel; it finally pulled its funding for the High Dam when Nasser announced the establishment of diplomatic relations with Communist China and broadened its military relationship with the Soviet bloc. The Soviets agreed to fund the dam and to supply Egypt with advanced weaponry and military advisors. In 1956, Nasser unilaterally nationalized the Suez Canal and threatened Israel's access to the Gulf of Aqaba. Israel, France, and Britain hatched a secret plan to attack Egypt and possibly oust Nasser. In October 1956, Israeli forces invaded the Sinai Peninsula and Gaza, quickly routing the Egyptian army. The British and French followed quickly on by seizing the Suez zone as a "peacekeeping" measure. The superpowers' response was instructive as to how the new world order would work. The Soviets, already facing insurrection in Hungary, warned that they might intervene to defend Egypt. The United States placed financial pressure on Britain, France, and Israel to get them to quit what was broadly deemed an illegal military action. The UN dispatched a peacekeeping mission to monitor the Gulf of Aqaba. Nasser emerged from the apparent military defeat diplomatically triumphant. He became the champion of a new wave of anti-imperialist Arab nationalism. Egypt would be the most important Soviet-aligned state in MENA until 1975, when it abruptly switched camps and fell under the US umbrella. The United States meanwhile became more reliant on Israel and the conservative Arab monarchies. Nonetheless, intra-regional dynamics were still the most dominant element. As Malcom Kerr, a political scientist and president of the American University of Beirut, put it in his masterful study of the Arab Cold War, "even the most influential foreigners are peripheral to the Arab's own conceptions of their world and their vision of the future."[34] Washington, London, Moscow, and Jerusalem were largely bit players.

Regional wars may have involved local and regional issues, but they were often quickly embroiled within Cold War geopolitics. The impact, however, was equivocal and often contradictory. There is a lengthy historiographical debate regarding the origins of the 1967 Arab–Israeli war, for example. Historians have pored over diplomatic communiqués, intelligence assessments, diaries, and memoirs to find evidence that the superpowers commissioned their proxies to engage in war. Did the Soviets feed false information to Egypt and Syria to provoke a confrontation with Israel? Did the United States give Israel an "amber light" to launch a pre-emptive strike before Egypt could mount its assault?[35] The uncertainty surrounding these events and the fact there is no conclusive evidence feeds hoary conspiracy theories. A simpler explanation, though, is miscalculation, when policy-makers fail to foresee and anticipate results or counteractions.[36] Miscalculations are the production of misperception, miscommunication, and mistrust often rooted in geopolitical imaginings about who the antagonists are and what they are capable of doing.

Cold War geopolitics enabled regional actors to enact wars in their own time and for their own agendas. MENA was awash with foreign weapons, as shown in Table 5.2. Egypt was the second largest importer of weapons in the 1960s, according to the comprehensive data of the Stockholm International Peace Research Institute, with Israel, Iran, Syria, Iraq, Algeria, and Saudi Arabia all in the top fifty. By the 1970s, Iran was the global leader, with Libya, Syria, Israel, and Iraq in the top ten. In the 1980s, Iraq was the global leader, with Saudi Arabia, Syria, Egypt, and Libya close behind. Outside powers provided some of the most advanced armored vehicles and aircraft in the region. They intended the provision of military aid, typically coupled with smaller sums of development assistance, to assure their sway over regional client states. The result, though, was often the exact opposite.

Regional actors tried to maximize their autonomy and leverage within the global hierarchy. They skillfully invoked the mantras and slogans that superpowers wanted to hear. They obfuscated aims and outlooks. In appealing to the USSR, the so-called "Arab socialists" were never close to enacting doctrinaire communism. Likewise, the conservative Arab monarchies that treated with the United States were far from democratic. As historian Peter Sluglett observes: "the amount of manipulation exercised by individuals such as Gamal Abd al-Nasser, Hafiz al-Asad, Saddam Hussein, and others should not be underestimated; the phenomenon of the 'tail wagging the dog' was very much in evidence."[37] Similarly, the United States turned a blind eye to Israel's diversion of a peaceful nuclear program toward warhead development. Nasser's calculation that he needed to win a war with Israel before those weapons became operational may have contributed to his seemingly rash escalation of the conflict in May and June 1967.[38] Israel was hardly unique in

Table 5.2 MENA states among the world's top fifty arms importers, 1950–89

1950–9		1960–9		1970–9		1980–9	
Country, rank	Total (millions US$)	Country, rank	Total (millions US$)	Country, rank	Total (millions US$)	Country, rank	Total (millions US$)
Egypt, 21	3,429	Egypt, 2	10,123	Iran, 1	28,710	Iraq, 1	30,213
Israel, 34	1,636	Israel, 18	4,703	Libya, 2	18,027	Saudi Arabia, 4	16,138
Syria, 39	898	Iran, 22	3,641	Syria, 3	15,615	Syria, 5	15,459
Iraq, 43	691	Syria, 28	3,325	Israel, 6	13,432	Egypt, 6	12,690
Iran, 45	607	Iraq, 32	2,791	Egypt, 7	12,565	Libya, 7	12,598
		Algeria, 41	1,741	Iraq, 8	10,765	Israel, 17	7,759
		Saudi Arabia, 45	1,387	Algeria, 23	5,007	Algeria, 20	6,500
				Saudi Arabia, 29	4,525	Iran, 27	5,137
				Jordan, 40	2,564	Jordan, 35	4,112
				Kuwait, 49	1,681	Morocco, 47	2,521
						UAE, 49	2,428

Source: Stockholm International Peace Research Institute, "SIPRI Arms Transfers Database." Multiple years.

turning foreign military assistance to its own ulterior ends. It was difficult for the superpowers to monitor clients' misuse of aid. Even if they could, they were reluctant to punish their wayward clients, as neither the United States nor the USSR believed it could afford to lose a client in a zero-sum global competition. At the same time, both were wary of being dragged into localized conflicts.

Often caught flatfooted when conflicts erupted, the superpowers became deeply involved in trying to contain or de-escalate them. They attempted to create firewalls that bracketed regional conflicts from each other and prevented region-wide conflagration. This urge, paradoxically, contributed to the inconclusiveness of so many conflicts and their tendency to flare up again and again. Because the superpowers would always intervene to bolster either Israel or the Arabs, victory was never definitive.[39] The 1973 October War was the closest any Arab states had come to defeating Israel since 1948. Israel eventually fought back, thanks in part to a massive airlift of American arms. The United States launched its customary round of diplomacy to find agreement on a ceasefire. Egyptian President Anwar Sadat proved willing to break with the Soviets, his long-standing allies, in return for American support. In 1975, Sadat abruptly expelled Soviet military advisors and sought a separate peace under US auspices. The USSR fell back on its secondary alliance with Syria, which became the epicenter of resistance against normalization. Other Arab countries refused to engage in a peace process that did not address Palestinians' demands. Thus, a comprehensive regional settlement remained elusive.

The superpowers' involvement in MENA's internal conflicts during the Cold War era was even more complicated and attenuated. Some saw the wars in North Yemen, Dhofar (Oman), Iraqi Kurdistan, Lebanon, and Western Sahara (Morocco) as far-off but essential fulcrums in the global superpower competition. In reality, neither the United States nor the USSR was willing to wager much on the outcome, however. Instead, their key allies often served as conduits for support to the domestic belligerents. Sometimes regional allies dispatched their own expeditionary forces. Iran dispatched forces to Oman, Egypt invaded during Yemen's civil war, and Israel and Syria both set up zones of influence and occupation in Lebanon. More common, though, was simple subvention of local forces, creating the kind of multi-tiered clientelist ties in which superpowers were distant patrons. However consequential these conflicts were for those who fought and died in them, they had little geopolitical significance.

By the late 1970s, the ground beneath the superpowers' feet was shifting. The Soviets' ability to counterbalance the United States declined precipitously with Egypt's defection in 1975. In December 1979, the Soviets invaded Afghanistan. Some US geopolitical strategists believed, using a convoluted cartographic logic, that the invasion presaged a Soviet advance on the Persian

Gulf. In fact, the invasion bespoke the desperation of a waning superpower expending enormous resources on an inefficacious client regime in a poor and landlocked country. The United States, though, also suffered blows. The most significant was the Iranian Revolution and the emergence of the Islamic Republic of Iran in 1979. The United States responded by realigning its own network of clients. It strengthened ties to Iraq, regarded as a Soviet client only a few years before, and reinforced its long-standing relationship with Saudi Arabia. This shift enabled Iraq's invasion of Iran in September 1980, beginning one of the longest and bloodiest wars since World War II. Saddam feared Iran would try to export its revolution to his country but was also convinced that he had the opportunity to vault to leadership in the Arab world. He expected at least tacit US backing and active financial support from Saudi Arabia, Kuwait, and richer Arab oil states.[40] The Iraqi army fielded a hodgepodge of Soviet, French, British, and American equipment. Iraq's advanced chemical weapons program derived largely from materials imported from the West. Its nascent nuclear program included components from a number of countries. Iran had stockpiles of older American weapons and learned to jerry-rig technologies to new purposes. Although the United States generally supported Iraq, it also cut secret deals to provide weapons to Iran (the so-called "Iran–Contra Affair"). The primary US concern was not who won the war, but how the war affected the traffic of oil tankers through the Persian Gulf. Both Iran and Iraq attacked oil facilities and tankers. Most of the US naval effort was devoted to deterring or punishing Iran. In April 1988, the United States attacked Iranian oil platforms and warships in retaliation for the mining of a US frigate. In July, it shot down an Iranian airliner which it mistook for a warplane. These demonstrations of American resolve convinced Iranian leaders of the futility of continued fighting and prompted them to accept UN-brokered peace terms. While neither Iran nor Iraq could claim victory in the war, the United States had emphatically demonstrated its ability to ensure the global oil supply.[41]

The definitive proof of US primacy in MENA came at the twilight of the Cold War in the Gulf War of 1990–1. Again, despite the conspiracy theories that the United States invited Iraq's invasion of Kuwait, the documentary evidence suggests more a string of misimpressions and faulty assumptions about how the United States and the USSR would react. The invasion and annexation of a neighbor violated the fundamental norm against wars of aggression and the violation of territorial integrity. US officials were keenly aware that Iraq now threatened both Israel and the global oil supply. Saddam hoped to pull off a feat similar to Nasser's triumph in 1956, turning a military defeat into a political and diplomatic victory. Yet no one, not the UN, Russia, or any other Arab actors, came to his rescue. The UN condemned the invasion and authorized the use of force against Iraq. The United States amassed some 540,000 troops in the region. Saudi Arabia, Britain, Egypt, France, and other members of the international coalition supplied another 150,000. These partners were largely superfluous, however. The United States was so far ahead in the use of advanced technologies like satellite surveillance, guided munitions, and aerial supremacy that even close allies struggled to keep up. American military planners saw the Gulf War as the first step in their mastery of the revolution in military affairs (RMA). The Iraqi army, vaunted as the best in the Arab world, could offer little resistance.[42] By the war's end, the United States had taken its deepest steps into MENA's geographic core.

MENA's wars never fitted neatly into the dichotomy of Cold War geopolitics. The provision of military, political, and economic support from abroad was supposed to render regional states pawns for the United States and the USSR. In fact, actors within the region often put that support to ulterior ends and waged wars that were, at best, orthogonal to their patron's agendas. No client state was completely docile and the leeway diminished as the United States moved to undisputed global primacy.

Case Study: *Pax Americana*, Counterterrorism, and the Greater West Asian Crisis

Just as the transition from colonialism to Cold War geopolitics realigned power structures and norms, the end of the Cold War introduced new ambiguities and uncertainties to the geopolitical order. At the dawn of the twenty-first century, the United States enjoyed unparalleled military, political, and economic dominance. Some spoke of a new era of global peace under the American aegis. MENA was no exception to this global dominance. As Michael Hudson skeptically put it:

> the balance of power has shifted so decisively in favour of the USA that the USA is now capable of "ordering" the region far more effectively than in the past. Regional governments can no longer use the Soviet Union as a strategic or tactical counterweight to the USA. . . . [T]he Gulf crisis and war decisively altered the balance of power in a more stable direction through the defeat, not just of the Saddam Hussein government, but of Iraq as a state capable of challenging the existing order of things.[43]

The United States tried to block both Iran and Iraq from asserting their power in the region. President Bill Clinton also plunged the United States into negotiations that promised to end the Arab–Israeli conflict. Regimes across the region undertook painful, albeit often half-hearted, economic and political reforms in response to the neoliberal Washington Consensus espoused by the IMF and championed by the United States. Yet the fall from this apex was steep and violent. By the mid-2000s, US forces would be mired in what Fred Halliday called the Great West Asian Crisis, a string of wars spanning Afghanistan, Iraq, Yemen, Lebanon, and Israel/Palestine. At the same time, US engagement indirectly enabled and provoked regional actors to wage wars of their own.[44]

What is doubly striking about the geopolitics of the post-Cold War era is how much effort was devoted to fighting a nebulously defined category of enemies: radical Islamic terrorists. There were some exceptions, such as the 250,000 US troops committed to defeat the ramshackle Iraqi army in 2003; the ongoing military commitment to check Iran in the Persian Gulf; and the airstrikes against the Libyan army in 2011. But in an era of US global hegemony, few states could be credible enemies. The United States devoted the bulk of its military, political, and economic energies to battling a non-state actor that lacked even a fraction of its resources and reach. The battle was not waged by US troops alone. On the one hand, allied regional states continued to use US equipment and training, often to their own ends. On the other hand, deepening US encroachment elicited counter-responses from states and non-state actors in the region which precipitated further conflict.

Islam had been on the minds of US geopolitical thinkers since the Iranian Revolution of 1979. As media scholar Melani McAlister put it, following the revolution, when American embassy personnel were taken hostage:

> "Militant Islam" quickly became the primary narrative device for the US new media; long essays and editorials in many major publications explained "Islam" as a single, unchanging cultural proclivity to mix faith with politics, and to express both through violence. The vast variety of Muslim beliefs and practices, spread across four continents, were summarized in simplistic, often overtly hostile summaries of the "essence" of Islam, which was now allegedly on display in Tehran.[45]

Various movements in MENA claimed that Islam offered a total solution to contemporary social and political challenges. This offered an attractive contrast to the hollow promises of secular nationalism or Marxism.[46] The practical programs of Islamist movements varied. The largest and most successful, such as the Egyptian Muslim Brotherhood, focused on providing social services and representation to communities that seemed to be left out of the old authoritarian bargains. By and large, Islamist movements were willing to abide by rules set by the regimes and work through civil society. Few were bent on violence. Most were too immersed in domestic affairs and the struggle to survive repression to threaten the United States.[47] Nevertheless, US strategic thinkers began to sound the alarm about Islam as a new kind of geopolitical foe. This rival was not a nation-state or a discrete ideology but an entire "civilization" which stood in opposition to the West, as political scientist Samuel Huntington put it in an empirically dubious but highly influential essay.[48] This slippery idea would become a common trope in geopolitical discourse.

Islamist groups themselves, though, also found the notion of civilizational chasm useful to justify their defiance of the United States. The most prominent radical was al-Qaeda and its leader, Osama bin Laden. In many ways, the growth of al-Qaeda amounted to a kind of blowback from the US effort to support the Afghan resistance to the Soviet invasion of 1979. Most of the US effort involved funneling arms and money through Saudi Arabia and Pakistan. Bin Laden, the scion of one of Saudi Arabia's richest families, had provided financial and logistical support to recruit Arabs to join the anti-Soviet campaign in Afghanistan in the 1980s. The Afghan jihad, as it was known, bled the occupying Soviet army dry. After the Soviet evacuation, the former rebels turned on each other, each claiming ideological and religious purity. The Taliban seized power in the mid-1990s and imposed a version of Islamic rule that combined rural tribal customs with puritanical zeal. Bin Laden began to deploy his network of Arab Afghan war veterans to new fronts. Following Iraq's invasion of Kuwait, he suggested Saudi Arabia raise an Islamic army for self-defense. The Saudis demurred, instead inviting the United States to set up military bases within the kingdom. Bin Laden became militantly opposed to the Saudi royal family, accusing them of corrupting the Islamic heartland and prostituting themselves to the West. He cited Qur'anic injunctions against allowing non-Muslims to inhabit sacred Arabia. Bin Laden went into exile, first to Sudan, then to Taliban-controlled Afghanistan. His geopolitical vision broadened and grew more trenchant during his exile. Other regimes in MENA were declared equally hypocritical, burnishing Islamic laurels while suborning apostasy. Al-Qaeda ideologues deemed violence against unbelievers as obligatory upon all Muslims. Moreover, it was not enough to confront the odious regimes individually. Rather, it was imperative to take the fight to the "far enemy" that propped them up, the West in general and the United States in particular. Given the imbalance in global power and the West's own abuse of Muslims in Palestine, Chechnya, Kashmir, the Balkans, and elsewhere, every type of resistance was legitimate, including the killing of civilians. Indeed, for some theorists of jihad, violence itself had a redemptive, even chiliastic, potential. Al-Qaeda thus offered a blueprint for a global campaign of violence in which all was promised and nothing forbidden.[49]

Al-Qaeda's transnational agenda for jihad coincided with the weakening of states across the wider developing world. With the end of superpower economic subvention, client regimes faced increased pressure for political reform. State capacity withered and even collapsed in some areas. Civil wars erupted through Algeria, Afghanistan, Yemen, Somalia, and the Balkans and former Soviet Central Asia. Foreign Islamist fighters seeking new frontiers of battle were hardly welcome parties to these internal conflicts. But these foreign fighters had the advantages of combat experience, financing from networks in the Gulf, and an ideological stringency that attracted highly motivated (and perhaps psychopathic) fighters. Following the lessons of the Afghanistan war, these radicals sought ways to insert themselves into local battles, recruiting and absorbing the next generation of fighters.[50] Al-Qaeda operatives attacked the United States in a series of increasingly large-scale attacks, mostly focused on civilian targets, in the 1990s and early 2000s. The attacks of September 11,

2001, killing over 3,000 in New York and Washington were the most spectacular and deadly. Nearly all Islamic leaders deemed such indiscriminate violence
abhorrent, or at least ill advised. But the attacks succeeded in elevating al-
Qaeda's status to that of a global player. By the mid-2000s, it had reorganized
into a kind of franchising operation, inducting fighting groups in North Africa,
Yemen, and Iraq, as representatives of its global brand.[51]

The United States, in turn, made counterterrorism its new global priority, a
complement to the objectives of securing oil flow and Israel. Counterterrorism
policies boiled down to a kind a military-centered state-building project. To
block terrorist infiltration and prevent the appearance of safe havens, the
United States devoted greater sums of military training and assistance to
get states to monitor, regulate, and repress.[52] Notionally this training was
linked to wider initiatives of security sector reform, democratization, and
inculcation of humanitarian norms. Practically, though, the United States was
willing to overlook shortfalls in these domains in favor of brute effectiveness.
Thus, its counterterrorism agenda reinforced its alliances with authoritarian
regimes.[53]

The invasions of Afghanistan in 2001 and Iraq in 2003 carried this logic to
the fullest and perhaps most absurd conclusion. Afghanistan, where al-Qaeda
had established an alliance with the Taliban regime, was an easy and obvious target. But it was too poor, blighted, and peripheral to showcase the US
agenda effectively. George W. Bush and his circle soon turned their attention
to Iraq. The reasons and justifications for the invasion of Iraq were multi-
farious and often inconsistent. American officials cited both the dangers
of Iraq's chemical weapons program and the possible connections between
Saddam and al-Qaeda. For neoconservatives, the goal was democratization.
For others, this was a holy crusade. Iraq seemed a propitious target because
it was urbanized, politically central to MENA, and endowed with oil wealth.
At the same time, it was also militarily depleted, unlike Iran, itself another
element in what the United States deemed the "axis of evil." Unlike in 1990–1
or the invasion of Afghanistan two years earlier, though, there was no broad
international mandate for action against Iraq. The UN refused to authorize
what could only be deemed a war of pre-emption. Save for Britain, major US
allies offered little military support. Saudi Arabia and Israel saw the good in
being rid of Saddam, but also warned of the very heavy risks of intervention.
Such concerns hardly impeded the United States. Washington was confident
that its mastery of the RMA, including extensive use of drones and aerial
bombing, would suffice to deliver quick victory. Only 250,000 US troops
were committed to invasion and around 150,000 to the ensuing occupation
(less than half the total force involved in the 1991 campaign). Britain, the
second largest coalition partner, added 45,000 troops to the invasion force
and 20,000 to the occupation. US planners expected Iraqis, grateful for their
liberation, to do the bulk of the work. They would quickly take the reins of a

more effective, pluralistic, and moderate government that would become a model for its neighbors.

The outcomes that unfolded in Iraq belied nearly every one of these optimistic projections. Senior officials in the Bush and Blair administrations ignored or silenced skeptics and doctored intelligence assessments to bolster the case for war. Iraqis generally did not greet the coalition forces as liberators (except in the separatist stronghold of Kurdistan). The US decision to disband the Iraqi army and police, considered redoubts of Saddam loyalists, effectively obliterated the already weakened Iraqi state and left Iraqi civilians exposed to looting, crime, and attack. Some set up self-defense militias, which operated similarly to mafia extortionist rackets. Arming begot more arming. There was violence both between Iraqi factions and against the occupation forces. Al-Qaeda, which had little presence in Iraq prior to the war, soon exploited the conditions of state failure. It muscled and cajoled its way into Sunni areas of western Iraq, absorbing other insurgent groups. Al-Qaeda in Iraq (AQI) was responsible for some of the most devastating attacks of the war. Beside its campaign against US forces and Iraqi security personnel, it also assaulted mosques, markets, and the headquarters of the UN and Red Cross. In southern Iraq, Shi'i rejectionists launched their own insurgency. For the most part, though, the US invasion opened the door to Shi'i sectarian parties to take control of the state. Party militias were absorbed into the ministry of the interior or operated with the collusion of government officials. While they had made tactical alliances with the United States, they had much stronger and deeper ties to Tehran. These official ethno-sectarian militias in uniform waged campaigns of intimidation and extrajudicial killing against suspected Sunni "terrorists." The United States had hoped that standing up new Iraqi security forces would alleviate the burden, but also knew that training and equipping them often only enabled the ethnic cleansing campaign that was being conducted in the name of counterterrorism. The United States thus found itself in the middle of Iraq's worsening ethnic security dilemma.[54]

As a consequence of the invasion and occupation, Iraq exhibited exactly the conditions of civil war which the US counterterrorism doctrine had sought to prevent. American and coalition troops were literally caught in the middle of the battle. Bombings and other attacks accelerated, especially in Baghdad, central Iraq, and the west. Through the worst period of 2006 and 2007, there were around 6,000 attacks claiming 3,000 civilians per month. US forces sustained an average of sixty combat deaths per month, mostly from improvised explosive devices and sniper fire. Iraq's army and police suffered upwards of 150 combat deaths per month themselves. The United States reached out to the Sunni tribes, many of whom were already implicated in the insurgency. As security broke down, many tribal leaders had sought alliance with al-Qaeda, or, alternatively, been forced to accede to their protection. The United States offered an alternative bargain: it would provide weapons and arms and allow them self-governance in western Iraq, to the exclusion of the central government. In return, the tribal fighters would help the United States to combat AQI. By the end of 2007, some 75,000 to 100,000 men joined what were dubbed Sunni Awakening militias.[55] Combined with the surge of an additional 40,000 US troops, these forces were able to root out AQI insurgents and dampen violence dramatically.

Coming to office in January 2008, Barack Obama made clear his intent to withdraw from Iraq and put the mess of MENA behind him. Negotiations between the US and Iraqi governments over the status of forces agreement that would allow the United States to leave behind forces in Iraq ended unsuccessfully. Obama realized that US popular opinion had turned against the war. Iraqi Prime Minister Nuri al-Maliki, too, faced popular pressure to show the United States out. America's future, senior officials opined, depended on a pivot to Asia, where there were more important strategic allies and more significant potential rivals, namely China.[56]

It is difficult to overstate the damage that the invasion of Iraq caused.[57] The drain on US forces was intense. At the peak, as shown in Figure 5.2, nearly one out of every five American soldiers was serving in MENA. Some 4,400 US troops died, plus several hundred more from other coalition countries. Hardly any of the key strategic objectives were met. The United States appeared inept, even malevolent. The false pretenses and disregard for international law in launching the war had been one thing; the seemingly indiscriminate use of violence and abuse of Iraqi prisoners confirmed some of the worst assumptions about US motives toward the Islamic world. Key global allies and those within the region treated the United States more warily. Israel, Saudi Arabia, and other Sunni Arab powers talked about Iran's influence casting a "Shi'i crescent" from Tehran to Baghdad, Damascus, and Beirut. Equally importantly, the American public at large and the foreign policy elite grew more skeptical of possibilities for foreign intervention and engagement.[58] Anti-Arab and anti-Muslim racist stereotypes hardened in some segments of the American public.

Iraq remained a dysfunctional state after the US withdrawal. The Iraqi government estimated the loss of 155,000 battle deaths, coupled with a far higher number of indirect deaths, as discussed in Chapter 1.[59] Whatever success the United States had in dampening violence and repressing Sunni radicals in 2008 proved temporary. The success of the US counterinsurgency campaign in Iraq, as political scientist Adeed Dawisha put it, came "not because of the state, but in spite of it."[60] The Iraqi government was never truly democratic and there was no real reconciliation between Sunnis and Shi'is. The Shi'i-dominated government in Baghdad regarded the American-backed Sunni militias as a threat and sought to dismantle them once the United States withdrew. This betrayal of the Sunnis reinforced radicalization and contributed to the reincarnation of AQI as the Islamic State (IS). The Iraqi security services, meanwhile, remained a shambles. Beside a handful of elite Iraqi counterterrorism units, the Iraqi army

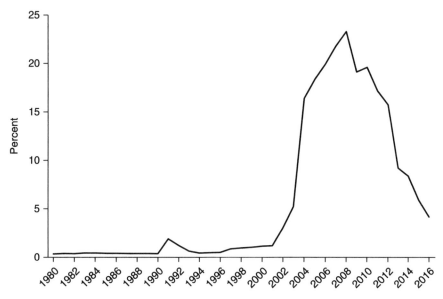

Figure 5.2 US troops deployed to MENA as percentage of forces worldwide, 1980–2016
Source: Kane, "Global US Troop Deployment, 1950–2003."

could hardly operate without US support. This continued to enflame sectarian tensions and leave the Iraqi state profoundly vulnerable to internal challenges.

Iraq and Afghanistan were not showcases of US power, but became proving grounds of a different sort. Through the late 2000s and into the 2010s, the United States honed its tactics for a grinding and interminable counterterrorism campaign that combined the advanced technical wizardry of the RMA with older quasi-colonial counterinsurgency tactics. Although the setbacks in Iraq and Afghanistan shook confidence in the decisive effect of drones and air power, by 2008 the United States had expanded and intensified its campaign based on its mastery of the RMA. The Obama administration expanded drone strikes across seemingly ungoverned territories in MENA, as well as Afghanistan, Pakistan, and Somalia. Drones seemed the perfect solution for a casualty-averse superpower.[61] Data collected by the New America Foundation think tank (Table 5.3) show the acceleration of drone strikes in Yemen, beginning with Obama and escalating further under Trump. With its operational requirements classified and rules of engagement lax, collateral damage, including civilian deaths, was a virtual certainty. Yet US policy-makers were convinced that the strategic gains of targeting terrorist leaders outweighed these deaths and the backlash they incited.

At the same time, though, the experience of the Iraqi insurgency demonstrated that ground troops remained essential for clearing out insurgents and holding off terrorist infiltration. Wary of the large-scale troop deployment

Table 5.3 US drone strikes in Yemen, 2000–June 2019

President	Time period	Total strikes	Average strikes per month	Civilian casualties	Militant casualties	Unknown
Bush II	2000–8	1	.01	0	6	0
Obama	2009–16	184	1.9	89–101	973–1,240	33–52
Trump	2017–June 2019	100	3.3	27–48	214–81	29–37
TOTAL		285	1.25	116–49	1,193–527	62–89

Source: New America Foundation, "Drone Strikes: Yemen," available at *https://www.newamerica.org/in-depth/americas-counterterrorism-wars/us-targeted-killing-program-yemen/.*

of Iraq and Afghanistan, the United States focused on developing special forces, essentially flexible light infantry, that could work in small units in far-flung locations. The success of this approach became apparent in the US raid that killed Osama bin Laden in Pakistan in 2011. The United States also redoubled its partnership with regional actors. Military training had traditionally been considered part of a broader set of programs for socio-economic modernization and development. These newer partnerships were more narrowly construed and often ad hoc. Again, special forces were crucial points of exchange and contact. The United States focused specifically on cultivating elite units with the unique training, armament, and skills required to operate with its forces.[62] Emblematic of this approach was the growth of Warrior Competition, a kind of special forces Olympiad held annually in Jordan. In its first years, in 2009 and 2010, the competition was relatively modest in scale, with a handful of teams representing Saudi Arabia, the United States, and Jordan. Over the next decade, however, it grew to involve over thirty teams from the US, Canada, Europe, Iraq, Lebanon, the UAE, several former Soviet republics, and even India and China. In addition to specialized shock troops, private military contractors (PMCs) also became an important source of supplemental training, intelligence support, facilities protection, and even direct combat operations.[63] Overall, these measures honed the military edge of state-building and concentrated more coercive power in state hands. If state security services were not available or up to the task, there were less orthodox approaches on hand by engaged warlords, tribal leaders, and others who maintained private military retinues. These armed non-state actors were even cheaper than PMCs and more expendable, but often lacked professional training. In the long term, reliance on armed non-state actors also countered the goals of centralizing coercive power.[64]

The US effort to externalize the risk of engagement left more room for local actors to defect or double-cross their sponsors. International relations specialist Stephen Tankel describes how US efforts to assist the Yemeni government of Ali Abdullah Saleh to counter infiltration from al-Qaeda affiliates often backfired:

> It often seemed to American officials that the [Yemeni] security forces were doing just enough to keep aid flowing. Assistance was more helpful in terms of securing access for small numbers of US forces and for air and missile strikes. Unilateral action was necessary because Yemeni forces were not getting it done – a result of their severely limited capacity and the government's questionable commitment. The United States spent large sums of money to build up the security forces, but the outcomes were mixed at best. US efforts to promote development and counter violent extremism were more limited and less successful.[65]

WikiLeaks documents detail how the Saleh regime tried to manipulate US military support in order to counter domestic opposition of all kinds. While Yemen was an extreme case with an already very weak central government, similar concerns could be evinced about collaboration across the region.[66] Transferring risk to regional partners entailed risk of its own.

US geopolitical retrenchment from MENA had a significant impact on the course of the civil wars that engulfed Syria, Yemen, Iraq, and Libya in the 2010s. These conflicts, like the uprisings that preceded them, were initially driven by domestic politics. Once they began, though, they quickly became elements in larger regional and even global contestations for power and supremacy. Most non-state opposition figures broadly appealed for foreign support in the name of freedom and democracy. Beleaguered regimes, meanwhile, tried to enlist international allies by posing as bulwarks of global order and stability. While we will examine these conflicts more fully in Chapter 6, several points about the geopolitical element in these conflicts bear special mention.

As the United States appeared to withdraw from the region, other actors stepped forward. Regional states all accelerated their purchase of weapons, adding to their already sizable arsenals. By the 2010s, five of the top ten and thirteen of the top fifty arms importers were in MENA, as shown in Table 5.4. Moreover, the source of these weapons became more diverse. Although the United States remained the leading supplier, states diversified their sources, as shown in Figure 5.3.

Other actors assumed more assertive positions within the region. Russia's influence in MENA seemed to have been waning since the mid-1970s. Moscow lacked the geopolitical means to save Saddam Hussein, first from the 1991 attack and then from the 2003 invasion. Its prime regional allies, Iran and Syria, were among a handful of regional actors that stood out for their defiance of US hegemony. Now Russia returned to geopolitical form. Russian intervention in Syria in 2015 tipped the balance in favor of the regime. Russia was also involved in the Libya conflict. This was part of a larger geopolitical assertiveness first in Georgia in the mid-2000s and then in Ukraine in the 2010s.[67]

Table 5.4 MENA states among the world's top fifty arms importers, 1990–2018

1990–9		2000–9		2010–18	
Country, rank	Total (millions US$)	Country, rank	Total (millions US$)	Country, rank	Total (millions US$)
Saudi Arabia, 2	17,571	UAE, 5	8,976	Saudi Arabia, 2	21,822
Egypt, 7	10,423	Egypt, 9	6,372	UAE, 5	10,626
Israel, 10	7,095	Israel, 12	5,776	Egypt, 6	9,701
Iran, 14	5,134	Algeria, 16	5,249	Algeria, 7	9,530
Kuwait, 15	5,028	Saudi Arabia, 16	3,867	Iraq, 10	7,187
UAE, 16	4,920	Iran, 25	2,714	Morocco, 16	4,447
Algeria, 26	2,876	Iraq, 32	1,621	Qatar, 19	3,569
Syria, 36	1,714	Yemen, 33	1,615	Israel, 20	3,355
Oman, 47	1,014	Jordan, 34	1,552	Oman, 23	3,018
Qatar, 50	931	Sudan, 38	1,103	Syria, 34	2,094
		Oman, 47	912	Jordan, 35	1,821
				Kuwait, 36	1,696
				Sudan, 48	948

Source: Stockholm International Peace Research Institute, "SIPRI Arms Transfers Database," available at *https://www.sipri.org/databases/armstransfers.*

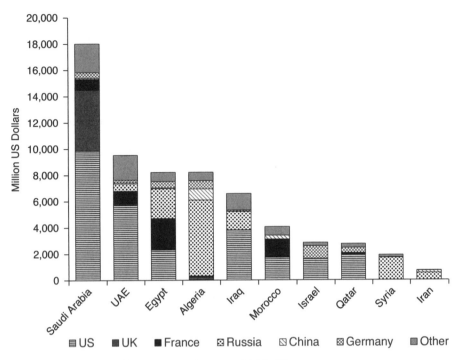

Figure 5.3 Sources of MENA arms imports, 2010–17
Source: Stockholm International Peace Research Institute, "SIPRI Arms Transfers Database," available at *https://www.sipri.org/databases/armstransfers.*

China's presumptive rise as the next superpower also cast a long shadow over MENA. China had managed to build economic and political ties to the most important regional actors, including Israel, Saudi Arabia, the UAE, Egypt, and Iran. Its connection to the region extended through overland traffic and was thus less susceptible to US naval interdiction. Since the United States restricted export of sensitive drone technology, China became a major arms supplier to Riyadh and Abu Dhabi and the largest trade partner for many of the Arab Gulf states. It offered a model of broad-scale economic development without social upheaval that might precipitate regime instability. Many MENA countries thus seemed to bide their time until China could arrive in full force in the region.[68]

It is important, though, not to overstate the scale or finality of US withdrawal from MENA. The United States retained a dense network of regional alliances. Its military presence through bases and naval forces remained unrivaled. US diplomatic pressure was critical in ousting autocrats in Tunisia, Egypt, and Yemen. Conversely, US inaction was essential for protecting Bahrain's Khalifa dynasty from internal pressure. The United States projected military power through aerial strikes and deployment of light infantry across the region, as it did in Libya and, more hesitantly, in Syria. But it ruled out large-scale and direct military intervention. Instead, it tried to orchestrate a response through regional allies, such as Saudi Arabia, the UAE, and Qatar, and NATO member states. It also sought to arm and equip armed non-state actors. This type of engagement from a distance allowed actors within the region to use American-provided resources to pursue their own military and strategic agendas. No one other actor matched the span of US engagements. Russia had a major role in Syria and Libya, but was far less influential in Yemen or Iraq. China's role as a military power was still hypothetical. Similarly, Turkey and France, among other traditional US allies, also plotted more activist and independent courses, but could never match the United States' breadth of reach.

Finally, the renewal of geopolitical competition within MENA did not preclude cooperation and collaboration among antagonists. This was most evident in the campaign against IS. IS emerged out of the battered remnants of AQI in western Iraq in the late 2000s. It established strongholds along the Iraqi–Syrian border as political turmoil worsened in both states. In the summer of 2014, it launched a major breakout, capturing most of the border posts and holding a huge span of territory from Mosul to Raqqa. Like al-Qaeda, it sought to recruit terrorist acolytes across the world. The international anti-IS coalition was ad hoc but ultimately highly effective. There was an informal division of labor. The United States, Russia, and other larger powers provided mostly aerial support, equipment, and training, while Syrian, Iraqi, and Kurdish troops operated on the ground either in formal units or in various pro-government militias. Even though these states had different and even contradictory geopolitical agendas, the possibility of a radical Islamist entity embedded in the MENA core was something they all could oppose.

Conclusion

Outside actors had a major role in shaping the course and conduct of war in MENA over the last century and a half. The conspiracy theorists, in a limited sense, were right. External actors did try to impose war on the region for their own geopolitical ends. These dynamics shifted historically through the course of the twentieth and twenty-first centuries, depending on the underlying configuration of global power and the animating norms of statehood. The colonial period saw Britain, Italy, and France wage war directly and intensely in the region. These campaigns helped assert state dominance over non-state actors and crucially shaped the institutions of coercion in the region. A new dichotomy emerged between the US and Soviet spheres of influence during the Cold War. Yet the superpowers often tried to restrain regional conflicts and prevent their escalation into a global conflagration. Outside actors generally relied on client states to man the bulwarks. This type of engagement granted regional states even greater ability to wage war against each other and against internal challengers alike. Finally, the period of American ascendance coincided with a period of state buckling and the rise of non-state adversaries under the ambiguous banner of radical Islam. The campaigns in Iraq and Afghanistan had many monikers, such as the greater war on terror, Enduring Freedom, and (more ominously) the Forever War. These ambiguities gestured toward how vaguely defined the enemy was and how the violence would proliferate.

Yet geopolitical modes of analysis can only partially account for MENA's conflict trap. First, geopolitical explanations necessarily minimize the agency and impact of actors within the region. As shown here, external intervention, particularly the supply of weaponry, strategy, and the import of ideologies, enabled states and non-state actors to launch violence on their own. The most consistent element of geopolitics in MENA is the inconsistency and unpredictability of these indirect effects. Throughout the wars and revolutions witnessed in MENA over the last century, belligerents derived technologies, armaments, and strategic cues from outside the region. They vied to gain support from more powerful, extra-regional actors. Yet their conflicts were often only tangential to larger global agendas. Great powers' most lasting and significant intervention, though, was likely in creating conditions that enacted and commissioned violence. Outside actors proved to have only limited and sporadic ability to channel or control their clients' aggression. Geopolitics trapped MENA into war in a different way.

Secondly, geopolitical imaginaries posit a dichotomous structure of violence, "us" and "them", insiders and outsiders, East and West, Global North and Global South. Yet war necessarily instigates relationships that are multidirectional and mutually constitutive. Edward Said asks:

> Who in India or Algeria today can confidently separate out the British or French component of the past from present actualities; and who in Britain and France can draw a clear circle around British London or French Paris that would exclude the impact of India or Algeria upon these two imperial cities?[69]

What is broadly true about culture is especially true of the unique cultural enactment of war. This is the obverse of traditional geopolitical analysis, where the balance between great powers drives military engagement at the peripheral regional level. In this sense, events at the regional and even the state level shaped and propelled changes at the global level. Britain and France had not intended to assume mandatory, as opposed to more traditional colonial, roles in the former Ottoman territory. But the mandates had to be invented in response both to geopolitical pressure and to the unwillingness of actors within the region to submit to a return to the discredited ideas of imperial dominion. In a similar vein, Cold War-era conflicts in MENA repeatedly played a part in the development of Soviet–US relations, even though Moscow and Washington could only intermittently contain and control the violence once it began.[70] The bouts of Arab–Israeli conflict, the Yemen war, and the other conflagrations originating within MENA spurred the superpowers to seek pathways for de-escalation and détente.

The travails of the United States as the singular superpower in the twenty-first century further confirm the practical limitations of external involvement. It is not enough to point out the setbacks and failures of American campaigns to defeat radical Islamic terrorism. It is more correct, but still insufficient, to consider the ancillary impact of these campaigns. US indirect engagements enabled Saudi Arabia, Israel, and others to follow their own courses. US policies also spurred retaliation and counter-responses from Iran, al-Qaeda, and others. To grasp the role of geopolitics in war most fully requires considering how the quagmire of MENA changed American understandings of geopolitics itself. Geopolitics, in this sense, is not about outside imposition but about processes of mutual constitution that weld local and global forms of violence together.

6

Fragmentation, Integration, and War in the 2010s

The 2010s began in MENA with optimism, even exuberance. The largely peaceful overthrow of autocratic regimes in Egypt, Tunisia, Libya, and Yemen seemed to augur a fundamental shift in the nature of regional politics.[1] By the middle of the decade, though, violence had return to MENA with a vengeance, leaving virtually no part of the region untouched. As the new decade begins, fighting continues in Syria, Yemen, and Libya. Iraq's transition to post-conflict reconstruction remains tentative, underscored by the violent repression of street protesters in 2019. The violence of the occupation of Palestinian territories endures. Regime repression has become more intensive in Egypt, Algeria, Sudan, and Bahrain as military dictatorships reign. Meanwhile, radical opposition forces have grown more desperate and aggressive.

There have been periods in MENA's modern history when bloodshed has been more prolific. There have also been wars in the region of greater consequence for global peace and stability. But it is difficult to think of a period when war so totally and thoroughly engulfed MENA. The most complete data on battle deaths, collected by the Uppsala Conflict Data Project, finds 8,200 deaths in Libya, 20,000 in Yemen, and 313,000 in Syria between 2011 and May 2018.[2] This amounts to the loss in battle of 1 in 1,000 Libyans, 7 in 1,000 Yemenis, and, astonishingly, 17 in 1,000 Syrians. The figures get grimmer when added to the mostly untallied non-lethal casualties, population displacement, and additional deaths due to destruction of infrastructure.

This chapter asks why and how the wars of the decade became at once so bloody and interminable. For some analysts, the key issue is the transformation of these conflicts into religious wars. What was at stake was not national security but sectarian supremacy. It was a battle, in other words, for the "soul of Islam." Iran posed as the standard-bearer of Shi'ism, Saudi Arabia as the self-appointed champion of Sunnism.[3] This chapter argues, however, that the key mechanism driving the proliferation and intensification of conflict is not the religiosity of the protagonists but their entrapment in modes of conflict that shifted the onus of battle to third-party actors, often non-state militias and other armed groups. The conduct of proxy wars in Yemen, Libya, Iraq, and Syria eroded the bedrock of statehood, making it difficult to reassert control over violence. But paralleling this fragmentation at the local and state level was also a process of integration of the conflict into larger regional and geopolitical scales. The interventions from Saudi Arabia, Iran, Qatar, and Turkey, to name some regional actors, plus the United States, Russia, and European powers, rendered the wars lengthy but inconclusive and prone to recurrence.

MENA had certainly seen proxy wars before. During the Cold War, there were geopolitical proxies, as greater powers adopted regional states as allies and partners. Not wanting to be dragged into a larger conflict by their Lilliputian allies, both the United States and the USSR often tried to restrain these engagements. Another form of proxy warfare involved regional states' engaging with non-state actors. Egypt and Saudi Arabia recruited rival Yemeni factions during the North Yemen civil war of 1960. Egypt helped to set up the Palestinian Fedayeen to attack Israel in the 1950s. Multiple regional states made alliances with militias involved in Lebanon's civil war. Again, however, these types of engagement tended to be on a limited scale and often served to bracket and contain conflicts, not expand them.

The proxy wars of the 2010s, however, saw the conjoining of elements that intensified, accelerated, and proliferated violence. First, as discussed in Chapter 2, there was the rash of state failures that occurred as regimes struggled to maintain control in the face of mass popular opposition and security sector defection. Secondly, there was a shifting of geopolitical conditions, particularly the United States' military retrenchment and the unsteadying of the normative principles for global order. Journalist Robert Marquand described how the response to the 2011 uprisings made apparent

> fading authority and consensus on the world stage. The cold war 'spheres of influence' between two powers are long gone. The new world order of American dominance has faded. But no clear leadership or rules have replaced this. New fights between trends of human rights and democracy – and sovereignty – have no rules as of yet.[4]

This compounding of a military vacuum with an ideological one gave room to regional actors to step in to fill the void. Thirdly, there was the continued availability of oil revenue that could help sustain the budgets of both local belligerents and intervening states. The final element was sectarianism. Competing actors used sectarian discourse to constitute or buttress proxy alliances. Still, sectarian discourse often merely served to mask gross power politics.[5] Overall, these conditions dramatically altered the scale and form of war and violence. Bypassing defunct states, the fighting interlinked the motivations and capacities of local armed actors with those of regional and global powers. What had been discrete civil wars became adjoining theaters in broader global and regional campaigns.

Proxy Wars and the Politics of Distant Proximities

Most discussions of the problems of proxy warfare begin with principal–agent (P–A) theory.[6] States adopt proxy warfare for the same reasons of cost and efficiency that a company hires a third-party contractor. They embark on proxy warfare in the belief that it is less risky or cheaper than direct engagement. Instead of directly committing their own forces, a sponsor provides arms and other support to local agents who will carry out the war – and suffer the damages – themselves. In some cases, states can maintain plausible deniability while their proxies are involved in crimes against humanity.[7]

Yet sponsor–proxy relationships are notoriously difficult to manage. The objectives and capabilities of sponsor and proxy are never perfectly aligned. Proxies themselves want to extract the most they can from the sponsor while incurring the lowest possible costs. P–A theory highlights two distinct problems or challenges inherent in proxy relationships. First, adverse selection occurs when a sponsoring state knows little about the capacities, motivations, and objectives of a proxy prior to establishing their relationship. In the rush to find suitable local partners, they overlook or underestimate how their agendas diverge. Secondly, moral hazard occurs when sponsoring states lack ways to monitor or oversee their proxy's actions, creating asymmetries of information. Proxies try to avoid their sponsor's scrutiny and keep their own internal operations hidden. Both factors increase the risk that proxies will misuse their sponsor's support. Proxies might overreach, expanding violence in ways the sponsor does not intend. Proxies might also refuse to attack those whom the patron wants to target. To overcome these problems, sponsoring states must carefully vet potential proxies for competence and compatibility. Once a proxy relationship congeals, sponsors closely monitor their agents' actions. Benefactors try to maintain the credible threat of withholding support to punish a recalcitrant agent. Sponsors must try to block any agent from having access to multiple sponsors in order to maintain their leverage and ensure that proxies abide by the sponsor's directives.[8]

But these remedies are easier said than done in the modern state system. Sponsoring states have only illusions of flexibility and control. Decision-makers typically underestimate the potential costs and risks of conducting policy through proxies.[9] With multiple centers of global and regional power, proxies inevitably have a chance to find alternative sponsors. In many instances, the ostensible proxy has greater capacity on the ground than the sponsor, allowing the agent effectively to pick the principal, instead of vice versa.[10]

States often rely on non-state proxies when they wish to avoid blame or responsibility for attacks but still maintain pressure on an adversary. But such obfuscation can lead to miscalculation and inadvertent escalation. Adversaries cannot accurately discern the level of a state's commitment to a secret proxy. Absent a clear signal of warning and deterrence, escalation can happen inadvertently.[11]

A sponsor's own bureaucratic culture can hinder effective oversight. In democracies like the United States, this allows executive officials to hide the proxy relationship from organizational oversight and control. Clandestine branches typically play a key role in proxy relationships. Secrecy, however, exacerbates the information asymmetries and adds volatility to sponsor–proxy relationships. Especially in covert policy spaces, bureaucratic factions can have an interest in continuing to invest in proxy relationships after they have proven ineffective or counterproductive. Since the policy itself is a secret, it is difficult to muster an effective critique or offer a substantial alternative.[12]

Even bad proxy relationships can be hard to escape. Ideological commitments between sponsors and proxies can sometimes overshadow cost–benefit analysis. Sponsors tend to align with proxy groups they consider ethnic kin and ideological partners, even when the benefits of such partnerships are equivocal.[13] As with other forms of identity construction, however, these efforts often involve the creation of narratives of common values, culture, and historical origins.[14]

Similar organizational problems exist on the proxy side of the equation. Proxy groups themselves can decentralize command and subcontract violence to others, increasing the risk of defection, cheating, or splintering.[15] Proxies that accept foreign assistance can lose their own operational and political autonomy and even legitimacy at home. Outside support, a kind of strategic rent, can be a crutch, allowing armed groups to ignore the wishes and complaints of the civilians under their control. The armed group loses touch with key constituencies and even loses credibility. This can lead to breakdowns of discipline and increases the propensity to alienate or even abuse civilians.[16]

Proxy wars involve simultaneous mechanisms of fragmentation and integration, breaking down states' capacities to manage violence but inviting outside states into the domestic arena.[17] Sponsors initiate engagement with proxies believing they offer an easy way to achieve strategic objectives at little cost. Sponsors are willing to fight to the last proxy. Yet proxies find ways to use violence for their own ends. The proliferation of violence only incites greater commitment from the sponsors, which lose control over the means by which their initial strategic goals could be attained. The result is a broader transformation in the global system itself, what international relations theorist James Rosenau calls the formation of "distant proximities" between disparate elements and actors of the global system.[18] States are still present, but are forced to compete and cooperate with non-state actors in new and uncertain ways.

From Local Disputes to Civil War

Nearly all of the optimistic discussions of the 2011 uprisings in MENA have shifted into the "what went wrong" genre. There was no single path from mass demonstrations to state failure, civil conflict, and proxy wars. Grievances were ubiquitous in MENA, but only in certain countries was the opposition able to muster large-scale political mobilization. Of these, only some protest movements truly challenged the regime, and these seldom sought to break apart the state. Rather, they largely demanded reform or removal of a specific regime. But these protests exacerbated the security predicament of individual regimes. Elite praetorian guards, staffed by the rulers' closest kin, were unlikely to defect to the protesters. But regular army, police, and even intelligence branches all had different calculations about their institutional and personal loyalties. Different configurations of civil–military relations, therefore, led to different outcomes. In Tunisia, more or less cohesive and professional military branches helped to oust Ben Ali. The transitional government, led by Ben Ali's own vice-president, appeared relatively quickly and with minimal slippage of state control. In Egypt, too, there were a few unsettled weeks of looting and street violence, some of which was itself covertly staged by Mubarak loyalists, which increased the popular sense of chaos on the street. There were also increased terrorist attacks in bombings in peripheral areas like Sinai and Upper Egypt. But when the Egyptian high command decided to jettison Mubarak, it quickly clamped down. Similarly, when the Bahrain security services proved unable to deal with street protests, the arrival of some 2,000 Saudi and Emirati troops reinforced the regime and crushed the opposition.

Civil wars began only where the entire apparatus of statehood was already more brittle. The patrimonial logic that sustained Qaddafi in Libya, Assad in Syria, and Saleh in Yemen prevented any mass defection by the military. Instead, it made the splintering of the security services more likely. Opposition factions struggled to reassemble some measure of centralized authority. The breakdown of the state left a kind of vortex that spurred two contradictory processes. First was the profound localization of violence. Militias, self-defense forces, and criminal organizations, as well as terrorist groups and other armed non-state actors, took security into their own hands. Many of these groups espoused ambitious agendas. They declared themselves revolutionary vanguards (*thuwar*) or stalwarts of the old regime. They adopted grandiose slogans of jihad, sectarian triumphalism, or national liberation. Most, however, could scarcely rule a single city or province. Some did better than others in addressing the core tasks of rebel governance: defending their territories against encroachment from other armed groups, be they states or rebels; maintaining discipline and order among their own fighters; and assuring quiescence, or even outright support, from civilians.[19]

The second process was the intervention of outside powers filling in the space where titular states had once stood. Incumbent regimes fell back on the familiar arguments about sovereignty and norms of interference, the normative foundations of statehood since the end of colonialism. They also described themselves as bulwarks of stability and appealed for outside support to help combat the scourge of radical Islamists. The rebels made their appeals to the international community on humanitarian grounds. Provisional governments cited the novel responsibility-to-protect (R2P) doctrine, arguing essentially that the regimes' own threats to their civilians made them dangers to the international community too and so warranted outside military action.[20] This idea, the rebels knew, undercut norms of sovereignty. Yet, as the exasperated chairman of Libya's Transitional National Council (TNC) put it, "We think that the Security Council can skip international sovereignty and protect the civilians by all means necessary."[21] On more practical terms, the rebels posed as responsible interlocutors who could help right dysfunctional states. By appealing for outside support, though, both pro- and anti-regime actors only made their own claims to statehood more implausible. What good was a purportedly sovereign state if it had to rely on external backers to sustain it?

The ideological and political hollowing of states, then, left more room for local and global forces of violence to converge. The result was a complex configuration of antagonisms, alliances, and proxy relationships that spanned the region and the globe. The involvement of the United States, Russia, Iran, Saudi Arabia, Qatar, the UAE, Turkey, and other regional and global powers knitted these networks of violence together into a fully regional crisis. The denser and more intricate these webs, the more difficult it was to control the outcome and the more contagious violence became. Perturbations affecting one node led to violent reactions in another.

Libya was to the first MENA country to involve outside intervention and the first to succumb to civil war. It is thus a natural starting point for describing how the combination of localized and fragmented violence and outside intervention conjoined in the vortex. Syria's tragic progression from civil unrest to proxy war syncopated with Libya's. In Syria, it was Iran's and Russia's efforts to defend the regime that induced an exponential escalation of violence. Syria's conflict also spilled over the border to Iraq, creating a true arc of crisis across the former mandate zones. In Yemen, the state was by far the weakest prior to the onset of the rebellion. Its regime transition involved the most pronounced foreign involvement and its descent into proxy war was the most abrupt.

Libya

Protests in Libya began in mid-February in Benghazi, the largest city of the east, and quickly spread to nearby towns and cities of the Green Mountains, then to Tripoli, Misrata, and the Nafusa Mountains region along the Algerian and Tunisian border. The TNC was founded in Benghazi within the first week. It featured a mix of exiled politicians, long-standing opposition activists, and recent regime defectors. The TNC established its own military council, naming a former general in the interior ministry forces as supreme commander.[22] Several of the leading local revolutionary factions announced their support for the TNC.[23] Still, it was racked by internal divisions, and several rebel commanders jockeyed for supremacy. As the uprising spread, violence became localized. Armed groups appeared organically, including militias associated with local revolutionary committees, tribal forces, and armed Islamist groups.[24]

The regime's resistance stiffened and the rebellion seemed to stall within a few weeks. Most of the regular army was still intact. Qaddafi could still call on the praetorian guards, tribal militias from loyalist strongholds in Sirte and Bani Walid, as well as mercenaries from sub-Saharan Africa. Government forces put down the uprising in Tripoli, encircled Misrata, and moved on the oil installations in the east.[25] Qaddafi's son and heir-apparent Saif made menacing statements about what would happen if the revolution proceeded: the end of oil revenue, the return of colonialism, and "rivers of blood." Qaddafi himself picked up these same themes, calling the rebels "rats who are getting paid by foreign powers," and warned that the uprising would produce civil war, infiltration by al-Qaeda and other radical Islamists, and foreign occupation similar to that experienced by Iraq, Afghanistan, and Pakistan. In response, the TNC lobbied more adamantly for international protection and opened the conflict fully to outside intervention.

Among the Arab states, Qatar was the first Arab country to come to the rebels' rescue. The tiny Gulf state had been on an unmistakable winning streak. The ouster of Mubarak and rapid ascent of the Muslim Brotherhood in Egypt was widely seen as a strategic victory for Qatar's form of soft power. Some saw in al-Jazeera, the influential satellite television station owned by the Qatari royal family, an arm of Qatar propaganda. As it was, al-Jazeera covered the situation in Benghazi with a similar pro-opposition angle. Qatar also pledged hundreds of millions of dollars to the TNC, plus provision of humanitarian relief to rebel-held areas.[26] Qatar successfully introduced an Arab League resolution placing sanctions on Libya. As the military situation grew more dire, Qatar pushed the League to make the unprecedented step of approving a no-fly zone (NFZ) and humanitarian safe haven for rebel enclaves.

Among Western countries, France took the lead in humanitarian involvement. Intellectuals and activists warned of a humanitarian disaster if the regime forces were to retake Benghazi. France extended diplomatic recognition to the TNC and began to call for a UN Security Council Resolution. Many European states saw Libya as a chance to substantiate the R2P doctrine. The United States, for its part, tried to keep Libya at arm's length, skeptical of the TNC's ability to actually command on the ground and worried that radical groups might hijack the transition process. The willingness of Qatar and France to lead the intervention helped convince the United States to back more aggressive action as well. China, Russia, Brazil, and India, traditionally skeptical of intervention, deferred to the Arab League and abstained from the vote.[27] On March 17, the UN Security Council formally approved the NFZ and humanitarian safe haven while explicitly excluding foreign occupation.

As it turned out, the international community could scarcely move on its humanitarian principles without US military backing. Many members of the coalition, including Turkey and Qatar, refused to accede to France's self-appointed position as spearhead of the operation. Initial airstrikes did little to hinder Qaddafi's advances. Finally, the United States agreed to take a more forward position, coordinating with NATO. Western forces, alongside the UAE, Jordan, and Qatar, set up training and support programs for rebel troops. Rebels were able at least to consolidate their lines.[28] Qatar provided tens of millions of dollars and some 20,000 tons of weapons. But as the front shifted away from the TNC's Benghazi beachhead, Doha concentrated efforts on independent militias operating in the west. Islamist groups like the Libyan Islamic Fighting Group and the Rafallah as-Shahati Brigades were lavished with Qatari equipment and funding.[29] Rebels accelerated their mobilization and, with it, relied more and more on local networks for leadership. Most revolutionary militias recruited their fighters from specific towns, cities, neighborhoods, or tribes. Various foreign sponsors tried to help the TNC bolster its organizational capacities and incorporate these disparate rebel groups into a solid chain of command. But these same foreign powers also maintained direct bilateral relationships with different armed factions, effectively bypassing the TNC. Saudi Arabia, Turkey, and the UAE set out to recruit their own militias, largely to counter Qatar's increasing sway. The United States and other NATO players, too, were concerned about the flow of money and arms eventually falling into the hands of hardline Islamist elements.[30]

Internecine conflict among the rebels persisted even as Qaddafi's forces fell back into isolated pockets around Tripoli and Sirte. A top TNC military commander was assassinated in Benghazi in July, most likely by Islamist militias that refused to accede to command from a former regime official. In August 2011, Islamist militias from Misrata and the Nafusa mountain region finally managed to capture Tripoli. Qatar provided significant logistical and communications support. Qaddafi was summarily executed in Sirte in October.

TNC officials repeatedly complained that outside support for armed groups fatally undercut their own ability to re-establish state control over coercion and disarm the rebel groups. As one member of the TNC complained, "I cannot claim to have control over these formations . . . [they take] matters into their own hands . . . and violate human rights."[31] But it was the TNC's own entreaties for international support that had invited intervention in the first place.

The beginning of electoral politics in Libya only heightened the fragmentation of coercive control and, in turn, hastened further outside interference. The results of the first parliamentary elections in 2012 were widely seen as a public refutation of Qatari influence in Libya. Parties aligned with the Muslim Brotherhood, many with close ties to Doha, lost to a more moderate Islamist faction. Yet electoral politics mattered little in a situation where most political parties fielded their own private militias. Revolutionary committees and fighters refused to stand down. The international community failed in its efforts to overcome the fragmentation of control by bringing former fighters from overseas for training and integration into a new national army. With no army to join, they simply took their training back to their original militias, or started new ones.[32] Fighters affiliated with al-Qaeda, the Islamic State, and other radical organizations, some returning from campaigns in Iraq or Syria, set up their own armed groups. Residents of Benghazi, Tripoli, Derna, and other cities saw these militias set up check-points, extort money from residents, and impose their own version of law and order. Kidnappings, assassinations, and bombings became more common. Key diplomatic facilities were also targeted, most famously with the attack on the US consulate in Benghazi on September 11, 2012, which killed the ambassador and numerous others.

Of all the countries the crisis of the 2010s touched, no place was more affected by the contest over oil than Libya. Although it was only a middling producer on the global scale, oil was the absolute lifeblood of the Libyan economy. Early in the revolution, tribal forces and others had threatened to sabotage pipelines or seize production and refinement facilities as a way to blackmail the central government. The TNC lobbied the international community to assume control over the sovereign wealth fund, the central bank, the national oil company, and other state assets. There were rumors of both Qaddafi and the TNC trading oil for political considerations. Still, most reputable foreign buyers refused to purchase oil of questionable provenance.[33] The pattern continued under the General National Council (GNC) government in 2012, which was supposed to draft Libya's constitution. Eastern separatist factions blockaded oil terminals, which cost the government an estimated $30 billion. The US navy eventually interdicted the contraband oil (as discussed in Chapter 3). But this only underscored the apparent inability of the central state to deal with its own domestic challengers.

The disputed 2014 parliamentary elections further fragmented what remained of the Libyan state, marking the beginning of another civil war. The top levels of the Libyan government split in two. After armed clashes in the capital, the newly elected House of Representatives (HoR) government retreated eastward to Tobruk. The holdovers from the old GNC remained in Tripoli and declared themselves the legitimate government. Both sought recognition and support from the international community or specific foreign states and the international community writ large. Likewise, both sought access to and authority over key state institutions like the supreme court, central bank, treasury, and security services.

But the fragmentation went far beyond a simple bifurcation or "dual sovereignty." Across Libya, there were networks of localized forces in loose alliance with either Tripoli or Tobruk. Crucially, the HoR government aligned with General Khalifa Haftar, a rogue Libyan military commander who had set up his own self-styled Libyan National Army (LNA). Haftar capitalized on popular disaffection with Tripoli. Many Libyans blamed the feckless Tripoli government for the poor security and economic performance of the country. Haftar faulted it for permitting – even abetting – the emergence of radical Islamist groups. His shifting network of allies and supporters included former regime members resentful of the revolutionaries' lustration policies, eastern separatists seeking to establish Cyrenaican autonomy, and militia fighters from the city of Zintan opposed to the dominance of Misratan forces in Tripoli. With support from the UAE and Saudi Arabia, Haftar also made alliances with Salafi Islamist groups that deemed the Muslim Brotherhood an infidel innovation and set out their own brand of austere and puritanical politics. Even within the Haftar alliance network there was constant tension between Islamist and tribal forces, as well as those forces personally loyal to Haftar himself. Manipulating these rivalries and setting these factions against each other helped Haftar remain in power, but also added further centrifugal momentum.[34]

An even looser galaxy of forces orbited the Tripoli government. Many hailed from Islamist forces that had emerged during the 2011 revolution. Misrata, probably Libya's most important mercantile city, had historically supported these factions and was closely associated with the Muslim Brotherhood movement. But there were other factions as well, including indigenous Islamists from Cyrenaica that opposed Haftar, as well as tribal forces in the south and far west. For a year, Haftar's forces battered Benghazi and other Cyrenaican cities, seeking to "cleanse" them of Islamist influence. There were similar confrontations over oil installations in the east. The result was a kind of pockmarked array of armed groups with multiple overlaps and fluid zones of control. The forces in both the Tripoli and Haftar networks exhibited varying degrees of professionalization, training, and equipment. Many combined political agendas with more pecuniary goals, trying to dominate lucrative smuggling routes, ports of entry (including Tripoli's international airport), and, of course, oil.

Some acted as free agents, shifting alliances between the Tripoli government and Haftar, depending on their own strategic circumstances.

These localized nodes within Libya were linked into a larger regional and global hierarchy. Qatar and Turkey had military and financial ties to the Tripoli government and maintained direct ties to specific non-state armed groups. The United States and UN recognized Tripoli as the seat of the new Government of National Accord (GNA) in December 2015. This meant that the GNA enjoyed greater access to the central bank and the revenues from Libyan oil sales with which to purchase weapons and pay salaries.

Haftar was adept at extracting financial and military support from international backers. Egypt's new military government under General Sisi, along with the UAE, served as Haftar's air force. The UAE and Saudi Arabia helped Haftar build ties to Islamist factions that opposed the Muslim Brotherhood. Moscow provided weaponry, military training, and crucial financial support, such as allowing Haftar to print his own Libyan currency outside the control of the central bank. When France became concerned that instability in southern Libya would spill over into Chad and other Sahel countries, Haftar capitalized by launching his own campaign to assert control in in the southern region. France became another one of Haftar's arms suppliers. Again, the United States played an important but inconsistent role. Ultimately, as Jalel Harchaoui and Mohamed Essaïd Lazib point out, "External interference [in Libya] has helped empower some actors by granting them financial, military, and political means. However, international backers are seldom able to dictate their proxies' actions. Local considerations impose stronger constraints on armed groups' trajectories, cohesion, and sustainability over time than any external patrons."[35] International interventions may not have been responsible for beginning the war in Libya. By enabling belligerents to offset costs and ignore opportunities for negotiation, however, foreign actors helped prolong the bloodletting.

Syria

Though geographically distant, Syria's fate was tied inextricably to Libya's. Nearly every actor involved in the conflict in Syria saw Libya as a cautionary tale, albeit for different reasons. On the one hand, the United States saw Syria as even more fractious than Libya, presenting even greater problems for cohesion. Indeed, a disjointed effort to funnel military aid to the Syrian rebels exacerbated the same problems of organizational control seen in Libya. On the other hand, the Syrian ambassador complained that the Arab League's approval of the Libyan NFZ "violates the sovereignty, independence and unity of Libyan territory," aware that the precedents used in Libya might soon be used against Syria.[36] Ultimately, it was less the rebels' invocation of R2P than the Assad regime's invocation of sovereignty that induced foreign military intervention. Iran's and Russia's rescue of the regime was by far the most the significant factor driving the acceleration of violence.

The Syrian opposition faced problems of coordination from the outset of the rebellion. The Syrian National Council (SNC), a government-in-exile, emerged in July 2011. Yet the Free Syrian Army (FSA) and most local revolutionary coordinating committees that had emerged from the ground up offered the SNC nominal allegiance at best. The SNC claimed to represent the full breadth of Syria's multi-ethnic society, but it was clearly dominated by the Sunni Muslim Brotherhood and beholden to Qatar and Turkey for financing and political support. Saudi Arabia and other regional states supported rival rebel factions, reinforcing the momentum of fragmentation.[37]

Violence escalated as the regime adopted more brutal tactics of aerial bombardment, including with chemical weapons and barrel bombs. The opposition shifted further into insurgency, relying mostly on weapons looted from armories or provided by foreign backers. Rebel armed groups multiplied as they tried to take advantage of multiple streams of foreign donations. Many of the rebels adopted starkly sectarian attitudes, claiming to fight on behalf of beleaguered Sunnis beset by the infidel Alawi regime. Regardless of ideology, though, all rebel groups strove to gain strategically valuable and economically lucrative areas in the east and north. By 2013, much of Syria's primary agricultural lands and most of its modest oil fields were in rebel hands.[38] Syria, like Libya, became a jumble of authorities and shifting networks of alliances, many with complicated and contradictory connections leading either to Damascus or to the rebels and their foreign backers.

The situation in Kurdish-inhabited areas along the Turkish border was especially complex. The Kurdish Democratic Union Party (PYD) carved out its own autonomous region called Rojava (Western Kurdistan), as discussed in Chapter 4. The PYD had emerged as the Syrian wing of the Turkish PKK (Kurdistan Workers' Party), which Ankara regarded as a terrorist organization. The PYD declared its loyalty to the Syrian state and to Assad. Practically, however, it acted unilaterally and without consulting the central government in setting up Kurdish self-rule.

Despite the similarities in the initial phases of revolution and state breakdown, the geopolitical circumstances of the Syrian war differed vastly from those of Libya. From the outset of the uprising, the Assad regime could rely on key strategic partnerships with Iran and Russia. Tehran saw the uprising as the stalking horse of Sunni radicals funded by Sunni Arab states and, more obliquely, from the United States. Iran sent its own expeditionary forces to reinforce the Syrian security services and recruited Shi'i sectarian militias from Lebanon, Iraq, and Afghanistan to fill in the ranks. Iran and its allied forces helped set up a bevy of pro-government Syrian militia forces. These forces mirrored the kind of localization seen in the opposition.

The Obama administration equivocated in its response to the Syrian uprising, just as it had in Libya. It did not want to provoke a fight with Russia or get
drawn into a quagmire like Iraq, whatever the severity of Assad's repression.
The United States also wanted to find a way to improve relations with Iran, as
made evident by its diplomatic outreach regarding the latter's nascent nuclear
program. Most importantly, though, US officials realized, however intuitively,
the dangers of proxy wars. The Syrian opposition was in shambles. Its victories
might only clear the field for more radical Islamist elements to gain momentum. The United States tried to limit support for the Syrian opposition to
non-lethal instruments. Other regional powers, though, violated the UN arms
embargos and kept up the flow of armaments to the rebels. The FSA floundered
and eventually broke up, with commanders transferring their training and
equipment to new armed groups. When Assad attacked rebels with chemical
weapons in 2012, a clear violation of both international law and Obama's own
self-declared "red line" warning, the United States did not take action.

The arrival of the Islamic State was in some ways the sum of all the foreign
actors' fears. IS originated as al-Qaeda in Iraq (see Chapter 4) and moved into
Syria in the first days of the civil war. Although it pronounced itself the champion of Sunni Islam against Shi'i heresy, most of its initial military campaigns
involved attacking fellow Sunni jihadi groups, including those affiliated with
al-Qaeda and the FSA. IS thus played a major role in the processes of sectarian
outbidding that turned the Syrian and Iraq conflicts into sectarian campaigns
(a topic also discussed in Chapter 4). In July 2014, IS forces stormed Mosul in
Iraq, establishing a sinuous zone of control that reached from the outskirts of
Aleppo all the way to the edges of Baghdad.

IS's emergence thus prompted an unprecedented period of international
collaboration. The international anti-IS coalition involved an ad hoc division
of labor that transcended geopolitical fault lines. Iran provided direct military
support to both Baghdad and Damascus, helping to establish pro-government
militias that supplemented the main security arms. Russia provided further
military backing to Assad, especially in air support. The United States, along
with Turkey, the UAE, Jordan, Saudi Arabia, and several NATO states, lent air
and drone strikes against IS in both Iraq and Syria. Turkey recruited a network
of militias in northern Syria, including remnants of the FSA.

The United States tried to stand up the Syrian Democratic Forces (SDF) to
replace the mostly defunct FSA. The SDF was supposed to include all the major
elements of the armed opposition. In practice, though, the PYD provided the
most important constituent. Under the SDF banner, PYD forces played a major
part in the reconquest of Raqqa and other IS strongholds in northeastern Syria.
Likewise, the United States backed the Iraqi Kurdish Regional Government's
campaign to retake Mosul.

Three particular features of the Syrian war aptly illustrate the compounding effects of violence and fractionalization stemming from state failure. First,

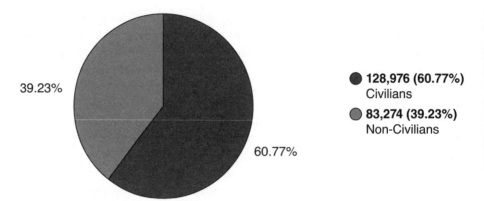

Figure 6.1 Battle-related deaths in Syria, March 2011–January 2020
Source: Violations Documentation Center in Syria, "Monthly Statistical Report on Casualties in Syria" (January 2020).

the war took an enormous toll on civilians. The Violations Documentation Center in Syria (VDCS), an opposition-aligned think tank, estimated that of the total 192,036 documented battle deaths, nearly two-thirds were of civilians (as shown in Figure 6.1).

Secondly, the violence became increasingly one-sided. At every point in the conflict, the Syrian state possessed far greater capacity for coercion than the rebels, and used that capacity to inflict the bulk of the damage. The influx of assistance from Iran and then Russia heightened this disparity. According to the VDCS, the regime and its Iranian-aligned forces accounted for 146,918 deaths of civilians and non-civilians, the opposition 23,027, IS 7,314, and Russian forces 6,213 (as shown in Figure 6.2). Of course, these data are highly disputed and potentially biased. Moreover, they reflect more the imbalance in the means than in motives to inflict violence. There is simply no telling what IS or other rebel groups would have done had they had an air force at their disposal or could call on an alliance with Russia.

The point about the one-sidedness of the violence concords with a less empirically controversial feature of the conflict: its spatial fractionalization. The Assad regime talked incessantly about preserving Syrian sovereignty, even when it allowed armed actors to run rampant in its territory. The talk of sovereignty served to extract greater resources from abroad, mirroring the way the opposition forces spoke of humanitarian ideals and R2P as a way to gain greater support from intervening powers. The regime required international aid agencies like the Red Cross and others to partner exclusively with state-controlled bodies like the Syrian Arab Red Crescent and funneled money and aid to state-controlled areas like the capital city of Damascus or the Mediterranean coastal areas, the Alawi heartland. These areas suffered economic decline and sporadic violence, including terrorist bombings, but nothing on the scale of what was seen in Raqqa, Aleppo, Homs, or other

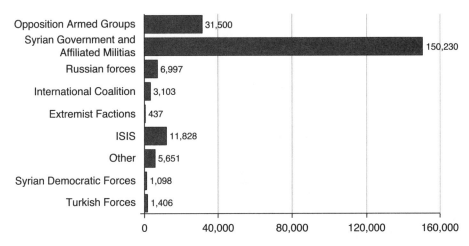

Figure 6.2 Deaths by parties responsible, Syria, March 2011–January 2020
Source: Violations Documentation Center in Syria, "Monthly Statistical Report on Casualties in Syria" (January 2020).

rebel-held cities. Syria's overall economy crumbled, but war-profiteers with close connections to the Assad regime still made fortunes. The rebel-held areas, in contrast, literally starved. Schools, healthcare, and other basic social services collapsed and hunger and disease prevailed. Survival depended on smuggling, black market trade, and occasional subventions from intrepid humanitarian agencies or sponsoring states.[39]

A sense of the spatial disparity in destruction comes from satellite imaging technology, which avoids the problems of bias in death toll reporting. Reflected light is broadly correlated with measures of economic activity, electrification, and population density. Across Syria, these measures fell by almost 8 percent from the start of the war in 2011 until 2017, as shown in Figure 6.3. Relatively peaceful regime strongholds like Latakia, Tartus, or Damascus held close to pre-war levels. In contrast, the provinces where rebels gained a foothold and where fighting was fiercest – Aleppo, Raqqa, Daraa, Deir Ezzour, and Idlib – essentially went dark. This suggests dramatic declines in population, owing to both casualties and flight. The Syrian war was responsible for the displacement of an estimated 13 million people. About 6 million became internally displaced, many joining the ranks of the urban poor and marginalized. Over 3 million Syrians moved to Turkey, 1 million to Lebanon, 660,000 to Jordan, and 250,000 to Iraq. An additional 1 million made the dangerous passage to seek asylum in Europe. This spillover had profoundly destabilizing effects for the region, straining local economies and broadly changing political dynamics.[40]

Concurrent findings are apparent when using satellite imaging to analyze damage to buildings and other physical infrastructure. A UN study of Syria's large cities did not even bother to examine damage to regime-held Latakia and

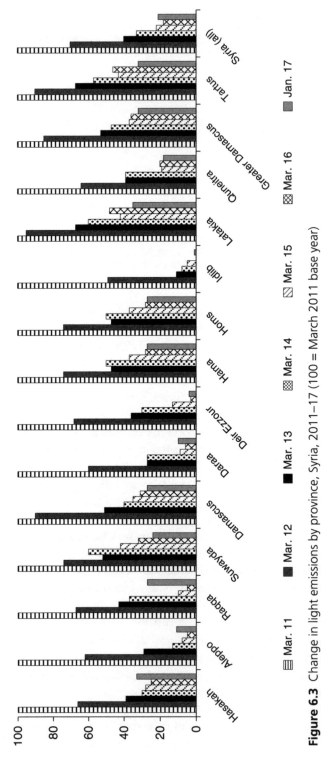

Figure 6.3 Change in light emissions by province, Syria, 2011–17 (100 = March 2011 base year)

Source: Alexander De Juan and André Bank, "The Ba'athist Blackout? Selective Goods Provision and Political Violence in the Syrian Civil War," *Journal of Peace Research* 52, no. 1 (2015): 91–104; Xi Li et al., "Intercalibration between DMSP/OLS and VIIRS Night-Time Light Images to Evaluate City Light Dynamics of Syria's Major Human Settlement during Syrian Civil War," *International Journal of Remote Sensing* 38, no. 21 (2017): 5934–51.

Tartus. It was Aleppo that suffered the most damage in absolute terms, and Raqqa, the IS capital, the most totalizing destruction.[41]

Ultimately, the combination of civil war and foreign intervention reduced Syria to a fierce but weak form of statehood. Neither the Assad regime nor the nascent rebel rulers could control territory without support from external patrons and armed non-state actors. By the time Turkey, Russia, Iran, and the Assad regime began peace negotiations, it was a peace of the victor. No major rebel groups were involved. This, however, only ensured the violence would continue.

Yemen

Yemen was a frail state even before 2010. There was no monopoly over violence and the country was awash in small arms. By some estimates, there was one firearm for every two households.[42] For at least a decade, Yemen was roiled by three distinct conflicts. First, in the far north, Houthi insurgents fought government forces and allied tribal and Sunni Islamist militias. The Houthi movement capitalized on disaffection among the Zaydi Muslim population, an early offshoot of Shi'ism unique to Yemen's northern highlands. Secondly, in the south, the separatist Southern Movement demanded political devolution or even outright independence for areas that had comprised the People's Democratic Republic of Yemen until the unification of 1990. Both the Houthis and the southern separatists received support from Iran, which was eager to recruit potential proxies in Saudi Arabia's southern flank. Thirdly, al-Qaeda and similar radical Islamist groups had infiltrated Yemen's porous borders, using it as an outpost for larger regional and global campaigns. Yemeni President Ali Abdullah Saleh had adeptly extracted military and economic assistance from Saudi Arabia and the United States to counter these threats through the 1990s and 2000s.

The international community thus took a special interest when protests began in February 2011 in Sana'a and other Yemeni cities. The protests themselves followed a familiar script. Youth and local activists, often unconnected to the established opposition parties, led the first wave. The regime lurched between efforts to coopt and intimidate the rebels, blaming outside instigators for endangering Yemeni sovereignty. Regime loyalists, particularly senior military commanders and tribal leaders, defected.

The UN Security Council authorized Saudi Arabia and its Gulf allies to manage Saleh's exit so as to avoid state collapse. One-time Saleh loyalists flocked to Riyadh to consult with the presumed king-maker. Saleh remained intransigent. Saleh was wounded in a bombing at his compound in Sana'a, leaving a constitutional and political void. Much global attention naturally focused on the violence in the streets of Sana'a or the politicking in the salons of Riyadh. In the meantime, though, armed actors – separatists, Houthis, al-Qaeda, and others – seized the initiative at the periphery. Saleh agreed to resign in favor of his vice-president, Mansur Abd al-Rabbo Hadi, assuring the continued dominance of the ruling General People's Congress. The transitional government, such as it was, lobbied the international community for military and economic assistance to push back al-Qaeda and other enemies. It promised to use Gulf and Western aid to expand political participation and inclusion. Yet one commentator likened the nation-wide dialog conference intended to start processes of reconciliation to "a spectacular wedding where no one wants to get married."[43] The Houthis and southern separatist factions withdrew their delegates from the meeting in 2013, claiming that the entire endeavor was stage-managed by Hadi and his foreign backers to assure continuity. Each retained or expanded their military presence in the far north and the south. Saleh sought an alliance with the Houthis, whom he had waged war against in the previous decade. Saleh himself hailed from a highlander Zaydi background. Units of the Yemeni Republican Guard, many under the command of his closest kin, joined the Houthis. They stormed Sana'a in late 2014 and had moved southward on Taiz, Hodeidah, and even Aden by early 2015. The Hadi government retreated in disarray, first to Aden, then to Riyadh. Meanwhile radical Islamist groups, including al-Qaeda activists and IS sympathizers, seized power over provincial cities and remote areas across the country.

To defend the Hadi government from what it deemed joint Houthi–Iranian aggression, Saudi Arabia marshaled a broad coalition of Sunni states. Some Saudi officials even analogized their response to the humanitarian intervention in Libya. Riyadh dispatched some 150,000 troops and 100 combat aircrafts. The UAE was a significant, but still junior, partner in the coalition. Its newly created conscript army was also deployed, including a special forces contingent. Around 30 UAE jets were also dispatched to Yemen. Sudan supplied 6,000 troops, many veterans of the Darfur campaign, to the task. Egypt provided air and naval patrols. Kuwait, Bahrain, and even Qatar, which had its own acrimonious relationship with Saudi Arabia, made nominal military contributions. Jordan and Morocco also voiced diplomatic support for the endeavor. There was also a significant contingent of PMCs attached to campaign in various capacities.

As the primary arms supplier to Saudi Arabia and the UAE, the United States loomed behind the coalition. Efforts to restrict how the Gulf states used these armaments proved half-hearted and ultimately futile. In fact, the more the United States seemed intent on stepping back from MENA, the more aggressive Saudi and Emirati policies seemed to become.

The Saudis used their air supremacy less as a scalpel, as prescribed in RMA doctrine, than a bludgeon. The coalition blockaded Houthi-held territories in the north and the central plateau. The siege denied millions of already impoverished Yemenis food and medicine. Aerial bombardment destroyed key pieces of civilian infrastructure, including hospitals and water-treatment facilities. Conflict-affected areas of northern and central Yemen faced the largest cholera epidemic since World War II and near-famine conditions.[44] By 2018, the UN described Yemen as "the world's worst humanitarian crisis." An estimated 18 million Yemenis suffered food insecurity and millions lacked access to safe drinking water, causing cholera and other epidemic diseases.[45]

At the same time, the Houthis matured from a relatively low-skilled insurgency into a fully fledged army with Iran's foreign sponsorship. The Houthis absorbed weaponry and training from Saleh's Republican Guard units. Advisors from Iran and Lebanese Hezbollah offered them an expanded arsenal, including ballistic missiles, anti-shipping weapons, and drones. Houthi forces launched missiles and drone attacks at targets in the south, as well as at Saudi cities and oil facilities.[46] The Houthi leaders dealt harshly with any signs of internal opposition. UN officials concluded that the Houthis systematically recruited child soldiers. They often cashiered and diverted aid supplies. Saleh himself was assassinated in 2017 after he broke with the Houthis and sought to ally with the Aden-based government.

Indigenous Yemeni actors realigned in response to this foreign intervention. Hadi's government, still basically encamped in Riyadh, invited the Saudi rescue. Saudi Arabia was the primary benefactor of the rump of the Yemeni National Army, the mainstay of the official security services, totaling some 400,000 troops. But the Saudis, as well as the Emiratis, also maintained direct funding and training programs with smaller and more localized non-state actors. These militias waged their own campaigns against the Houthis and against al-Qaeda under the coalition's umbrella. Former Republican Guard commanders, including some of Saleh's own kin, came to join the medley of coalition forces following the break with the Houthis in 2017. However, both the Gulf sponsors tried to prevent any single commander from gaining too much power and, notoriously, withdrew fiscal support from commanders who grew too independent.

The separatist movement in southern Yemen saw its position shift even more dramatically. Until 2014, the separatists had seen the Houthis as a tactical ally in their battle with the central government. Moreover, both had received some support from Iran. As Houthi forces threatened Aden, however, the separatists struck a tactical alliance with the UAE and, by extension, the Hadi government, to defend Aden from the Houthis. The UAE cultivated particularly close ties with the Southern Transitional Council (STC). The STC became the primary conduit for international humanitarian aid to the city. The STC-affiliated Security Belt militias, comprised largely of Salafi-inspired fighters, patrolled in and around Aden. The gap between the state's juridical authority and the material power of the separatists became glaring in

2017 when STC and pro-Hadi forces fought for control over Aden's port. Hadi accused the STC of sedition and moved to sack several of its officials and defeat its militias. The STC responded with massive demonstrations that paralyzed Aden and declared southern independence. Although no outside state accepted the independence of southern Yemen, separatists remained in place as a major power in Aden and elsewhere in the south.

Yemen, like Libya, witnessed multiple civil wars concurrently. While Houthi and government forces fought in the north and center, other groups contended for power in cities and provinces of the south. Just one example comes from the Indian Ocean ports of Mukalla and ash-Shihr in Hadramat. Just a week into the Decisive Storm campaign in May 2015, al-Qaeda seized these ports with the help of local tribal elites. For nearly a year they ran their own municipal government, handling schools, electricity, public safety, and other essential services. They collected taxes from shipping and gasoline sales and even tried to siphon money from the state oil company and cell phone companies.[47] Although Saudi- and UAE-aligned forces eventually retook the cities, the possibilities for a return to such local self-rule loomed large. The inland province of Marib evinced an even fuller and more sustained exemption from central control. Marib had been one of the hardest fought-over areas in the beginning of the fighting, resting on the seam between Houthi and coalition forces' control. As the Houthi forces retreated, however, the central government in Aden was still in no position to resume governing. Instead, Marib's local elite capitalized on the region's oil wealth, commercial connections to Saudi Arabia, and the influx of foreign investment to defend what was essentially an island of prosperity and stability in a sea of conflict.[48]

The ability of Yemeni factions to stand up a more or less autonomous local governance apparatus mirrored the localization in the conflict. Nation-wide surveys conducted by the Yemen Polling Center in 2018 showed profound differences in attitudes and experiences of insecurity from one governorate to another. In the most fought-over areas of Sana'a, Jawf, and Amran, 20 to 40 percent of respondents described feeling mostly or always unsafe. In Bayda, a central governorate astride the fluid line of control between Houthi- and Saudi-aligned forces, over 50 percent reported feeling a sense of insecurity. In the southern governorates of Lahj and Aden, that proportion was less than 10 percent, in Hadramat less than 5 percent, and in remote eastern Mahra less than 1 percent. Beyond the bare sense of danger, Yemenis disagreed also as to what represented the greatest dangers they faced. Some rated Saudi airstrikes as the most significant personal threats. Others listed random bombings or armed groups. Some deemed issues of poverty, lack of healthcare, and other externalities of state failure as the biggest threat.[49]

Networks Unwound

The networks of proxies and sponsors that sustained, enabled, and initiated violence in MENA in the 2010s were never stable. Coalitions among states often suffered a kind of entropy induced by the problems of collective action, assuring that one state didn't free-ride on the efforts of the others. Similarly, sponsor–proxy relationships often enervated or shifted as a result of the problems of moral hazard, as each side tried to induce the other to overcommit. This transferred and transmitted violence to new nodes and locations within the region.

One way to take account of the durability of violence is to examine the most central node in the network: the United States. As discussed previously, no actor in the 2010s catastrophe could match the US for overall reach and impact. However reluctantly, it remained the pivotal actor. Changes in US policy, therefore, should have been decisive. But even the United States could not impose its will over the sprawling networks of proxy violence. This was made most apparent with the transition from the Obama to the Trump administration in 2017. Trump had criticized Obama's negotiations with Iran. Indeed, the new administration overall seemed to adopt the geopolitical discourses emanating from Riyadh and Jerusalem that identified two co-equal enemies: on one hand, there was Iran, a fount of Shi'i terrorism and open advocate of Islamic revolution; on the other hand, there was the Muslim Brotherhood, a vast and shadowy network backed by Qatar and other states to serve as a kind of front for a conspiracy of Sunni radicalism. Trump tried to demonstrate resolve and commitment to traditional allies like Saudi Arabia and Israel. He recognized Israel's sovereignty over the Golan Heights and moved the US embassy from Tel Aviv to Jerusalem. He withdrew from the Obama-era nuclear agreement with Iran and instead adopted a more aggressive posture of economic pressure toward Tehran. The administration also designated the Muslim Brotherhood as a terrorist organization.

Despite these new priorities, the United States remained inconsistent and hesitant in the actual application of its power and demonstrated fear of sinking into another indefinite campaign in the region. Even when it was engaged, the effects were unexpected. In Libya, the United States seemed to back away from its commitment to the Tripoli-based GNA, which remained the internationally recognized government. Haftar tried to capitalize on the international tilt in his favor. He calculated that demonstrable foreign support from the United States, along with his long-standing relationships with Russia, Saudi Arabia, the UAE, Egypt, and France, would help convince "free agent" militias in Libya to join his side. As Haftar's LNA and allied forced encircled and attacked Tripoli in 2019, White House spokespersons praised Haftar and suggested that Trump had verbally consulted with the renegade general. But Haftar's gamble only led to more indeterminate fighting. His air and ground assault killed over 1,000 in a few months, but did little to shift the political calculus. Many of the militias that had seemed eager to align with the LNA before Haftar's offensive held back or even came to defend Tripoli. Haftar himself became more reliant on Russian military trainers and mercenaries.[50]

The Trump administration similarly redoubled its support for the Saudi campaign in Yemen, overriding Congressional majorities. Still, the coalition behind Saudi Arabia eroded. Qatar effectively quit in 2017 when Saudi Arabia and the UAE announced a blockade of the island in retaliation for its backing of radical Islamists. Other coalition partners simply reneged on their pledged contributions. As the humanitarian crisis worsened and public opinion in the United States and Europe tended to blame Saudi Arabia and the UAE, the signals were clear. In late 2018, Saudi Arabia and the Hadi government agreed to a ceasefire for the besieged port of Hodeidah. Implementation was spotty and short-lived, but the accord opened up an important humanitarian corridor and suggested possibilities for negotiations between Aden and Sana'a. Still, shifts in the international coalition changed the dynamics of violence again. The UAE, long seen as Saudi's junior partner, took an increasingly independent path. It redoubled its financial and military support to Yemen's southern separatists, disquieting the nominal Hadi government and Saudi Arabia. Southern Yemen was part of a larger Emirati adventure in the Indian Ocean, which included new naval bases on the Yemeni island of Socotra, in Eritrea, and in the self-proclaimed Republic of Somaliland. In 2019, the UAE announced that it, too, would withdraw its military forces from Yemen. Although Emirati officials claimed that these measures were intended to reallocate forces to the Persian Gulf and in anticipation of a confrontation with Iran, the effect further weakened the Hadi government and emboldened the separatists. The fractal violence in southern Yemen provided opportunities for both the Houthis and al-Qaeda to advance. While the STC remained the dominant separatist movement in the south, the Hadi government built alliances with other southern factions that opposed the STC. Riyadh's attempts to broker an agreement between the STC and Hadi further complicated efforts to negotiate with the Houthis in the north.[51]

The unwieldy anti-IS coalition witnessed the most complicated unwinding. It was obvious from the outset that Assad, Russia, and Iran equated every element of Syrian opposition with IS and intended to carry the momentum of victory to crush the rebels completely. Anyone inhabiting rebel-controlled territory was automatically a target. The Russian aerial campaign targeted areas like Aleppo that were held by non-IS opposition groups. Idlib held out as the last sanctuary city for the rebels. Security forces and allied militias moved in to mop up, often committing atrocities to punish civilians – mostly Sunnis – for their betrayal. With even ostensibly pro-government militias operating with more and more autonomy and direct ties to foreign backers, the Syrian state often could not contain the very violence it had sought to instigate.[52]

The fate of the Kurdish factions in Syria and Iraq is another node illustrative of the dissemination and proliferation of violence. Kurdish forces had made key contributions to the anti-IS alliance. Both the PYD and the KRG had managed to take new territories in the ground war against IS. But their position quickly eroded as regional and geopolitical circumstances changed. Turkey launched incursions that liquidated the Rojava cantons of Afrin and Kobani. Within Syria, the PYD had alienated many Arab tribes and Turkomen groups living in Syria. The Syrian government, which had once regarded the PYD as at least a tacit ally, criticized it for secessionist tendencies. The United States wanted to keep the SDF alive through the PYD, but would not commit the forces necessary to protect Rojava. Instead, it helped negotiate a ceasefire with Turkey and evacuated the PYD forces to Hasakah in the far northeast. The Trump administration's withdrawal of all but a handful of American troops from northeastern Syria in 2019 left the PYD further exposed. PYD leaders sought to re-establish ties to Assad or Russia to avoid falling under the Turkish hammer.

Kurdish leaders in Iraq made an even brasher – and more futile – effort to capitalize on their success in the anti-IS campaign. Defying the objections of Baghdad, the United States, and nearly every regional state, Kurdish leaders held a referendum on independence in 2018 that sparked a military and political crisis. Ultimately, Baghdad forced the Kurds to abandon Kirkuk and other newly captured territory. Iraq's Kurdish factions turned on each other, each accusing the other of betraying the nation and siding with Baghdad.[53]

A Thirty Years' War?

As optimism about the 2011 uprising fizzled, commentators and analysts struggled to make sense of the escalating bloodshed. Many likened the wars in MENA to the Thirty Years' War that ravaged Europe between 1618 and 1648. Veteran US diplomat Richard Haas described MENA in 2014 as the "chief cauldron of contemporary disorder."

> What is taking place in the region today most resembles the Thirty Years' War, three decades of conflict that ravaged much of Europe in the first half of the seventeenth century. As with Europe back then, in coming years, the Middle East is likely to be filled with mostly weak states unable to police large swaths of their territories, militias and terrorist groups acting with increasing sway, and both civil war and interstate strife. Sectarian and communal identities will be more powerful than national ones. Fueled by vast supplies of natural resources, powerful local actors

will continue to meddle in neighboring countries' internal affairs, and major outside actors will remain unable or unwilling to stabilize the region.[54]

There were new initiatives aimed at finding pathways to "de-sectarianize" regional politics and devise a new "Westphalian accord" that would stabilize the relationship between religion and state and create a basis for a more livable order.[55]

The comparison to the Thirty Years' War illuminates some aspects of the contemporary conflict in MENA but obscures others. Certainly, much of the conflict seemed to unfold along a sectarian seam. This was especially prominent as Saudi Arabia and Iran confronted each other. Both Riyadh and Tehran used sectarian discourse to depict the other as an existential threat rather than merely a strategic rival. Partisans in Syria, Iraq, and Yemen echoed this framing, each calling their opponents various synonyms of infidels and heretics.

But sectarianism alone was an inefficient compass by which to measure the arrays of state and non-state armed actors. The very insistence that this was in fact a sectarian war served to police social boundaries at the micro-level, summoning a sense of communalism that was at best latent prior to the onset of violence. There was clearly an ethnic structure to the mobilization in Syria, with Sunnis on the side of the opposition, Alawis and other minorities on the side of the regime. Nevertheless, as discussed in Chapter 4, there were many instances of cross-sectarian alliances: Sunnis who sided with the regime and Alawis and other minorities who joined the opposition.[56]

Some of the major belligerents in MENA wars did not fit within the Sunni–Shi'i binary. Israel, for example, was an important regional player with little at stake in the sectarian ramifications. Israel's alignment with Saudi Arabia and its periodic attacks on Hezbollah positions in Lebanon and Syria reflected a purely strategic calculation of Iran as a greater threat. Even some Muslim groups were immune to the sectarian pull. Although the war induced overt competition between the PYD and its PKK allies and the Iraqi branch of the KDP, it also precipitated a renewed sense of pan-Kurdish national solidarity. Kurds in Iraq were horrified by the IS onslaught on the PYD enclave of Kobani. IS killing, abduction, and enslavement of Kurdish-speaking Yezidis was a cause of concern. And, finally, the KRG's futile bid for independence seemed to garner broad sympathy in Syria as well. Despite the efforts of some Kurdish Salafi groups to initiate purges of non-Sunni groups, Kurdish politics became more focused on ethnic solidarity than sectarian polarization.[57]

Intra-sectarian tensions and violence were as significant as inter-sectarian clashes in MENA, although less often remarked upon. Just as France refused to align with fellow Catholic Austria during the Thirty Years' War, infighting among co-sectarians in MENA was often as salient as fighting across sectarian lines. The contest in the Sunni bloc was especially pronounced and apparent. Intra-Sunni battles played out as fiercely as the more commonly remarked upon Sunni–Shi'i strife. Saudi Arabia, custodian of the holy cities of Mecca and Medina, asserted that it had the strongest theological claim to purity and authenticity through its Wahhabi doctrine. The fact that Riyadh controlled the largest oil reserves gave it enormous economic clout as well. However, there were numerous other contestants. Early in the decade it looked as if tiny Qatar might emerge as the Sunni champion. Qatar, like Saudi Arabia, follows the Wahhabi traditions of an austere, even puritanical, Islamic doctrine. But Qatar refused to fall in behind its larger Gulf neighbor. Using its own oil and gas wealth, it shaped a vision of Islamic politics that was open to the kinds of political debate and social innovation that Saudi Arabia rejected.[58] The Muslim Brotherhood and its affiliates and fellow-travelers carried this vision to Egypt and Tunisia, as well as Syria, Libya, and Yemen. Turkey was an even more substantial military power. With the electoral ascendance of the Islamist Justice and Development Party (AKP), it seemed ideologically sympathetic with Doha and the Brotherhood. To counter these claimants, Saudi Arabia backed Salafi groups hostile to anything resembling the Brotherhood. This also meant attacking traditional practices that many regarded as intrinsically Islamic. In Libya, a country that is 99 percent Sunni Muslim, for example, Salafi groups declared veneration of Sufi tombs, a practice nearly ubiquitous in the Islamic world, as idolatry. In Iraq, IS made a tactical alliance with a local Sufi order that was dominated by ex-Ba'athists, but then quickly turned on its erstwhile allies. Even countries like Egypt and the UAE, which at times moved in lockstep with Riyadh, often took their own course when they saw the opportunity.[59]

Non-state actors, namely al-Qaeda and IS, also challenged Saudi pretensions to Islamic leadership. Both claimed Wahhabism as a legitimating ideology and could effectively quote the kingdom's own doctrine back to them in their respective claims to be the sole Islamic polity. Every other Muslim state had succumbed to compromise, corruption, and malfeasance. Although neither al-Qaeda nor IS had mass followings, their internal critique cut to the quick of Saudi society and its pretensions as an Islamic paradigm. Saudi Arabia's cooperation in the counterterrorism campaigns often involved policing and repressing its own ideologues. In sum, it is difficult to discern whether Saudi Arabia put its strategic objectives in the service of its creed, or developed a creed to suit its strategic objectives.[60]

Iran's championing of the Shi'i was more secure, but hardly assured. The seminaries of Qom in Iran and Najaf in Iraq had long vied for the status of the pre-eminent source of Shi'i theology and jurisprudence. With the 1979 Islamic Revolution, Iran set out to export its ideology of clerical rule, often through recruiting local partisans. Oil revenues were again enabling factors in Iran's power project. Lebanese Hezbollah and some of the most significant Shi'i political-military factions in Iraq openly subscribed to Iran's theological model. Both Hezbollah and sundry Iraqi militias proved extremely important in the campaigns in Syria and Yemen. Despite these definite theological affinities and close military cooperation, however, Iran could never assert absolute command over either Lebanese or Iraqi non-state actors. These militias, significant as they were, operated in a context of multi-ethnic electoral politics with its own requirements and demands. Hezbollah might have been the strongest single military force in Lebanon, but it had to cooperate with other ethno-sectarian factions to rule. It suffered political setbacks in the domestic arena for appearing to be the cat's paw of Tehran. Similarly, many Iraqi Shi'is (to say nothing of Sunnis and other Iraqis) were wary of Iranian influence in their country. The seminaries of Najaf, led by Grand Ayatollah Ali Sistani, opposed the Iranian vision of theocratic rule and invited electoral competition and a stronger sense of Iraqi national solidary. Iraq's 2018 election, in which the most avowedly pro-Iranian factions in the country were outpaced by a non-sectarian political faction (led by a Shi'i cleric), was further testament to the limits of Tehran's sway.[61] By 2019, protesters in Karbala and elsewhere in the Shi'i regions of Iraq were chanting anti-Iranian slogans and rejecting the role of Iranian-backed militias in domestic politics.[62]

Iran's relationships in Yemen and Syria were even more complicated. Neither the Houthis nor the Alawis subscribed to the main sub-sect of Ja'afari (Twelver) Shi'is predominant in Iran, Iraq, or Lebanon. In fact, until the 1970s, the Alawis were largely regarded as so heterodox that their status as Muslims was questionable. Syria's Alawi rulers had largely fashioned a discourse of Islamic ecumenicism, if not outright secularism. Iran's version of revolutionary clerical rule, therefore, had limited practical appeal or value to the regime in reconsolidating its control.[63] Thus, even as Tehran built strong military ties with the Houthi leadership and with Syrian state officials and associated militias, these relationships were evidence more of tactical affinities than of ideological comportment.

Another crucial difference between the contemporary conflict in MENA and the crucible of early modern Europe was that MENA's struggle took place in a distinctly subordinate global position. There were no Muslim states that could act as a great power, much less a superpower. For the largest actors – the United States, Russia, the European powers, and China – MENA's tragedy was but one of a larger set of global issues. This made it crucial for regional protagonists to enlist outside actors into their campaigns for sectarianism.[64] This was best exemplified in an exchange on the *New York Times* opinions page. Adel bin Ahmed al-Jubeir charged that Iran was incapable of being a normal and responsible state actor. It was theologically and constitutionally obliged to promote its idea of juridical rule and expand its revolutionary reach. Iran's military efforts in Yemen, Syria, Iraq, and the Gulf, then, were part of a larger sectarian strategy of domination. The United States had to block this dangerous power-play.[65] Iran's foreign minister, Mohammed Javad Zarif, responded that Saudi Arabia had propagated "reckless extremism" in the form of Sunni Wahhabi, ideas which inspired and justified al-Qaeda and IS. The United States and Iran, Zarif counseled, could work together to "rid the world of Wahhabism."[66] This, of course, was an oddly theological argument to have in a predominantly Christian country where most people – including senior politicians and lawmakers – couldn't locate the historical differences between Sunnis and Shi'is, much less the finer points of Islamic doctrine. But the point was not theological suasion at all. Rather, Iran and Saudi Arabia realized that their own ability to extend their networks of proxies and allies depended on framing their efforts as concording with the agenda of outside powers.

Ultimately, what made the 2010s in MENA most similar to early modern Europe was not the pantomime of sectarianism, but the sheer pointlessness of the war. Historian C. V. Wedgewood described the Thirty Years' War as the epitome of a "meaningless conflict . . . morally subversive, economically destructive, socially degrading, confused in its causes, devious in its course, futile in its result."[67] The same can be said of MENA's descent into regional warfare in the 2010s. Certainly, individual actors made strategic moves that led to and sustained the conflict. But as the process of fragmentation and integration generated wider and more intricate networks of violence, strategy became less determinative. The war, as in the 1600s, was one that almost no one wanted and that left everyone worse off. Perversely, often those who did the most to expand and intensify violence suffered the least. For all the efforts of Russia, the United States, Iran, Saudi Arabia, the UAE, and other meddlers, it was still Yemenis, Libyans, Iraqis, and Syrians who did most of the fighting. Moreover, it was overwhelmingly Yemeni, Libyan, Iraqi, and Syrian civilians who did the dying.

7

Peace and Peacemaking

Discussions of peace in MENA tend to be either very short or very long. The previous chapters painted a thoroughly bleak picture. War is bad and getting worse in the region. Violence and war inflected the very origins of MENA states. Calculations of regime security and state survival narrowed into a regional security predicament that made violence a recurrent feature in the region. Beyond the nature of states themselves, competitions over identity, oil, and geopolitics could work to trap MENA in more expansive and interminable conflicts. The dual process of state fragmentation and integration of conflict zones into larger regional and global competitions yielded a kind of perfect storm of violence. Still, war has never been the sum and substance of life in the region. War's impact is uneven both temporally and spatially. Even for people living close to the maelstrom, the conflicts can sometimes seem very far away. In this sense, peace is always on the horizon, however distant or obscure.

Studying war and studying peace are theoretically kindred, but practically often segregated. Peace, like war, has many definitions and can take many forms. Peace, like war, is a social endeavor that combines the exercise of power and the invocation of norms that justify and animate it. The ways that peace is defined and pursued reflect assumptions about legitimacy as much as feasibility. Finally, peace, like war, can itself become self-reinforcing, in this case a more virtuous cycle than the kind of conflict traps previously discussed in this book.[1]

First, this chapter discusses the long-standing distinction in the field of peace studies between "negative" and "positive" peace. Yet how to operationalize and use these definitions has proven challenging. Understanding these differences is important for evaluating the progress and possibilities of peace in MENA. Secondly, the chapter examines the institutions, mechanisms, resources, and skills through which conflicts have been resolved and peace has been sustained. This infrastructure of peacebuilding is variegated and complex. It includes major intergovernmental organizations charged with maintaining regional security and stability and humanitarian and human rights organizations. It also involves localized initiatives that manage conflict in individual neighborhoods and villages, a capillary scale far below the ken of the state or most international actors.[2] In different forms and at different levels, MENA has experienced more peace than many assume. Thirdly, the chapter examines the dynamics of peacebuilding in the recurrent Arab–Israeli conflict. Common formulas and instruments have had differing results there, delivering some dimensions of peace but not others. Finally, the chapter examines the infrastructure of peacebuilding that has emerged in response to the catastrophe of the 2010s. While local initiatives have sought to mitigate the effects of war, peacebuilding at the high diplomatic level is often at cross-purposes with them.

Defining Peace and Pursuing It

Many scholars who study the onset, conduct, and consequences of war and conflict are surprisingly silent when it comes to questions of peace. At most, they consider peace as merely the absence or cessation of war. Peace, then, is what happens in the intervals between wars. This is appealing arithmetically, if nothing else. If peace is simply a condition of "not war," we can easily identity the location and duration of peace. Consider Figure 1.3 in the first chapter of the book. Dark shading indicates a year of war for a MENA country. But most of the field is white – suggesting that war remains the exception, not the rule, in the region. The issue of body count looms large in this conceptualization of peace. If fatalities dip below a given number, war is effectively over. Alternatively, peace treaties, disarmaments, and other types of diplomatic and legal exchanges can mark the end of war and the beginning of peace.

Such a sparse definition of peace, though, does not accord with the lofty ideals of peace as many understand it. "They shall beat their swords into plowshares," propounds the biblical prophet Isaiah, "and their spears into pruning hooks, and nation shall not lift up sword against nation, neither shall they learn war anymore" (Isaiah 2:3–4). These words are now famously inscribed at United Nations Park in New York as a reminder of an august agenda for peace. In a similar vein, a number of modern scholars conceptualize peace not just as the cessation of war and violence but also as a condition in which war and violence are inconceivable, unthinkable – in effect, unlearned. Peace is not just the absence of war. Rather, it entails a disposition toward benevolence, confidence, and justice instead of violence, fear, and subjugation.[3]

Peace studies scholarship has often distinguished between "negative" and "positive" forms of peace, as discussed above.[4] Negative peace involves reducing or stopping direct physical violence – the lowest common denominator for what any concept of peace must entail.[5] This still leaves room for a grave range of harms. Negative peace, the absence of direct violence, does not preclude authoritarian oppression. It permits structural violence, the institutionalization of political, social, and economic structures that marginalize and exclude. Structural violence is diffuse but still dire. It involves a wide range of emotional, economic, and physical harm to a wide swath of the population. An example of negative peace combined with structural violence comes from the United States during the era of Jim Crow. After the end of the American Civil War in 1865, the United States had achieved negative peace in its internal politics. Nevertheless, systematic and structural racism continued to deny millions of African-Americans access to adequate healthcare, housing, and employment, much less a political voice. Separate was certainly unequal. Occasional spasms and outbursts of direct physical violence often reinforced structures of economic and social repression. Under American segregation, lynching, riots, and other forms of one-sided violence often occurred with the collusion or instigation of state authority. Overall, this system continued to diminish the life chances of a significant part of the population. At the same time, for white Americans the structural violence and its impact remained mostly imperceptible. The racial violence was justified as legitimate and proper. Moreover, the lack of overt violent resistance suggested acquiescence. Inequality seemed the natural order of things – until it wasn't. In reality, most African-Americans (and many others) would have preferred another arrangement. However, the overwhelming coercive threat posed by the state deterred most from pursuing such a change.

Oliver Richmond, a specialist on peace and conflict theory, equates negative peace with what he calls the "victor's peace." As such, it is "inherently limited, based upon military control and occupation, on colonialism and imperialism. At best it leads to a basic form of order created through domination, or alliances and balance of power whereby states and leaders perceive war as too costly to win because of their opponent's strength."[6] Others similarly describe a version of "tyrannical" peace to explain how authoritarian domination can perpetuate structural violence but still keep people alive.[7] This is perhaps a bit uncharitable to negative peace, but still suggestive of the moral quandaries involved in distinguishing war from other kinds of less intensive forms of harm.

The contrast to positive peace, in its idealized form, is stark. Positive peace requires much deeper-seated societal transformations that curb structural violence and progress equity, harmony, reconciliation, and conflict resolution. Richmond describes how positive peace and the attendant concept of human security involve resolution of conflicts through mutual and consensual processes.

> This [positive] peace is acceptable in everyday terms to ordinary people, not only to political and economic elites according to their interests. [Peace] transcends basic security concerns over power, territory, and material resources. ... Under such conditions social justice – human rights, democratic representation, relative material equality, and prosperity – the accountability of states and elites, as well as peace between states may be achieved.[8]

Peacebuilding takes these various notions of peace and places them temporally and analytically beside war. The quality of peace naturally depends on the form of incompatibility that leads to war and conflict. This allows us to consider more fully empirical variation in the practice and norms that uphold non-violence.[9] For example, international relations experts James Klein, Gary Goertz, and Paul Diehl offer a scalar approach to measuring peace between states. At one extreme is rivalry. Two states are rivals if they actively engage in or plan for war against one another. Militarized disputes are frequent, conflicts are unresolved, and diplomacy is often overtly hostile. Even if fighting is not underway, its possibility looms. At the other extreme, positive peace entails common involvement in a pluralistic security community of mutual defense. Not only is there no conflict, but there are no preparations or plans for war. There are extensive institutionalized diplomatic, economic, and even cultural exchanges that create conditions of interdependence. Negative peace rests between the poles of active rivalry and positive peace. Here war is thought about but rarely enacted. There are limited and isolated militarized disputes, skirmishes, and low-level conflicts. Some key areas of contention and disputed issues are beginning to be resolved. Diplomatic engagement may or may not be active in negative peace.[10]

Christian Davenport, Erik Melander, and Peter Regan, another group of political scientists, take a similar approach in their studies of domestic peace (i.e., peace within states). Negative peace is the lack of outright and direct physical violence against inhabitants. Such negative peace can often be accomplished through repression. A strong, violence-monopolizing state can marshal enough force to deter any potential challengers and impose its control. Such arrangements necessarily involve forms of structural violence. The fuller and higher-quality forms of positive peace, in contrast, require a sense of political mutuality. This ameliorates both direct and structural violence among citizens and between rulers and the ruled. High-quality peace involves political conduct that respects human rights, uses consensual decision-making, and provides for equality of values.[11] This is far more than just the cessation of direct physical violence. It further requires modes of democratic political participation and broader cultural changes amenable to equitable inclusion of women, minorities, and other historically marginalized groups.

One practical predicament for peacebuilding is whether to prioritize negative or positive peace. Much of what could be considered the high diplomacy of peacebuilding aims for obtaining negative peace. According to realist geopolitical thinking, the best assurance of peace between states is when there is a single hegemon able to enforce domination – the true victor's peace. In lieu of such hegemony, international alliances, arms control treaties, and other measures seek to maintain a balance of power whereby each side so intimidates the other that they avoid war – but only by a hair's breadth.

War preparation is constant, but war itself is too risky to undertake. Similar dynamics occur in the context of internal strife and civil war. Outright victory, especially by rebels, has proven to yield the most durable periods of peace precisely because the victorious party has demonstrably defeated its opponent and established a credible deterrent against any potential challengers. Similarly, the arrival of international peacekeepers, essentially a third-party enforcer, also increases the chances of peace. Post-conflict efforts to promote disarmament, demobilization, and reintegration and security sector reform also aim to increase the state's capacity to defeat any internal challenger.[12]

Yet there are also important efforts for thorough-going transformation aimed at positive peace. The European Union, for example, built elaborate networks of economic and cultural exchange between member states, some of whom had been avowed enemies as recently as 1945. The explicit goal of these measures was to promote integration such that another European war became impossible to conduct, even inconceivable.[13] Within the context of civilian control, initiatives for transitional justice, truth commissions, lustrations, and grassroots civil society efforts relate to wider goals of transformation, rather than just mitigation. Democratic elections following civil wars are similarly vital for legitimating post-war order through popular participation and mutuality.[14]

But is negative peace even compatible with the pursuit of positive peace? Consider the long-running discussion about conducting war crimes trials over the Balkans war. On the one hand, many self-described pragmatists argued that such trials would only incite violence, destabilize the balance of power, and lead to a recurrence of fighting. Transitional justice should be postponed or even cancelled. On the other hand, delaying justice and allowing perpetrators of mass rape and murder to walk free only leaves the victims of violence more vulnerable. This exacerbates popular alienation and distrust, which can make the entire political system more vulnerable to breakdown. Without justice, peace is just a veil for continued insecurity.[15]

Nowhere is this friction more evident than in the relationship between democracy and peace. Democracy promotion initiatives are often touted as complements or adjutants to conflict resolution and peacemaking. Many practitioners cite theories of democratic peace to explain why. Democratic states seldom make war against one another. Democracies tend to feel commonality with one another that makes it difficult to construe the other as an enemy. Moreover, democratic decision-making often constrains a leader's tendency to pursue war.[16] Stable democracies tend to deploy less domestic repression and are less vulnerable to civil wars.[17] But the path toward such stable democracy is often fraught. Democracies might be more pacific toward each other but often remain belligerent toward non-democracies. Moreover, moments of political opening are often chaotic. In their efforts to win electoral contests, leaders might have an incentive to foment violence, either against another state or against their own population. This undermines whatever negative domestic peace had tentatively obtained under more stable authoritarian rule.[18] Ultimately, democracy and peace may be less complementary than contradictory.

The Evolution of MENA's Peace Infrastructure

What has passed for peace in MENA has consisted almost entirely of the negative kind. Much of the internal stability within MENA states derives from authoritarianism. Repression, sometimes overt and sometimes more subtle, shuts down the opportunity for armed rebellion. The region is rife with structural violence. Communities and individuals are systematically excluded or underserved by the state. Moreover, as discussed earlier, the provision of oil revenues, the manipulation of identity, and the intervention of geopolitics often strengthen the hand of the autocracies. Seeming political openings, such as witnessed in Lebanon and more recently in Iraq, yielded more turmoil and ultimately civil war. Alternatively, these experiments in electoral politics degenerated into elite bargains that were only slightly more inclusive than traditions of one-man rule.[19]

Whether the allegedly pacifying influences of strongmen translate from the domestic to the international arena in MENA is unclear. Before the invasion of Iraq in 2003, there was some discussion that a turn toward democratic regimes might facilitate regional conflict resolution. MENA might became a zone of democratic peace. But the United States' cynical adoption of democracy promotion seemed to discredit this idea.[20] Dictators face a similar array of internal pressures that might constrain or enable their pursuit of war against neighbors.[21] Fear of internal insurrections and coups can goad leaders into aggressive stances. Many of the region's most prominent strongmen, from Nasser in Egypt in the 1950s and 1960s, to Saddam in Iraq in the 1980s and 1990s, to Crown Prince Mohammed bin Salman in Saudi Arabia in the 2010s, gained their notoriety through embroilment in foreign wars. Insofar as their proclivities for foreign aggression stem from domestic security concerns, war isn't so much averted as shifted from one arena to another.

But there have been long periods of non-war and even comity. Oncetroublesome border disputes, especially in the Arabian Peninsula, have been resolved amicably.[22] A most recent example is the December 2019 Saudi–Kuwait agreement on disputed oil fields along their shared borders.[23] Yet conflict and violence still occur too often to describe the Arab sphere as approaching positive peace. Beside the Iraq–Kuwait war of 1990, there have been violent border clashes between Algeria and Morocco, and Libya and Chad, to name a few examples. Historical rivalries between Egypt and Saudi Arabia, Iraq and Egypt, and other dyads have led to militarized disputes, if not outright war, in the last fifty years. Countries are on a carousel from enmity to alliance. The confrontation between Saudi Arabia and Qatar since 2011 further undercuts any hopes that positive peace might prevail. Moreover, relationships with non-Arab states, particularly Israel and Iran, are even less peaceful and are prone to violence.

It seems paradoxical or perverse to think about the peacebuilding infrastructure in MENA given the feebleness of the actual results. But it is exactly the seeming paucity of peace in MENA that deserves special attention. Just as MENA has set trends and served as a laboratory for different modes of conflictual engagement, it has also been precocious and replete with peace-making initiatives. A range of actors have effected peace in the region, from global and regional intergovernmental organs like the UN and Arab League, to humanitarian NGOs that operate in warzones, to more organic organizations that arise in response to violence

At the top echelons of high diplomacy, MENA's peace infrastructure – just like its wars – is heavily influenced and penetrated by outside powers. Middle East peace involves a virtually endless parade of mostly failed trial balloons, diplomatic missions, working plans, and summits. Equally important as how these efforts ended is where they began. Indicatively, most took the names of the locales in which they were held: Geneva, Stockholm, Madrid, Oslo, and Camp David – all located outside the region. Beyond such impressionistic evidence, though, a clearer sense of the extraverted peacebuilding in MENA comes from examining the record of peace operations conducted in the region, as shown in Table 7.1. Peace operations are military expeditions that assist in preventing armed conflict, observe or assist ceasefire implementation, or enforce the terms of ceasefires and peace agreements. How and when peace operations are initiated and by whom are windows into the way peacebuilding proceeds at the upper diplomatic levels.

MENA has been a global pacesetter in peace operations. The very first UN-approved peacekeeping mission came in 1948 with the UN Truce Supervision Organization (UNTSO). Numbering only a few hundred, UNTSO played a minimal role in curbing the fighting itself, but its presence did help maintain the ceasefire and border disengagement between Israel, Egypt, Syria, and Jordan and established a pattern of extra-regional engagement in MENA's peacemaking initiatives. After UNTSO came the UN Emergency Force (UNEF), deployed in the wake of the 1956 Sinai war. Another contingent of UN forces came to Egypt and Syria following the 1973 war and another multinational force monitored the Egypt–Israel peace treaty from Sinai in the 1980s. Peace operations worked best when third-party forces stood between two belligerent states. These forces, therefore, did not have to overawe anyone to act as a deterrent. In fact, UN forces were almost always exposed and at the mercy of larger national armies. The first UN Emergency Force simply got up and left its monitoring post at Nasser's request in 1967. This is often cited as a

Table 7.1 International peace operations in MENA, 1948–2019

Mission	Location	Dates	Deployed size (est. max. uniformed)
UN Truce Supervision Organization (UNTSO)	Israel, Egypt, Lebanon, Syria	1948–	570
UN Emergency Force (UNEF I)	Israel, Egypt	1956–67	6,073
UN Observation Group in Lebanon (UNOGIL)	Lebanon	1958	591
Arab League Force	Kuwait	1961–3	5,000
UN Yemen Observation Mission (UNYOM)	Yemen	1963–4	190
Arab League Military Observers	Yemen	1967	Unclear
Arab Ceasefire Observer Mission	Jordan	1970–1	Unclear
Arab League Observers	Yemen	1972	Unclear
UN Emergency Force II (UNEF II)	Israel, Egypt	1973–9	6,973
UN Disengagement Observation Force (UNDOF)	Israel, Syria	1974–	1,100
Arab League Arab Security Forces (SASF)	Lebanon	1976	2,500
UN Interim Force in Lebanon (UNIFIL)	Lebanon	1978–	12,700
Multinational Force & Observers (MFO)	Egypt (Sinai)	1982–	2,600
Multinational Force in Lebanon (MNF)	Lebanon	1982	2,285
Multinational Force Lebanon II (MNF II)	Lebanon	1982–4	4,800
UN Iran–Iraq Military Observer Group (UNIIMOG)	Iran, Iraq	1988–91	400
UN Mission for the Referendum in Western Sahara (MINURSO)	Western Sahara	1991–	237
Organization of African Unity (OAU) Mission to Western Sahara	Western Sahara	1991–2002	Unclear
UN Iraq–Kuwait Observation Mission (UNIKOM-a)	Kuwait, Iraq	1991–3	320
UN Iraq–Kuwait Observation Mission (UNIKOM-b)	Kuwait, Iraq	1993–2003	1,174
Joint Monitoring Contingent	Yemen	1994	Unclear
Joint Military Commission & International Monitoring Unit	Sudan	2002–05	24
OAU Mission to Sudan	Sudan	2004–7	7,700
UN Mission in Sudan (UNMIS)	Sudan	2005–11	10,519
EU Support to OAU Mission in Sudan 2	Sudan	2005–7	50
UN Interim Security Force for Abyei (UNISFA)	Sudan	2011–	4,250
Arab League Observer Mission	Syria	2011–12	30

Source: Paul D. Williams with Alex J. Bellamy, *Understanding Peacekeeping*, third edition (Cambridge: Polity, 2021), Appendix.

trigger in the escalation to the June 1967 war. But the positioning of outside troops set a symbolic precedent. They are held safe by international norms. Molesting these forces would constitute an attack on the global community writ large, something few regional actors would risk. The semi-effective model that worked in Sinai and Syria was transported to the Iran–Iraq border in 1988 and then the Iraq–Kuwait border in 1991.[24]

Responding to civil wars posed a much greater challenge. The UN sent an observation mission, backed by American warships, to arrest Lebanon's brief 1958 civil war. Its observation mission to Yemen's far bloodier war of 1963–4 was inconsequential. Lebanon's civil war of the 1970s occasioned a slew of peacebuilding initiatives. The Arab League's security force failed. The UN Interim Force in Lebanon (UNFIL) came in 1978, followed by a US-led multinational force (MNF) in the 1980s. Unlike in international wars, it is far more difficult in internal disputes to monitor lines of control and contain belligerents spatially. Here, expeditionary forces played a delicate role. They were, on the one hand, a constabulary force meant to keep the peace between opposing factions. On the other hand, they were also a training and advising mission, tasked to impart new skills and capacities to the central government so that it could conduct coercion on its own. These ostensibly neutral missions inevitably got caught up in the political crossfire. In 1982, Hezbollah fighters bombed the MNF barracks in Beirut, killing 242 American and 58 French soldiers. While the Americans withdrew, the UNFIL mission itself grew progressively more robust, including the involvement of French and NATO troops. The goal of peace operations mostly went no further than maintaining the barest negative peace. So long as bullets are not flying, peace operations are a success.

The prominence of the UN and other extra-regional powers in MENA's peacekeeping is both cause and effect of the relative paucity of efforts originating from within the region itself. Peace was not the Arab League's priority. Its 1945 charter makes only two references to peace, both suggesting the need to defer to larger intergovernmental organizations like the UN. The Arab League's mission served only its member states, which necessarily meant that it discounted several of the predominant military powers in MENA, notably Israel and Iran. UNFIL stepped in after the Arab League Security Forces failed in Lebanon, although with scarcely better results. An area where the Arab League could have had a significant impact on peace was to prevent aggression among member states. Indeed, in the 1960s, the Arab League enjoyed modest success in positioning forces to protect Kuwait from the blustering Iraqi strongman Abd al-Karim Abd al-Qassim. But when Saddam invaded and annexed Kuwait in 1990, the organization offered only rhetorical disapproval. It required a UN action authorizing the United States to take action to restore Kuwaiti sovereignty.[25]

There were attempts to muster an Arab League response during the crisis of 2011. Qatar, fortuitously holding the rotating chair of the organization when the crisis began, argued that if Arab states did not take actions to end the wars, outside actors would once again intrude on the region. Qatar's approach suggested an effort to bolster the Arab League in a way comparable to the energetic efforts of the African Union to take on regional peacekeeping duties and avoid meddling from the UN or outside powers. In the previous decade, the AU had sent peace missions to Sudan, Western Sahara, Nigeria, Somalia, and elsewhere.[26] The Arab League's initiatives on Libya seemed off to a good start. By endorsing the no-fly zone and humanitarian protection areas, it could at least claim some role in what became the larger NATO intervention. By the time it came to Syria, though, the League was flummoxed. Its efforts to mediate the conflict went nowhere. Damascus agreed to the League's peace plan in late 2011, only to undermine and obstruct its meager peace observer mission.[27] The mission lasted only a few months. MENA states collectively threw their collective challenges back into the global forum. Peace, just like war, depended on outside actors.

The 2015 Iran nuclear deal, known as the Joint Comprehensive Plan of Action (JCPOA), similarly demonstrates how deeply extra-regional actors were involved in regional peacebuilding. Formally, the JCPOA covered a narrow set of issues. In return for allowing UN inspectors and limits on its nuclear enrichment program, Iran benefited from an easing of international sanctions. In another sense, though, the JCPOA must be viewed as part of a larger US effort to find common ground with Iran in Syria and Iraq. Some Iranian negotiators saw the deal as "a window that would open to Sana'a, Beirut, Damascus, and Baghdad."[28] Apart from Iran, however, every other signature from the so-called P5+1 group (i.e., the United States, Britain, France, Germany, Russia, and China) came from outside the region. Excluded from the negotiations were Saudi Arabia and Israel, the two countries most directly threatened by Iran's military power. Both considered the JCPOA a betrayal from the United States and spent the next three years trying to block further rapprochement between Washington and Tehran. The United States under President Trump formally withdrew from the agreement and unilaterally imposed stronger sanctions on Iran in 2018. Again, a contemporary comparison is telling of how involved outside actors are in MENA's peacemaking. In the multi-party talks over North Korea's nuclear program, virtually concomitant with those in Iran, every participating country (save the United States) was a regional neighbor.

One notable and somewhat exceptional case of high-level peacebuilding from within the region is the Taif Accord, which ended the Lebanese civil war in 1989. Taif further demonstrates how negative peace became the default mode of conflict resolution. At least superficially, Taif rehashed the formula used to end the violence of 1958, declaring that there was to be "no victor, no vanquished." Lebanon was to have new elections following the same procedures of a confessional pact. In practice, though, Lebanon's sovereignty was hollowed out. The agreement effectively acceded to Syrian hegemony, with Damascus making sure that no party could destabilize the system again. Israeli troops, meanwhile, still occupied a security zone in the far south, working with Maronite proxy militias. Corruption and organized crime, which had grown more rampant during the war, became further embedded in the fabric of societal and state institutions.[29] This bargain for negative peace was worth the trade-off for war-weary people. Certainly it was worthwhile for Lebanon's neighbors. But decades later, processes of reconciliation remain stalled. Lebanon remains in a kind of purgatory, with conflicts erupting swiftly and the danger of the "war to come" constantly looming.[30]

Moving below the high politics of diplomatic engagement and peace expeditions, the peacebuilding infrastructure in MENA gets denser and more variegated. Humanitarianism is often treated as apart from peacebuilding. Humanitarian agencies are involved in aiding victims of war, not stopping war. But as notions of peace tilt toward more positive versions, humanitarian provision becomes a way of mitigating and resisting war and carving out zones of peaceful interaction.[31] Thus, relief agencies like the UN refugee agencies, the International Committee of the Red Cross (ICRC), Doctors without Borders (MSF), Islamic Relief USA, and a myriad of government and non-governmental groups, international and domestic, faith-based and secular, must be counted in the peacebuilding infrastructure. So, too, must global human rights groups which seek to prevent abuses through naming-and-shaming policies, such as Amnesty International and Human Rights Watch, and locally based ones like Btselem in Israel or the Lebanese Center for Human Rights.[32]

These types of humanitarian and human rights peacebuilding organizations operate in a complex environment, caught between the demands of armed groups (including states), international sponsors and funders, and the civilians whom they are supposed to preserve and protect. They have their own internal dynamics, opaque bureaucracies that can at times impugn their organizational mission. UN agencies tend to defer to state claims on sovereignty and operate only when and how states let them. The ICRC's traditional code of neutrality allows it to win the trust of combatants and to attend to casualties from all parties. But this also means that ICRC operations are at times coopted into the agendas of different conflicting parties. Faith-based organizations have their own codes of conduct and priorities. The more swashbuckling and outspoken MSF has insisted on naming abuses and sought to operate in areas of greatest need. This, however, has at times put its own operators in harm's way and limited its actual ability to provide aid.[33]

Many of the key ideas and institutions of global humanitarianism were born or at least matured in MENA. The mass killings and refugee outflows that occurred in the Ottoman empire during World War I, the arrival of Jewish refugees to Palestine after World War II, and the fresh waves of Palestinian refugees after the 1948–9 war were critical junctures in the development of global humanitarian and human rights institutions.[34] These peacebuilding institutions thus form odd siblings of the region's institutions of violence.

The shortcomings of these humanitarian and human rights organizations are easy to spot. Navigating such a complicated political landscape leads inevitably to compromises, double standards, and even scandals. For example, while Iraqis faced severe food and medicine shortages in the 1990s, a group of UN administrators, Iraqi government officials, and oil company executives colluded to skim from the humanitarian funds.[35] But more damning than malfeasance is a sense of futility. The provision of humanitarian aid or voicing a human rights critique, even in the best of circumstances, cannot compensate for such massive damage. Mere humanitarian response never seems morally commensurate with the scale of suffering that wars produce.[36] But this is not a reason to discount organizations that at least make war more survivable.

Peacebuilding also occurs at an even smaller, local scale. Although always limited, civilians have agency to take measures that protect not just their physical persons, but also their social connectivity in the midst of war. Civilians can "nudge" armed actors to respect human rights through moral arguments and discourse that reframe violence as something that is shameful or an anathema, rather than necessary or even laudable.[37] These kinds of initiatives are often too small and idiosyncratic to gain much attention.

Nonetheless, it is exactly at the capillary level where peace has been most resilient and persistent in MENA. Palestinian political discourse has long stressed the need for steadfastness (*sumud*) in the face of the physical and structural violence of the occupation. *Sumud* inspired the non-violent tactics of the Palestinian uprising in the 1980s. Even after the collapse of the uprising, the concept offered a vision of social resilience and peace that refused to accommodate repression. *Sumud* often had a specifically gendered connotation. It was associated with the perseverance of women in the face of a political circumstance that made normal living impossible.[38] A similar notion appeared during the Lebanese civil war of 1975–90, as well. "We carried on," writes Mona Takieddine Amyuni about her life in Beirut.

> We looked after our families and went to work. Schools, universities, hospitals, banks and offices continued to function, which seemed incredible to many of our foreign friends. In fact, life went on in the midst of a very violent war, where combat took place in the inhabited streets of Beirut in quite an uncommon style. Daily life was organized by quarters and sectors of cities, by villages and larger areas of the country, and depended totally on citizens themselves since most of our governmental institutions were paralyzed.[39]

As in Palestine, women were especially prominent in these localized efforts. As Amyuni put it:

Women were largely responsible for the support system ... sustained family, society, and the mental health of the Lebanese as a whole. Women queued for gas, water, and bread, for they felt safer moving around when their men were kidnapped. Women recreated a semblance of a home when a quarter of the population of the country was displaced within its own homeland ... [this] was our silent protest against the war and its atrocities. The silent majority of my country, men and women, resisted the fanaticism and the hatred. Suddenly, in this mute resistance, men and women walked, side by side, worked, and helped each other.[40]

In rural Lebanon, many local conflict resolution and peacebuilding measures blended civil and tribal law and were overseen by sheikhs and other older authorities.[41]

Still, the same challenges, limitations, and ambiguities that affect large humanitarian and human rights organizations inhere in more localized peacebuilding initiatives. Peacebuilding can be captured by or dependent on international or governmental patrons. This renders them more a source of rents than a means of reconciliation or protection. In times of open war, there may be a thin line dividing a local peace committee and a militia. Both, after all, emerge from the same hyper-localized milieu, respond to the same challenges of communal and personal insecurity, and involve the same kinds of mobilization and collective action. While civilians might espouse ideals of positive peace, their survival ultimately rests on the beneficence of warlords or even the distant state. Thus, civilian mobilization in peacebuilding is vulnerable to being coopted or even dominated, degrading the possibilities of positive peace into a less satisfying peace of the victor. Yet even in this attenuated form, the experience of locally initiated peace in the midst of wartime has longer-term effects on post-conflict reconstruction and reconciliation. Wars, as political scientist Reyko Huang notes, can "dislodge the old order at the top while galvanizing political action in the grassroots."[42] Civilians may thus acquire greater voice and organizational capacity to demand rights that have been denied them.

Arab–Israeli Conflicts and the Question of Peace

The Arab–Israeli conflicts, the focus of such great regional peacebuilding energies, bear special mention. Just as warfare between Israel and its neighbors established the pace and pattern for future conflicts in the region more broadly, so too did peacemaking efforts. As mentioned above, some of the key elements of regional peacebuilding infrastructure, such as the UN Relief and Works Agency and the American Friends Service Committee, effectively began in response to the 1947–9 war. Likewise, most of the cavalcade of failed peace plans for MENA dealt with Israel and its neighbors. There are competing and partially contradictory narratives about the Arab–Israel conflict – who started it, who perpetuated it, and why it has not (yet) been resolved. It is tempting to point fingers at bad actors and bad faith for missing opportunities for peace. This is not the place to offer a lengthy historical summary of the conflict's evolution or to adjudicate blame for its continuation. Rather, the goal here is to examine the effect, for good and ill, of the MENA peacebuilding infrastructure in ending these wars.[43]

Nearly every initiative for Arab–Israel peace involves the same basic formula: Israel offers to withdraw from conquered territories; the United States offers both parties economic subventions, military aid, and political support aimed to sweeten the deal and offset perceived risks. This formula has had two major successes. The first was the Egyptian–Israeli peace treaties of 1978, often referred to as the Camp David Accords because initial drafting took place at the American presidential retreat. The agreements stipulated Israeli withdrawal from the Sinai Peninsula, which Israel had held since 1967. In return, Egypt offered Israel full diplomatic recognition, the first Arab country to do so. Ancillary parts of the agreements assured Israel access to Sinai's oil and gas reserves. The signing of the agreements also cemented Cairo's realignment with Washington. Egypt received massive amounts of American military and economic aid, at one point becoming the second largest recipient in the world. The Egyptian–Israeli peace was no small achievement. It represented a negotiated agreement that ended an interstate rivalry responsible for five wars in less than three decades. Israeli Prime Minister Menachem Begin and Egyptian President Anwar Sadat shared the Nobel Peace Prize in 1978. The Jordanian–Israeli peace in 1994, again signed in Washington, was less groundbreaking. There were fewer territorial issues at stake. Jordan had renounced claims to the West Bank in favor of Palestinians. The last war between Jordan and Israel had been three decades earlier. Moreover, the peace treaty came in the wake of the far more significant agreement between Israel and the Palestinians.[44]

Both sets of accords yielded an unequivocally negative or "cold peace." Jordan, Egypt, and Israel have more intensive, although often covert, security cooperation, mostly geared toward suppressing domestic opposition. Israel relies on Jordan and Egypt for assistance in suppressing Palestinian radicalism. Egypt and Jordan work with Israel to counter the Muslim Brotherhood, whom they mutually regard as an enemy, plus any number of other elements. The peace is unpopular among Egyptians and Jordanians, who generally regard the treaties as a betrayal of the Palestinian cause. Cultural or interpersonal exchange, including tourism and trade, are rare, despite efforts from the United States, Europe, and private philanthropies to encourage Arab–Israeli contacts. Still, even in its rather unsatisfactory quality, negative peace between Israel and Egypt and Israel and Jordan seems better that the recurrent militarized disputes that occur along Israel's border with Lebanon and Syria.

The mixed success of the Israel–Egypt and Israel–Jordan negotiations poses an obvious contrast with the failure of the land-for-peace formula seen in the case of the Palestinian–Israel track. The Oslo Accords, signed in Washington in 1993 after extensive back-channel negotiations hosted in Norway, followed the same basic logic as the Egypt plan. There were proposed territorial exchanges. There was a new set of Nobel Peace Prizes for Israeli Prime Minister Yitzhak Rabin, Foreign Minister Shimon Peres, and Palestine Liberation Organization (PLO) Chairman Yasser Arafat. There was a flood of foreign aid. No conflict saw more intensive investments in people-to-people exchanges and civil society dialogs, all intended to assure the transformation into a fuller, more positive peace.

Peace between Israel and Palestine differed from any other venue because it required not just the division of territory but also building an entirely new state. The process of turning the Palestinian Authority (PA), which Arafat's PLO dominated, into a fully functional state was inextricable from the process of negotiating peace with Israel, and vice versa. Israeli interlocutors regarded Palestinian statehood as an end point or destination, a kind of culmination and finalization of land exchange and confidence-building measures. For the Palestinian leadership, however, it became clear that they could not proceed with the peace process without a functional state already in place that could assert physical control over territories and garner some kind of popular legitimacy.[45]

Territorial issues were the key sticking point. Israelis and Palestinians lived cheek by jowl in a relationship of inequality but also interdependence. Such economic, political, and even physical proximity made demarcation of territorial control and authorities more difficult than in other cases. The working assumption throughout the Oslo process was that Israel would relinquish territories occupied during the 1967 war, as specified in UN Security Council Resolution 242 of 1967. The PA would presumptively assume a wider span of control over governance and security and eventually proceed to full sovereignty. The Oslo agreements also specified differentiated zones of control, creating a brindled map designating areas of PA, Israeli, and mixed authority. The seldom-read but vital annexes of the Oslo agreements laid out plans for a thorough-going conflict transformation through cooperation on water, electricity, energy, finance, transportation and communication, trade and commerce, labor, social welfare, and the environment. It was, in essence, a microcosm of the kind of transformation underway within Europe. But as interim agreements dragged into interminable delays, the idea of some new-fangled hybridized sovereignty seemed fanciful.[46]

Beside the perceived intransigence of the other side, political leaders who favored continued negotiations faced outbidding from their own camps.[47] Even members of the dovish Israeli Labor governments were reluctant to relinquish settlement blocs in and near Jerusalem. Israel's ascendant and increasingly violent right wing maintained that there could be no sacrifice of sacred Jewish soil and sought to make any transfer of territory impossible. They pushed to expand settlements deeper into Arab territory. Israel's electoral democracy turned factionalized and violent, most graphically illustrated when a Jewish extremist associated with a pro-settlement group assassinated Rabin in 1995. Jewish militias, some with backing from right-wing factions in the government, launched campaigns of intimidation of Arabs as well, including vigilante attacks and land seizures.[48]

For their part, Palestinians had their own reasons to be dissatisfied with territorial arrangements. The continuation of settlements imperiled the viability of any future Palestinian state, denying it territorial contiguity and preventing the possibility of making Jerusalem its capital city. Many Palestinians themselves refused to accept the 1967 border as a maximal limit for their claims. Palestinians' insistence on the right of refugees and their descendants to return to and resettle inside Israel caused further obstruction, as Israel saw this as a means to shift the demographic balance and endanger Israel's Jewish majority status.

Moreover, Hamas (the Islamic Resistance Movement), an outgrowth of the Palestinian Muslim Brotherhood, insisted in its charter of 1988 that the entirety of Palestine through its 1948 borders was consecrated and inalienable (*waqf*). With backing from Iran, Hamas and other smaller rejectionist factions launched attacks on Israeli civilians aimed at provoking a militarized Israeli response and challenging the PA.[49] The PA fell back in disarray. It alternatively tried to partner with Israel to root out militants or to coopt the militants to maintain pressure on Israel. Palestinian governance became increasingly a shambles: undemocratic, exclusive, and reliant on a small cadre of exiles. Many Palestinians, especially the younger generation and those attracted to the Islamist parties, saw the PA as an Israeli stooge.[50] Ultimately, none of the key actors were willing to run the risks or incur the costs that peace required.

By the turn of the twenty-first century, amid worsening violence, it seemed that Palestinians and Israelis disagreed fundamentally about what peace even meant, much less how to attain it. Israeli public opinion and policy approaches focused increasingly on a negative version of peace as in the absence of violence. Given Israel's dominance in the use of force, negotiations seemed irrelevant to achieve this end. Rather, such solutions could be imposed unilaterally.[51] In some cases, this involved tactical withdrawal, such as the evacuation of Jewish settlement blocks from Gaza in 2005. Mostly, though, it entailed new and more intensive uses of surveillance and coercion. This strategy also redoubled the violence inherent in the Israeli occupation. Palestinian lives were subject to arbitrary forms of Israeli control. The ultimate emblem of this was the erection of security barriers enveloping the West Bank and Gaza. The barriers – part concrete wall, part electronically monitored fence – acted as a forward position point for Israel's system of surveillance and control. Drone strikes and targeted assassination could disrupt most militant activities. When necessary, larger-scale incursions, such as in Gaza in 2008–9 and again in 2014, could suppress the more obstreperous actors.[52]

For the many Israelis who measured peace by negative metrics, these efforts have been resoundingly successful. The sight of guards checking bags at cafés or on buses in Tel Aviv, common in the late 1990s and early 2000s, is a thing of the past. According to official Israeli statistics, terrorism deaths fell from a high of over 400 in 2002 to just six by 2013 (these figures count active duty police and soldiers). Of course, there were periodic military incursions. Thirteen Israeli soldiers died during the invasion of Gaza in 2008–9 and 67 during the 2014 Gaza war, but these were largely considered unavoidable.[53]

As with any such victor's peace, the cost of violence in the Palestinian–Israeli conflict was borne unevenly. Palestinian deaths and casualties always outnumbered those of Israelis. Over 1,000 Palestinians died in the 2008–9 war and over 2,000 in 2014, including hundreds of civilians. Gaza remains an open-air prison, its perimeter jointly patrolled by Israel and Egypt. The West Bank barrier maximized connectivity between Israeli settlements and Israel proper while encircling Palestinian villages and towns in a labyrinth of military checkpoints and barriers. Any Palestinians appearing to pose a security threat can be arrested or killed. Such conditions impinge upon even the most basic economic and social life, let alone the far-reaching goals of political independence and sovereignty associated with positive peace. As historian Salim Tamari put it, "The conditions of creating normalcy for the Israeli public, through a regime of segregation and insularity, was predicated on making life abnormal for Palestinians through a system of separation, confinement, and control."[54] Palestinian violence seemed intent mainly on denying Israelis the sense of normal security and peace that they had gone so far to impose. Scattershot sniper, mortar, and rocket attacks, suicide bombings, vehicular homicides, and improvised incendiaries, mostly against civilians, were dangerous and destructive. But they accomplished nothing to roll back the Israeli occupation. They reminded Israel and the world, rather, that even the most meager negative peace is still not assured.

The Arab–Israeli conflict illustrates the capabilities and limitations of MENA's peace infrastructure. The record of intensive war followed by flailing peacebuilding is hardly encouraging. For a long time, one of MENA's strategic truisms held that the Arab–Israeli conflict served as a kind of lodestone toward which other regional actors oriented themselves. The path to Israeli–Arab peace therefore intersected with other regional conflicts.[55] The fate of the Palestinians remains a considerable concern for the Arab general public. A recent poll conducted by the Arab Center for Research and Policy Studies in Doha found that 77 percent of respondents considered the Palestinian issue to be a cause for all Arabs, not just Palestinians.[56] Politically, though, the substance of these linkages must be asserted and constructed, not just assumed. Arab states have gradually but steadily lost interest in the fate of the Palestinians and focus instead on their own narrow interests within the regional system.[57] Egypt insisted that clauses for Palestinian autonomy be included in its treaty with Israel but did little to push for their actual implementation. As it was, the Arab League expelled Egypt in punishment for its pursuit of a separate peace at the Palestinians' expense. Many other regional actors have claimed that their struggle is waged, indirectly, on behalf of the Palestinians and against the Israelis. Khomeini proclaimed that the road to Jerusalem went through Karbala during the Iran–Iraq War, suggesting that the overthrow of Saddam Hussein would somehow lead to the liberation of Palestine. Saddam made his own attempt at linkage during the 1990–1 Gulf War. He insisted that his withdrawal from Kuwait was conditional on Israeli concessions to the Palestinians and lobbed over three dozen missiles at Israel in the vain hopes of inciting retaliation that would fracture the US coalition. After the war, though, the United States did put pressure on Israel to get involved in the multilateral Madrid peace talks, which indirectly led to the Oslo process. How persistent and substantial these linkages ultimately are, however, is unclear. The recurrent wars between Israel and its neighbors have never been the region's bloodiest conflicts. Achieving Arab–Israeli peace, in whatever form, offers no obvious assurances for improving conditions in Yemen, Libya, Syria, or Iraq, and could, in fact, generate unexpected consequences.

The Future of Peace, 2011 and Beyond

As in other periods of strife and war, MENA has seen new peacebuilding initiatives in response to the wars of the 2010s. One of the most remarkable characteristics of the recent peacebuilding initiatives was the alacrity of bottom-up initiatives that came from civil society. In part, this reflected the momentum of the popular mobilizations that set off the crisis in the first place. Equally important was the ensuing fragmentation of the state and fractionalization of violence, which added urgency to localized peacebuilding efforts. At the same time, though, the higher-level diplomatic engagements have followed the familiar pattern of foreign-initiated peace plans. They seek to return the region to what international relations specialists Michael Mandelbaum calls a workable "hegemonic truce."[58] Mediation and outside security guarantees will buttress a top-down oligopolistic bargain. The persistent disjuncture between the integrative, top-down peacebuilding efforts and the fragmentation of bottom-up peacebuilding critically defines the contours of peace in MENA in the 2010s.

The emergence of islands of stability during the 2010s catastrophe depended on local grassroots organizations that could resolve conflicts without resort to violence. Across the war-torn areas, civilians launched their own efforts to assure safety, recovery, and even restitution. Some of these islands were no bigger than a neighborhood or village. Others encompassed multiple districts, even whole provinces. Their boundaries were often blurry and operations opaque, but they offered glimmers of hope for the possibilities of peace.[59]

Syria witnessed an efflorescence of citizen-led organizations and associations in the midst of war and displacement. Civilian groups endeavored to monitor and expose violations of human rights and international law and to alleviate some of the war's most destructive consequences.[60] This was especially evident as rebel forces expanded their control over cities and towns in the north and east. Some rebel factions were barely disguised criminal gangs, kidnapping, pillaging, and killing civilians. The commanders of the FSA, backed by the Syrian National Congress government-in-exile, promulgated codes of conduct that mandated rebel fighters abide by international humanitarian law and respect human rights. Yet no one had the ability to monitor or enforce these rules from the top. Instead, local coordinating committees and community elders negotiated with rebels in Idlib and other cities to maintain peace and security for local residents.[61]

The most famous element of civilian-led peacebuilding in Syria was the paramedical Syrian Civil Defense group known as the White Helmets. The White Helmets' paramedical responders helped to evacuate civilians from battle zones, conducted rescue and recovery measures, and maintained basic services in the midst of protracted siege. The White Helmets received funding and training from NGOs and government sources and by 2013 had some 3,000 volunteers operating in 111 local committees.[62] Again, the impact of this group on the overall course of the war is hard to judge. The White Helmets claim to have helped save 100,000 lives – a figure which is impossible to confirm. At the most basic level, they improved the chances of human survival. Yet again, this humanitarian instinct must be seen on the wider scale, as a counter to the conduct of war that deliberately maximized damage and made no distinction between combatants and civilians.

Where there had been prior civil wars in recent memory, such as in Iraq and Yemen, foreign NGOs had pre-existing contacts with local peacebuilding initiatives. Peacebuilding had become a veritable mini-industry in Iraq, involving youth forums, tribal congresses, women's councils, and other means to promote or preserve local ties even when politicians turned to war. Of course, this bureaucratization of peace had its own drawbacks, but suggested the underlying power of civil society to maintain stability even when states are weak or breaking down.[63] Yemenis have a long history of relying on tribal leaders as mediators in the absence of effective state authority. In areas like Marib and parts of Hadramat, tribal mobilization helped contribute to buttressing islands of peace in the midst of violence. However, when national and international actors inducted tribal forces into their campaigns as proxies, the possibilities of peace based on tribal values become remote. Newer civil society initiatives came about to respond to fighting and humanitarian needs. Similar to the discussion of civil society responses to war in Lebanon, Yemeni women and youth played especially prominent roles in these grassroots initiatives.[64] Libya also had its own form of local peacebuilding. Instead of trying to deal with the national-level conflict pitting eastern and western governments against each other, these often focused on resolving the micro-scale disputes among neighbors over land and housing that drove individuals to take up arms in the first place.[65]

Efforts at local peacebuilding were always limited in both time and space. Some succumbed to cooptation. What began with a vision of peace with equity became simply a form of petty dictatorship where local strongmen replaced the state as the final arbiter of violence. This was still peace, but in the barest negative sense. Others gave way entirely as fighting and the acceleration of violence overwhelmed them. Still, these represented notable examples of peacebuilding from actors that would seem to have almost no power in a time of war.

The higher-level diplomatic engagements, in contrast, more or less followed the pattern of previous peacebuilding measures. They originated outside the region, operating under the auspices of third-party, extra-regional mediation. Addressing the predicaments of proxy warfare, they uniformly sought to affirm states' sovereignty but also to enlist outside powers as its guarantors. Issues of democratization, reconciliation, and transitional justice were all delayed, pending the arrival of negative peace. But the emphasis of external and even extra-regional powers in peacebuilding meant that there was almost necessarily less room for the myriad of armed non-state actors doing the bulk of the actual fighting. Repeated European initiatives to draw Haftar into some kind of concord with the GNA ignored many of the largely autonomous factions that operated alternatively as part of the Tripoli- or Tobruk-based networks. Similarly, Yemen's southern separatists denounced the proceedings of the Stockholm agreement of late 2018, signed between the Houthis and the Hadi government, for failing to treat southern demands on par with those of the Houthis. By the same token, Riyadh's efforts to reconcile Hadi with the southern separatists in late 2019 further complicated efforts to negotiate with the Houthis in the north.[66]

Syria's civil war presents the starkest example of a victor's peace. The Astana talks of the late 2010s featured representatives from the Syrian government as well as Iran, Turkey, and Russia, but had no delegates from any major Syrian opposition body or the Kurdish PYD. With the US effort to extricate itself from Syria, Astana eclipsed the more inclusive UN-backed negotiations in Geneva. The final withdrawal of US forces from the northeast left Syrian Kurdish forces with little option but to seek protection from Damascus or face the onslaught from Turkey.[67]

Besides ignoring potential domestic spoilers, though, these diplomatic peace engagements proceed as if local peacebuilding never occurred. Nowhere has the war on local peace been more severe than in Syria. Syrian and Russian state propaganda depicts the White Helmets as a terrorist organization. Airstrikes appear to deliberately target first responders and other medical personnel. In 2018, Bashar al-Assad told Russian media that "[t]he fate of the White Helmets will be the same as for any other terrorists. They have two choices: to lay down their arms and use the amnesty we have offered over the last four or five years, or be killed like other terrorists."[68] Several hundred of the White Helmets have gone into exile. Some have been assassinated. As more territory fell under state control, tens of thousands of displaced Syrians have sought to return to their homes under promises of amnesty. The process of reconstruction, however, has itself been turned into a tool to ensure and extend state control. Vacant properties have been expropriated to make room for massive building projects. Some returnees have been subject to arrest, despite initial promises of amnesty.[69] Humanitarian missions always face moral and ethical dilemmas. These dilemmas, though, have become especially pronounced as Syria has transitioned to a post-conflict footing. It is one thing to provide basic assistance to civilians in periods of chaotic war; it is another to assist Damascus in reasserting its power. Cooperating with the government, accepting its rules about how to allocate aid and assistance, has challenged the principles of independence, impartiality, and neutrality by which humanitarian organizations operate.[70]

Even in Yemen, though, where there was well-established history of indigenous bottom-up peacebuilding, international diplomacy basically sidelined civil society. Yemen's National Dialog Conference (NDC) of 2014 intended to incorporate civil society, including youth and women's organizations, in the discussion on national reconciliation. In fact, the NDC proved a stage-managed disaster. Representatives of civil society actors that have actually maintained peace at a local level are nowhere to be seen in the most recent high-level talks. Their absence, though, misses opportunities to shift toward a fuller, comprehensive, and positive version of peace.

Conclusion

Peace is present in many forms and on many scales in MENA, contrary to received wisdom. Non-violence has prevailed among most Arab states since the advent of the regional system. Inter-Arab rivalry is common, but actual war has been rare. Similarly, peace between Israel and its Arab neighbors is also expanding. This is largely a negative peace derived from the balance of power, making war too costly to pursue. Peace in the domestic arena depends even more heavily on deterrence and coercion. For the most part, MENA's states rely heavily on authoritarian means to preserve their rule. This does not just mean direct threats of military force and infliction of damage, but also the selective distribution of resources to reward compliance. Even when physical violence is not overt, systematic structural violence prevails. Semi-democratic systems like Iraq's and Lebanon's operate largely as pacts where elites maintain control over their own communities and then agree to divvy up spoils between them. Tunisia's democratic consolidation is still questionable. Israel's democratic system is consistently ethnocratic and selectively inclusive.

A different kind of peace exists in the capillaries of MENA's societies. Even in the midst of war and repression, people go about their lives as best they can, trying to preserve themselves and their families. They salvage whatever bits of decency and dignity they can. These measures are typically the most fragile and ephemeral. They are at the mercy of more powerful, armed actors. But they also perhaps come closest to representing the ideals of a fuller, more positive peace. They pursue peace with justice and conciliation, not just non-belligerence.

The challenge for peacemaking is to aggregate from this disparate infrastructure. Peace can only be self-sustaining when these elements of peace mutually reinforce each other. This is difficult to envisage, let alone implement. Most of the international diplomacy aimed at bringing peace to civil wars has focused on reinstating the trappings of territorial integrity and sovereignty. National-level peace negotiations often aim to re-establish some version of a victor's peace, either by asserting a single party's dominance or by reaching an oligopolistic balance of power. External actors, in an ideal circumstance, act as guarantors. Their own balance of power in the regional environment allows them to take measures for enforcement. But such top-down initiatives are liable to crush more localized peacebuilding infrastructure oriented toward inclusivity, participation, and reconciliation, rather than domination.[71] States may be as essential for peace as they are for war. But as James Rosenau observes, those dual processes of fragmentation and integration that generate contemporary global conflicts render states increasingly incapable of "initiating, sustaining, and controlling an appropriate rebuilding processes."[72] States may have made these wars, but the wars made many states increasingly obsolete.

Such challenges demand unorthodox approaches that belie the conventional peacebuilding-as-state-building model. A hybrid peace seeks to make bottom-up and top-down approaches to peacebuilding compatible. Local peacebuilding need not automatically yield to demands emanating from national and/or international powers. Rather, national and international actors must grant communities broader space to resolve conflicts according to local custom and necessities. Hybrid peace thus takes a radically different shape than what is described in peace treaties.[73]

One of the key themes of this volume has been the centrality of MENA's states to the conduct of war and violence. States are not the only protagonists in the region's wars, but they are typically the most dominant. Even when states have atrophied, fighting is often about them. Even more importantly, there is little question that a strong, effective, and representative state is the best insurer of peace. But in MENA – as in many other regions – there has been a wide gap between the pacific theories of statehood and the practice. In 2009, a group of Arab intellectuals and scholars associated with the UN-sponsored Arab Human Development report noted that "weak institutional curbs on state power; a fragile and fragmented civil society; dysfunctional elected assemblies, both national and local; and disproportionately powerful security apparatuses often combine to turn the state into a menace to human security, rather than its chief supporter."[74] One does not need to point to the flagrant violence of the 2010s to realize that the record of MENA states meeting their demands for physical protection or economic opportunity is disheartening.[75] The prevailing regional security predicament and the various conflict traps impede efforts to shift states toward a more peaceful and productive relationship with their neighbors or their citizens.

Negative peace – a cessation of violence – is a worthy goal in the midst of horrible war, but it need not be the end of peacebuilding. Considerations of positive peace, including reconciliation, representation, and justice, must also be part of the agenda. To some, this might appear the height of naïveté and wishful thinking, sacrificing pragmatic concerns about human safety for a distant ideal. But the last century has shown how brittle and inconstant negative peace alone can be. There is no reason to sell peace short.

The instrumentation of peace in MENA might also shift away from the singular focus on enhancing and refining state power and capacity to find ways to incorporate local actors and bottom-up initiatives more readily. States in MENA, as in many other regions, are not up to the task. Wishing for strong states to arrive is not the solution. Rather, the atrophy and reorientation of states is an opportunity to open up room for new kinds of political communities and institutions. Already, the flow of foreign military and economic aid to MENA has proven to generate externalities that embolden, instead of mitigate, states' repression and aggression. Moreover, outsiders often sponsor armed non-state actors as proxies for dealing with specific security concerns. Civilians have found ways of coping that circumvent the hollow state. Rather than continuing with the hypocrisies and inconsistencies of sovereignty, it is worth considering jettisoning them entirely. New institutions of governance – city-states, protectorates, and frontiers – could emerge as states recede. These new or revived modes of governance offer ways to construe the relationship between political authority, territory, and populations that reduce the risks of war and afford a broad peace, albeit in different forms and locations.

Conclusion

On May 9, 1915, Ihsan Hasan al-Turjman, a low-level clerk in the Ottoman army, wrote in his diary about the anxiety and fatigue of what was then called the Great War:

> I cannot think of anything except our present misfortune. When will we finish with this wretched war, and what will happen to us next? Our lives are threatened from all sides: a European war and an Ottoman war, prices are skyrocketing, a financial crisis, and the locusts are attacking the country north and south. On top of all this, now infectious diseases are spreading through the Ottoman lands. May God protect us. I can hardly walk in the streets and talk to anybody for fear of facing these misfortunes. . . . I have stopped caring. Hasan told me today that the Dardanelles are about to fall.[1]

Turjman spent the war living in the comfort of his family home in Jerusalem and never saw the front lines. He was far luckier in this respect than many others. Tens of thousands of Ottoman citizens fought and died in the Caucasus, Iraq, and the Dardanelles Straits and Gallipoli Peninsula. Most were conscripts, living under a brutal military discipline far from family and home. Jews and Christians, whom the Ottoman leadership generally regarded as untrustworthy, were often consigned to heavy labor battalions instead of battle units. Provision and supply were constant problems with the Ottoman armies fighting on multiple fronts. European observers were shocked to find frontline Ottoman troops lacking adequate winter wear or even shoes. Besides combat, soldiers succumbed to poor hygiene, hunger, and disease. Desertion and mutiny were rampant across the ranks. Civilians, too, lived under the shadow of deprivation, repression, and foreign invasion. Millions fled their homes as displaced refugees. The worst suffering were Armenian Christians, regarded as a traitorous fifth column by the Ottoman authorities. As their strategic position deteriorated, Ottoman leaders took increasingly drastic and brutal measures against Armenians, deporting tens of thousands to desert camps and certain death.[2] Turjman wrote only sporadically and often inconsistently about the larger political questions of the war. He generally wished for victory against the Entente, but he showed marked disaffection toward the empire's Turkish elite, especially the blundering and pompous Turkish officers under whom he served. Turjman was proud of his Arabic literary and cultural heritage. Indeed, his literacy made him valuable at staff work, a key factor keeping him in the relatively safe rear echelon. He expressed hope for the Arab revolt, launched by the Hashemites in the Hejaz with British support. He was also concerned about the encroachment of the Zionists into Palestine as they, too, entered a political alliance with Britain.[3]

Beyond the experience of World War I, Turjman's diary touches upon some of the perennial themes about war and conflict in MENA throughout the modern era. The key premise of this book is that war is an inherently social process and must be examined as such. Thus, the important questions about war and conflict are not simply about victory or defeat, but also about who fights and who dies in the process. As sociologist Siniša Malešević points out, "there is no military violence and war without social organization."[4] The organization of society, the political, economic, and cultural ligatures that connect individuals together, also grant meaning and order to acts of violence. They crucially enable or retard the ability to coordinate campaigns of violence against another group. Social arrangements sustain hierarchies (often through intra-group violence and coercion) that shift the burdens of fighting and dying onto particular categories of people. Likewise, these arrangements selectively allocate the benefits of victory and costs of defeat to individuals and groups. The relationship between war and social organization, though, is reciprocal and interdependent. War shapes societies, too, both through direct battle or through preparation for future battles. Wars test and challenge old institutions to marshal sufficient powers for self-defense and spur the search for new social, economic, and political arrangements when old ones prove lacking.[5]

Based on this premise, the book broadly considered three key themes about war and conflict in the modern Middle East and North Africa. First, it probed the widely held presumption that MENA is a region rife with violence and bellicosity. Using cross-national statistics, it examined the frequency, form, and severity of conflict in MENA in comparison to other regions of the world. There is no question that the period since the turn of the twenty-first century has been exceptionally violent in MENA. It has suffered higher frequencies and greater intensities of war than any other region during this era. But this has not always been the case. The largest and most consequential wars of the 1950s to 1970s occurred not in MENA but in East Asia, where the two superpowers engaged in local conflicts. Moreover, the incidence and impact of war in MENA were highly uneven. Some countries were only tangentially affected while others saw nearly constant war.

Lurking beyond the effort to enumerate and catalog wars and casualties is a more fundamental question about what and who really matters in MENA. Debates about defining terrorism and whether specific acts of violence constitute legitimate forms of war and violent resistance or are, rather, illegitimate and criminal deviations defy empirical solution. They are fundamentally normative, requiring definitions of who is entitled to enact violence, who is a legitimate target, and who should be afforded protection. Efforts to count combatants, civilians, or violent events inevitably assign value and worth to some individuals and deny it to others.[6]

The book's second goal was to examine the relationship between war-fighting and state-making in MENA. Written just a few cataclysmic years after Turjman's diary entry, Weber's description of the state as the entity possessing the monopoly over legitimate force within a given territory reflects an intimate understanding that violence and statehood work together. Force, legitimacy, and territory position states as the predominant organizations in the preparation for and conduct of war. Indeed, the need to fight internal challengers and external enemies was a key driver in the formation of relatively strong, competent, and homogeneous states in Europe.[7] Many scholars contrast Europe's "successful" state formation with MENA's seemingly defective or dysfunctional statehood. MENA's states are often depicted as the artificial implants of colonialism. Invented, unwanted, and internally divided, these states are bound to certain failure.[8]

This book challenges these assumptions. MENA states responded to the same sets of internal and external challengers as seen in Europe. Indeed, MENA's regional security predicament and the need to confront internal and external challengers at once was very similar to the conditions witnessed in early modern Europe. One of the crucial differences was the role of superpowers and the hierarchical nature of the global system. The provision of rents and protections from abroad changed the decision calculus for both rulers and opposition. Often inadvertently, external involvements tipped the scales toward violent confrontation. Regimes tended to be narrow and exclusive, even as they seemed to offer populations some measure of economic or cultural incentives to comply. Recognizing the divergence between state, regime, and human security in MENA, it is important to retain a view of how everyday people experience security and insecurity and the resultant compulsions for state-building.

Finally, the book considered how geopolitics, resources, and identity could trap MENA into self-perpetuating wars. Each of these factors, in certain cases, affects state formation in ways that served to consolidate political and economic inequalities. These durable inequalities, in turn, help to make conflict a perennial feature in regional affairs, rather than a sporadic and episodic occurrence. They define interaction among rulers and opposition and the relationship between rulers and broader populations. They create incentive structures and propensities for dealing with political challenges through violence and exclusion. But these same elements work in other ways in different circumstances. The presence of oil, geopolitical intervention, and ethnic diversity can compel cooperation and provide a measure of peace. Ultimately, none of these factors are immediate triggers of war. Rather, they collectively and individually affect propensities and inscribe practices of both war and peace.

Can MENA escape these conflict traps? Might peace come? As discussed in the final chapter, changes will have to come in the ways states engage with international society and with their own populations. Peace – just like war – has many forms. Most regional peace initiatives amount to top-down plans for dividing power among elites and their foreign backers. They are, in other words, externally sponsored state-building projects. But state-building initiatives are often oblivious to the ways small communities, neighborhoods, and villages manage to provide for common stability and safety in the midst of state collapse. These bottom-up solutions are hardly perfect. They create hybrid political orders, where prerogatives of violence fall to armed non-state actors, typically the leaders of tribes, clans, and local strongmen. Yet these coping mechanisms, however limited, often seem better than a return to MENA's bloody and interminable processes of state-building and war-making.[9] Pursuing such solutions requires both impressive political will and expansive political imagination. It means finding other ways to organize political life that de-emphasize statehood as the ideal end-goal. It rearranges the key elements of state power: violence, legitimacy, and territory. This approach may loosen the binding logic of the contemporary security predicament and finally offer a way for MENA to escape war and conflict.

Notes

INTRODUCTION

1 Joshua S. Goldstein, *Winning the War on War: The Decline of Armed Conflict Worldwide* (New York: Penguin, 2012); Nils Petter Gleditsch et al., "The Forum: The Decline of War," *International Studies Review* 15, no. 3 (2013): 396–419.

2 Stockholm International Peace Research Institute, *SIPRI Yearbook 2017* (New York: Oxford University Press, 2017), 3.

3 Robert Malley, "The Unwanted Wars: Why the Middle East Is More Combustible Than Ever," *Foreign Affairs*, November 1, 2019.

4 Miguel A. Centeno and Elaine Enriquez, *War and Society* (Cambridge: Polity, 2016), 175. See also Wim A. Smit, "Military Technologies and Politics," in *The Oxford Handbook of Contextual Political Analysis*, edited by Charles Tilly and Robert E. Goodin (New York: Oxford University Press, 2009).

5 Paul Collier, *Breaking the Conflict Trap: Civil War and Development Policy* (Washington, DC: World Bank Publications, 2003), 13.

6 Charles Tilly, *Coercion, Capital, and European States, AD 990–1990* (Cambridge, Mass.: Basil Blackwell, 1990); Joel S. Migdal, *Strong Societies and Weak States: State–Society Relations and State Capabilities in the Third World* (Princeton, NJ: Princeton University Press, 1988); Kalevi J. Holsti, "War, Peace, and the State of the State," *International Political Science Review* 16, no. 4 (1995): 319–39; Dan Slater, "Violent Origins of Authoritarian Variation: Rebellion Type and Regime Type in Cold War Southeast Asia," *Government and Opposition* 55, no. 1 (2020): 21–40.

7 Alexander Bellamy, *World Peace (and How We Can Achieve It)* (New York: Oxford University Press, 2019), 126.

8 Michael Mann, *The Sources of Social Power, Volume 1: A History of Power from the Beginning to AD 1760* (New York: Cambridge University Press, 1986), 11.

9 Douglass C. North, John Joseph Wallis, and Barry R. Weingast, *Violence and Social Orders: A Conceptual Framework for Interpreting Recorded Human History* (New York: Cambridge University Press, 2009).

10 Edward W. Said, *Orientalism* (New York: Vintage, 1979), 83.

11 Abbas Amanat, *Is There a Middle East? The Evolution of a Geopolitical Concept* (Stanford, Calif.: Stanford University Press, 2012).

12 Fred Halliday, *The Middle East in International Relations: Power, Politics and Ideology* (New York: Cambridge University Press, 2005), 81.

13 Nikki R. Keddie, "Is There a Middle East?," *International Journal of Middle East Studies* 4, no. 3 (1973): 255–71 (258).

14 Yaniv Voller, "From Periphery to the Moderates: Israeli Identity and Foreign Policy in the Middle East," *Political Science Quarterly* 130, no. 3 (2015): 505–36; Kamal S. Salibi, "The Lebanese Identity," *Journal of Contemporary History* 6, no. 1 (1971): 76–86.

15 Martin W. Lewis and Kären E. Wigen, eds., *The Myth of Continents: A Critique of Metageography* (Berkeley: University of California Press, 1997); Ariel I. Ahram, Patrick Köllner, and Rudra Sil, eds., *Comparative Area Studies: Methodological Rationales and Cross-Regional Applications* (New York: Oxford University Press, 2018).

16 For one example, see Paul Salem and Ross Harrison, eds., *Escaping the Conflict Trap: Toward Ending Civil Wars in the Middle East* (Washington, DC: Middle East Institute, 2019).

17 One recent exception is Anders Jägerskog, Michael Schulz, and Ashok Swain, eds., *Routledge Handbook on Middle East Security* (London: Routledge, 2019).

18 Hazem Adam Ghobarah, Paul Huth, and Bruce Russett, "The Post-War Public Health Effects of Civil Conflict," *Social Science & Medicine* 59, no. 4 (2004): 869–84; Christopher J. L. Murray et al., "Armed Conflict as a Public Health Problem," *BMJ* 324, no. 7333 (2002): 346–9; Michael Palmer et al., "Long-Lasting Consequences of War on Disability," *Journal of Peace Research* 56, no. 6 (2019): 860–75.

19 Michael N. Barnett, *Confronting the Costs of War: Military Power, State, and Society in Egypt and Israel* (Princeton, NJ: Princeton University Press, 2012); Thierry Gongora, "War Making and State Power in the Contemporary Middle East," *International Journal of Middle East Studies* 29, no. 3 (1997): 323–40.

20 Steven Heydemann, "Introduction," in *War, Institutions, and Social Change in the Middle East*, edited by Steven Heydemann (Berkeley: University of California Press, 2000), 1.

21 Lingyu Lu and Cameron G. Thies, "War, Rivalry, and State Building in the Middle East," *Political Research Quarterly* 66, no. 2 (2013): 239–53; Mehran Kamrava, *Inside the Arab State* (New York: Oxford University Press, 2018); Daniel Neep, "War, State Formation, and Culture," *International Journal of Middle East Studies* 45, no. 4 (2013): 795–7; Rolf Schwarz, "Does War Make States? Rentierism and the Formation of States in the Middle East," *European Political Science Review* 3, no. 3 (2011): 419–43.

22 Bent Flyvbjerg, *Making Social Science Matter: Why Social Inquiry Fails and How It Can Succeed Again* (New York: Cambridge University Press, 2001); Karl Spracklen, *Making the Moral Case for Social Sciences: Stemming the Tide* (New York: Springer, 2015).

CHAPTER 1 ACCOUNTING FOR WAR IN THE MIDDLE EAST AND NORTH AFRICA

1 Fred Charles Iklé, *Every War Must End* (New York: Columbia University Press, 2005 [1971]), 35–6.
2 Alan Page Fiske and Tage Shakti Rai, *Virtuous Violence: Hurting and Killing to Create, Sustain, End, and Honor Social Relationships* (New York: Cambridge University Press, 2014).
3 Jeremy Black, "What Is War?," in *What Is War? An Investigation in the Wake of 9/11*, edited by Mary Ellen O'Connell (Leiden: Martinus Nijhoff Publishers, 2012), 177.
4 Peter Wallensteen, "The Origins of Contemporary Peace Research," in *Understanding Peace Research*, edited by Kristine Höglund and Magnus Öberg (New York: Taylor & Francis, 2011); Barry Buzan and Lene Hansen, *The Evolution of International Security Studies* (New York: Cambridge University Press, 2009).
5 Mary Kaldor, *New and Old Wars*, second edition (Stanford, Calif.: Stanford University Press, 2007); Siniša Malešević, "The Sociology of New Wars? Assessing the Causes and Objectives of Contemporary Violent Conflicts," *International Political Sociology* 2, no. 2 (2008): 97–112.
6 John E. Mueller, *Remnants of War* (Ithaca, NY: Cornell University Press, 2004); Jacob Mundy, "Deconstructing Civil Wars: Beyond the New Wars Debate," *Security Dialogue* 42, no. 3 (2011): 279–95.
7 Edward Newman, "The 'New Wars' Debate: A Historical Perspective Is Needed," *Security Dialogue* 35, no. 2 (2004): 173–89.
8 Stathis N. Kalyvas and Laia Balcells, "International System and Technologies of Rebellion: How the End of the Cold War Shaped Internal Conflict," *American Political Science Review* 104, no. 3 (2010): 415–29.
9 Tarak Barkawi and Mark Laffey, "The Postcolonial Moment in Security Studies," *Review of International Studies* 32, no. 2 (2006): 329–54.
10 Jack P. Gibbs, "Conceptualization of Terrorism," *American Sociological Review* 54, no. 3 (1989): 329–41; Asafa Jalata, "Conceptualizing and Theorizing Terrorism in the Historical and Global Context," *Humanity & Society* 34, no. 4 (2010): 317–49; Leonard Weinberg, Ami Pedahzur, and Sivan Hirsch-Hoefler, "The Challenges of Conceptualizing Terrorism," *Terrorism and Political Violence* 16, no. 4 (2004): 777–94.
11 James Derrick Sidaway, "Geopolitics, Geography, and 'Terrorism' in the Middle East," *Environment & Planning D: Society & Space* 12, no. 3 (1994): 357–72.
12 Rosa Brooks, *How Everything Became War and the Military Became Everything: Tales from the Pentagon* (New York: Simon & Schuster, 2016), 61.
13 Heritage Foundation, "Assessing Threats to US Vital Interests: Middle East" (2018).
14 Mirjam E. Sørli, Nils Petter Gleditsch, and Håvard Strand, "Why Is There

So Much Conflict in the Middle East?," *Journal of Conflict Resolution* 49, no. 1 (2005): 141–65.

15 John E. Mueller, "The Obsolescence of Major War," *Bulletin of Peace Proposals* 21, no. 3 (1990): 321–8; Joshua S. Goldstein, *Winning the War on War: The Decline of Armed Conflict Worldwide* (New York: Penguin, 2012); Arie M. Kacowicz, *Zones of Peace in the Third World: South America and West Africa in Comparative Perspective* (Albany, NY: SUNY Press, 1998).

16 William Eckhardt, "Civilian Deaths in Wartime," *Bulletin of Peace Proposals* 20, no. 1 (1989): 89–98; Adam Roberts, "Lives and Statistics: Are 90% of War Victims Civilians?," *Survival* 52, no. 3 (2010): 115–36.

17 Madeline Edwards, "Syrian Author Khaled Khalifa on Latest Novel About 'Fear, in All Its Manifestations'," *SyriaDirect*, February 27, 2019, *https://syria direct.org/news/syrian-author-khaled-khalifa-on-latest-novel-about-%E2%80%98fear-in-all-its-manifestations%E2%80%99/*.

18 Nicholas P. Jewell, Michael Spagat, and Britta L. Jewell, "Accounting for Civilian Casualties: From the Past to the Future," *Social Science History* 42, no. 3 (2018): 379–410; Peter Andreas and Kelly M. Greenhill, eds., *Sex, Drugs, and Body Counts: The Politics of Numbers in Global Crime and Conflict* (Ithaca, NY: Cornell University Press, 2011).

19 Megan Price, Anita Gohdes, and Patrick Ball, "Documents of War: Understanding the Syrian Conflict," *Significance* 12, no. 2 (2015): 14–19.

20 Nils B. Weidmann, "A Closer Look at Reporting Bias in Conflict Event Data," *American Journal of Political Science* 60, no. 1 (2016): 206–18.

21 John Broder, "A Nation at War: The Casualties; US Military Has No Count of Iraqi Dead in Fighting," *New York Times*, April 2, 2003. It was only in 2018 that the US military was required to keep track and report on civilian casualties caused by US airstrikes and other military actions. Cf. Neta Crawford, "Human Costs of the Post 9/11 Wars: Lethality and the Need for Transparency" (Brown University, Watson Institute for International and Public Affairs, 2018).

22 Hannah Fischer, "Iraqi Civilian Deaths Estimates," in *Economics and Geopolitics of the Middle East*, edited by Richard Dralonge (New York: Nova Science 2008).

23 Hazem Adam Ghobarah, Paul Huth, and Bruce Russett, "The Post-War Public Health Effects of Civil Conflict," *Social Science & Medicine* 59, no. 4 (2004): 869–94; Hazem Adam Ghobarah, Paul Huth, and Bruce Russett, "Civil Wars Kill and Maim People – Long after the Shooting Stops," *The American Political Science Review* 97, no. 2 (2003): 189–202; Bethany Lacina and Nils Petter Gleditsch, "Monitoring Trends in Global Combat: A New Dataset of Battle Deaths," *European Journal of Population* 21, nos. 2–3 (2005): 145–66.

24 Zachary J. Foster, "The 1915 Locust Attack in Syria and Palestine and Its Role in the Famine during the First World War," *Middle Eastern Studies* 51,

no. 3 (2015): 370–94; Leila Tarazi Fawaz, *A Land of Aching Hearts: The Middle East in the Great War* (Cambridge, Mass.: Harvard University Press, 2014).

25 Firdausi Qadri, Taufiqul Islam, and John D. Clemens, "Cholera in Yemen – an Old Foe Rearing Its Ugly Head," *New England Journal of Medicine* 377 (2017): 2005–7.

26 United Nations Office for the Coordination of Humanitarian Affairs, "Largest Consolidated Humanitarian Appeal for Yemen to Provide a Lifeline to 13.1 Million People" (2018).

27 Les Roberts et al., "Mortality before and after the 2003 Invasion of Iraq: Cluster Sample Survey," *The Lancet*, no. 9448 (2004): 1857–64. A. Hagopian et al., "Navigating a Four-University, Three-Country Collaboration to Estimate Mortality in Iraq after the 2003 Invasion and Occupation," *The Lancet Global Health*, no. S1 (2014): S49.

28 Iraq Family Health Survey Study Group, "Violence-Related Mortality in Iraq from 2002 to 2006," *The New England Journal of Medicine*, no. 5 (2008): 484–93.

29 Lacina and Gleditsch, "Monitoring Trends in Global Combat: A New Dataset of Battle Deaths."

30 For data, Pierre Razoux, *The Iran–Iraq War* (Cambridge, Mass.: Harvard University Press, 2015).

31 Joost R. Hiltermann, *A Poisonous Affair: America, Iraq, and the Gassing of Halabja* (New York: Cambridge University Press, 2007).

32 Thérése Pettersson and Kristine Eck, "Organized Violence, 1989–2017," *Journal of Peace Research* 55, no. 4 (2018): 535–47.

33 Neil Bowie and Alex Schmid, "Databases on Terrorism," in *Routledge Handbook of Terrorism Research*, edited by Alex Schmid (New York: Routledge, 2011).

34 Additionally, GTD requires two of the following three criteria to be present: (1) the act must be motivated by a political, economic, religious, or social goal; (2) there must be evidence of an intention to coerce, intimidate, or convey some other message to a larger audience (or audiences) than the immediate victims; (3) and the action must be outside the context of legitimate warfare activities and transgress international humanitarian law concerning civilians or non-combatants. See National Consortium for the Study of Terrorism and Responses to Terrorism, "Global Terrorism Database" (College Park, Md.: START, University of Maryland, 2019).

35 Paul D. Williams, *War and Conflict in Africa* (Cambridge: Polity, 2016), 42.

CHAPTER 2 THE MENA SECURITY PREDICAMENT

1 Tarak Barkawi, *Globalization and War* (Lanham, Md.: Rowman & Littlefield, 2006), 169–72.

2 Morten Bøås, *The Politics of Conflict Economies: Miners, Merchants and Warriors in the African Borderland* (New York: Routledge, 2014). See also Miguel A. Centeno and Elaine Enriquez, *War and Society* (Cambridge: Polity, 2016).

3 Pinar Bilgin, "The 'Western-Centrism' of Security Studies: 'Blind Spot' or Constitutive Practice?," *Security Dialogue* 41, no. 6 (2010): 615–22; Steve Smith, "The Increasing Insecurity of Security Studies: Conceptualizing Security in the Last Twenty Years," *Contemporary Security Policy* 20, no. 3 (1999): 72–101; Amitav Acharya, "The Periphery as the Core: The Third World and Security Studies," in *Critical Security Studies*, edited by Keith Krause (New York: Routledge).

4 Mohammed Ayoob, "Security in the Third World: The Worm About to Turn?," *International Affairs* 60, no. 1 (1983): 41–51 (43).

5 Alexander Bellamy, *World Peace (and How We Can Achieve It)* (New York: Oxford University Press, 2019), 126–7.

6 Fred Halliday, *The Middle East in International Relations: Power, Politics and Ideology* (New York: Cambridge University Press, 2005), 75.

7 J. David Singer, "The Level-of-Analysis Problem in International Relations," *World Politics* 14, no. 1 (1961): 77–92; Nils Petter Gleditsch and Håvard Hegre, "Peace and Democracy: Three Levels of Analysis," *Journal of Conflict Resolution* 41, no. 2 (1997): 283–310; Owen Temby, "What Are Levels of Analysis and What Do They Contribute to International Relations Theory?," *Cambridge Review of International Affairs* 28, no. 4 (2015): 721–42.

8 Charles Tilly and Robert E. Goodin, "It Depends," in *The Oxford Handbook of Contextual Political Analysis*, edited by Robert E. Goodin and Charles Tilly (New York: Oxford University Press 2006); Clayton Roberts, *Logic of Historical Explanation* (State College: Pennsylvania State University Press, 2010).

9 Tareq Y. Ismael and Glenn E. Perry, "Toward a Framework for Analysis," in *The International Relations of the Contemporary Middle East*, edited by Tareq Y. Ismael and Glenn E. Perry (New York: Routledge, 2013), 7.

10 Ann Hironaka, *Neverending Wars: The International Community, Weak States, and the Perpetuation of Civil War* (Cambridge, Mass.: Harvard University Press, 2005), 11.

11 F. Gregory Gause, "Systemic Approaches to Middle East International Relations," *International Studies Review* 1, no. 1 (1999): 11–31.

12 Stephen Zunes, "The United States: A Hegemon Challenged," in *The International Relations of the Contemporary Middle East*, edited by Tareq Y. Ismael and Jacqueline S. Ismael (New York: Routledge, 2013).

13 Halliday, *The Middle East in International Relations*, 176.

14 Yezid Sayigh and Avi Shlaim, eds., *The Cold War and the Middle East* (New York: Clarendon Press, 1997); Bassam Tibi, *Conflict and War in the Middle East: From Interstate War to New Security* (New York: Springer, 1998), 28–9.

15 Ian S. Lustick, "The Absence of Middle Eastern Great Powers: Political 'Backwardness' in Historical Perspective," *International Organization* 51, no. 4 (1997): 653–83 (662).

16 Thomas J. Volgy et al., "The Case for Comparative Regional Analysis in International Politics," *International Studies Review* 19, no. 3 (2017): 452–80;

Morten Valbjørn and André Bank, "The New Arab Cold War: Rediscovering the Arab Dimension of Middle East Regional Politics," *Review of International Studies* 38, no. 1 (2012): 3–24.

17 Bassam Tibi, *Arab Nationalism: Between Islam and the Nation-State* (New York: St. Martin's Press, 1997).

18 Adeed Dawisha, *Arab Nationalism in the Twentieth Century: From Triumph to Despair* (Princeton, NJ: Princeton University Press, 2016); Fred Lawson, *Constructing International Relations in the Arab World* (Stanford, Calif.: Stanford University Press, 2006).

19 Ewan Stein, "Beyond Arabism vs. Sovereignty: Relocating Ideas in the International Relations of the Middle East," *Review of International Studies* 38, no. 4 (2012): 881–905.

20 Louise Fawcett, "Regionalism and Alliances in the Middle East," in *International Relations of the Middle East*, fifth edition, edited by Louise Fawcett (New York: Oxford University Press, 2019).

21 Halliday, *The Middle East in International Relations*, 75.

22 Mohammed Ayoob, "Unravelling the Concept: 'National Security' in the Third World," in *The Many Faces of National Security in the Arab World*, edited by Rex Brynen, Bahgat Korany, and Paul Noble (New York: Springer, 1993), 40. See also Tibi, *Conflict and War in the Middle East*, 475.

23 Keith Krause, "State-Making and Region-Building: The Interplay of Domestic and Regional Security in the Middle East," *Journal of Strategic Studies* 26, no. 3 (2003): 99–124 (101).

24 Nazih N. Ayubi, *Over-Stating the Arab State: Politics and Society in the Middle East* (London: I. B. Tauris, 1996), 449.

25 Cullen S. Hendrix and Joseph K. Young, "State Capacity and Terrorism: A Two-Dimensional Approach," *Security Studies* 23, no. 2 (2014): 329–63.

26 Bassel F. Salloukh and Rex Brynen, eds., *Persistent Permeability? Regionalism, Localism, and Globalization in the Middle East* (New York: Routledge, 2017).

27 Steven R. David, "Explaining Third World Alignment," *World Politics* 43, no. 2 (1991): 233–56.

28 Roger Owen, *The Rise and Fall of Arab Presidents for Life* (Cambridge, Mass.: Harvard University Press, 2014).

29 Ofra Bengio, "Shi'is and Politics in Ba'thi Iraq," *Middle Eastern Studies* 21, no. 1 (1985): 1–14.

30 Holger Albrecht, "The Myth of Coup-Proofing: Risk and Instances of Military Coups d'état in the Middle East and North Africa, 1950–2013," *Armed Forces & Society* 41, no. 4 (2015): 659–87; James T. Quinlivan, "Coup-Proofing: Its Practice and Consequences in the Middle East," *International Security* 24, no. 2 (1999): 131–65; Steffen Hertog, "Rentier Militaries in the Gulf States: The Price of Coup-Proofing," *International Journal of Middle East Studies* 43, no. 3 (2011): 400–2.

31 Dexter Filkins, *The Forever War* (New York: Vintage, 2009); Mark Danner, *Spiral: Trapped in the Forever War* (New York: Simon & Schuster, 2016).

32 Lisa Blaydes, "State Building in the Middle East," *Annual Review of Political Science* 20 (2017): 487–504.

33 Carter V. Findley, *Bureaucratic Reform in the Ottoman Empire: The Sublime Porte, 1789–1922* (Princeton, NJ: Princeton University Press, 1980).

34 Iliya Harik, "The Origins of the Arab State System," in *The Arab State*, edited by Giacomo Luciani (Berkeley: University of California Press, 1990), 25.

35 Nikki R. Keddie, "The Revolt of Islam, 1700 to 1993: Comparative Considerations and Relations to Imperialism," *Comparative Studies in Society and History* 36, no. 3 (1994): 463–87.

36 Israel Gershoni and James P. Jankowski, *Egypt, Islam, and the Arabs: The Search for Egyptian Nationhood, 1900–1930* (New York: Oxford University Press, 1987).

37 Juan R. Cole, "Of Crowds and Empires: Afro-Asian Riots and European Expansion, 1857–1882," *Comparative Studies in Society and History* 31, no. 1 (1989): 106–33; Keddie, "The Revolt of Islam, 1700 to 1993"; Joel Beinin, *Workers and Peasants in the Modern Middle East* (New York: Cambridge University Press, 2001).

38 Jonathan Wyrtzen, "Reimagining Political Space: Jihad, Empire, and the Interwar Making of the Modern Middle East and North Africa" (UCLA African Studies Center, 2016).

39 Elizabeth F. Thompson, *Justice Interrupted* (Cambridge, Mass.: Harvard University Press, 2013); Erez Manela, *The Wilsonian Moment: Self-Determination and the International Origins of Anticolonial Nationalism* (New York: Oxford University Press, 2007).

40 Rashid Khalidi, *Palestinian Identity: The Construction of Modern National Consciousness* (New York: Columbia University Press, 1997); Reidar Visser, "Proto-Political Conceptions of Iraq in Late Ottoman Times," *International Journal of Contemporary Iraqi Studies* 3, no. 2 (2009): 143–54; Eyal Zisser, "Who's Afraid of Syrian Nationalism? National and State Identity in Syria," *Middle Eastern Studies* 42, no. 2 (2006): 179–98.

41 Eliezer Tauber, *The Emergence of the Arab Movements* (New York: Routledge, 1993); Aula Hariri, "State Formation as an Outcome of the Imperial Encounter: The Case of Iraq," *Review of International Studies*, 45, no. 5 (2019): 848–69; Susan Pedersen, "Getting out of Iraq – in 1932: The League of Nations and the Road to Normative Statehood," *The American Historical Review* 115, no. 4 (2010): 975–1000.

42 Ariel I. Ahram, "War-Making, State-Making, and Non-State Power in Iraq," *Yale Program on Governance and Local Development Working Paper* 1 (2015), *https://cpb-us-w2.wpmucdn.com/campuspress.yale.edu/dist/e/439/files/2015/03/Ariel_War-MakingFinal.pdf*; Toby Dodge, "Iraq: The Contradictions of Exogenous State-Building in Historical Perspective," *Third World Quarterly* 27, no. 1 (2006): 187–2000.

43 Mark Tessler, *A History of the Israeli–Palestinian Conflict* (Bloomington: Indiana University Press, 2009), 123–85.

44 Sami Zubaida, "Contested Nations: Iraq and the Assyrians," *Nations and Nationalism* 6, no. 3 (2000): 363–82.

45 N. E. Bou-Nacklie, "Les Troupes Spéciales: Religious and Ethnic Recruitment, 1916–46," *International Journal of Middle East Studies* 25, no. 4 (1993): 645–60.

46 William B. Cohen, "The Harkis," in *Algeria & France, 1800–2000: Identity, Memory, Nostalgia*, edited by Patricia Lorcin (Syracuse, NY: Syracuse University Press, 2006), 164–81; Vincent Crapanzano, *The Harkis: The Wound That Never Heals* (Chicago: University of Chicago Press, 2011).

47 Kirsten E. Schulze, "The 1948 War: The Battle over History," in *Routledge Handbook on the Israeli–Palestinian Conflict*, edited by Joel Peters (New York: Routledge, 2013); Benny Morris, *1948: A History of the First Arab–Israeli War* (New Haven: Yale University Press, 2008); Rashid Khalidi, Eugene L. Rogan, and Avi Shlaim, eds., *The War for Palestine: Rewriting the History of 1948* (New York: Cambridge University Press, 2001).

48 Hillel Cohen, *Good Arabs: The Israeli Security Agencies and the Israeli Arabs, 1948–1967* (Berkeley: University of California Press, 2011).

49 Wendy Pearlman and Boaz Atzili, *Triadic Coercion: Israel's Targeting of States That Host Nonstate Actors* (New York: Columbia University Press, 2018); Yezid Sayigh, *Armed Struggle and the Search for a State: The Palestinian National Movement, 1949–1993* (New York: Clarendon Press, 1997).

50 Elia Zureik, "Colonialism, Surveillance, and Population Control," in *Surveillance and Control in Israel/Palestine: Population, Territory and Power*, edited by Elia Zureik, David Lyon, and Yasmeen Abu-Laban (New York: Routledge, 2011); Eyal Weizman, *Hollow Land: Israel's Architecture of Occupation* (New York: Verso, 2012).

51 Elie Podeh, "The Emergence of the Arab State System Reconsidered," *Diplomacy and Statecraft* 9, no. 3 (1998): 50–82.

52 Malik Mufti, *Sovereign Creations: Pan-Arabism and Political Order in Syria and Iraq* (Ithaca, NY: Cornell University Press, 1996); Stein, "Beyond Arabism vs. Sovereignty."

53 Mohammad Ayatollahi Tabaar, "Factional Politics in the Iran–Iraq War," *Journal of Strategic Studies* 42, nos. 3–4 (2019): 480–506.

54 Michael N. Barnett, *Confronting the Costs of War: Military Power, State, and Society in Egypt and Israel* (Princeton, NJ: Princeton University Press, 2012).

55 Shibley Telhami, "Kenneth Waltz, Neorealism, and Foreign Policy," *Security Studies* 11, no. 3 (2002): 158–70.

56 Fawaz A. Gerges, *The Far Enemy: Why Jihad Went Global* (New York: Cambridge University Press, 2009).

57 Barry R. Posen, "The Security Dilemma and Ethnic Conflict," *Survival* 35, no. 1 (1993): 27–47; Oren Barak, "Dilemmas of Security in Iraq," *Security Dialogue* 38, no. 4 (2007): 455–75.

58 Fanar Haddad, "Shi'a-Centric State Building and Sunni Rejection in Post-2003 Iraq," in *Beyond Sunni and Shia: The Roots of Sectarianism in a Changing Middle East*, edited by Frederic Wehrey (New York: Oxford University Press, 2016); Charles Tripp, "Theatres of Blood: Performative Violence in Iraq," *International Journal of Contemporary Iraqi Studies* 12, no. 2 (2018): 167–81.

59 Jillian Schwedler, "Spatial Dynamics of the Arab Uprisings," *PS: Political Science and Politics* 46, no. 2 (2013): 230–4.

60 Holger Albrecht, Aurel Croissant, and Fred H. Lawson, eds., *Armies and Insurgencies in the Arab Spring* (Philadelphia: University of Pennsylvania Press, 2016); John Gledhill, "Assessing (In)Security after the Arab Spring: Editor's Introduction," *PS: Political Science & Politics* 46, no. 4 (2013): 709–15.

61 Vali Nasr, *The Dispensable Nation: American Foreign Policy in Retreat* (New York: Anchor, 2014).

62 Zoltan Barany, "Why Have Three Gulf States Introduced the Draft? Bucking the Trend on Conscription in Arabia," *The RUSI Journal* 162, no. 6 (2017): 16–26.

63 Waleed Hazbun, "The Politics of Insecurity in the Arab World: A View from Beirut," *PS: Political Science & Politics*, no. 3 (2017): 656–9 (656).

64 Samer Abboud et al., "Towards a Beirut School of Critical Security Studies," *Critical Studies on Security* 6, no. 3 (2018): 273–95 (289).

PART II (INTRODUCTION)

1 See Dyan Mazurana, Karen Jacobsen, and Lacey Andrews Gale, *Research Methods in Conflict Settings: A View from Below* (New York: Cambridge University Press, 2013); Elisabeth Jean Wood, "The Ethical Challenges of Field Research in Conflict Zones," *Qualitative Sociology* 29, no. 3 (2006): 373–86; Nissim Cohen and Tamar Arieli, "Field Research in Conflict Environments: Methodological Challenges and Snowball Sampling," *Journal of Peace Research* 48, no. 4 (2011): 423–35. On the Middle East particularly, see David Romano, "Conducting Research in the Middle East's Conflict Zones," *PS: Political Science & Politics* 39, no. 3 (2006): 439–41; Sarah E. Parkinson, "Seeing beyond the Spectacle: Research on and Adjacent to Violence," in *Political Science Research in the Middle East and North Africa*, edited by Francesco Cavatorta and Janine Clark (New York: Oxford University Press, 2018).

2 John Gerring, "Causation: A Unified Framework for the Social Sciences," *Journal of Theoretical Politics* 17, no. 2 (2005): 163–98; Craig Parsons, *How to Map Arguments in Political Science* (New York: Oxford University Press, 2007).

3 Annika Mombauer, *The Origins of the First World War: Diplomatic and Military Documents* (Manchester: Manchester University Press, 2013).

4 Clayton Roberts, *Logic of Historical Explanation* (State College: Pennsylvania State University Press, 2010).

5 Kenneth Neal Waltz, *Man, the State, and War: A Theoretical Analysis* (New York:

Columbia University Press, 2001); Stephen Van Evera, *Causes of War: Power and the Roots of Conflict* (Ithaca, NY: Cornell University Press, 2013).

6 Azar Gat, *War in Human Civilization* (New York: Oxford University Press, 2008); Bradley A. Thayer, *Darwin and International Relations: On the Evolutionary Origins of War and Ethnic Conflict* (Lexington: University Press of Kentucky, 2009).

7 Hidemi Suganami, "Explaining War: Some Critical Observations," *International Relations* 16, no. 3 (2002): 307–26.

8 There is some debate as to how severe this risk is. Cf. Astri Suhrke and Ingrid Samset, "What's in a Figure? Estimating Recurrence of Civil War," *International Peacekeeping* 14, no. 2 (2007): 195–203.

9 Paul Collier, *Breaking the Conflict Trap: Civil War and Development Policy* (Washington, DC: World Bank Publications, 2003), 4.

10 Barbara F. Walter, "Does Conflict Beget Conflict? Explaining Recurring Civil War," *Journal of Peace Research* 41, no. 3 (2004): 371–88; Jacob Bercovitch and Karl DeRouen Jr., *Unraveling Internal Conflicts in East Asia and the Pacific: Incidence, Consequences, and Resolution* (Lanham, Md.: Lexington Books, 2011).

11 Gary Goertz and Paul F. Diehl, "The Empirical Importance of Enduring Rivalries," *International Interactions* 18, no. 2 (1992): 151–63.

12 Bruce G. Link and Jo Phelan, "Social Conditions as Fundamental Causes of Disease," *Journal of Health and Social Behavior* 35 [extra issue] (1995): 80–94.

CHAPTER 3 OIL AS CONFLICT TRAP

1 Daniel Yergin, *The Prize: The Epic Quest for Oil, Money and Power* (New York: Simon & Schuster, 2011).

2 Michael L. Ross, *The Oil Curse : How Petroleum Wealth Shapes the Development of Nations* (Princeton, NJ: Princeton University Press, 2012), 3.

3 Daveed Gartenstein-Ross, "Osama's Oil Obsession," *Foreign Policy*, May 23, 2011, *https://foreignpolicy.com/2011/05/23/osamas-oil-obsession-2/*.

4 Jonathan Swan and Alayna Treene, "Trump to Iraqi PM: How About That Oil?," *Axios*, November 25, 2018, *https://www.axios.com/trump-to-iraqi-pm-how-about-that-oil-1a31cbfa-f20c-4767-8d18-d518ed9a6543.html*; Patrick McDonnell and Nabhi Bulos, "Trump Says He Wants to Keep Syria's Oil. Here's the Problem," *Los Angeles Times*, November 4, 2019.

5 Marian Kent, *Moguls and Mandarins: Oil, Imperialism and the Middle East in British Foreign Policy 1900–1940* (New York: Routledge, 2013); Brian Stuart McBeth, *British Oil Policy, 1919–1939* (New York: Routledge, 2013).

6 Stacy L. Eller, Peter R. Hartley, and Kenneth B. Medlock, "Empirical Evidence on the Operational Efficiency of National Oil Companies," *Empirical Economics* 40, no. 3 (2011): 623–43; Valerie Marcel, *Oil Titans: National Oil Companies in the Middle East* (Washington, DC: Brookings Institution Press, 2006).

7 Terry Lynn Karl, *The Paradox of Plenty: Oil Booms and Petro-States* (Berkeley: University of California Press, 1997).

8 Timothy Mitchell, *Carbon Democracy: Political Power in the Age of Oil* (New York: Verso Books, 2011).

9 Lutz Kilian, "Oil Price Shocks: Causes and Consequences," *Annual Review of Resource Economics* 6, no. 1 (2014): 133–54.

10 Simon Bromley, "The United States and the Control of World Oil," *Government and Opposition* 40, no. 2 (2005): 225–55; Emily Meierding, "Dismantling the Oil Wars Myth," *Security Studies* 25, no. 2 (2016): 258–88.

11 Jeff D. Colgan, *Petro-Aggression: When Oil Causes War* (New York: Cambridge University Press, 2013).

12 Gawdat Bahgat, "Energy and the Arab–Israeli Conflict," *Middle Eastern Studies* 44, no. 6 (2008): 937–44.

13 Mehran Kamrava, "Iran–Qatar Relations," in *Security and Bilateral Issues between Iran and Its Arab Neighbours*, edited by Anoush Ehteshami, Neil Quilliam, and Gawdat Bahgat (New York: Palgrave, 2017).

14 Jeff D. Colgan, "Fueling the Fire: Pathways from Oil to War," *International Security* 38, no. 2 (2013): 147–80 (157).

15 "Speech at the Second Meeting of the Arab Cooperation Council in Amman, Jordan (1989)" *https://www.youtube.com/watch?v=yjvTaUB-iRA*.

16 Toby Craig Jones, "America, Oil, and War in the Middle East," *The Journal of American History* 99, no. 1 (2012): 208–18 (217). See also Bromley, "The United States and the Control of World Oil."

17 Rachel Bronson, *Thicker Than Oil: America's Uneasy Partnership with Saudi Arabia* (New York: Oxford University Press, 2006).

18 Kenneth M. Pollack, *Arabs at War: Military Effectiveness, 1948–1991* (Lincoln: University of Nebraska Press, 2004), 446.

19 F. Gregory Gause, III, "Saudi Arabia's Regional Security Strategy," in *International Politics of the Persian Gulf*, edited by Mehran Kamrava (Syracuse, NY: Syracuse University Press, 2011), 170.

20 Steven A. Yetiv and Katerina Oskarsson, *Challenged Hegemony: The United States, China, and Russia in the Persian Gulf* (Stanford, Calif.: Stanford University Press, 2018).

21 Benoit Faucon, Summer Said, and Warren Strobel, "Saudi Arabia Seeks to Ease Tensions with Iran," *Wall Street Journal*, December 12, 2019.

22 Cullen S. Hendrix, "Oil Prices and Interstate Conflict," *Conflict Management and Peace Science* 34, no. 6 (2017): 575–96.

23 Hossein Askari, "Conflicts, Oil Prices, and International Financial Stability," *Georgetown Journal of International Affairs* 14 (2013): 57–64; James D. Hamilton, "What Is an Oil Shock?," *Journal of Econometrics* 113, no. 2 (2003): 363–98.

24 Amy Myers Jaffe and Jareer Elass, "War and the Oil Price Cycle," *Journal of International Affairs* 69, no. 1 (2015): 121–37.

25 Cited in Ariel I. Ahram, *Break All the Borders: Separatism and the Reshaping of the Middle East* (New York: Oxford University Press, 2019), 49.

26 Lisa Anderson, *The State and Social Transformation in Tunisia and Libya, 1830–1980* (Princeton, NJ: Princeton University Press, 2014); Michael Herb, *All in the Family: Absolutism, Revolution, and Democracy in Middle Eastern Monarchies* (Albany, NY: SUNY Press, 1999); Steffen Hertog, *Princes, Brokers, and Bureaucrats: Oil and the State in Saudi Arabia* (Ithaca, NY: Cornell University Press, 2011); Benjamin B. Smith, *Hard Times in the Lands of Plenty: Oil Politics in Iran and Indonesia* (Ithaca, NY: Cornell University Press, 2007).

27 Holger Albrecht, "The Myth of Coup-Proofing: Risk and Instances of Military Coups d'état in the Middle East and North Africa, 1950–2013," *Armed Forces & Society* 41, no. 4 (2015): 659–87; Steffen Hertog, "Rentier Militaries in the Gulf States: The Price of Coup-Proofing," *International Journal of Middle East Studies* 43, no. 3 (2011): 400–2; Shana Marshall, "Military Prestige, Defense-Industrial Production, and the Rise of Gulf Military Activism," in *Armies and Insurgencies in the Arab Spring*, edited by Holger Albrecht, Aurel Croissant, and Fred Lawson (Philadelphia: University of Pennsylvania Press, 2017).

28 Simon Mabon, "Kingdom in Crisis? The Arab Spring and Instability in Saudi Arabia," *Contemporary Security Policy* 33, no. 3 (2012): 530–53; Afshon Ostovar, *Vanguard of the Imam: Religion, Politics, and Iran's Revolutionary Guards* (New York: Oxford University Press, 2016).

29 Human Rights Watch, "Testimony by Tom Malinowski, Human Rights Watch Washington Advocacy Director to House of Representatives," news release, June 14, 2007, *https://www.hrw.org/news/2007/06/14/there-human-rights-double-standard-us-policy-toward-saudi-arabia-iran-uzbekistan-and#*.

30 Calvin H. Allen, Jr., *Oman: The Modernization of the Sultanate* (New York: Routledge, 2016); Zoltan D. Barany, *The Bahrain Defence Force: The Monarchy's Second-to-Last Line of Defense* (Washington, DC: Center for Strategic & International Studies, 2016).

31 Mark Mazzetti and Emily Hager, "Secret Desert Force Set up by Blackwater's Founder," *New York Times*, May 14, 2011.

32 Reuters, "How UAE Used US Mercenaries and a Cyber Super-Weapon to Spy on iPhones of Foes," January 30, 2018, *https://www.nbcnews.com/tech/security/how-uae-used-u-s-mercenaries-cyber-super-weapon-spy-n964436*; Marcus Weisgerber, "US Defense Firms Eye Expansion into Saudi Arabia," *Defense One*, April 4, 2018, *https://www.defenseone.com/business/2018/04/us-defense-firms-eye-expansion-saudi-arabia/147182/*.

33 Abeer Abdulaziz al-Sarrani, "From Soil to Oil: The Resistance of the Environment in the Cities of Salt," *International Journal of Comparative Literature and Translation Studies* 3, no. 4 (2015): 20–6.

34 Farah al-Nakib, "Kuwait's Modern Spectacle: Oil Wealth and the Making of a New Capital City, 1950–90," *Comparative Studies of South Asia, Africa and the Middle East* 33, no. 1 (2013): 7–25.

35 Mohammed al-Zaidi, "Between Black Gold, Bleak Prospects: Visiting the Iraqi Shanty Town between Two Oil Fields," *Niqash*, n.d., *http://www.niqash.org/en/articles/economy/5198/*.

36 Mitchell, *Carbon Democracy*, 102–4; Nelida Fuccaro, "Introduction: Histories of Oil and Urban Modernity in the Middle East," *Comparative Studies of South Asia, Africa and the Middle East* 33, no. 1 (2013): 1–6.

37 Päivi Lujala, "The Spoils of Nature: Armed Civil Conflict and Rebel Access to Natural Resources," *Journal of Peace Research* 47, no. 1 (2010): 15–28; Philippe Le Billon and Alejandro Cervantes, "Oil Prices, Scarcity, and Geographies of War," *Annals of the Association of American Geographers* 99, no. 5 (2009): 836–44; Philipp Hunziker and Lars-Erik Cederman, "No Extraction without Representation: The Ethno-Regional Oil Curse and Secessionist Conflict," *Journal of Peace Research* 54, no. 3 (2017): 365–81; Gudrun Østby, Ragnhild Nordås, and Jan Ketil Rød, "Regional Inequalities and Civil Conflict in Sub-Saharan Africa," *International Studies Quarterly* 53, no. 2 (2009): 301–24.

38 Robert Vitalis, *America's Kingdom: Mythmaking on the Saudi Oil Frontier* (Stanford, Calif.: Stanford University Press, 2007).

39 Frederic Wehrey, *The Forgotten Uprising in Eastern Saudi Arabia* (Washington, DC: Carnegie Endowment for International Peace, 2013).

40 Brookings Institution, "Brookings Iraq Index" (Washington, DC: Brookings Institution, 2006).

41 Keith Crane, *The Role of Oil in ISIL Finances* (Washington, DC: RAND, 2015); Feryaz Ocakli and Matthew Scotch, "Oil-Fueled Insurgencies: Lootable Wealth and Political Order in Syria, Iraq, and Nigeria," *Journal of Global Security Studies* 2, no. 1 (2017): 74–88; Quy-Toan Do et al., "Terrorism, Geopolitics, and Oil Security: Using Remote Sensing to Estimate Oil Production of the Islamic State," *Energy Research & Social Science* 44 (2018): 411–18.

42 Michael L. Ross, "How Do Natural Resources Influence Civil War? Evidence from Thirteen Cases," *International Organization* 58, no. 1 (2004): 35–67.

43 Liam Anderson and Gareth Stansfield, *Crisis in Kirkuk: The Ethnopolitics of Conflict and Compromise* (Philadelphia: University of Pennsylvania Press, 2011).

44 David McDowall, *Modern History of the Kurds* (New York: I. B. Tauris, 2003), 333.

45 Robin Mills, *Under the Mountains: Kurdish Oil and Regional Politics* (Oxford: Oxford Institute for Energy Studies, 2016); Yaniv Voller, "Kurdish Oil Politics in Iraq: Contested Sovereignty and Unilateralism," *Middle East Policy* 20, no. 1 (2013): 68–82; Alessandro Tinti, "Contested Geographies of Kurdistan: Oil and Kurdish Self-Determination in Iraq" (Sant'Anna Scuola Universitaria Superiore, Pisa, 2019).

46 Dirk J. Vandewalle, *A History of Modern Libya* (New York: Cambridge

University Press, 2012); Judith Gurney, *Libya: The Political Economy of Oil* (New York: Oxford University Press, 1996).

47 Lisa Anderson, "Rogue Libya's Long Road," *Middle East Report*, no. 241 (2006): 42–7; George Joffé, "Libya and Europe," *The Journal of North African Studies* 6, no. 4 (2001): 75–92; Yehudit Ronen, *Qaddafi's Libya in World Politics* (Boulder, Colo.: Lynne Rienner, 2008).

48 Stefan A. G. Talmon, "Recognition of the Libyan National Transitional Council," *ASIL Insight* 15, no. 16 (2011); Christopher S. Chivvis, *Toppling Qaddafi: Libya and the Limits of Liberal Intervention* (New York: Cambridge University Press, 2013); Leonardo Bellodi, "Libya's Assets and the Question of Sovereignty," *Survival* 54, no. 2 (2012): 39–45.

49 Anthony Loyd, "Rebel Choking Libya's Oil Exports Steps up His Bid for Power; Libya," *The Times*, October 30, 2013.

50 Ahram, *Break All the Borders*, 87–93.

51 On Libyan banknotes, see Abdulkader Assad, "Libya's Parallel Central Bank Admits Printing 9.7 Billion Dinar Banknotes in Russia," *Libya Observer*, November 20, 2018; MercyCorp, "Libya's Shadow Economy" (2017). On the banking sector, see International Crisis Group, "Of Tanks and Banks: Stopping a Dangerous Escalation in Libya" (2019), *https://www.crisisgroup.org/middle-east-north-africa/north-africa/libya/201-tanks-and-banks-stopping-dangerous-escalation-libya*.

52 David Sheppard and Heba Saleh, "Libyan Oil Chief Warns Renewed Fighting Threatens Production," *Financial Times*, April 11, 2019.

CHAPTER 4 IDENTITY AS CONFLICT TRAP

1 Carleton S. Coon, *Caravan: The Story of the Middle East*, revised edition (New York: Holt, 1958); Bernard Lewis, *A Middle East Mosaic: Fragments of Life, Letters, and History* (New York: Modern Library, 2001).

2 Fred Kaplan, "Why the Middle East Is Still a Mess a Century after the Sykes–Picot Agreement," *Slate*, May 19, 2016, *https://slate.com/news-and-politics/2016/05/its-not-surprising-the-middle-east-is-a-mess-100-years-after-sykes-picot.html*.

3 Richard Engel, *And Then All Hell Broke Loose: Two Decades in the Middle East* (New York: Simon & Schuster, 2017), 28.

4 Michael C. Hudson, *Arab Politics: The Search for Legitimacy* (New Haven: Yale University Press, 1977), 59.

5 Milton J. Esman, "Ethnic Politics: How Unique Is the Middle East?," in *Ethnicity, Pluralism, and the State in the Middle East*, edited by Milton J. Esman and Itamar Rabinovich (Ithaca, NY: Cornell University Press, 1988), 275.

6 Raymond A. Hinnebusch, *The International Politics of the Middle East* (Manchester: Manchester University Press 2003), 174.

7 Enid Schildkrout, "Ethnicity and Generational Differences among Urban Immigrants in Ghana," in *Urban Ethnicity*, edited by Abner Cohen (New York: Routledge, 1974), 204.

8 Linda T. Darling, "Social Cohesion ('Asabiyya) and Justice in the Late Medieval Middle East," *Comparative Studies in Society & History* 49, no. 2 (2007): 329–57.

9 Yael Tamir, "A Strange Alliance: Isaiah Berlin and the Liberalism of the Fringes," *Ethical Theory & Moral Practice* 1, no. 2 (1998): 279–89.

10 Eugen Weber, *Peasants into Frenchmen: The Modernization of Rural France, 1870–1914* (Stanford, Calif.: Stanford University Press, 1976).

11 Harris Mylonas, *The Politics of Nation-Building: Making Co-Nationals, Refugees, and Minorities* (New York: Cambridge University Press, 2013).

12 Karen Barkey and George Gavrilis, "The Ottoman Millet System: Non-Territorial Autonomy and Its Contemporary Legacy," *Ethnopolitics* 15, no. 1 (2016): 24–42; Stanford J. Shaw, "The Ottoman Millet System: An Evaluation," in *Tolerance and Movements of Religious Dissent in Eastern Europe*, edited by Béla K. Király (New York: Columbia University Press, 1975).

13 M. Şükrü Hanioğlu, *The Young Turks in Opposition* (New York: Oxford University Press, 1995).

14 Rogers Brubaker, "Ethnicity without Groups," *European Journal of Sociology* 43, no. 2 (2002): 163–89.

15 William L. Cleveland, *Making of an Arab Nationalist* (Princeton, NJ: Princeton University Press, 2016); Michael Provence, *The Last Ottoman Generation and the Making of the Modern Middle East* (New York: Cambridge University Press, 2017).

16 David D. Laitin, *Nations, States, and Violence* (New York: Oxford University Press, 2007), 11.

17 Rasmus Christian Elling, *Minorities in Iran: Nationalism and Ethnicity after Khomeini* (New York: Palgrave Macmillan, 2013); A. William Samii, "The Nation and Its Minorities: Ethnicity, Unity, and State Policy in Iran," *Comparative Studies of South Asia, Africa and the Middle East* 20, nos. 1–2 (2000): 128–37; Richard W. Cottam, *Nationalism in Iran* (Pittsburgh: University of Pittsburgh Press, 1964).

18 Ephraim Ya'ar, "Continuity and Change in Israeli Society: The Test of the Melting Pot," *Israel Studies* 10, no. 2 (2005): 91–128.

19 Sammy Smooha, "Minority Status in an Ethnic Democracy: The Status of the Arab Minority in Israel," *Ethnic and Racial Studies* 13, no. 3 (1990): 389–413.

20 Bruce Maddy-Weitzman, *The Berber Identity Movement and the Challenge to North African States* (Austin: University of Texas Press, 2011), 65–6.

21 Arab Barometer, *https://www.arabbarometer.org/survey-data/data-downloads/*.

22 Sarah Sunn Bush et al., "The Effects of Authoritarian Iconography: An Experimental Test," *Comparative Political Studies* 49, no. 13 (2016): 1704–38.

23 Lisa Wedeen, *Ambiguities of Domination: Politics, Rhetoric, and Symbols in Contemporary Syria* (Chicago: University of Chicago Press, 1999); *Peripheral*

Visions: Publics, Power, and Performance in Yemen (Chicago: University of Chicago Press, 2008).

24 Iliya F. Harik, "The Ethnic Revolution and Political Integration in the Middle East," *International Journal of Middle East Studies* 3, no. 3 (1972): 303–23 (304).

25 Imad Salamey and Rhys Payne, "Parliamentary Consociationalism in Lebanon: Equal Citizenry vs. Quotated Confessionalism," *The Journal of Legislative Studies* 14, no. 4 (2008): 451–73; Richard Hrair Dekmejian, "Consociational Democracy in Crisis: The Case of Lebanon," *Comparative Politics* 10, no. 2 (1978): 251–65.

26 Samii, "The Nation and Its Minorities."

27 Eliz Sanasarian, *Religious Minorities in Iran* (New York: Cambridge University Press, 2000).

28 Maddy-Weitzman, *The Berber Identity Movement and the Challenge to North African States*, 119.

29 Dina Rizk Khoury, "The Security State and the Practice and Rhetoric of Sectarianism in Iraq," *International Journal of Contemporary Iraqi Studies* 4, no. 3 (2010): 325–38; Joseph Sassoon, *Saddam Hussein's Ba'th Party: Inside an Authoritarian Regime* (New York: Cambridge University Press, 2012).

30 "Constitution of the Republic of Iraq" (Constitution Project, 2005). *https://www.constituteproject.org/constitution/Iraq_2005.pdf?lang=en.*

31 Hiba Bou Akar, *For the War Yet to Come: Planning Beirut's Frontiers* (Stanford, Calif.: Stanford University Press, 2018). See also Melani Cammett and Sukriti Issar, "Bricks and Mortar Clientelism: Sectarianism and the Logics of Welfare Allocation in Lebanon," *World Politics* 62, no. 3 (2010): 381–421.

32 Max Weiss, "The Historiography of Sectarianism in Lebanon," *History Compass* 7, no. 1 (2009): 141–54.

33 John Nagle, "Between Entrenchment, Reform and Transformation: Ethnicity and Lebanon's Consociational Democracy," *Democratization* 23, no. 7 (2016): 1144–61.

34 Andreas Wimmer, Lars-Erik Cederman, and Brian Min, "Ethnic Politics and Armed Conflict: A Configurational Analysis of a New Global Data Set," *American Sociological Review* 74, no. 2 (2009): 316–37.

35 Manal A. Jamal, "The 'Tiering' of Citizenship and Residency and the 'Hierarchization' of Migrant Communities: The United Arab Emirates in Historical Context," *International Migration Review* 49, no. 3 (2015): 601–32; Virginia N. Sherry, *Syria, the Silenced Kurds* (New York: Human Rights Watch/Middle East Watch, 1996), *https://www.hrw.org/sites/default/files/reports/SYRIA96.pdf.*

36 Nikolaos van Dam, "Middle Eastern Political Clichés: 'Takriti' and 'Sunni Rule' in Iraq, 'Alawi Rule' in Syria: A Critical Appraisal," *Orient* 21, no. 1 (1980): 42–57.

37 Bassam Haddad, *Business Networks in Syria: The Political Economy of Authoritarian Resilience* (Stanford, Calif.: Stanford University Press, 2012).
38 Oren Yiftachel, *Ethnocracy: Land and Identity Politics in Israel/Palestine* (Philadelphia: University of Pennsylvania Press, 2006).
39 Fanar Haddad, "Shi'a-Centric State Building and Sunni Rejection in Post-2003 Iraq," in *Beyond Sunni and Shia: The Roots of Sectarianism in a Changing Middle East*, edited by Frederic Wehrey (New York: Oxford University Press, 2016).
40 Gregoy Kruczek, "Christian Minorities and the Struggle for Nineveh: The Assyrian Democratic Movement in Iraq and the Nineveh Plains Protection Units" (Virginia Tech, 2018).
41 Rebecca Murray, "Libya's Tebu: Living in the Margins," in *The Libyan Revolution and Its Aftermath*, edited by Peter Cole and Brian McQuinn (New York: Oxford University Press, 2015).
42 Jennifer M. Brinkerhoff, "Diaspora Identity and the Potential for Violence: Toward an Identity-Mobilization Framework," *Identity: An International Journal of Theory and Research* 8, no. 1 (2008): 67–88; Avi Kay, "Citizen Rights in Flux: The Influence of American Immigrants to Israel on Modes of Political Activism," *Jewish Political Studies Review* 13, nos. 3–4 (2001): 143–58.
43 Rami Siklawi, "The Dynamics of the Amal Movement in Lebanon 1975–90," *Arab Studies Quarterly* 34, no. 1 (2012): 4–26.
44 Liam D. Anderson and Gareth R. V. Stansfield, *Crisis in Kirkuk: The Ethnopolitics of Conflict and Compromise* (Philadelphia: University of Pennsylvania Press, 2009), 43. See also Arbella Bet-Shlimon, *City of Black Gold: Oil, Ethnicity, and the Making of Modern Kirkuk* (Stanford, Calif.: Stanford University Press, 2019).
45 Maddy-Weitzman, *The Berber Identity Movement and the Challenge to North African States*, 66.
46 John Gledhill, "When State Capacity Dissolves: Explaining Variation in Violent Conflict and Conflict Moderation," *European Journal of International Security* 2, no. 2 (2017): 153–78.
47 Barry R. Posen, "The Security Dilemma and Ethnic Conflict," *Survival* 35, no. 1 (1993): 27–47.
48 David A. Lake and Donald S. Rothchild, "Containing Fear," *International Security* 21, no. 2 (1996): 41–75; Stathis Kalyvas, "Ethnic Defection in Civil War," *Comparative Political Studies* 41, no. 8 (2008): 1043–68.
49 Michael Edward Brown, ed., *The International Dimensions of Internal Conflict* (Cambridge, Mass.: MIT Press, 1996).
50 Jill Ricotta, "The Arab Shi'a Nexus: Understanding Iran's Influence in the Arab World," *Washington Quarterly* 39, no. 2 (2016): 139–54; Babak Rahimi, "Iran's Declining Influence in Iraq," *Washington Quarterly* 35, no. 1 (2012): 25–40.
51 Douglas Ollivant and Erica Gaston, "The Problem with the Narrative of

'Proxy War' in Iraq," *War on the Rocks*, May 31, 2019, *https://warontherocks.com/2019/05/the-problem-with-the-narrative-of-proxy-war-in-iraq/*.

52 Andrew Tabler, "How Syria Came to This," *Atlantic*, April 15, 2018, *https://www.theatlantic.com/international/archive/2018/04/syria-chemical-weapons/558065/*; M. Zuhdi Jasser, "Sectarian Conflict in Syria," *PRISM* 4 (2014): 58–67.

53 Kevin Mazur, "State Networks and Intra-Ethnic Group Variation in the 2011 Syrian Uprising," *Comparative Political Studies* 52, no. 7 (2018): 995–1027.

54 Raymond Hinnebusch and Morten Valbjørn, "Sectarianism and Governance in Syria," *Studies in Ethnicity and Nationalism* 19, no. 1 (2019): 41–66.

55 Abu Musab Zarqawi, "February 2004 Coalition Provisional Authority English Translation of Terrorist Musab Al Zarqawi Letter Obtained by United States Government in Iraq" (US Department of State, 2004).

56 Arie Perliger and Daniel Milton, "From Cradle to Grave: The Lifecycle of Foreign Fighters in Iraq and Syria" (US Military Academy–Combating Terrorism Center West Point United States, 2016); Meirav Mishali-Ram, "Foreign Fighters and Transnational Jihad in Syria," *Studies in Conflict and Terrorism* 41, no. 3 (2018): 169–90.

57 Ariel I. Ahram, "Sexual Violence, Competitive State Building, and Islamic State in Iraq and Syria," *Journal of Intervention and Statebuilding* 13, no. 2 (2019): 180–96; Miriam Cooke, "Murad vs. ISIS: Rape as a Weapon of Genocide," *Journal of Middle East Women's Studies* 15, no. 3 (2019): 261–85.

58 Harout Akdedian, "On Violence and Radical Theology in the Syrian War: The Instrumentality of Spectacular Violence and Exclusionary Practices from Comparative and Local Standpoints," *Politics, Religion & Ideology* 20, no. 3 (2019): 361–80.

59 Charles R. Lister, *The Islamic State: A Brief Introduction* (Washington, DC: Brookings Institution Press, 2015), 48–9; Ali Nehme Hamdan, "Breaker of Barriers? Notes on the Geopolitics of the Islamic State in Iraq and Sham," *Geopolitics* 21, no. 3 (2016): 605–27.

60 Mara Revkin and Ariel I. Ahram, "Exit, Voice, and Loyalty under the Islamic State," in *Adaptation Strategies of Islamist Movements* (Washington, DC: Project on Middle East Political Science, 2017), *http://pomeps.org/wp-content/uploads/2017/04/POMEPS_Studies_26_Adaptation_Draft2.pdf#page=27*.

61 Christopher Phillips, "Sectarianism and Conflict in Syria," *Third World Quarterly* 36, no. 2 (2015): 357–76.

62 Wendy Pearlman, "Narratives of Fear in Syria," *Perspectives on Politics* 14, no. 1 (2016): 21–37.

CHAPTER 5 GEOPOLITICS AS CONFLICT TRAP

1 Sadik J. al-Azm, "Islam, Terrorism and the West Today," *Welt des Islams* 44, no. 1 (2004): 114–28 (116).

2 Jon W. Anderson, "Conspiracy Theories, Premature Entextualization, and Popular Political Analysis," *The Arab Studies Journal* 4, no. 1 (1996):

96–102; Matthew Gray, "Explaining Conspiracy Theories in Modern Arab Middle Eastern Political Discourse: Some Problems and Limitations of the Literature," *Critique: Critical Middle Eastern Studies* 17, no. 2 (2008): 155–74; Brendan Nyhan and Thomas Zeitzoff, "Conspiracy and Misperception Belief in the Middle East and North Africa," *Journal of Politics* 80, no. 4 (2018): 1400–4.

3 Stephen Zunes, "The United States Middle East Policy: The Need for Alternatives," *Peace Research* 25, no. 3 (1993): 105–16 (115).

4 Aharon Klieman, "Introduction," in *Great Powers and Geopolitics: International Affairs in a Rebalancing World*, edited by Aharon Klieman (New York: Springer, 2015), 4.

5 Daniel Deudney, "Geopolitics as Theory: Historical Security Materialism," *European Journal of International Relations* 6, no. 1 (2000): 77–107; Lucian M. Ashworth, "Mapping a New World: Geography and the Interwar Study of International Relations," *International Studies Quarterly* 57, no. 1 (2013): 138–49; Mackubin T. Owens, "In Defense of Classical Geopolitics," *Orbis* 59, no. 4 (2015): 463–78; Zhengyu Wu, "Classical Geopolitics, Realism and the Balance of Power Theory," *Journal of Strategic Studies* 41, no. 6 (2018): 786–823.

6 Edward W. Said, *Orientalism* (New York: Vintage, 1979); James Derrick Sidaway, "Geopolitics, Geography, and 'Terrorism' in the Middle East," *Environment and Planning D: Society and Space* 12, no. 3 (1994): 357–72.

7 Eid Mohamed, *Arab Occidentalism: Images of America in the Middle East* (New York: I. B. Tauris, 2015).

8 Sadik J. al-Azm, "Orientalism, Occidentalism, and Islamism," *Comparative Studies of South Asia, Africa and the Middle East* 30, no. 1 (2010): 6–13 (8).

9 Michiel Foulon, "Neoclassical Realism: Challengers and Bridging Identities," *International Studies Review* 17, no. 4 (2015): 635–61.

10 Karen Culcasi, "Constructing and Naturalizing the Middle East," *Geographical Review* 100, no. 4 (2010): 583–97.

11 Janet L. Abu-Lughod, *Before European Hegemony: The World System AD 1250–1350* (New York: Oxford University Press, 1991); Lisa Blaydes and Christopher Paik, "Muslim Trade and City Growth before the Nineteenth Century: Comparative Urbanization in Europe, the Middle East and Central Asia," *British Journal of Political Science* (2019), https://doi.org/10.1017/S0007123419000267.

12 Andrew Wheatcroft, *The Enemy at the Gate: Habsburgs, Ottomans, and the Battle for Europe* (New York: Basic Books, 2009).

13 Gerrit W. Gong, *The Standard of "Civilization" in International Society* (Oxford: Clarendon Press, 1984); Umut Özsu, Florian Hoffmann, and Anne Orford, "The Ottoman Empire, the Origins of Extraterritoriality, and International Legal Theory," in *The Oxford Handbook of the Theory of International Law*, edited by Anne Orford and Florian Hoffmann (New York: Oxford University Press, 2016).

14 Osama bin Laden, "Among a Band of Knights," translated by James Howarth, in *Messages to the World: The Statements of Osama bin Laden*, edited by Bruce Lawrence (London: Verso, 2005), 18.

15 Cited in James Gelvin, "Don't Blame Sykes–Picot," *OUPblog*, February 7, 2015, *https://blog.oup.com/2015/02/dont-blame-sykes-picot/*.

16 Robin Wright, "How the Curse of Sykes–Picot Still Haunts the Middle East," *The New Yorker*, April 30, 2016, *https://www.newyorker.com/news/news-desk/how-the-curse-of-sykes-picot-still-haunts-the-middle-east*.

17 Ariel I. Ahram, *Break All the Borders: Separatism and the Reshaping of the Middle East* (New York: Oxford University Press, 2019), 22. See also Elizabeth F. Thompson, *Justice Interrupted* (Cambridge, Mass.: Harvard University Press, 2013); Erez Manela, *The Wilsonian Moment: Self-Determination and the International Origins of Anticolonial Nationalism* (New York: Oxford University Press, 2007).

18 Priya Satia, "The Defense of Inhumanity: Air Control and the British Idea of Arabia," *The American Historical Review* 111, no. 1 (2006): 16–51; David E. Omissi, *Air Power and Colonial Control: The Royal Air Force, 1919–1939* (Manchester: Manchester University Press, 1990).

19 On the novelty of the mandate and the empowerment of mandatory leaders, see Michelle Burgis, "Mandated Sovereignty? The Role of International Law in the Construction of Arab Statehood during and after Empire," in *Sovereignty after Empire: Comparing the Middle East and Central Asia*, edited by Raymond Hinnebusch and Sally Cummings (Edinburgh: Edinburgh University Press, 2011); David Kenneth Fieldhouse, *Western Imperialism in the Middle East, 1914–1958* (New York: Oxford University Press, 2006), 340–8; Peter Sluglett, "An Improvement on Colonialism? The 'A' Mandates and Their Legacy in the Middle East," *International Affairs* 90, no. 2 (2014): 413–27; Susan Pedersen, "The Meaning of the Mandates System: An Argument," *Geschichte und Gesellschaft* 32, no. 4 (2006): 560–82.

20 David Siddharta Patel, "Repartitioning the Sykes–Picot Middle East? Debunking Three Myths," in *Middle East Brief* (Brandeis University Crown Center, 2016).

21 Katherine E. Hoffman, "Purity and Contamination: Language Ideologies in French Colonial Native Policy in Morocco," *Comparative Studies in Society and History* 50, no. 3 (2008): 724–52; Jonathan Wyrtzen, "Colonial Legitimization–Legibility Linkages and the Politics of Identity in Algeria and Morocco," *European Journal of Sociology* 58, no. 2 (2017): 205–35.

22 Christian Koller, "The Recruitment of Colonial Troops in Africa and Asia and Their Deployment in Europe during the First World War," *Immigrants & Minorities* 26, nos. 1–2 (2008): 111–33; Kaushik Roy, *The Indian Army in the Two World Wars* (Leiden: Brill, 2011); Stephen Russell Cox, "Britain and the Origin of Israeli Special Operations: SOE and Palmach during the Second World War," *Dynamics of Asymmetric Conflict* 8, no. 1 (2015): 60–78.

23 Avi Shlaim, "Britain and the Arab–Israeli War of 1948," *Journal of Palestine Studies* 16, no. 4 (1987): 50–76; Mark Heller, "Politics and the Military in Iraq and Jordan, 1920–1958: The British Influence," *Armed Forces & Society* 4, no. 1 (1977): 75–99.

24 Aula Hariri, "State Formation as an Outcome of the Imperial Encounter: The Case of Iraq," *Review of International Studies* 45, no. 5 (2019): 848–69.

25 Massimiliano Fiore, *Anglo-Italian Relations in the Middle East, 1922–1940* (New York: Routledge, 2016).

26 Joost Hiltermann, "The Middle East in Chaos: Of Orders and Borders," *Al Sharq Forum*, May 25, 2018, *https://www.crisisgroup.org/middle-east-north-africa/ middle-east-chaos-orders-and-borders*.

27 Steven L. Spiegel, *The Other Arab–Israeli Conflict: Making America's Middle East Policy, from Truman to Reagan* (Chicago: University of Chicago Press, 1986); John J. Mearsheimer and Stephen M. Walt, "Is It Love or the Lobby? Explaining America's Special Relationship with Israel," *Security Studies* 18, no. 1 (2009): 58–78.

28 Karen Dawisha, "Soviet Policy in the Arab World: Permanent Interests and Changing Influence," *Arab Studies Quarterly* 2, no. 1 (1980): 19–37.

29 Vincent Crapanzano, *The Harkis: The Wound That Never Heals* (Chicago: University of Chicago Press, 2011).

30 Simon C. Smith, *Ending Empire in the Middle East: Britain, the United States and Post-War Decolonization, 1945–1973* (New York: Routledge, 2013).

31 Melvyn P. Leffler, *For the Soul of Mankind: The United States, the Soviet Union, and the Cold War* (New York: Macmillan, 2007); Michael E. Latham, *The Right Kind of Revolution: Modernization, Development, and US Foreign Policy from the Cold War to the Present* (Ithaca, NY: Cornell University Press, 2010).

32 Louise Fawcett, *Iran and the Cold War: The Azerbaijan Crisis of 1946.* (New York: Cambridge University Press, 2009).

33 Mark J. Gasiorowski and Malcolm Byrne, *Mohammad Mosaddeq and the 1953 Coup in Iran* (Syracuse, NY: Syracuse University Press, 2015).

34 Malcolm H. Kerr, *The Arab Cold War: Gamal 'abd Al-Nasir and His Rivals, 1958– 1970* (New York: Oxford University Press, 1971), vi.

35 Michael B. Oren, *Six Days of War: June 1967 and the Making of the Modern Middle East* (New York: Presidio Press, 2017); Wm. Roger Louis and Avi Shlaim, *The 1967 Arab–Israeli War: Origins and Consequences* (New York: Cambridge University Press, 2012).

36 Richard Bordeaux Parker, *The Politics of Miscalculation in the Middle East* (Bloomington: Indiana University Press 1993), x.

37 Peter Sluglett and Andrew Payne, "The Cold War in the Middle East," in *International Relations of the Middle East*, fifth edition, edited by Louise Fawcett (New York: Oxford University Press, 2019), 64.

38 Avner Cohen, *Israel and the Bomb* (New York: Columbia University Press, 1998).

39 Benjamin Miller, *International and Regional Security: The Causes of War and Peace* (New York: Routledge, 2016), 83.
40 Hal Brands, "Saddam Hussein, the United States, and the Invasion of Iran: Was There a Green Light?," *Cold War History* 12, no. 2 (2012): 319–43; Chad E. Nelson, "Revolution and War: Saddam's Decision to Invade Iran," *The Middle East Journal* 72, no. 2 (2018): 246–66.
41 The Iran–Iraq War is surprisingly understudied given its importance. For recent work, see Pierre Razoux, *The Iran–Iraq War* (Cambridge, Mass.: Harvard University Press, 2015); Nigel Ashton and Bryan Gibson, eds., *The Iran–Iraq War: New International Perspectives* (New York: Routledge, 2013).
42 Keith L. Shimko, *The Iraq Wars and America's Military Revolution* (New York: Cambridge University Press, 2010).
43 Michael C. Hudson, "The Middle East under *Pax Americana*: How New, How Orderly?," *Third World Quarterly* 13, no. 2 (1992): 301–16 (309).
44 Fred Halliday, *The Middle East in International Relations: Power, Politics and Ideology* (New York: Cambridge University Press, 2005), 161.
45 Melani McAlister, *Epic Encounters: Culture, Media, and US Interests in the Middle East since 1945* (Berkeley: University of California Press, 2005), 211.
46 Sadik al-Azm, *Self-Criticism after the Defeat* (London: Saqi, 2012).
47 Shadi Hamid, *Temptations of Power: Islamists and Illiberal Democracy in a New Middle East* (New York: Oxford University Press, 2014).
48 Samuel P. Huntington, "The Clash of Civilizations," *Foreign Affairs* 72, no. 3 (1993): 22–49. For just one of many empirical critiques, see Errol A. Henderson, "Not Letting Evidence Get in the Way of Assumptions: Testing the Clash of Civilizations Thesis with More Recent Data," *International Politics* 42, no. 4 (2005): 458–69.
49 Fawaz A. Gerges, *The Far Enemy: Why Jihad Went Global* (New York: Cambridge University Press, 2009); Gilles Kepel, *Jihad: The Trail of Political Islam* (New York: I. B. Tauris, 2006).
50 Thomas Hegghammer, "The Rise of Muslim Foreign Fighters: Islam and the Globalization of Jihad," *International Security* 35, no. 3 (2010): 53–94; David Malet, *Foreign Fighters: Transnational Identity in Civil Conflicts* (New York: Oxford University Press, 2013).
51 Barak Mendelsohn, *The al-Qaeda Franchise: The Expansion of al-Qaeda and Its Consequences* (New York: Oxford University Press, 2015); Katherine Zimmerman, "The al-Qaeda Network: A New Framework for Defining the Enemy," in *AEI Paper & Studies* (Washington, DC: The American Enterprise Institute, 2013).
52 Ronald Crelinsten, *Counterterrorism* (New York: John Wiley & Sons, 2013).
53 Stephen Tankel, *With Us and Against Us: How America's Partners Help and Hinder the War on Terror* (New York: Columbia University Press, 2018); Daniel Byman, "Remaking Alliances for the War on Terrorism," *Journal of Strategic Studies* 29, no. 5 (2006): 767–811.

54 Oren Barak, "Dilemmas of Security in Iraq," *Security Dialogue* 38, no. 4 (2007): 455–75; Ahmed Hashim, *Insurgency and Counter-Insurgency in Iraq* (Ithaca, NY: Cornell University Press, 2005), 303–6.

55 Ariel I. Ahram, *Proxy Warriors: The Rise and Fall of State-Sponsored Militias* (Stanford, Calif.: Stanford University Press, 2011), 90.

56 Hal Brands, "Barack Obama and the Dilemmas of American Grand Strategy," *The Washington Quarterly* 39, no. 4 (2016): 101–25.

57 Peter Feaver and Hal Brands, "Lessons from the Iraq War " *National Review*, June 20, 2019.

58 Craig Kafura, "Ten Years On: American Public Opinion on the War in Iraq," *Chicago Council on Global Affairs*, March 22, 2013, *https://www.thechicagocouncil. org/blog/running-numbers/ten-years-american-public-opinion-war-iraq?page=9*.

59 Claire Lauterbach, "The Costs of Cooperation: Civilian Casualty Counts in Iraq," *International Studies Perspectives* 8, no. 4 (2007): 429–45.

60 Adeed Dawisha, *Iraq: A Political History* (Princeton, NJ: Princeton University Press, 2013), 272.

61 John Kaag and Sarah Kreps, *Drone Warfare* (Cambridge: Polity, 2014).

62 Alastair Finlan, *Special Forces, Strategy and the War on Terror: Warfare by Other Means* (New York: Routledge, 2009).

63 Deborah D. Avant, "Pragmatic Networks and Transnational Governance of Private Military and Security Services," *International Studies Quarterly* 60, no. 2 (2016): 330–42; Micah Zenko, "Mercenaries Are the Silent Majority of Obama's Military," *Foreign Policy*, May 18, 2016, *https://foreignpolicy.com/2016/ 05/18/private-contractors-are-the-silent-majority-of-obamas-military-mercenaries-iraq- afghanistan/*.

64 Matthew P. Dearing, "Turning Gangsters into Allies: The American Way of War in Northern Afghanistan," *Small Wars & Insurgencies* 30, no. 1 (2019): 101–39.

65 Tankel, *With Us and Against Us*, 207.

66 Andreas Krieg, "Externalizing the Burden of War: The Obama Doctrine and US Foreign Policy in the Middle East," *International Affairs* 92, no. 1 (2016): 97–113; Seyom Brown, "Purposes and Pitfalls of War by Proxy: A Systemic Analysis," *Small Wars & Insurgencies* 27, no. 2 (2016): 243–57.

67 James Sladden et al., *Russian Strategy in the Middle East* (Washington, DC: RAND Corporation, 2017); Roy Allison, "Russia and Syria: Explaining Alignment with a Regime in Crisis," *International Affairs* 89, no. 4 (2013): 795–823.

68 Jon B. Alterman and John W. Garver, *The Vital Triangle: China, the United States, and the Middle East* (Washington, DC: Center for Strategic and International Studies, 2008); Andrew Scobell and Alireza Nader, *China in the Middle East: The Wary Dragon* (Washington DC: RAND Corporation, 2016); European Council on Foreign Relations, "China's Great Game in the Middle East" (2019).

69 Edward W. Said, *Culture and Imperialism* (New York: Vintage, 2012), 15.
70 Fred Halliday, "The Great Powers and the Middle East," *Middle East Report* 18, no. 151 (1988): 3–6 (5).

CHAPTER 6 FRAGMENTATION, INTEGRATION, AND WAR IN THE 2010S

1 Marc Lynch, *The Arab Uprising: The Unfinished Revolutions of the New Middle East* (New York: PublicAffairs, 2013).
2 Therése Pettersson and Kristine Eck, "Organized Violence, 1989–2017," *Journal of Peace Research* 55, no. 4 (2018): 535–47.
3 Helle Malmvig, "Power, Identity and Securitization in Middle East: Regional Order after the Arab Uprisings," *Mediterranean Politics* 19, no. 1 (2014): 145–8; Simon Mabon, *Saudi Arabia and Iran: Power and Rivalry in the Middle East* (New York: I. B. Tauris, 2015).
4 Robert Marquand, "Amid BRICS' Rise and 'Arab Spring,' a New Global Order Forms," *Christian Science Monitor*, October 18, 2011.
5 Nader Hashemi and Danny Postel, eds., *Sectarianization: Mapping the New Politics of the Middle East* (New York: Oxford University Press, 2017); Simon Mabon and Lucia Ardovini, eds., *Sectarianism in the Contemporary Middle East* (New York: Routledge, 2018); F. Gregory Gause, "Beyond Sectarianism: The New Middle East Cold War" (Brookings Doha Center, 2014).
6 Idean Salehyan, "The Delegation of War to Rebel Organizations," *Journal of Conflict Resolution* 54, no. 3 (2010): 493–515; R. Kim Cragin, "Semi-Proxy Wars and US Counterterrorism Strategy," *Studies in Conflict & Terrorism* 38, no. 5 (2015): 311–27; Andrew Mumford, *Proxy Warfare* (New York: John Wiley & Sons, 2013).
7 Sabine C. Carey and Neil J. Mitchell, "Pro-Government Militias and Conflict," in *Oxford Research Encyclopedia of Politics* (2016).
8 Salehyan, "The Delegation of War to Rebel Organizations."
9 Seyom Brown, "Purposes and Pitfalls of War by Proxy: A Systemic Analysis," *Small Wars & Insurgencies* 27, no. 2 (2016): 243–57 (244).
10 Belgin San Akca, "Supporting Non-State Armed Groups: A Resort to Illegality?," *Journal of Strategic Studies* 32, no. 4 (2009): 589–613.
11 Boaz Atzili and Wendy Pearlman, "Triadic Deterrence: Coercing Strength, Beaten by Weakness," *Security Studies* 21, no. 2 (2012): 301–35; Austin Carson, *Secret Wars: Covert Conflict in International Politics* (Princeton, NJ: Princeton University Press, 2018).
12 Erica Borghard, "Friends with Benefits? Power and Influence in Proxy Warfare" (Ph.D. thesis, Columbia University, 2014); Geraint Hughes, *My Enemy's Enemy: Proxy Warfare in International Politics* (Chicago: Sussex Academic Press, 2012).
13 Niklas Karlén, "Turning Off the Taps: The Termination of State Sponsorship," *Terrorism and Political Violence* 31, no. 4 (2019): 733–58; Daniel Byman and Sarah Kreps, "Agents of Destruction? Applying Principal-Agent

Analysis to State-Sponsored Terrorism," *International Studies Perspectives* 11, no. 1 (2010): 1–18.

14 Eric Rittinger, "Arming the Other: American Small Wars, Local Proxies, and the Social Construction of the Principal–Agent Problem," *International Studies Quarterly* 61, no. 2 (2017): 396–409.

15 Milos Popovic, "Fragile Proxies: Explaining Rebel Defection against Their State Sponsors," *Terrorism and Political Violence* 29, no. 5 (2017): 922–42.

16 Jeremy M. Weinstein, *Inside Rebellion: The Politics of Insurgent Violence* (New York: Cambridge University Press, 2006); Daniel Byman, "Why Be a Pawn to a State? Proxy Wars from a Proxy's Perspective," *Brookings*, May 22, 2018, *https://www.brookings.edu/blog/order-from-chaos/2018/05/22/why-be-a-pawn-to-a-state-proxy-wars-from-a-proxys-perspective/*.

17 Ersel Aydinli and James N. Rosenau, *Globalization, Security, and the Nation-State: Paradigms in Transition* (Albany, NY: SUNY Press, 2005).

18 James N. Rosenau, *Distant Proximities: Dynamics beyond Globalization* (Princeton, NJ: Princeton University Press, 2003).

19 Zachariah Cherian Mampilly, Nelson Kasfir, and Ana Arjona, eds., *Rebel Governance in Civil War* (Cambridge: Cambridge University Press, 2015).

20 Aidan Hehir, "Assessing the Influence of the Responsibility to Protect on the UN Security Council during the Arab Spring," *Cooperation and Conflict* 51, no. 2 (2016): 166–83; Andrew Garwood-Gowers, "The Responsibility to Protect and the Arab Spring: Libya as the Exception, Syria as the Norm," *University of New South Wales Law Journal* 36 (2013): 594–618.

21 Cited in Ariel I. Ahram, *Break All the Borders: Separatism and the Reshaping of the Middle East* (New York: Oxford University Press, 2019), 50.

22 Ethan Chorin, *Exit the Colonel: The Hidden History of the Libyan Revolution* (New York: PublicAffairs, 2012), 204–5.

23 Youssef M. Sawani, "The February 17 Intifada in Libya: Disposing of the Regime and Issues of State-Building," in *Revolution, Revolt and Reform in North Africa*, edited by Ricardo Laremont (New York: Routledge, 2013), 73; Sean Kane, "Barqa Reborn? Eastern Regionalism and Libya's Political Transition," in *The Libyan Revolution and Its Aftermath* edited by Peter Cole and Brian McQuinn (New York: Oxford University Press, 2015), 211.

24 William Taylor, *Military Responses to the Arab Uprisings and the Future of Civil–Military Relations in the Middle East: Analysis from Egypt, Tunisia, Libya, and Syria* (New York: Springer, 2014), 148; Jihad Awdeh, Mahmud Jawdeh, and Ahmed al-Khatib, *Militishiyat wa al-Harakat al-Musallahah fi Libya* (Cairo: Maktab al-'Arabi lil t'arouf, 2015).

25 Taylor, *Military Responses to the Arab Uprisings and the Future of Civil–Military Relations in the Middle East*, 152–4.

26 Kristian Coates Ulrichsen, "The Rationale and Implications of Qatar's Intervention in Libya," in *Political Rationale and International Consequences of*

the War in Libya, edited by Dag Henriksen and Ann Karin Larsen (New York: Oxford University Press, 2016).

27 Christopher S. Chivvis, *Toppling Qaddafi: Libya and the Limits of Liberal Intervention* (New York: Cambridge University Press, 2013), 60–2.

28 Alan J. Kuperman, "A Model Humanitarian Intervention? Reassessing Nato's Libya Campaign," *International Security* 38, no. 1 (2013): 105–36 (114).

29 Kristian Coates Ulrichsen, *Qatar and the Arab Spring* (New York: Oxford University Press, 2014), 127; Sam Dagher, Charles Levinson, and Margaret Coker, "Tiny Kingdom's Huge Rule in Libya Draws Concern," *Wall Street Journal*, October 17, 2011.

30 Chivvis, *Toppling Qaddafi*, 105–8.

31 Cited in Ahram, *Break All the Borders*, 59.

32 Lisa Anderson, "'They Defeated Us All': International Interests, Local Politics, and Contested Sovereignty in Libya," *The Middle East Journal* 71, no. 2 (2017): 229–47 (242).

33 Ulrichsen, "The Rationale and Implications of Qatar's Intervention in Libya," 126. See also Leonardo Bellodi, "Libya's Assets and the Question of Sovereignty," *Survival* 54, no. 2 (2012): 39–45.

34 Frederic Wehrey, "A Minister, a General, & the Militias: Libya's Shifting Balance of Power," *New York Review of Books*, March 19, 2019.

35 Jalel Harchaoui and Mohamed-Essaïd Lazib, *Proxy War Dynamics in Libya* (Blacksburg: Virginia Tech Press, 2019).

36 Luke Glanville, *Sovereignty and the Responsibility to Protect: A New History* (Chicago: University of Chicago Press, 2013), 333–6; Ethan Bromer and David Sanger, "Arab League Endorses No-Flight Zone over Libya," *New York Times*, March 12, 2011.

37 Rustum Mahmoud and Stephan Rosiny, "Opposition Visions for Preserving Syria's Ethnic-Sectarian Mosaic," *British Journal of Middle Eastern Studies* 45, no. 2 (2018): 231–50.

38 Christopher Phillips, *The Battle for Syria: International Rivalry in the New Middle East* (New Haven: Yale University Press, 2016), 163.

39 Reinoud Leenders and Antonio Giustozzi, "Outsourcing State Violence: The National Defence Force, 'Stateness' and Regime Resilience in the Syrian War," *Mediterranean Politics* 24, no. 2 (2019): 157–80; Ariel I. Ahram, "Territory, Sovereignty, and New Statehood in the Middle East and North Africa," *The Middle East Journal* 71, no. 3 (2017): 345–62.

40 Phillip Connor, "Most Displaced Syrians Are in the Middle East, and About a Million Are in Europe" (Pew Research Center, 2018).

41 United Nations Institute for Training and Research–Operational Satellite Applications Program, "Syrian Cities Damage Atlas," (2019).

42 Small Arms Survey, "Yemen Armed Violence Assessment" (2010), *http:// www.smallarmssurvey.org/focus-projects/yemen-armed-violence-assessment.html*.

43 Cited in Ahram, *Break All the Borders*, 63.

44 Anthony Hardwood, "Saudi Arabia Using Famine as Weapon in War," *Newseek*, November 28, 2017; Kate Lyons, "Yemen's Cholera Outbreak Worst in History," *The Guardian*, October 12, 2017.

45 Office of the UN Secretary-General, "Remarks by the Secretary-General to the Pledging Conference on Yemen," news release, April 3, 2018, *https://www.unog.ch/unog/website/news_media.nsf/(httpNewsByYear_en)/27F6CCAD7178F3E9C1258264003311FA?OpenDocument*; Amnesty International, "Yemen: Huthi Forces Recruiting Child Soldiers for Front-Line Combat," press release, February 28, 2017, *https://www.amnesty.org.uk/press-releases/yemen-huthi-forces-recruiting-child-soldiers-front-line-combat*.

46 Michael Knights, "The Houthi War Machine: From Guerrilla War to State Capture," *CTC Sentinel* 11, no. 8 (2018), *https://ctc.usma.edu/houthi-war-machine-guerrilla-war-state-capture/*.

47 Michael Horton, "Fighting the Long War: The Evolution of Al-Qa'ida in the Arabian Peninsula," *CTC Sentinel* 10, no. 1 (2017), *https://ctc.usma.edu/fighting-the-long-war-the-evolution-of-al-qaida-in-the-arabian-peninsula/*.

48 Adam Baron, "The Marib Paradox" (European Council on Foreign Relations, 2018).

49 Marie-Christine Heinze and Hafez Albukari, "Yemen's War as Seen from the Local Level," in *Politics, Governance, and Reconstruction in Yemen* (Washington, DC: Project on Middle East Political Science, 2018), *https://pomeps.org/wp-content/uploads/2018/02/POMEPS_Studies_29_Yemen_Web-REV.pdf*.

50 David Kirkpatrick, "Russian Snipers, Missiles and Warplanes Try to Tilt Libyan War," *New York Times*, November 5, 2019.

51 April Longley Alley and Peter Salisbury, "Peace Is Possible in Yemen," *Foreign Affairs*, November 11, 2019, *https://www.foreignaffairs.com/articles/iran/2019-11-11/peace-possible-yemen*.

52 Raymond Hinnebusch, "State De-construction in Iraq and Syria," *PVS Politische Vierteljahresschrift* 57, no. 4 (2016): 560–85.

53 Henri J. Barkey, "The Kurdish Awakening: Unity, Betrayal, and the Future of the Middle East," *Foreign Affairs* 98, no. 2 (2019): 107–18.

54 Richard N. Haass, "The Unraveling: How to Respond to a Disordered World," *Foreign Affairs* 93, no. 6 (2014): 70–80.

55 Patrick Milton, Michael Axworthy, and Brendan Simms, *Towards a Westphalia for the Middle East* (New York: Oxford University Press, 2019); Simon Mabon, *Saudi Arabia and Iran: Islam and Foreign Policy in the Middle East* (New York: Routledge, 2019).

56 Kevin Mazur, "State Networks and Intra-Ethnic Group Variation in the 2011 Syrian Uprising," *Comparative Political Studies* 52, no. 7 (2019): 995–1027 (1021); Christopher Phillips, "Sectarianism and Conflict in Syria," *Third World Quarterly* 36, no. 2 (2015): 357–76.

57 Barkey, "The Kurdish Awakening."

58 James M. Dorsey, "Qatar's Challenge to Saudi Arabia," *RSIS Commentaries*

(2013), *https://www.rsis.edu.sg/rsis-publication/rsis/1907-qatars-challenge-to-saudi-ara/#.XmfhmKj7SUk*; David Roberts, "Qatar and the Muslim Brotherhood: Pragmatism or Preference?," *Middle East Policy* 21, no. 3 (2014): 84–94.

59 Frederic Wehrey, "The Authoritarian Resurgence: Saudi Arabia's Anxious Autocrats," *Journal of Democracy* 26, no. 2 (2015): 71–85; Madawi al-Rasheed, "Saudi Arabia: Local and Regional Challenges," *Contemporary Arab Affairs* 6, no. 1 (2013): 28–40.

60 Cole Bunzel, "The Kingdom and the Caliphate: Saudi Arabia and the Islamic State," in *Beyond Sunni and Shia*, edited by Frederic Wehrey (New York: Oxford University Press, 2018); Gause, "Beyond Sectarianism."

61 Phillip Smyth, "The Battle for the Soul of Shi'ism," *MERIA Journal* 16, no. 3 (2012): 1–20; Caroleen Marji Sayej, *Patriotic Ayatollahs: Nationalism in Post-Saddam Iraq* (Ithaca, NY: Cornell University Press, 2018).

62 Qassim Abdul-Zahra and Joseph Krauss, "Protests in Iraq Reveal a Long-Simmering Anger at Iran," *Washington Post*, November 6, 2019.

63 Yvette Talhamy, "The Fatwas and the Nusayri/Alawis of Syria," *Middle Eastern Studies* 46, no. 2 (2010): 175–94.

64 Afshon Ostovar, "Sectarianism and Iranian Foreign Policy," in *Beyond Sunni and Shia*, edited by Frederic Wehrey (New York: Oxford University Press, 2018).

65 Adel Bin Ahmed Al-Jubeir, "Can Iran Change?," *New York Times*, January 19, 2016.

66 Mohammad Javad Zarif, "Rid the World of Wahhabism," *New York Times*, September 14, 2016.

67 C. V. Wedgwood, *The Thirty Years War* (New York: New York Review of Books, 2016 [1938]).

CHAPTER 7 PEACE AND PEACEMAKING

1 John Gledhill and Jonathan Bright, "Studying Peace and Studying Conflict: Complementary or Competing Projects?," *Journal of Global Security Studies* 4, no. 2 (2019): 259–66; Barry Buzan and Lene Hansen, *The Evolution of International Security Studies* (New York: Cambridge University Press, 2009).

2 For more on infrastructures for peace, see UN Development Program, *https://peaceinfrastructures.org/SitePages/Thematic.aspx?IdThematic=1*. See also Tobi P. Dress, *Designing a Peacebuilding Infrastructure: Taking a Systems Approach to the Prevention of Deadly Conflict* (New York: UN Non-Governmental Liaison Services 2005); Balázs Áron Kovács, *Peace Infrastructures and State-Building at the Margins* (New York: Springer, 2018).

3 Yaacov Bar-Siman-Tov, *From Conflict Resolution to Reconciliation* (New York: Oxford University Press, 2004); Kenneth E. Boulding, *Stable Peace* (Austin: University of Texas Press, 1978).

4 Johan Galtung, "Peace," in *International Encyclopedia of the Social & Behavioral Sciences*, second edition, edited by James D. Wright (Oxford: Elsevier, 2015).

5 Christian Davenport, Erik Melander, and Patrick M. Regan, *The Peace Continuum: What It Is and How to Study It* (New York: Oxford University Press, 2018), 37.

6 Oliver P. Richmond, *Peace: A Very Short Introduction* (New York: Oxford University Press, 2014), 52.

7 Christian Davenport, "State Repression and the Tyrannical Peace," *Journal of Peace Research* 44, no. 4 (2007): 485–504; David Lewis, John Heathershaw, and Nick Megoran, "Illiberal Peace? Authoritarian Modes of Conflict Management," *Cooperation and Conflict* 53, no. 4 (2018): 486–506.

8 Richmond, *Peace*, 10.

9 Peter Wallensteen, *Quality Peace: Peacebuilding, Victory, and World Order* (New York: Oxford University Press, 2015).

10 James P. Klein, Gary Goertz, and Paul F. Diehl, "The Peace Scale: Conceptualizing and Operationalizing Non-Rivalry and Peace," *Conflict Management and Peace Science* 25, no. 1 (2008): 67–80.

11 Davenport et al., *The Peace Continuum*, 127.

12 Caroline A. Hartzell, "Settling Civil Wars: Armed Opponents' Fates and the Duration of the Peace," *Conflict Management and Peace Science* 26, no. 4 (2009): 347–65; Lise Morjé Howard and Alexandra Stark, "How Civil Wars End: The International System, Norms, and the Role of External Actors," *International Security* 42, no. 3 (2017/18): 127–71; Monica Duffy Toft, "Ending Civil Wars," *International Security* 34, no. 4 (2010): 7–36.

13 Harry Anastasiou, "The EU as a Peace Building System," *International Journal of Peace Studies* 12, no. 2 (2007); Vicki L. Birchfield, John Krige, and Alasdair R. Young, "European Integration as a Peace Project," *The British Journal of Politics and International Relations* 19, no. 1 (2017): 31–50.

14 Kristine Höglund and Mimmi Söderberg Kovacs, "Beyond the Absence of War: The Diversity of Peace in Post-Settlement Societies," *Review of International Studies* 36, no. 2 (2010): 367–90.

15 Chandra Lekha Sriram, "Beyond Transitional Justice: Peace, Governance, and Rule of Law," *International Studies Review* 19, no. 1 (2017): 53–69; Nir Eisikovits, "Peace versus Justice in Transitional Settings," *Quinnipiac Law Review (QLR)* 32, no. 3 (2014): 705–22.

16 James Lee Ray, "Does Democracy Cause Peace?," *Annual Review of Political Science* 1, no. 1 (1998): 27–46.

17 Christian Davenport, *State Repression and the Domestic Democratic Peace* (New York: Cambridge University Press, 2007); Håvard Hegre, "Toward a Democratic Civil Peace? Democracy, Political Change, and Civil War, 1816–1992," *American Political Science Review* 95, no. 1 (2001): 33–48.

18 Thad Dunning, "Fighting and Voting: Violent Conflict and Electoral Politics," *Journal of Conflict Resolution* 55, no. 3 (2011): 327–39; Edward D. Mansfield and Jack Snyder, *Electing to Fight: Why Emerging Democracies Go to War* (Cambridge, Mass.: MIT Press, 2007).

19 Toby Dodge, "Enemy Images, Coercive Socio-Engineering and Civil War in Iraq," *International Peacekeeping* 19, no. 4 (2012): 461–77; Paul Salem, "Framing Post-War Lebanon: Perspectives on the Constitution and the Structure of Power," *Mediterranean Politics* 3, no. 1 (1998): 13–26.

20 Katerina Dalacoura, "US Democracy Promotion in the Arab Middle East since 11 September 2001: A Critique," *International Affairs* 81, no. 5 (2005): 963–79; Piki Ish-Shalom, "Theorization, Harm, and the Democratic Imperative: Lessons from the Politicization of the Democratic-Peace Thesis," *International Studies Review* 10, no. 4 (2008): 680–92.

21 Jessica L. P. Weeks, *Dictators at War and Peace* (Ithaca, NY: Cornell University Press, 2014); Bruce Bueno de Mesquita and Alastair Smith, "Domestic Explanations of International Relations," *Annual Review of Political Science* 15, no. 1 (2012): 161–81.

22 Gwenn Okruhlik and Patrick J. Conge, "The Politics of Border Disputes: On the Arabian Peninsula," *International Journal* 54, no. 2 (1999): 230–48.

23 Anthony Dipaola, "Kuwait Could Agree in Days with Saudis on Neutral-Zone Oil," *Bloomberg*, December 23, 2019, *https://www.bloomberg.com/news/articles/2019-12-22/kuwait-could-agree-with-saudis-on-neutral-zone-oil-by-end-2019*.

24 Marrack Goulding, "The Evolution of United Nations Peacekeeping," *International Affairs* 69, no. 3 (1993): 451–64; Duane Bratt, "Assessing the Success of UN Peacekeeping Operations," *International Peacekeeping* 3, no. 4 (1996): 64–81.

25 Marco Pinfari, *Nothing but Failure? The Arab League and the Gulf Cooperation Council as Mediators in Middle Eastern Conflicts* (Crisis States Research Centre, 2009); Louise Fawcett, "League of Arab States," in *Handbook of Governance and Security*, edited by James Spreling (Cheltenham: Edward Elgar Publishing, 2014).

26 Paul D. Williams, "The African Union's Peace Operations: A Comparative Analysis," *African Security* 2, nos. 2–3 (2009): 97–118.

27 Mohammed Nuruzzaman, "Qatar and the Arab Spring: Down the Foreign Policy Slope," *Contemporary Arab Affairs* 8, no. 2 (2015): 226–38.

28 Mohammad Ayatollahi Tabaar, "How Iranians Are Debating the Nuclear Deal," *Washington Post*, April 21, 2015.

29 Salem, "Framing Post-War Lebanon," 25. See also Sandra M. Saseen, "The Taif Accord and Lebanon's Struggle to Regain Its Sovereignty," *American University Journal of International Law & Policy* 6, no. 1 (1990): 57–75.

30 Faten Ghosn and Amal Khoury, "Lebanon after the Civil War: Peace or the Illusion of Peace?," *The Middle East Journal* 65, no. 3 (2011): 381–97.

31 Mahmoud Abdou, "Humanitarian Assistance and Peacebuilding: Congruence as a By-Product of Incompatibility," *University for Peace & Conflict Monitor*, June 18, 2014, *http://www.monitor.upeace.org/innerpg.cfm?id_article=1050*.

32 Kevin Dwyer, *Arab Voices: The Human Rights Debate in the Middle East* (New

York: Routledge, 2016). Daphna Golan and Zvika Orr, "Translating Human Rights of the 'Enemy': The Case of Israeli NGOs Defending Palestinian Rights," *Law & Society Review* 46, no. 4 (2012): 781–814.

33 Michael Barnett, *Empire of Humanity: A History of Humanitarianism* (Ithaca, NY: Cornell University Press, 2011).

34 Keith David Watenpaugh, *Bread from Stones: The Middle East and the Making of Modern Humanitarianism* (Berkeley: University of California Press, 2015); Laura Robson, *States of Separation: Transfer, Partition, and the Making of the Modern Middle East* (Berkeley: University of California Press, 2017).

35 Paul Heaton, "Oil for What? Illicit Iraqi Oil Contracts and the UN Security Council," *Journal of Economic Perspectives* 19, no. 4 (2005): 193–206.

36 David Rieff, *A Bed for the Night: Humanitarianism in Crisis* (New York: Simon & Schuster, 2003). Barnett, *Empire of Humanity*.

37 Oliver Kaplan, *Resisting War: How Communities Protect Themselves* (New York: Cambridge University Press, 2017).

38 Nijmeh Ali, "Active and Transformative *Sumud* among Palestinian Activists in Israel," in *Palestine and Rule of Power: Local Dissent vs. International Governance*, edited by Alaa Tartir and Timothy Seidel (New York: Springer, 2019); Caitlin Ryan, "Everyday Resilience as Resistance: Palestinian Women Practicing *Sumud*," *International Political Sociology* 9, no. 4 (2015): 299–315; Ilana Feldman, "Looking for Humanitarian Purpose: Endurance and the Value of Lives in a Palestinian Refugee Camp," *Public Culture* 27, no. 3 (2015): 427–47.

39 Mona Takieddine Amyuni, "And Life Went On . . .: In War-Torn Lebanon," *Arab Studies Quarterly* 15, no. 2 (1993): 1–13 (2–3).

40 Ibid., 3.

41 Sune Haugbolle, "Dealing with Lebanon's Past," in *Reconciliation, Reform and Resilience: Postive Peace for Lebanon*, edited by Elizabeth Picard and Alexander Ramsbotham (Conciliation Resources, 2012), *https://www.c-r.org/accord/leba non/civil-mobilisation-and-peace-lebanon*.

42 Reyko Huang, *The Wartime Origins of Democratization: Civil War, Rebel Governance, and Political Regimes* (New York: Cambridge University Press, 2016).

43 Laura Zittrain Eisenberg and Neil Caplan, *Negotiating Arab–Israeli Peace: Patterns, Problems, Possibilities* (Bloomington: Indiana University Press, 2010); Arie M. Kacowicz, "Rashomon in the Middle East: Clashing Narratives, Images, and Frames in the Israeli–Palestinian Conflict," *Cooperation and Conflict* 40, no. 3 (2005): 343–60; Elie Podeh, *Chances for Peace: Missed Opportunities in the Arab–Israeli Conflict* (Austin: University of Texas Press, 2015).

44 Bahgat Korany, "The Cold Peace, the Sixth Arab–Israeli War, and Egypt's Public," *International Journal* 38, no. 4 (1983): 652–73; Rami G. Khouri, "The Arab–Israeli Peace Process: Lessons from the Five Years since Oslo," *Security Dialogue* 29, no. 3 (1998): 333–44.

45 Yezid Sayigh, "Redefining the Basics: Sovereignty and Security of the Palestinian State," *Journal of Palestine Studies* 24, no. 4 (1995): 5–19.

46 Joel Peters, "The Camp David Summit: A Tale of Two Narratives," in *Routledge Handbook on the Israeli–Palestinian Conflict*, edited by Joel Peters and David Newman (New York: Routledge, 2013).

47 Robert H. Mnookin, Ehud Eiran, and Sreemati Mitter, "Barriers to Progress at the Negotiation Table: Internal Conflicts among Israelis and among Palestinians," *Nevada Law Journal* 6 (2005): 299–366; Wendy Pearlman, "Spoiling Inside and Out: Internal Political Contestation and the Middle East Peace Process," *International Security* 33, no. 3 (2009): 79–109.

48 Ehud Sprinzak, "Extremism and Violence in Israel: The Crisis of Messianic Politics," *The Annals of the American Academy of Political and Social Science* 555, no. 1 (1998): 114–26; Ehud Eiran and Peter Krause, "Old (Molotov) Cocktails in New Bottles? 'Price-Tag' and Settler Violence in Israel and the West Bank," *Terrorism and Political Violence* 30, no. 4 (2018): 637–57.

49 Beverley Milton-Edwards and Alastair Crooke, "Elusive Ingredient: Hamas and the Peace Process," *Journal of Palestine Studies* 33, no. 4 (2004): 39–52.

50 Yezid Sayigh, "Inducing a Failed State in Palestine," *Survival* 49, no. 3 (2007): 7–39.

51 Dalia Gavriely-Nuri, "The Idiosyncratic Language of Israeli 'Peace': A Cultural Approach to Critical Discourse Analysis (CCDA)," *Discourse & Society* 21, no. 5 (2010): 565–85; Yifat Biton and Gavriel Salomon, "Peace in the Eyes of Israeli and Palestinian Youths: Effects of Collective Narratives and Peace Education Program," *Journal of Peace Research* 43, no. 2 (2006): 167–80.

52 Daniel Byman, "Curious Victory: Explaining Israel's Suppression of the Second Intifada," *Terrorism and Political Violence* 24, no. 5 (2012): 825–52.

53 Israel Ministry of Foreign Affairs, "Wave of Terror 2015–2019," December 31, 2019, *https://mfa.gov.il/MFA/ForeignPolicy/Terrorism/Palestinian/Pages/Wave-of-terror-October-2015.aspx*.

54 Salim Tamari, "Normalcy and Violence: The Yearning for the Ordinary in Discourse of the Palestinian–Israeli Conflict," *Journal of Palestine Studies* 42, no. 4 (2013): 48–60 (59).

55 Fred Halliday, *The Middle East in International Relations: Power, Politics and Ideology* (New York: Cambridge University Press, 2005), 307.

56 Arab Center for Research and Policy Studies, "Al Mu'ashar Al'arabi 2017/2018 fi Niqat" (Doha, 2018), *https://www.dohainstitute.org/ar/Lists/ACRPS-PDFDocumentLibrary/Arab-Index-2017-2018-in-Brief.pdf*.

57 Avraham Sela, *The Decline of the Arab–Israeli Conflict: Middle East Politics and the Quest for Regional Order* (Albany, NY: SUNY Press, 2012).

58 Michael Mandelbaum, *The Rise and Fall of Peace on Earth* (New York: Oxford University Press, 2019).

59 Séverine Autesserre, *Peaceland: Conflict Resolution and the Everyday Politics of International Intervention* (New York: Cambridge University Press, 2014).

60 Deborah Avant et al., eds., *Civil Action and the Dynamics of Violence in Conflicts* (New York: Oxford University Press, 2019).

61 Oliver Kaplan, "Nudging Armed Groups: How Civilians Transmit Norms of Protection," *Stability: International Journal of Security and Development* 2, no. 3 (2013), *http://doi.org/10.5334/sta.cw*; Center for Civilians in Conflict, "Issue Brief: Civilian Protection in Syria (December 2012)," December 6, 2012, *https://civiliansinconflict.org/publications/policy/issue-brief-civilian-protection-syria-december-2012/*.

62 Jared Malsin, "As the War Worsens, Rescue Workers Risk Their Lives on the Front Lines," *Time*, October 17, 2016; Fouad M. Fouad et al., "Health Workers and the Weaponisation of Health Care in Syria: A Preliminary Inquiry for the Lancet–American University of Beirut Commission on Syria," *The Lancet* 390, no. 10111 (2017): 2516–26.

63 Wolfram Lacher, "Iraq: Exception to, or Epitome of Contemporary Post-Conflict Reconstruction?," *International Peacekeeping* 14, no. 2 (2007): 237–50.

64 Marekie Transfeld and Marie-Christine Heizne, "Understanding Peace Requirements in Yemen: Needs and Roles for Civil Soviet, Women, Youth, the Media" (Center for Applied Research in Partnership with the Orient, 2019).

65 John Braithwaite and Tamim Rashed, "Nonviolence and Reconciliation among the Violence in Libya," *Restorative Justice* 2, no. 2 (2014): 185–204.

66 April Longley Alley and Peter Salisbury, "Peace Is Possible in Yemen," *Foreign Affairs*, Fall 2019, *https://www.foreignaffairs.com/articles/iran/2019-11-11/peace-possible-yemen*.

67 Ariel Ahram, "Breaking and Mending," *Wilson Quarterly*, November 12, 2019, *https://www.wilsonquarterly.com/quarterly/borders-and-beyond/breaking-and-mending/*; André Bank, "The 'Victor's Peace' in Syria and the Limits of Multilateral Policies," *GIGA Middle East Focus* 7 (2019), *https://www.giga-hamburg.de/en/system/files/publications/gf_nahost_1907_en.pdf*.

68 "White Helmets Are Terrorists, Can Choose Surrender or Death – Assad," *RT*, July 26, 2018, *https://www.rt.com/news/434368-white-helmets-surrender-death-assad/*.

69 Omar Imady, "The Weaponization of Syria's Reconstruction," *Syria Studies* 11, no. 1 (2019): 6–21; Steven Heydemann, "Beyond Fragility: Syria and the Challenges of Reconstruction in Fierce States," *The New Geopolitics: Middle East*, June 2018, *https://www.brookings.edu/research/beyond-fragility-syria-and-the-challenges-of-reconstruction-in-fierce-states/*.

70 Haid Haid, "Principled Aid in Syria: A Framework for International Agencies," Chatham House, July 4, 2019, *https://www.chathamhouse.org/publication/principled-aid-syria-framework-international-agencies*.

71 Giulia Piccolino, "Local Peacebuilding in a Victor's Peace: Why Local Peace Fails without National Reconciliation," *International Peacekeeping* 26, no. 3 (2019): 354–79.

72 James N. Rosenau, *Distant Proximities: Dynamics beyond Globalization* (Princeton, NJ: Princeton University Press, 2003).
73 Roger Mac Ginty and Oliver Richmond, "The Fallacy of Constructing Hybrid Political Orders: A Reappraisal of the Hybrid Turn in Peacebuilding," *International Peacekeeping* 23, no. 2 (2016): 219–39; Volker Boege, M. Anne Brown, and Kevin P. Clements, "Hybrid Political Orders, Not Fragile States," *Peace Review* 21, no. 1 (2009): 13–21.
74 United Nations Development Programme, "Arab Human Development Report 2009" (2015), 54.
75 Lisa Anderson, "The State and Its Competitors," *International Journal of Middle East Studies* 40, no. 2 (2018): 317–22; Lisa Blaydes, "State Building in the Middle East," *Annual Review of Political Science* 20 (2017): 487–504.

CONCLUSION

1 Salim Tamari, *Year of the Locust: A Soldier's Diary and the Erasure of Palestine's Ottoman Past* (Berkeley: University of California Press, 2011), 118.
2 Dominik J. Schaller and Jürgen Zimmerer, eds., *Late Ottoman Genocides: The Dissolution of the Ottoman Empire and Young Turkish Population and Extermination Policies* (New York: Routledge, 2013); Ronald Grigor Suny, *"They Can Live in the Desert but Nowhere Else": A History of the Armenian Genocide* (Princeton, NJ: Princeton University Press, 2017).
3 For more on the Ottoman experience during World War I, see Kristian Coates Ulrichsen, *The First World War in the Middle East* (London: Hurst, 2014); Leila Tarazi Fawaz, *A Land of Aching Hearts: The Middle East in the Great War* (Cambridge, Mass.: Harvard University Press, 2014).
4 Siniša Malešević, "The Organization of Military Violence in the 21st Century," *Organization* 24 (2017), 456–74 (458).
5 Miguel A. Centeno and Elaine Enriquez, *War and Society* (Cambridge: Polity, 2016).
6 Tarak Barkawi and Mark Laffey, "The Postcolonial Moment in Security Studies," *Review of International Studies* 32, no. 2 (2006): 329–54; Keith Krause, "Challenges to Counting and Classifying Victims of Violence in Conflict, Post-Conflict, and Non-Conflict Settings," in *Counting Civilian Casualties: An Introduction to Recording and Estimating Nonmilitary Deaths in Conflict*, edited by Taylor Seybolt, Jay Aronson, and Baruch Fischhoff (New York: Oxford University Press, 2013).
7 Charles Tilly, *Coercion, Capital, and European States, AD 990–1990* (Cambridge, Mass.: Basil Blackwell, 1990).
8 Dietrich Jung, "War and State in the Middle East: Reassessing Charles Tilly in a Regional Context," in *Does War Make States? Investigations of Charles Tilly's Historical Sociology*, edited by Lars Bo Kaspersen and Jeppe Strandsbjerg (New York: Cambridge University Press, 2017).

9 Volker Boege, M. Anne Brown, and Kevin P. Clements, "Hybrid Political Orders, Not Fragile States," *Peace Review* 21, no. 1 (2009): 13–21; Ariel I. Ahram, "Learning to Live with Militias: Toward a Critical Policy on State Frailty," *Journal of Intervention and Statebuilding* 5, no. 2 (2011): 175–92.

Bibliography

Abboud, Samer, Omar S. Dahi, Waleed Hazbun, Nicole Sunday Grove, Coralie Pison Hindawi, Jamil Mouawad, and Sami Hermez. "Towards a Beirut School of Critical Security Studies." *Critical Studies on Security* 6, no. 3 (2018): 273–95.

Abdou, Mahmoud. "Humanitarian Assistance and Peacebuilding: Congruence as a By-Product of Incompatibility." *University for Peace & Conflict Monitor*, June 18, 2014. *http://www.monitor.upeace.org/innerpg.cfm?id_article=1050*.

Abdul-Zahra, Qassim, and Joseph Krauss. "Protests in Iraq Reveal a Long-Simmering Anger at Iran." *Washington Post*, November 6, 2019.

Abu-Lughod, Janet L. *Before European Hegemony: The World System AD 1250–1350*. New York: Oxford University Press, 1991.

Acharya, Amitav. "The Periphery as the Core: The Third World and Security Studies." In *Critical Security Studies*, edited by Keith Krause. New York: Routledge, 2002.

Ahram, Ariel I. *Break All the Borders: Separatism and the Reshaping of the Middle East.* New York: Oxford University Press, 2019.

Ahram, Ariel. "Breaking and Mending." *Wilson Quarterly*, November 12, 2019. *https://www.wilsonquarterly.com/quarterly/borders-and-beyond/breaking-and-mending/*.

Ahram, Ariel I. "Learning to Live with Militias: Toward a Critical Policy on State Frailty." *Journal of Intervention and Statebuilding* 5, no. 2 (2011): 175–92.

Ahram, Ariel I. *Proxy Warriors: The Rise and Fall of State-Sponsored Militias*. Stanford, Calif.: Stanford University Press, 2011.

Ahram, Ariel I. "Sexual Violence, Competitive State Building, and Islamic State in Iraq and Syria." *Journal of Intervention and Statebuilding* 13, no. 2 (2019): 180–96.

Ahram, Ariel I. "Territory, Sovereignty, and New Statehood in the Middle East and North Africa." *The Middle East Journal* 71, no. 3 (2017): 345–62.

Ahram, Ariel I. "War-Making, State-Making, and Non-State Power in Iraq." *Yale Program on Governance and Local Development Working Paper* 1 (2015). *https://cpb-us-w2.wpmucdn.com/campuspress.yale.edu/dist/e/439/files/2015/03/Ariel_War-MakingFinal.pdf*.

Ahram, Ariel I., Patrick Köllner, and Rudra Sil, eds. *Comparative Area Studies: Methodological Rationales and Cross-Regional Applications*. New York: Oxford University Press, 2018.

Akdedian, Harout. "On Violence and Radical Theology in the Syrian War: The Instrumentality of Spectacular Violence and Exclusionary Practices from Comparative and Local Standpoints." *Politics, Religion & Ideology* 20, no. 3 (2019): 361–80.

al-Azm, Sadik J. "Islam, Terrorism and the West Today." *Welt des Islams* 44, no. 1 (2004): 114–28.

al-Azm, Sadik J. "Orientalism, Occidentalism, and Islamism." *Comparative Studies of South Asia, Africa and the Middle East* 30, no. 1 (2010): 6–13.

al-Azm, Sadik. *Self-Criticism after the Defeat*. London: Saqi, 2012.

Albrecht, Holger. "The Myth of Coup-Proofing: Risk and Instances of Military Coups d'état in the Middle East and North Africa, 1950–2013." *Armed Forces & Society* 41, no. 4 (2015): 659–87.

Albrecht, Holger, Aurel Croissant, and Fred H. Lawson, eds. *Armies and Insurgencies in the Arab Spring*. Philadelphia: University of Pennsylvania Press, 2016.

Alesina, Alberto, Arnaud Devleeschauwer, William Easterly, Sergio Kurlat, and Romain Wacziarg. "Fractionalization." *Journal of Economic Growth* 8, no. 2 (2003): 155–94.

Ali, Nijmeh. "Active and Transformative *Sumud* among Palestinian Activists in Israel." In *Palestine and Rule of Power: Local Dissent vs. International Governance*, edited by Alaa Tartir and Timothy Seidel. New York: Springer, 2019.

Al-Jubeir, Adel Bin Ahmed. "Can Iran Change?" *New York Times*, January 19, 2016.

Allen, Calvin H., Jr. *Oman: The Modernization of the Sultanate*. New York: Routledge, 2016.

Alley, April Longley, and Peter Salisbury. "Peace Is Possible in Yemen." *Foreign Affairs*, November 11, 2019. *https://www.foreignaffairs.com/articles/iran/2019-11-11/peace-possible-yemen*.

Allison, Roy. "Russia and Syria: Explaining Alignment with a Regime in Crisis." *International Affairs* 89, no. 4 (2013): 795–823.

al-Nakib, Farah. "Kuwait's Modern Spectacle: Oil Wealth and the Making of a New Capital City, 1950–90." *Comparative Studies of South Asia, Africa and the Middle East* 33, no. 1 (2013): 7–25.

al-Rasheed, Madawi. "Saudi Arabia: Local and Regional Challenges." *Contemporary Arab Affairs* 6, no. 1 (2013): 28–40.

al-Sarrani, Abeer Abdulaziz. "From Soil to Oil: The Resistance of the Environment in the Cities of Salt." *International Journal of Comparative Literature and Translation Studies* 3, no. 4 (2015): 20–6.

Alterman, Jon B., and John W. Garver. *The Vital Triangle: China, the United States, and the Middle East*. Washington, DC: Center for Strategic and International Studies, 2008.

al-Zaidi, Mohammed. "Between Black Gold, Bleak Prospects: Visiting the Iraqi Shanty Town between Two Oil Fields." *Niqash* (n.d.). *http://www.niqash.org/en/articles/economy/5198/*.

Amanat, Abbas. *Is There a Middle East? The Evolution of a Geopolitical Concept.* Stanford, Calif.: Stanford University Press, 2012.

Amnesty International. "Yemen: Huthi Forces Recruiting Child Soldiers for Front-Line Combat." Press release, February 28, 2017. *https://www.amnesty.org. uk/press-releases/yemen-huthi-forces-recruiting-child-soldiers-front-line-combat.*

Amyuni, Mona Takieddine. "And Life Went On . . . In War-Torn Lebanon." *Arab Studies Quarterly* 15, no. 2 (1993): 1–13.

Anastasiou, Harry. "The EU as a Peace Building System." *International Journal of Peace Studies* 12, no. 2 (2007): 31–50.

Anderson, Jon W. "Conspiracy Theories, Premature Entextualization, and Popular Political Analysis." *The Arab Studies Journal* 4, no. 1 (1996): 96–102.

Anderson, Liam D., and Gareth R. V. Stansfield. *Crisis in Kirkuk: The Ethnopolitics of Conflict and Compromise.* Philadelphia: University of Pennsylvania Press, 2009.

Anderson, Lisa. "Rogue Libya's Long Road." *Middle East Report*, no. 241 (2006): 42–7.

Anderson, Lisa. "'They Defeated Us All': International Interests, Local Politics, and Contested Sovereignty in Libya." *The Middle East Journal* 71, no. 2 (2017): 229–47.

Anderson, Lisa. "The State and Its Competitors." *International Journal of Middle East Studies* 40, no. 2 (2018): 317–22.

Anderson, Lisa. *The State and Social Transformation in Tunisia and Libya, 1830–1980.* Princeton, NJ: Princeton University Press, 2014.

Andreas, Peter, and Kelly M. Greenhill, eds. *Sex, Drugs, and Body Counts: The Politics of Numbers in Global Crime and Conflict.* Ithaca, NY: Cornell University Press, 2011.

Arab Center for Research and Policy Studies. "Al Mu'ashar Al'arabi 2017/2018 fi Niqat." Doha, 2018. *https://www.dohainstitute.org/ar/Lists/ACRPS-PDFDocumentLibrary/Arab-Index-2017-2018-in-Brief.pdf.*

Ashton, Nigel, and Bryan Gibson, eds. *The Iran–Iraq War: New International Perspectives.* New York: Routledge, 2013.

Ashworth, Lucian, M. "Mapping a New World: Geography and the Interwar Study of International Relations." *International Studies Quarterly* 57, no. 1 (2013): 138–49.

Askari, Hossein. "Conflicts, Oil Prices, and International Financial Stability." *Georgetown Journal of International Affairs* 14 (2013): 57–64.

Assad, Abdulkader. "Libya's Parallel Central Bank Admits Printing 9.7 Billion Dinar Banknotes in Russia." *Libya Observer*, November 20, 2018.

Atzili, Boaz, and Wendy Pearlman. "Triadic Deterrence: Coercing Strength, Beaten by Weakness." *Security Studies* 21, no. 2 (2012): 301–35.

Autesserre, Séverine. *Peaceland: Conflict Resolution and the Everyday Politics of International Intervention.* New York: Cambridge University Press, 2014.

Avant, Deborah D. "Pragmatic Networks and Transnational Governance of

Private Military and Security Services." *International Studies Quarterly* 60, no. 2 (2016): 330–42.

Avant, Deborah, Marie Berry, Erica Chenoweth, Rachel Epstein, Cullen Hendrix, Oliver Kaplan, and Timothy Sisk, eds. *Civil Action and the Dynamics of Violence in Conflicts*. New York: Oxford University Press, 2019.

Awdeh, Jihad, Mahmud Jawdeh, and Ahmed al-Khatib. *Militishiyat wa al-Harakat al-Musallahah fi Libya* Cairo: Maktab al-'Arabi lil t'arouf, 2015.

Aydinli, Ersel, and James N. Rosenau. *Globalization, Security, and the Nation-State: Paradigms in Transition*. Albany, NY: SUNY Press, 2005.

Ayoob, Mohammed. "Security in the Third World: The Worm About to Turn?" *International Affairs* 60, no. 1 (1983): 41–51.

Ayoob, Mohammed. "Unravelling the Concept: 'National Security' in the Third World." In *The Many Faces of National Security in the Arab World*, edited by Rex Brynen, Baghat Korany, and Paul Noble. New York: Springer, 1993.

Ayubi, Nazih N. *Over-Stating the Arab State: Politics and Society in the Middle East*. London: I. B. Tauris, 1996.

Bahgat, Gawdat. "Energy and the Arab–Israeli Conflict." *Middle Eastern Studies* 44, no. 6 (2008): 937–44.

Bank, André, "The 'Victor's Peace' in Syria and the Limits of Multilateral Policies." *GIGA Middle East Focus* 7 (2019), *https://www.giga-hamburg.de/en/system/files/publications/gf_nahost_1907_en.pdf*.

Barak, Oren. "Dilemmas of Security in Iraq." *Security Dialogue* 38, no. 4 (2007): 455–75.

Barany, Zoltan D. *The Bahrain Defence Force: The Monarchy's Second-to-Last Line of Defense*. Washington, DC: Center for Strategic & International Studies, 2016.

Barany, Zoltan. "Why Have Three Gulf States Introduced the Draft? Bucking the Trend on Conscription in Arabia." *The RUSI Journal* 162, no. 6 (2017): 16–26.

Barkawi, Tarak. *Globalization and War*. Lanham, Md.: Rowman & Littlefield, 2006.

Barkawi, Tarak, and Mark Laffey. "The Postcolonial Moment in Security Studies." *Review of International Studies* 32, no. 2 (2006): 329–54.

Barkey, Henri J. "The Kurdish Awakening: Unity, Betrayal, and the Future of the Middle East." *Foreign Affairs* 98, no. 2 (2019): 107–18.

Barkey, Karen, and George Gavrilis. "The Ottoman Millet System: Non-Territorial Autonomy and Its Contemporary Legacy." *Ethnopolitics* 15, no. 1 (2016): 24–42.

Barnett, Michael N. *Confronting the Costs of War: Military Power, State, and Society in Egypt and Israel*. Princeton, NJ: Princeton University Press, 2012.

Barnett, Michael. *Empire of Humanity: A History of Humanitarianism*. Ithaca, NY: Cornell University Press, 2011.

Baron, Adam. "The Marib Paradox." European Council on Foreign Relations, 2018.

Bar-Siman-Tov, Yaacov. *From Conflict Resolution to Reconciliation*. New York: Oxford University Press, 2004.

Beinin, Joel. *Workers and Peasants in the Modern Middle East*. New York: Cambridge University Press, 2001.

Bellamy, Alexander. *World Peace (and How We Can Achieve It)*. New York: Oxford University Press, 2019.

Bellodi, Leonardo. "Libya's Assets and the Question of Sovereignty." *Survival* 54, no. 2 (2012): 39–45.

Bengio, Ofra. "Shi'is and Politics in Ba'thi Iraq." *Middle Eastern Studies* 21, no. 1 (1985): 1–14.

Bercovitch, Jacob, and Karl DeRouen, Jr. *Unraveling Internal Conflicts in East Asia and the Pacific: Incidence, Consequences, and Resolution*. Lanham, Md.: Lexington Books, 2011.

Bet-Shlimon, Arbella. *City of Black Gold: Oil, Ethnicity, and the Making of Modern Kirkuk*. Stanford, Calif.: Stanford University Press, 2019.

Bilgin, Pinar. "The 'Western-Centrism' of Security Studies: 'Blind Spot' or Constitutive Practice?" *Security Dialogue* 41, no. 6 (2010): 615–22.

bin Laden, Osama. "Among a Band of Knights." Translated by James Howarth. In *Messages to the World: The Statements of Osama Bin Laden*, edited by Bruce Lawrence. London: Verso, 2005.

Birchfield, Vicki L., John Krige, and Alasdair R. Young. "European Integration as a Peace Project." *The British Journal of Politics and International Relations* 19, no. 1 (2017): 3–12.

Birnir, Jóhanna K., David D. Laitin, Jonathan Wilkenfeld, David M. Waguespack, Agatha S. Hultquist, and Ted R. Gurr. "Introducing the AMAR (All Minorities at Risk) Data." *Journal of Conflict Resolution* 62, no. 1 (2018): 203–26.

Biton, Yifat, and Gavriel Salomon. "Peace in the Eyes of Israeli and Palestinian Youths: Effects of Collective Narratives and Peace Education Program." *Journal of Peace Research* 43, no. 2 (2006): 167–80.

Black, Jeremy. "What Is War?" In *What Is War? An Investigation in the Wake of 9/11*, edited by Mary Ellen O'Connell. Leiden: Martinus Nijhoff Publishers, 2012.

Blaydes, Lisa. "State Building in the Middle East." *Annual Review of Political Science* 20 (2017): 487–504.

Blaydes, Lisa, and Christopher Paik. "Muslim Trade and City Growth before the Nineteenth Century: Comparative Urbanization in Europe, the Middle East and Central Asia." *British Journal of Political Science* (2019). *https://doi.org/10.1017/S0007123419000267*.

Bøås, Morten. *The Politics of Conflict Economies: Miners, Merchants and Warriors in the African Borderland*. New York: Routledge, 2014.

Boege, Volker, M. Anne Brown, and Kevin P. Clements. "Hybrid Political Orders, Not Fragile States." *Peace Review* 21, no. 1 (2009): 13–21.

Borghard, Erica. "Friends with Benefits? Power and Influence in Proxy Warfare." Ph.D. thesis, Columbia University, 2014.

Bou Akar, Hiba. *For the War Yet to Come: Planning Beirut's Frontiers*. Stanford, Calif.: Stanford University Press, 2018.

Boulding, Kenneth E. *Stable Peace*. Austin: University of Texas Press, 1978.

Bou-Nacklie, N. E. "Les Troupes Spéciales: Religious and Ethnic Recruitment, 1916–46." *International Journal of Middle East Studies* 25, no. 4 (1993): 645–60.

Bowie, Neil, and Alex Schmid. "Databases on Terrorism." In *Routledge Handbook of Terrorism Research*, edited by Alex Schmid. New York: Routledge, 2011.

Braithwaite, John, and Tamim Rashed. "Nonviolence and Reconciliation among the Violence in Libya." *Restorative Justice* 2, no. 2 (2014): 185–204.

Brands, Hal. "Barack Obama and the Dilemmas of American Grand Strategy." *Washington Quarterly* 39, no. 4 (2016): 101–25.

Brands, Hal. "Saddam Hussein, the United States, and the Invasion of Iran: Was There a Green Light?" *Cold War History* 12, no. 2 (2012): 319–43.

Bratt, Duane. "Assessing the Success of UN Peacekeeping Operations." *International Peacekeeping* 3, no. 4 (1996): 64–81.

Brinkerhoff, Jennifer M. "Diaspora Identity and the Potential for Violence: Toward an Identity-Mobilization Framework." *Identity: An International Journal of Theory and Research* 8, no. 1 (2008): 67–88.

Broder, John. "A Nation at War: The Casualties; US Military Has No Count of Iraqi Dead in Fighting." *New York Times*, April 2, 2003.

Bromer, Ethan, and David Sanger. "Arab League Endorses No-Flight Zone over Libya." *New York Times*, March 12, 2011.

Bromley, Simon. "The United States and the Control of World Oil." *Government and Opposition* 40, no. 2 (2005): 225–55.

Bronson, Rachel. *Thicker Than Oil: America's Uneasy Partnership with Saudi Arabia*. New York: Oxford University Press, 2006.

Brookings Institution. "Brookings Iraq Index." Washington, DC: Brookings Institution, 2006.

Brooks, Rosa. *How Everything Became War and the Military Became Everything: Tales from the Pentagon*. New York: Simon & Schuster, 2016.

Brown, Michael Edward, ed. *The International Dimensions of Internal Conflict*. Cambridge, Mass.: MIT Press, 1996.

Brown, Seyom. "Purposes and Pitfalls of War by Proxy: A Systemic Analysis." *Small Wars & Insurgencies* 27, no. 2 (2016): 243–57.

Brubaker, Rogers. "Ethnicity without Groups." *European Journal of Sociology* 43, no. 2 (2002): 163–89.

Bueno de Mesquita, Bruce, and Alastair Smith. "Domestic Explanations of International Relations." *Annual Review of Political Science* 15, no. 1 (2012): 161–81.

Bunzel, Cole. "The Kingdom and the Caliphate: Saudi Arabia and the Islamic State." In *Beyond Sunni and Shia*, edited by Frederic Wehrey. New York: Oxford University Press, 2018.

Burgis, Michelle. "Mandated Sovereignty? The Role of International Law in the Construction of Arab Statehood during and after Empire." In *Sovereignty after Empire: Comparing the Middle East and Central Asia*, edited by Raymond Hinnebusch and Sally Cummings. Edinburgh: Edinburgh University Press, 2011.

Bush, Sarah Sunn, Aaron Erlich, Lauren Prather, and Yael Zeira. "The Effects of Authoritarian Iconography: An Experimental Test." *Comparative Political Studies* 49, no. 13 (2016): 1704–38.

Buzan, Barry, and Lene Hansen. *The Evolution of International Security Studies*. New York: Cambridge University Press, 2009.

Byman, Daniel. "Curious Victory: Explaining Israel's Suppression of the Second Intifada." *Terrorism and Political Violence* 24, no. 5 (2012): 825–52.

Byman, Daniel. "Remaking Alliances for the War on Terrorism." *Journal of Strategic Studies* 29, no. 5 (2006): 767–811.

Byman, Daniel. "Why Be a Pawn to a State? Proxy Wars from a Proxy's Perspective." *Brookings*, May 22, 2018. *https://www.brookings.edu/blog/order-from-chaos/2018/05/22/why-be-a-pawn-to-a-state-proxy-wars-from-a-proxys-perspective/*.

Byman, Daniel, and Sarah Kreps. "Agents of Destruction? Applying Principal–Agent Analysis to State-Sponsored Terrorism." *International Studies Perspectives* 11, no. 1 (2010): 1–18.

Cammett, Melani, and Sukriti Issar. "Bricks and Mortar Clientelism: Sectarianism and the Logics of Welfare Allocation in Lebanon." *World Politics* 62, no. 3 (2010): 381–421.

Carey, Sabine C., and Neil J. Mitchell. "Pro-Government Militias and Conflict." In *Oxford Research Encyclopedia of Politics*, 2016.

Carson, Austin. *Secret Wars: Covert Conflict in International Politics*. Princeton, NJ: Princeton University Press, 2018.

Centeno, Miguel A., and Elaine Enriquez. *War and Society*. Cambridge: Polity, 2016.

Center for Civilians in Conflict. "Issue Brief: Civilian Protection in Syria (December 2012)." December 6, 2012. *https://civiliansinconflict.org/publications/policy/issue-brief-civilian-protection-syria-december-2012/*.

Central Intelligence Agency, "Communist Aid Activities in Non-Communist Less Developed Countries, 1979 and 1954–1979." October 1980. *https://www.cia.gov/library/readingroom/docs/DOC_0000499891.pdf*.

Chivvis, Christopher S. *Toppling Qaddafi: Libya and the Limits of Liberal Intervention*. New York: Cambridge University Press, 2013.

Chorin, Ethan. *Exit the Colonel: The Hidden History of the Libyan Revolution*. New York: PublicAffairs, 2012.

Cleveland, William L. *Making of an Arab Nationalist*. Princeton, NJ: Princeton University Press, 2016.

Cohen, Avner. *Israel and the Bomb*. New York: Columbia University Press, 1998.

Cohen, Hillel. *Good Arabs: The Israeli Security Agencies and the Israeli Arabs, 1948–1967*. Berkeley: University of California Press, 2011.

Cohen, Nissim, and Tamar Arieli. "Field Research in Conflict Environments: Methodological Challenges and Snowball Sampling." *Journal of Peace Research* 48, no. 4 (2011): 423–35.

Cohen, William B. "The Harkis." In *Algeria & France, 1800–2000: Identity, Memory, Nostalgia*, edited by Patricia Lorcin. Syracuse, NY: Syracuse University Press, 2006.

Cole, Juan R. "Of Crowds and Empires: Afro-Asian Riots and European Expansion, 1857–1882." *Comparative Studies in Society and History* 31, no. 1 (1989): 106–33.

Colgan, Jeff D. "Fueling the Fire: Pathways from Oil to War." *International Security* 38, no. 2 (2013): 147–80.

Colgan, Jeff D. *Petro-Aggression: When Oil Causes War*. New York: Cambridge University Press, 2013.

Collier, Paul. *Breaking the Conflict Trap: Civil War and Development Policy*. Washington, DC: World Bank Publications, 2003.

Connor, Phillip. "Most Displaced Syrians Are in the Middle East, and About a Million Are in Europe." Pew Research Center, 2018.

"Constitution of the Republic of Iraq." Constitution Project, 2005. *https://www.constituteproject.org/constitution/Iraq_2005.pdf?lang=en*.

Cooke, Miriam. "Murad vs. ISIS: Rape as a Weapon of Genocide." *Journal of Middle East Women's Studies* 15, no. 3 (2019): 261–85.

Coon, Carleton S. *Caravan: The Story of the Middle East*. Revised edition. New York: Holt, 1958.

Cottam, Richard W. *Nationalism in Iran*. Pittsburgh: University of Pittsburgh Press, 1964.

Cox, Stephen Russell. "Britain and the Origin of Israeli Special Operations: SOE and Palmach during the Second World War." *Dynamics of Asymmetric Conflict* 8, no. 1 (2015): 60–78.

Cragin, R. Kim. "Semi-Proxy Wars and US Counterterrorism Strategy." *Studies in Conflict & Terrorism* 38, no. 5 (2015): 311–27.

Crane, Keith. *The Role of Oil in ISIL Finances*. Washington DC: RAND, 2015.

Crapanzano, Vincent. *The Harkis: The Wound That Never Heals*. Chicago: University of Chicago Press, 2011.

Crawford, Neta. "Human Costs of the Post 9/11 Wars: Lethality and the Need for Transparency." Brown University, Watson Institute for International and Public Affairs, 2018.

Crelinsten, Ronald. *Counterterrorism*. New York: John Wiley & Sons, 2013.

Culcasi, Karen. "Constructing and Naturalizing the Middle East." *Geographical Review* 100, no. 4 (2010): 583–97.

Dagher, Sam, Charles Levinson, and Margaret Coker. "Tiny Kingdom's Huge Rule in Libya Draws Concern." *Wall Street Journal*, October 17, 2011.

Dalacoura, Katerina. "US Democracy Promotion in the Arab Middle East since 11 September 2001: A Critique." *International Affairs* 81, no. 5 (2005): 963–79.

Danner, Mark. *Spiral: Trapped in the Forever War.* New York: Simon & Schuster, 2016.

Darling, Linda T. "Social Cohesion ('Asabiyya) and Justice in the Late Medieval Middle East." *Comparative Studies in Society & History* 49, no. 2 (2007): 329–57.

Davenport, Christian. *State Repression and the Domestic Democratic Peace.* New York: Cambridge University Press, 2007.

Davenport, Christian. "State Repression and the Tyrannical Peace." *Journal of Peace Research* 44, no. 4 (2007): 485–504.

Davenport, Christian, Erik Melander, and Patrick M. Regan. *The Peace Continuum: What It Is and How to Study It.* New York: Oxford University Press, 2018.

David, Steven R. "Explaining Third World Alignment." *World Politics* 43, no. 2 (1991): 233–56.

Dawisha, Adeed. *Arab Nationalism in the Twentieth Century: From Triumph to Despair.* Princeton, NJ: Princeton University Press, 2016.

Dawisha, Adeed. *Iraq: A Political History.* Princeton, NJ: Princeton University Press, 2013.

Dawisha, Karen. "Soviet Policy in the Arab World: Permanent Interests and Changing Influence." *Arab Studies Quarterly* 2, no. 1 (1980): 19–37.

De Juan, Alexander, and André Bank. "The Ba'athist Blackout? Selective Goods Provision and Political Violence in the Syrian Civil War." *Journal of Peace Research* 52, no. 1 (2015): 91–104.

Dearing, Matthew P. "Turning Gangsters into Allies: The American Way of War in Northern Afghanistan." *Small Wars & Insurgencies* 30, no. 1 (2019): 101–39.

Dekmejian, Richard Hrair. "Consociational Democracy in Crisis: The Case of Lebanon." *Comparative Politics* 10, no. 2 (1978): 251–65.

Deudney, Daniel. "Geopolitics as Theory: Historical Security Materialism." *European Journal of International Relations* 6, no. 1 (2000): 77–107.

Dipaola, Anthony, "Kuwait Could Agree in Days with Saudis on Neutral-Zone Oil." *Bloomberg,* December 23, 2019. *https://www.bloomberg.com/news/articles/2019-12-22/kuwait-could-agree-with-saudis-on-neutral-zone-oil-by-end-2019.*

Do, Quy-Toan, Jacob N. Shapiro, Christopher D. Elvidge, Mohamed Abdel-Jelil, Daniel P. Ahn, Kimberly Baugh, Jamie Hansen-Lewis, Mikhail Zhizhin, and Morgan D. Bazilian. "Terrorism, Geopolitics, and Oil Security: Using Remote Sensing to Estimate Oil Production of the Islamic State." *Energy Research & Social Science* 44 (2018): 411–18.

Dodge, Toby. "Enemy Images, Coercive Socio-Engineering and Civil War in Iraq." *International Peacekeeping* 19, no. 4 (2012): 461–77.

Dodge, Toby. "Iraq: The Contradictions of Exogenous State-Building in Historical Perspective." *Third World Quarterly* 27, no. 1 (2006): 187–200.

Dorsey, James M. "Qatar's Challenge to Saudi Arabia." RSIS Commentaries (2013). *https://www.rsis.edu.sg/rsis-publication/rsis/1907-qatars-challenge-to-saudi-ara/#.XmfhmKj7SUk.*

Dress, Tobi P. *Designing a Peacebuilding Infrastructure: Taking a Systems Approach to the Prevention of Deadly Conflict*. UN Non-Governmental Liaison Services, 2005.

Dunning, Thad. "Fighting and Voting: Violent Conflict and Electoral Politics." *Journal of Conflict Resolution* 55, no. 3 (2011): 327–39.

Dwyer, Kevin. *Arab Voices: The Human Rights Debate in the Middle East*. New York: Routledge, 2016.

Eckhardt, William. "Civilian Deaths in Wartime." *Bulletin of Peace Proposals* 20, no. 1 (1989): 89–98.

Edwards, Madeline. "Syrian Author Khaled Khalifa on Latest Novel About 'Fear, in All Its Manifestations'." *SyriaDirect*, February 27, 2019. *https://syriadirect. org/news/syrian-author-khaled-khalifa-on-latest-novel-about-%E2%80%98fear-in-all-its-manifestations%E2%80%99/*.

Eiran, Ehud, and Peter Krause. "Old (Molotov) Cocktails in New Bottles? 'Price-Tag' and Settler Violence in Israel and the West Bank." *Terrorism and Political Violence* 30, no. 4 (2018): 637–57.

Eisenberg, Laura Zittrain, and Neil Caplan. *Negotiating Arab–Israeli Peace: Patterns, Problems, Possibilities*. Bloomington: Indiana University Press, 2010.

Eisikovits, Nir. "Peace versus Justice in Transitional Settings." *Quinnipiac Law Review (QLR)* 32, no. 3 (2014): 705–22.

Eller, Stacy L., Peter R. Hartley, and Kenneth B. Medlock. "Empirical Evidence on the Operational Efficiency of National Oil Companies." *Empirical Economics* 40, no. 3 (2011): 623–43.

Elling, Rasmus Christian. *Minorities in Iran: Nationalism and Ethnicity after Khomeini*. New York: Palgrave Macmillan, 2013.

Engel, Richard. *And Then All Hell Broke Loose: Two Decades in the Middle East*. London: Simon & Schuster, 2017.

Esman, Milton J. "Ethnic Politics: How Unique Is the Middle East?" In *Ethnicity, Pluralism, and the State in the Middle East*, edited by Milton J. Esman and Itamar Rabinovich. Ithaca, NY: Cornell University Press, 1988.

European Council on Foreign Relations. "China's Great Game in the Middle East." 2019.

Faucon, Benoit, Summer Said, and Warren Strobel. "Saudi Arabia Seeks to Ease Tensions with Iran." *Wall Street Journal*, December 12, 2019.

Fawaz, Leila Tarazi. *A Land of Aching Hearts: The Middle East in the Great War*. Cambridge, Mass.: Harvard University Press, 2014.

Fawcett, Louise. *Iran and the Cold War: The Azerbaijan Crisis of 1946*. New York: Cambridge University Press, 2009.

Fawcett, Louise. "League of Arab States." In *Handbook of Governance and Security*, edited by James Spreling. Cheltenham: Edward Elgar Publishing, 2014.

Fawcett, Louise. "Regionalism and Alliances in the Middle East." In *International Relations of the Middle East*, fifth edition, edited by Louise Fawcett. New York: Oxford University Press, 2016.

Feaver, Peter, and Hal Brands. "Lessons from the Iraq War." *National Review*, June 20, 2019.

Feldman, Ilana. "Looking for Humanitarian Purpose: Endurance and the Value of Lives in a Palestinian Refugee Camp." *Public Culture* 27, no. 3 (2015): 427–47.

Fieldhouse, David Kenneth. *Western Imperialism in the Middle East, 1914–1958.* New York: Oxford University Press, 2006.

Filkins, Dexter. *The Forever War.* New York: Vintage, 2009.

Findley, Carter V. *Bureaucratic Reform in the Ottoman Empire: The Sublime Porte, 1789–1922.* Princeton, NJ: Princeton University Press, 1980.

Finlan, Alastair. *Special Forces, Strategy and the War on Terror: Warfare by Other Means.* New York: Routledge, 2009.

Fiore, Massimiliano. *Anglo-Italian Relations in the Middle East, 1922–1940.* New York: Routledge, 2016.

Fischer, Hannah. "Iraqi Civilian Deaths Estimates." In *Economics and Geopolitics of the Middle East*, edited by Richard Dralonge. New York: Nova Science, 2008.

Fiske, Alan Page, and Tage Shakti Rai. *Virtuous Violence: Hurting and Killing to Create, Sustain, End, and Honor Social Relationships.* New York: Cambridge University Press, 2014.

Flyvbjerg, Bent. *Making Social Science Matter: Why Social Inquiry Fails and How It Can Succeed Again.* New York: Cambridge University Press, 2001.

Foster, Zachary J. "The 1915 Locust Attack in Syria and Palestine and Its Role in the Famine during the First World War." *Middle Eastern Studies* 51, no. 3 (2015): 370–94.

Fouad, Fouad M., Annie Sparrow, Ahmad Tarakji, Mohamad Alameddine, Fadi El-Jardali, Adam P. Coutts, Nour El Arnaout, et al. "Health Workers and the Weaponisation of Health Care in Syria: A Preliminary Inquiry for the Lancet–American University of Beirut Commission on Syria." *The Lancet* 390, no. 10111 (2017): 2516–26.

Foulon, Michiel. "Neoclassical Realism: Challengers and Bridging Identities." *International Studies Review* 17, no. 4 (2015): 635–61.

Fuccaro, Nelida. "Introduction: Histories of Oil and Urban Modernity in the Middle East." *Comparative Studies of South Asia, Africa and the Middle East* 33, no. 1 (2013): 1–6.

Galtung, Johan. "Peace." In *International Encyclopedia of the Social & Behavioral Sciences*, second edition, edited by James D. Wright. Oxford: Elsevier, 2015.

Gartenstein-Ross, Daveed. "Osama's Oil Obsession." *Foreign Policy*, May 23, 2011. *https://foreignpolicy.com/2011/05/23/osamas-oil-obsession-2/*.

Garwood-Gowers, Andrew. "The Responsibility to Protect and the Arab Spring: Libya as the Exception, Syria as the Norm." *University of New South Wales Law Journal* 36 (2013): 594–618.

Gasiorowski, Mark J., and Malcolm Byrne. *Mohammad Mosaddeq and the 1953 Coup in Iran.* Syracuse, NY: Syracuse University Press, 2015.

Gat, Azar. *War in Human Civilization.* New York: Oxford University Press, 2008.

Gause, F. Gregory. "Beyond Sectarianism: The New Middle East Cold War." Brookings Doha Center, 2014.

Gause, F. Gregory. "Saudi Arabia's Regional Security Strategy." In *International Politics of the Persian Gulf*, edited by Mehran Kamrava. Syracuse, NY: Syracuse University Press, 2011.

Gause, F. Gregory. "Systemic Approaches to Middle East International Relations." *International Studies Review* 1, no. 1 (1999): 11–31.

Gavriely-Nuri, Dalia. "The Idiosyncratic Language of Israeli 'Peace': A Cultural Approach to Critical Discourse Analysis (CCDA)." *Discourse & Society* 21, no. 5 (2010): 565–85.

Gelvin, James. "Don't Blame Sykes–Picot." *OUPblog*, February 7, 2015. *https://blog.oup.com/2015/02/dont-blame-sykes-picot/*.

Gerges, Fawaz A. *The Far Enemy: Why Jihad Went Global.* New York: Cambridge University Press, 2009.

Gerring, John. "Causation: A Unified Framework for the Social Sciences." *Journal of Theoretical Politics* 17, no. 2 (2005): 163–98.

Gershoni, Israel, and James P. Jankowski. *Egypt, Islam, and the Arabs: The Search for Egyptian Nationhood, 1900–1930.* New York: Oxford University Press, 1987.

Ghobarah, Hazem Adam, Paul Huth, and Bruce Russett, "Civil Wars Kill and Maim People – Long after the Shooting Stops." *The American Political Science Review* 97, no. 2 (2003): 189–202.

Ghobarah, Hazem Adam, Paul Huth, and Bruce Russett. "The Post-War Public Health Effects of Civil Conflict." *Social Science & Medicine* 59, no. 4 (2004): 869–84.

Ghosn, Faten, and Amal Khoury. "Lebanon after the Civil War: Peace or the Illusion of Peace?" *The Middle East Journal* 65, no. 3 (2011): 381–97.

Gibbs, Jack P. "Conceptualization of Terrorism." *American Sociological Review* 54, no. 3 (1989): 329–41.

Glanville, Luke. *Sovereignty and the Responsibility to Protect: A New History.* Chicago: University of Chicago Press, 2013.

Gledhill, John. "Assessing (In)Security after the Arab Spring: Editor's Introduction." *PS: Political Science & Politics* 46, no. 4 (2013): 709–15.

Gledhill, John. "When State Capacity Dissolves: Explaining Variation in Violent Conflict and Conflict Moderation." *European Journal of International Security* 2, no. 2 (2017): 153–78.

Gledhill, John, and Jonathan Bright. "Studying Peace and Studying Conflict: Complementary or Competing Projects?" *Journal of Global Security Studies* 4, no. 2 (2019): 259–66.

Gleditsch, Nils Petter, and Håvard Hegre. "Peace and Democracy: Three Levels of Analysis." *Journal of Conflict Resolution* 41, no. 2 (1997): 283–310.

Gleditsch, Nils Petter, Steven Pinker, Bradley A. Thayer, Jack S. Levy, and William R. Thompson. "The Forum: The Decline of War." *International Studies Review* 15, no. 3 (2013): 396–419.

Gleditsch, Nils Petter, Peter Wallensteen, Mikael Eriksson, Margareta

Sollenberg, and Håvard Strand, "Armed Conflict 1946–2001: A New Dataset." *Journal of Peace Research* 39, no. 5 (2002): 615–37.

Goertz, Gary, and Paul F. Diehl. "The Empirical Importance of Enduring Rivalries." *International Interactions* 18, no. 2 (1992): 151–63.

Golan, Daphna, and Zvika Orr. "Translating Human Rights of the 'Enemy': The Case of Israeli NGOs Defending Palestinian Rights." *Law & Society Review* 46, no. 4 (2012): 781–814.

Goldstein, Joshua S. *Winning the War on War: The Decline of Armed Conflict Worldwide.* New York: Penguin, 2012.

Gong, Gerrit W. *The Standard of "Civilization" in International Society.* Oxford: Clarendon Press, 1984.

Gongora, Thierry. "War Making and State Power in the Contemporary Middle East." *International Journal of Middle East Studies* 29, no. 3 (1997): 323–40.

Goulding, Marrack. "The Evolution of United Nations Peacekeeping." *International Affairs* 69, no. 3 (1993): 451–64.

Gray, Matthew. "Explaining Conspiracy Theories in Modern Arab Middle Eastern Political Discourse: Some Problems and Limitations of the Literature." *Critique: Critical Middle Eastern Studies* 17, no. 2 (2008): 155–74.

Gurney, Judith. *Libya: The Political Economy of Oil.* New York: Oxford University Press, 1996.

Haass, Richard N. "The Unraveling: How to Respond to a Disordered World." *Foreign Affairs* 93, no. 6 (2014): 70–80.

Haber, Stephen, and Victor Menaldo. "Do Natural Resources Fuel Authoritarianism? A Reappraisal of the Resource Curse." *American Political Science Review* 105, no.1 (2011): 1–26.

Haddad, Bassam. *Business Networks in Syria: The Political Economy of Authoritarian Resilience.* Stanford, Calif.: Stanford University Press, 2012.

Haddad, Fanar. "Shi'a-Centric State Building and Sunni Rejection in Post-2003 Iraq." In *Beyond Sunni and Shia*, edited by Frederic Wehrey. New York: Oxford University Press, 2016.

Hagopian, Amy, Abraham Flaxman, Tim K. Takaro, Lindsay Galway, Berj Hadi Al-Yasseri, and Gilbert Burnham. "Navigating a Four-University, Three-Country Collaboration to Estimate Mortality in Iraq after the 2003 Invasion and Occupation." *The Lancet Global Health*, no. S1 (2014): S49.

Haid, Haid. "Principled Aid in Syria: A Framework for International Agencies." Chatham House, July 4, 2019. *https://www.chathamhouse.org/publication/principled-aid-syria-framework-international-agencies.*

Halliday, Fred. "The Great Powers and the Middle East." *Middle East Report* 18, no. 151 (1988): 3–6.

Halliday, Fred. *The Middle East in International Relations: Power, Politics and Ideology.* New York: Cambridge University Press, 2005.

Hamdan, Ali Nehme. "Breaker of Barriers? Notes on the Geopolitics of the Islamic State in Iraq and Sham." *Geopolitics* 21, no. 3 (2016): 605–27.

Hamid, Shadi. *Temptations of Power: Islamists and Illiberal Democracy in a New Middle East.* New York: Oxford University Press, 2014.

Hamilton, James D. "What Is an Oil Shock?" *Journal of Econometrics* 113, no. 2 (2003): 363–98.

Hanioğlu, M. Şükrü. *The Young Turks in Opposition.* New York: Oxford University Press, 1995.

Harchaoui, Jalel, and Mohamed-Essaïd Lazib. *Proxy War Dynamics in Libya.* Blacksburg: Virginia Tech Press, 2019.

Hardwood, Anthony. "Saudi Arabia Using Famine as Weapon in War." *Newsweek*, November 28, 2017.

Harik, Iliya F. "The Ethnic Revolution and Political Integration in the Middle East." *International Journal of Middle East Studies* 3, no. 3 (1972): 303–23.

Harik, Iliya. "The Origins of the Arab State System." In *The Arab State*, edited by Giacomo Luciani. Berkeley: University of California Press, 1990.

Hariri, Aula. "State Formation as an Outcome of the Imperial Encounter: The Case of Iraq." *Review of International Studies* 45, no. 5 (2019): 848–69.

Hartzell, Caroline A. "Settling Civil Wars: Armed Opponents' Fates and the Duration of the Peace." *Conflict Management and Peace Science* 26, no. 4 (2009): 347–65.

Hashemi, Nader, and Danny Postel, eds. *Sectarianization: Mapping the New Politics of the Middle East.* New York: Oxford University Press, 2017.

Hashim, Ahmed. *Insurgency and Counter-Insurgency in Iraq.* Ithaca, NY: Cornell University Press, 2005.

Haugbolle, Sune. "Dealing with Lebanon's Past." In *Reconciliation, Reform and Resilience: Positive Peace for Lebanon*, edited by Elizabeth Picard and Alexander Ramsbotham. Conciliation Resources, 2012. *https://www.c-r.org/accord/lebanon/civil-mobilisation-and-peace-lebanon.*

Hazbun, Waleed. "The Politics of Insecurity in the Arab World: A View from Beirut." *PS: Political Science & Politics*, no. 3 (2017): 656–9.

Heaton, Paul. "Oil for What? Illicit Iraqi Oil Contracts and the UN Security Council." *Journal of Economic Perspectives* 19, no. 4 (2005): 193–206.

Hegghammer, Thomas. "The Rise of Muslim Foreign Fighters: Islam and the Globalization of Jihad." *International Security* 35, no. 3 (2010): 53–94.

Hegre, Håvard. "Toward a Democratic Civil Peace? Democracy, Political Change, and Civil War, 1816–1992." *American Political Science Review* 95, no. 1 (2001): 33–48.

Hehir, Aidan. "Assessing the Influence of the Responsibility to Protect on the UN Security Council during the Arab Spring." *Cooperation and Conflict* 51, no. 2 (2016): 166–83.

Heinze, Marie-Christine, and Hafez Albukari. "Yemen's War as Seen from the Local Level." In *Politics, Governance, and Reconstruction in Yemen.* Washington, DC: Project on Middle East Political Science, 2018. *https://pomeps.org/wp-content/uploads/2018/02/POMEPS_Studies_29_Yemen_Web-REV.pdf.*

Heller, Mark. "Politics and the Military in Iraq and Jordan, 1920–1958: The British Influence." *Armed Forces & Society* 4, no. 1 (1977): 75–99.

Henderson, Errol A. "Not Letting Evidence Get in the Way of Assumptions: Testing the Clash of Civilizations Thesis with More Recent Data." *International Politics* 42, no. 4 (2005): 458–69.

Hendrix, Cullen S. "Oil Prices and Interstate Conflict." *Conflict Management and Peace Science* 34, no. 6 (2017): 575–96.

Hendrix, Cullen S., and Joseph K. Young. "State Capacity and Terrorism: A Two-Dimensional Approach." *Security Studies* 23, no. 2 (2014): 329–63.

Herb, Michael. *All in the Family: Absolutism, Revolution, and Democracy in Middle Eastern Monarchies.* Albany, NY: SUNY Press, 1999.

Heritage Foundation. "Assessing Threats to US Vital Interests: Middle East." 2018.

Hertog, Steffen. *Princes, Brokers, and Bureaucrats: Oil and the State in Saudi Arabia.* Ithaca, NY: Cornell University Press, 2011.

Hertog, Steffen. "Rentier Militaries in the Gulf States: The Price of Coup-Proofing." *International Journal of Middle East Studies* 43, no. 3 (2011): 400–2.

Heydemann, Steven. "Beyond Fragility: Syria and the Challenges of Reconstruction in Fierce States." *The New Geopolitics: Middle East*, June 2018. *https://www.brookings.edu/research/beyond-fragility-syria-and-the-challenges-of-reconstruction-in-fierce-states/.*

Heydemann, Steven. "Introduction." In *War, Institutions, and Social Change in the Middle East*, edited by Steven Heydemann. Berkeley: University of California Press, 2000.

Hiltermann, Joost. "The Middle East in Chaos: Of Orders and Borders." *Al Sharq Forum*, May 25, 2018. *https://www.crisisgroup.org/middle-east-north-africa/middle-east-chaos-orders-and-borders.*

Hiltermann, Joost R. *A Poisonous Affair: America, Iraq, and the Gassing of Halabja.* New York: Cambridge University Press, 2007.

Hinnebusch, Raymond. *The International Politics of the Middle East.* Manchester: Manchester University Press 2003.

Hinnebusch, Raymond. "State De-construction in Iraq and Syria." *Politische Vierteljahresschrift* 57, no. 4 (2016): 560–85.

Hinnebusch, Raymond, and Morten Valbjørn. "Sectarianism and Governance in Syria." *Studies in Ethnicity and Nationalism* 19, no. 1 (2019): 41–66.

Hironaka, Ann. *Neverending Wars: The International Community, Weak States, and the Perpetuation of Civil War.* Cambridge, Mass.: Harvard University Press, 2005.

Hoffman, Katherine E. "Purity and Contamination: Language Ideologies in French Colonial Native Policy in Morocco." *Comparative Studies in Society and History* 50, no. 3 (2008): 724–52.

Höglund, Kristine, and Mimmi Söderberg Kovacs. "Beyond the Absence of War: The Diversity of Peace in Post-Settlement Societies." *Review of International Studies* 36, no. 2 (2010): 367–90.

Holsti, Kalevi J. "War, Peace, and the State of the State." *International Political Science Review* 16, no. 4 (1995): 319–39.

Horton, Michael. "Fighting the Long War: The Evolution of Al-Qaʻida in the Arabian Peninsula." *CTC Sentinel* 10, no. 1 (2017). *https://ctc.usma.edu/fighting-the-long-war-the-evolution-of-al-qaida-in-the-arabian-peninsula/*.

Howard, Lise Morjé, and Alexandra Stark. "How Civil Wars End: The International System, Norms, and the Role of External Actors." *International Security* 42, no. 3 (2017/18): 127–71.

Huang, Reyko. *The Wartime Origins of Democratization: Civil War, Rebel Governance, and Political Regimes.* New York: Cambridge University Press, 2016.

Hudson, Michael C. *Arab Politics: The Search for Legitimacy.* New Haven: Yale University Press, 1977.

Hudson, Michael C. "The Middle East under *Pax Americana*: How New, How Orderly?" *Third World Quarterly* 13, no. 2 (1992): 301–16.

Hughes, Geraint. *My Enemy's Enemy: Proxy Warfare in International Politics.* Chicago: Sussex Academic Press, 2012.

Human Rights Watch. "Testimony by Tom Malinowski, Human Rights Watch Washington Advocacy Director to House of Representatives." News release, June 14, 2007, *https://www.hrw.org/news/2007/06/14/there-human-rights-double-standard-us-policy-toward-saudi-arabia-iran-uzbekistan-and#*.

Huntington, Samuel P. "The Clash of Civilizations." *Foreign Affairs* 72 (1993): 22–49.

Hunziker, Philipp, and Lars-Erik Cederman. "No Extraction without Representation: The Ethno-Regional Oil Curse and Secessionist Conflict." *Journal of Peace Research* 54, no. 3 (2017): 365–81.

Iklé, Fred Charles. *Every War Must End.* New York: Columbia University Press, 2005 [1971].

Imady, Omar. "The Weaponization of Syria's Reconstruction." *Syria Studies* 11, no. 1 (2019): 6–21.

International Crisis Group. "Of Tanks and Banks: Stopping a Dangerous Escalation in Libya." 2019. *https://www.crisisgroup.org/middle-east-north-africa/north-africa/libya/201-tanks-and-banks-stopping-dangerous-escalation-libya*.

Iraq Family Health Survey Study Group. "Violence-Related Mortality in Iraq from 2002 to 2006." *New England Journal of Medicine*, no. 5 (2008): 484–93.

Ish-Shalom, Piki. "Theorization, Harm, and the Democratic Imperative: Lessons from the Politicization of the Democratic-Peace Thesis." *International Studies Review* 10, no. 4 (2008): 680–92.

Ismael, Tareq Y., and Glenn E. Perry. "Toward a Framework for Analysis." In *The International Relations of the Contemporary Middle East*, edited by Tareq Y. Ismael and Glenn E. Perry. New York: Routledge, 2013.

Israel Ministry of Foreign Affairs. "Wave of Terror 2015–2019." December 31, 2019. *https://mfa.gov.il/MFA/ForeignPolicy/Terrorism/Palestinian/Pages/Wave-of-terror-October-2015.aspx*.

Jaffe, Amy Myers, and Jareer Elass. "War and the Oil Price Cycle." *Journal of International Affairs* 69, no. 1 (2015): 121–37.

Jägerskog, Anders, Michael Schulz, and Ashok Swain, eds., *Routledge Handbook on Middle East Security*. London: Routledge, 2019.

Jalata, Asafa. "Conceptualizing and Theorizing Terrorism in the Historical and Global Context." *Humanity & Society* 34, no. 4 (2010): 317–49.

Jamal, Manal A. "The 'Tiering' of Citizenship and Residency and the 'Hierarchization' of Migrant Communities: The United Arab Emirates in Historical Context." *International Migration Review* 49, no. 3 (2015): 601–32.

Jasser, M. Zuhdi. "Sectarian Conflict in Syria." *PRISM* 4 (2014): 58–67.

Jewell, Nicholas P., Michael Spagat, and Britta L. Jewell. "Accounting for Civilian Casualties: From the Past to the Future." *Social Science History* 42, no. 3 (2018): 379–410.

Joffé, George. "Libya and Europe." *Journal of North African Studies* 6, no. 4 (2001): 75–92.

Jones, Toby Craig. "America, Oil, and War in the Middle East." *Journal of American History* 99, no. 1 (2012): 208–18.

Jung, Dietrich. "War and State in the Middle East: Reassessing Charles Tilly in a Regional Context." In *Does War Make States? Investigations of Charles Tilly's Historical Sociology*, edited by Lars Bo Kaspersen and Jeppe Strandsbjerg. New York: Cambridge University Press, 2017.

Kaag, John, and Sarah Kreps. *Drone Warfare*. Cambridge: Polity, 2014.

Kacowicz, Arie M. "Rashomon in the Middle East: Clashing Narratives, Images, and Frames in the Israeli–Palestinian Conflict." *Cooperation and Conflict* 40, no. 3 (2005): 343–60.

Kacowicz, Arie M. *Zones of Peace in the Third World: South America and West Africa in Comparative Perspective*. Albany, NY: SUNY Press, 1998.

Kafura, Craig. "Ten Years On: American Public Opinion on the War in Iraq." *Chicago Council on Global Affairs*, March 22, 2013. https://www.thechicagocouncil. org/blog/running-numbers/ten-years-american-public-opinion-war-iraq?page=9.

Kaldor, Mary. *New and Old Wars*. Second edition. Stanford, Calif.: Stanford University Press, 2007.

Kalyvas, Stathis. "Ethnic Defection in Civil War." *Comparative Political Studies* 41, no. 8 (2008): 1043–68.

Kalyvas, Stathis N., and Laia Balcells. "International System and Technologies of Rebellion: How the End of the Cold War Shaped Internal Conflict." *American Political Science Review* 104, no. 3 (2010): 415–29.

Kamrava, Mehran. *Inside the Arab State*. New York: Oxford University Press, 2018.

Kamrava, Mehran. "Iran–Qatar Relations." In *Security and Bilateral Issues between Iran and Its Arab Neighbours*, edited by Anoush Ehteshami, Neil Quilliam, and Gawdat Bahgat. New York: Palgrave, 2017.

Kane, Sean. "Barqa Reborn? Eastern Regionalism and Libya's Political

Transition." In *The Libyan Revolution and Its Aftermath*, edited by Peter Cole and Brian McQuinn New York: Oxford University Press, 2015.

Kane, Tim. "Global US Troop Deployment, 1950–2003." *Heritage Foundation*, October 27, 2004. *https://www.heritage.org/defense/report/global-us-troop-deployment-1950-2003*.

Kaplan, Fred. "Why the Middle East Is Still a Mess a Century after the Sykes-Picot Agreement." *Slate*, May 19, 2016. *https://slate.com/news-and-politics/2016/05/its-not-surprising-the-middle-east-is-a-mess-100-years-after-sykes-picot.html*.

Kaplan, Oliver. "Nudging Armed Groups: How Civilians Transmit Norms of Protection." *Stability: International Journal of Security and Development* 2, no. 3 (2013). *http://doi.org/10.5334/sta.cw*.

Kaplan, Oliver. *Resisting War: How Communities Protect Themselves*. New York: Cambridge University Press, 2017.

Karl, Terry Lynn. *The Paradox of Plenty: Oil Booms and Petro-States*. Berkeley: University of California Press, 1997.

Karlén, Niklas. "Turning Off the Taps: The Termination of State Sponsorship." *Terrorism and Political Violence* 31, no. 4 (2019): 733–58.

Kay, Avi. "Citizen Rights in Flux: The Influence of American Immigrants to Israel on Modes of Political Activism." *Jewish Political Studies Review* 13, nos. 3–4 (2001): 143–58.

Keddie, Nikki R. "Is There a Middle East?" *International Journal of Middle East Studies* 4, no. 3 (1973): 255–71.

Keddie, Nikki R. "The Revolt of Islam, 1700 to 1993: Comparative Considerations and Relations to Imperialism." *Comparative Studies in Society and History* 36, no. 3 (1994): 463–87.

Kent, Marian. *Moguls and Mandarins: Oil, Imperialism and the Middle East in British Foreign Policy 1900–1940*. New York: Routledge, 2013.

Kepel, Gilles. *Jihad: The Trail of Political Islam*. New York: I. B. Tauris, 2006.

Kerr, Malcolm H. *The Arab Cold War: Gamal 'abd Al-Nasir and His Rivals, 1958–1970*. New York: Oxford University Press, 1971.

Khalidi, Rashid. *Palestinian Identity: The Construction of Modern National Consciousness*. New York: Columbia University Press, 1997.

Khalidi, Rashid, Eugene L. Rogan, and Avi Shlaim, eds. *The War for Palestine: Rewriting the History of 1948*. New York: Cambridge University Press, 2001.

Khouri, Rami G. "The Arab–Israeli Peace Process: Lessons from the Five Years since Oslo." *Security Dialogue* 29, no. 3 (1998): 333–44.

Khoury, Dina Rizk. "The Security State and the Practice and Rhetoric of Sectarianism in Iraq." *International Journal of Contemporary Iraqi Studies* 4, no. 3 (2010): 325–38.

Kilian, Lutz. "Oil Price Shocks: Causes and Consequences." *Annual Review of Resource Economics* 6, no. 1 (2014): 133–54.

Kirkpatrick, David. "Russian Snipers, Missiles and Warplanes Try to Tilt Libyan War." *New York Times*, November 5, 2019.

Klein, James P., Gary Goertz, and Paul F. Diehl. "The Peace Scale: Conceptualizing and Operationalizing Non-Rivalry and Peace." *Conflict Management and Peace Science* 25, no. 1 (2008): 67–80.

Klieman, Aharon. "Introduction." In *Great Powers and Geopolitics: International Affairs in a Rebalancing World*, edited by Aharon Klieman. New York: Springer, 2015.

Knights, Michael. "The Houthi War Machine: From Guerrilla War to State Capture." *CTC Sentinel* 11, no. 8 (2018). *https://ctc.usma.edu/houthi-war-machine-guerrilla-war-state-capture/*.

Koller, Christian. "The Recruitment of Colonial Troops in Africa and Asia and Their Deployment in Europe during the First World War." *Immigrants & Minorities* 26, nos. 1–2 (2008): 111–33.

Korany, Bahgat. "The Cold Peace, the Sixth Arab–Israeli War, and Egypt's Public." *International Journal* 38, no. 4 (1983): 652–73.

Kovács, Balázs Áron. *Peace Infrastructures and State-Building at the Margins*. New York: Springer, 2018.

Krause, Keith. "Challenges to Counting and Classifying Victims of Violence in Conflict, Post-Conflict, and Non-Conflict Settings." In *Counting Civilian Casualties: An Introduction to Recording and Estimating Nonmilitary Deaths in Conflict*, edited by Taylor Seybolt, Jay Aronson, and Baruch Fischhoff. New York: Oxford University Press, 2013.

Krause, Keith. "State-Making and Region-Building: The Interplay of Domestic and Regional Security in the Middle East." *Journal of Strategic Studies* 26, no. 3 (2003): 99–124.

Krieg, Andreas. "Externalizing the Burden of War: The Obama Doctrine and US Foreign Policy in the Middle East." *International Affairs* 92, no. 1 (2016): 97–113.

Kruczek, Gregoy. "Christian Minorities and the Struggle for Nineveh: The Assyrian Democratic Movement in Iraq and the Nineveh Plains Protection Units." Virginia Tech, 2018.

Kuperman, Alan J. "A Model Humanitarian Intervention? Reassessing NATO's Libya Campaign." *International Security* 38, no. 1 (2013): 105–36.

Lacher, Wolfram. "Iraq: Exception to, or Epitome of Contemporary Post-Conflict Reconstruction?" *International Peacekeeping* 14, no. 2 (2007): 237–50.

Lacina, Bethany, and Nils Petter Gleditsch. "Monitoring Trends in Global Combat: A New Dataset of Battle Deaths." *European Journal of Population* 21, nos. 2–3 (2005): 145–66.

Laitin, David D. *Nations, States, and Violence*. New York: Oxford University Press, 2007.

Lake, David A., and Donald S. Rothchild. "Containing Fear." *International Security* 21, no. 2 (1996): 41–75.

Latham, Michael E. *The Right Kind of Revolution: Modernization, Development, and US Foreign Policy from the Cold War to the Present*. Ithaca, NY: Cornell University Press, 2010.

Lauterbach, Claire. "The Costs of Cooperation: Civilian Casualty Counts in Iraq." *International Studies Perspectives* 8, no. 4 (2007): 429–45.

Lawson, Fred. *Constructing International Relations in the Arab World.* Stanford, Calif.: Stanford University Press, 2006.

Le Billon, Philippe, and Alejandro Cervantes. "Oil Prices, Scarcity, and Geographies of War." *Annals of the Association of American Geographers* 99, no. 5 (2009): 836–44.

Leenders, Reinoud, and Antonio Giustozzi. "Outsourcing State Violence: The National Defence Force, 'Stateness' and Regime Resilience in the Syrian War." *Mediterranean Politics* 24, no. 2 (2019): 157–80.

Leffler, Melvyn P. *For the Soul of Mankind: The United States, the Soviet Union, and the Cold War.* New York: Macmillan, 2007.

Lewis, Bernard. *A Middle East Mosaic: Fragments of Life, Letters, and History.* New York: Modern Library, 2001.

Lewis, David, John Heathershaw, and Nick Megoran. "Illiberal Peace? Authoritarian Modes of Conflict Management." *Cooperation and Conflict* 53, no. 4 (2018): 486–506.

Lewis, Martin W., and Kären E. Wigen, eds. *The Myth of Continents: A Critique of Metageography.* Berkeley: University of California Press, 1997.

Li, Xi, Deren Li, Huimin Xu, and Chuanqing Wu. "Intercalibration between DMSP/OLS and VIIRS Night-Time Light Images to Evaluate City Light Dynamics of Syria's Major Human Settlement during Syrian Civil War." *International Journal of Remote Sensing* 38, no. 21 (2017): 5934–51.

Link, Bruce G., and Jo Phelan. "Social Conditions as Fundamental Causes of Disease." *Journal of Health and Social Behavior* 35 [extra issue] (1995): 80–94.

Lister, Charles R. *The Islamic State: A Brief Introduction.* Washington, DC: Brookings Institution Press, 2015.

Louis, Wm Roger, and Avi Shlaim. *The 1967 Arab–Israeli War: Origins and Consequences.* New York: Cambridge University Press, 2012.

Loyd, Anthony. "Rebel Choking Libya's Oil Exports Steps up His Bid for Power; Libya." *The Times*, October 30, 2013.

Lu, Lingyu, and Cameron G. Thies. "War, Rivalry, and State Building in the Middle East." *Political Research Quarterly* 66, no. 2 (2013): 239–53.

Lujala, Päivi. "The Spoils of Nature: Armed Civil Conflict and Rebel Access to Natural Resources." *Journal of Peace Research* 47, no. 1 (2010): 15–28.

Lustick, Ian S. "The Absence of Middle Eastern Great Powers: Political 'Backwardness' in Historical Perspective." *International Organization* 51, no. 4 (1997): 653–83.

Lynch, Marc. *The Arab Uprising: The Unfinished Revolutions of the New Middle East.* New York: PublicAffairs, 2013.

Lyons, Kate. "Yemen's Cholera Outbreak Worst in History." *The Guardian*, October 12, 2017.

Mabon, Simon. "Kingdom in Crisis? The Arab Spring and Instability in Saudi Arabia." *Contemporary Security Policy* 33, no. 3 (2012): 530–53.

Mabon, Simon. *Saudi Arabia and Iran: Islam and Foreign Policy in the Middle East.* New York: Routledge, 2019.

Mabon, Simon. *Saudi Arabia and Iran: Power and Rivalry in the Middle East.* New York: I. B. Tauris, 2015.

Mabon, Simon, and Lucia Ardovini, eds. *Sectarianism in the Contemporary Middle East.* New York: Routledge, 2018.

Mac Ginty, Roger, and Oliver Richmond. "The Fallacy of Constructing Hybrid Political Orders: A Reappraisal of the Hybrid Turn in Peacebuilding." *International Peacekeeping* 23, no. 2 (2016): 219–39.

Maddy-Weitzman, Bruce. *The Berber Identity Movement and the Challenge to North African States.* Austin: University of Texas Press, 2011.

Mahmoud, Rustum, and Stephan Rosiny. "Opposition Visions for Preserving Syria's Ethnic-Sectarian Mosaic." *British Journal of Middle Eastern Studies* 45, no. 2 (2018): 231–50.

Malešević, Siniša. "The Organization of Military Violence in the 21st Century." *Organization* 24 (2017), 456–74.

Malešević, Siniša. "The Sociology of New Wars? Assessing the Causes and Objectives of Contemporary Violent Conflicts." *International Political Sociology* 2, no. 2 (2008): 97–112.

Malet, David. *Foreign Fighters: Transnational Identity in Civil Conflicts.* New York: Oxford University Press, 2013.

Malley, Robert. "The Unwanted Wars: Why the Middle East Is More Combustible Than Ever." *Foreign Affairs,* November 1, 2019.

Malmvig, Helle. "Power, Identity and Securitization in Middle East: Regional Order after the Arab Uprisings." *Mediterranean Politics* 19, no. 1 (2014): 145–8.

Malsin, Jared. "As the War Worsens, Rescue Workers Risk Their Lives on the Front Lines." *Time,* October 17, 2016.

Mampilly, Zachariah Cherian, Nelson Kasfir, and Ana Arjona, eds. *Rebel Governance in Civil War.* Cambridge: Cambridge University Press, 2015.

Mandelbaum, Michael. *The Rise and Fall of Peace on Earth.* New York: Oxford University Press, 2019.

Manela, Erez. *The Wilsonian Moment: Self-Determination and the International Origins of Anticolonial Nationalism.* New York: Oxford University Press, 2007.

Mann, Michael. *The Sources of Social Power, Volume 1: A History of Power from the Beginning to AD 1760.* New York: Cambridge University Press, 1986.

Mansfield, Edward D., and Jack Snyder. *Electing to Fight: Why Emerging Democracies Go to War.* Cambridge, Mass.: MIT Press, 2007.

Marcel, Valerie. *Oil Titans: National Oil Companies in the Middle East.* Washington, DC: Brookings Institution Press, 2006.

Marquand, Robert. "Amid BRICS's Rise and 'Arab Spring,' a New Global Order Forms." *Christian Science Monitor,* October 18, 2011.

Marshall, Shana. "Military Prestige, Defense-Industrial Production, and the Rise of Gulf Military Activism." In *Armies and Insurgencies in the Arab Spring*, edited by Holger Albrecht, Aurel Croissant, and Fred Lawson. Philadelphia: University of Pennsylvania Press, 2017.

Mazur, Kevin. "State Networks and Intra-Ethnic Group Variation in the 2011 Syrian Uprising." *Comparative Political Studies* 52, no. 7 (2018): 995–1027.

Mazurana, Dyan, Karen Jacobsen, and Lacey Andrews Gale. *Research Methods in Conflict Settings: A View from Below*. New York: Cambridge University Press, 2013.

Mazzetti, Mark, and Emily Hager. "Secret Desert Force Set up by Blackwater's Founder." *New York Times*, May 14, 2011.

McAlister, Melani. *Epic Encounters: Culture, Media, and US Interests in the Middle East since 1945*, Berkeley: University of California Press, 2005.

McBeth, Brian Stuart. *British Oil Policy, 1919–1939*. New York: Routledge, 2013.

McDonnell, Patrick, and Nabhi Bulos. "Trump Says He Wants to Keep Syria's Oil. Here's the Problem." *Los Angeles Times*, November 4, 2019.

McDowall, David. *Modern History of the Kurds*. New York: I. B. Tauris, 2003.

Mearsheimer, John J., and Stephen M. Walt. "Is It Love or the Lobby? Explaining America's Special Relationship with Israel." *Security Studies* 18, no. 1 (2009): 58–78.

Meierding, Emily. "Dismantling the Oil Wars Myth." *Security Studies* 25, no. 2 (2016): 258–88.

Mendelsohn, Barak. *The al-Qaeda Franchise: The Expansion of al-Qaeda and Its Consequences*. New York: Oxford University Press, 2015.

MercyCorp. "Libya's Shadow Economy." 2017.

Migdal, Joel S. *Strong Societies and Weak States: State–Society Relations and State Capabilities in the Third World*. Princeton, NJ: Princeton University Press, 1988.

Miller, Benjamin. *International and Regional Security: The Causes of War and Peace*. New York: Routledge, 2016.

Mills, Robin. *Under the Mountains: Kurdish Oil and Regional Politics*. Oxford: Oxford Institute for Energy Studies, 2016.

Milton, Patrick, Michael Axworthy, and Brendan Simms. *Towards a Westphalia for the Middle East*. New York: Oxford University Press, 2019.

Milton-Edwards, Beverley, and Alastair Crooke. "Elusive Ingredient: Hamas and the Peace Process." *Journal of Palestine Studies* 33, no. 4 (2004): 39–52.

Mishali-Ram, Meirav. "Foreign Fighters and Transnational Jihad in Syria." *Studies in Conflict and Terrorism* 41, no. 3 (2018): 169–90.

Mitchell, Timothy. *Carbon Democracy: Political Power in the Age of Oil*. London: Verso Books, 2011.

Mnookin, Robert H., Ehud Eiran, and Sreemati Mitter. "Barriers to Progress at the Negotiation Table: Internal Conflicts among Israelis and among Palestinians." *Nevada Law Journal* 6 (2005): 299–366.

Mohamed, Eid. *Arab Occidentalism: Images of America in the Middle East.* New York: I. B. Tauris, 2015.

Mombauer, Annika. *The Origins of the First World War: Diplomatic and Military Documents.* Manchester: Manchester University Press, 2013.

Morris, Benny. *1948: A History of the First Arab–Israeli War.* New Haven: Yale University Press, 2008.

Mueller, John E. "The Obsolescence of Major War." *Bulletin of Peace Proposals* 21, no. 3 (1990): 321–8.

Mueller, John E. *Remnants of War.* Ithaca, NY: Cornell University Press, 2004.

Mufti, Malik. *Sovereign Creations: Pan-Arabism and Political Order in Syria and Iraq.* Ithaca, NY: Cornell University Press, 1996.

Mumford, Andrew. *Proxy Warfare.* New York: John Wiley & Sons, 2013.

Mundy, Jacob. "Deconstructing Civil Wars: Beyond the New Wars Debate." *Security Dialogue* 42, no. 3 (2011): 279–95.

Murray, Christopher J. L., Gary King, Alan D. Lopez, Niels Tomijima, and Etienne G. Krug. "Armed Conflict as a Public Health Problem." *BMJ* 324, no. 7333 (2002): 346–9.

Murray, Rebecca. "Libya's Tebu: Living in the Margins." In *The Libyan Revolution and Its Aftermath*, edited by Peter Cole and Brian McQuinn, 303–20. New York: Oxford University Press, 2015.

Mylonas, Harris. *The Politics of Nation-Building: Making Co-Nationals, Refugees, and Minorities.* New York: Cambridge University Press, 2013.

Nagle, John. "Between Entrenchment, Reform and Transformation: Ethnicity and Lebanon's Consociational Democracy." *Democratization* 23, no. 7 (2016): 1144–61.

Nasr, Vali. *The Dispensable Nation: American Foreign Policy in Retreat.* New York: Anchor, 2014.

National Consortium for the Study of Terrorism and Responses to Terrorism. "Global Terrorism Database." College Park, Md.: START, University of Maryland, 2019.

Neep, Daniel. "War, State Formation, and Culture." *International Journal of Middle East Studies* 45, no. 4 (2013): 795–7.

Nelson, Chad E. "Revolution and War: Saddam's Decision to Invade Iran." *The Middle East Journal* 72, no. 2 (2018): 246–66.

Newman, Edward. "The 'New Wars' Debate: A Historical Perspective Is Needed." *Security Dialogue* 35, no. 2 (2004): 173–89.

North, Douglass C., John Joseph Wallis, and Barry R. Weingast. *Violence and Social Orders: A Conceptual Framework for Interpreting Recorded Human History.* New York: Cambridge University Press, 2009.

Nuruzzaman, Mohammed. "Qatar and the Arab Spring: Down the Foreign Policy Slope." *Contemporary Arab Affairs* 8, no. 2 (2015): 226–38.

Nyhan, Brendan, and Thomas Zeitzoff. "Conspiracy and Misperception Belief in the Middle East and North Africa." *Journal of Politics* 80, no. 4 (2018): 1400–4.

Ocakli, Feryaz, and Matthew Scotch. "Oil-Fueled Insurgencies: Lootable Wealth and Political Order in Syria, Iraq, and Nigeria." *Journal of Global Security Studies* 2, no. 1 (2017): 74–88.

Office of the UN Secretary-General. "Remarks by the Secretary-General to the Pledging Conference on Yemen." News release, April 3, 2018, *https://www. unog.ch/unog/website/news_media.nsf/(httpNewsByYear_en)/27F6CCAD7178F3E9C125 8264003311FA?OpenDocument.*

Okruhlik, Gwenn, and Patrick J. Conge. "The Politics of Border Disputes: On the Arabian Peninsula." *International Journal* 54, no. 2 (1999): 230–48.

Ollivant, Douglas, and Erica Gaston. "The Problem with the Narrative of 'Proxy War' in Iraq." *War on the Rocks*, May 31, 2019. *https://warontherocks.com/2019/05/ the-problem-with-the-narrative-of-proxy-war-in-iraq/.*

Omissi, David E. *Air Power and Colonial Control: The Royal Air Force, 1919–1939.* Manchester: Manchester University Press, 1990.

Oren, Michael B. *Six Days of War: June 1967 and the Making of the Modern Middle East.* New York: Presidio Press, 2017.

Østby, Gudrun, Ragnhild Nordås, and Jan Ketil Rød. "Regional Inequalities and Civil Conflict in Sub-Saharan Africa." *International Studies Quarterly* 53, no. 2 (2009): 301–24.

Ostovar, Afshon. "Sectarianism and Iranian Foreign Policy." In *Beyond Sunni and Shia*, edited by Frederic Wehrey, 87–114. New York: Oxford University Press, 2018.

Ostovar, Afshon. *Vanguard of the Imam: Religion, Politics, and Iran's Revolutionary Guards.* New York: Oxford University Press, 2016.

Owen, Roger. *The Rise and Fall of Arab Presidents for Life.* Cambridge, Mass.: Harvard University Press, 2014.

Owens, Mackubin T. "In Defense of Classical Geopolitics." *Orbis* 59, no. 4 (2015): 463–78.

Özsu, Umut, Florian Hoffmann, and Anne Orford. "The Ottoman Empire, the Origins of Extraterritoriality, and International Legal Theory." In *The Oxford Handbook of the Theory of International Law*, edited by Anne Orford and Florian Hoffmann. New York: Oxford University Press, 2016.

Palmer, Michael, Cuong Viet Nguyen, Sophie Mitra, Daniel Mont, and Nora Ellen Groce. "Long-Lasting Consequences of War on Disability." *Journal of Peace Research* 56, no. 6 (2019): 860–75.

Parker, Richard Bordeaux. *The Politics of Miscalculation in the Middle East.* Bloomington: Indiana University Press 1993.

Parkinson, Sarah E. "Seeing beyond the Spectacle: Research on and Adjacent to Violence" in *Political Science Research in the Middle East and North Africa: Methodological and Ethical Challenges*, edited by Janine A. Clark and Francesco Cavatorta. New York: Oxford University Press, 2018.

Parsons, Craig. *How to Map Arguments in Political Science*. New York: Oxford University Press, 2007.

Patel, David Siddharta. "Repartitioning the Sykes–Picot Middle East? Debunking Three Myths." In *Middle East Brief*: Brandeis University Crown Center, 2016.

Pearlman, Wendy. "Narratives of Fear in Syria." *Perspectives on Politics* 14, no. 1 (2016): 21–37.

Pearlman, Wendy. "Spoiling Inside and Out: Internal Political Contestation and the Middle East Peace Process." *International Security* 33, no. 3 (2009): 79–109.

Pearlman, Wendy, and Boaz Atzili. *Triadic Coercion: Israel's Targeting of States That Host Nonstate Actors*. New York: Columbia University Press, 2018.

Pedersen, Susan. "Getting out of Iraq – in 1932: The League of Nations and the Road to Normative Statehood." *American Historical Review* 115, no. 4 (2010): 975–1000.

Pedersen, Susan. "The Meaning of the Mandates System: An Argument." *Geschichte und Gesellschaft* 32, no. 4 (2006): 560–82.

Perliger, Arie, and Daniel Milton. "From Cradle to Grave: The Lifecycle of Foreign Fighters in Iraq and Syria." US Military Academy–Combating Terrorism Center West Point United States, 2016.

Peters, Joel. "The Camp David Summit: A Tale of Two Narratives." In *Routledge Handbook on the Israeli–Palestinian Conflict*, edited by Joel Peters and David Newman. New York: Routledge, 2013.

Pettersson, Thérése, and Kristine Eck. "Organized Violence, 1989–2017." *Journal of Peace Research* 55, no. 4 (2018): 535–47.

Phillips, Christopher. *The Battle for Syria: International Rivalry in the New Middle East*. New Haven: Yale University Press, 2016.

Phillips, Christopher. "Sectarianism and Conflict in Syria." *Third World Quarterly* 36, no. 2 (2015): 357–76.

Piccolino, Giulia. "Local Peacebuilding in a Victor's Peace: Why Local Peace Fails without National Reconciliation." *International Peacekeeping* 26, no. 3 (2019): 354–79.

Pinfari, Marco. *Nothing but Failure? The Arab League and the Gulf Cooperation Council as Mediators in Middle Eastern Conflicts*. Crisis States Research Centre, 2009.

Podeh, Elie. *Chances for Peace: Missed Opportunities in the Arab–Israeli Conflict*. Austin: University of Texas Press, 2015.

Podeh, Elie. "The Emergence of the Arab State System Reconsidered." *Diplomacy and Statecraft* 9, no. 3 (1998): 50–82.

Pollack, Kenneth M. *Arabs at War: Military Effectiveness, 1948–1991*. Lincoln: University of Nebraska Press, 2004.

Popovic, Milos. "Fragile Proxies: Explaining Rebel Defection against Their State Sponsors." *Terrorism and Political Violence* 29, no. 5 (2017): 922–42.

Posen, Barry R. "The Security Dilemma and Ethnic Conflict." *Survival* 35, no. 1 (1993): 27–47.

Price, Megan, Anita Gohdes, and Patrick Ball. "Documents of War: Understanding the Syrian Conflict." *Significance* 12, no. 2 (2015): 14–19.

Provence, Michael. *The Last Ottoman Generation and the Making of the Modern Middle East*. New York: Cambridge University Press, 2017.

Qadri, Firdausi, Taufiqul Islam, and John D. Clemens. "Cholera in Yemen: An Old Foe Rearing Its Ugly Head." *New England Journal of Medicine* 377 (2017): 2005–7.

Quinlivan, James T. "Coup-Proofing: Its Practice and Consequences in the Middle East." *International Security* 24, no. 2 (1999): 131–65.

Rahimi, Babak. "Iran's Declining Influence in Iraq." *Washington Quarterly* 35, no. 1 (2012): 25–40.

Ray, James Lee. "Does Democracy Cause Peace?" *Annual Review of Political Science* 1, no. 1 (1998): 27–46.

Razoux, Pierre. *The Iran–Iraq War*. Cambridge, Mass.: Harvard University Press, 2015.

Reuters. "How UAE Used US Mercenaries and a Cyber Super-Weapon to Spy on iPhones of Foes." *NBC News*, January 30, 2019. *https://www.nbcnews.com/tech/security/how-uae-used-u-s-mercenaries-cyber-super-weapon-spy-n964436*.

Revkin, Mara, and Ariel I. Ahram. "Exit, Voice, and Loyalty under the Islamic State." In *Adaptation Strategies of Islamist Movements*. Washington, DC: Project on Middle East Political Science, 2017. *http://pomeps.org/wp-content/uploads/2017/04/POMEPS_Studies_26_Adaptation_Draft2.pdf#page=27*.

Richmond, Oliver P. *Peace: A Very Short Introduction*. New York: Oxford University Press, 2014.

Ricotta, Jill. "The Arab Shi'a Nexus: Understanding Iran's Influence in the Arab World." *Washington Quarterly* 39, no. 2 (2016): 139–54.

Rieff, David. *A Bed for the Night: Humanitarianism in Crisis*. New York: Simon & Schuster, 2003.

Rittinger, Eric. "Arming the Other: American Small Wars, Local Proxies, and the Social Construction of the Principal–Agent Problem." *International Studies Quarterly* 61, no. 2 (2017): 396–409.

Roberts, Adam. "Lives and Statistics: Are 90% of War Victims Civilians?" *Survival* 52, no. 3 (2010): 115–36.

Roberts, Clayton. *Logic of Historical Explanation*. State College: Penn State Press, 2010.

Roberts, David. "Qatar and the Muslim Brotherhood: Pragmatism or Preference?" *Middle East Policy* 21, no. 3 (2014): 84–94.

Roberts, Les, Riyadh Lafta, Richard Garfield, Jamal Khudhairi, and Gilbert Burnham. "Mortality before and after the 2003 Invasion of Iraq: Cluster Sample Survey." *The Lancet*, no. 9448 (2004): 1857–64.

Robson, Laura. *States of Separation: Transfer, Partition, and the Making of the Modern Middle East*. Berkeley: University of California Press, 2017.

Romano, David. "Conducting Research in the Middle East's Conflict Zones." *PS: Political Science & Politics* 39, no. 3 (2006): 439–41.

Ronen, Yehudit. *Qaddafi's Libya in World Politics*. Boulder, Colo.: Lynne Rienner, 2008.

Rosenau, James N. *Distant Proximities: Dynamics beyond Globalization*. Princeton, NJ: Princeton University Press, 2003.

Ross, Michael L. "How Do Natural Resources Influence Civil War? Evidence from Thirteen Cases." *International Organization* 58, no. 1 (2004): 35–67.

Ross, Michael L. *The Oil Curse: How Petroleum Wealth Shapes the Development of Nations*. Princeton, NJ: Princeton University Press, 2012.

Roy, Kaushik. *The Indian Army in the Two World Wars*. Leiden: Brill, 2011.

Ryan, Caitlin. "Everyday Resilience as Resistance: Palestinian Women Practicing *Sumud*." *International Political Sociology* 9, no. 4 (2015): 299–315.

Said, Edward W. *Culture and Imperialism*. New York: Vintage, 2012.

Said, Edward W. *Orientalism*. New York: Vintage, 1979.

Salamey, Imad, and Rhys Payne. "Parliamentary Consociationalism in Lebanon: Equal Citizenry vs. Quotated Confessionalism." *Journal of Legislative Studies* 14, no. 4 (2008): 451–73.

Salehyan, Idean. "The Delegation of War to Rebel Organizations." *Journal of Conflict Resolution* 54, no. 3 (2010): 493–515.

Salem, Paul. "Framing Post-War Lebanon: Perspectives on the Constitution and the Structure of Power." *Mediterranean Politics* 3, no. 1 (1998): 13–26.

Salem, Paul, and Ross Harrison, eds. *Escaping the Conflict Trap: Toward Ending Civil Wars in the Middle East*. Washington, DC: Middle East Institute, 2019.

Salibi, Kamal S. "The Lebanese Identity." *Journal of Contemporary History* 6, no. 1 (1971): 76–86.

Salloukh, Bassel F., and Rex Brynen, eds. *Persistent Permeability? Regionalism, Localism, and Globalization in the Middle East*. New York: Routledge, 2017.

Samii, A. William. "The Nation and Its Minorities: Ethnicity, Unity, and State Policy in Iran." *Comparative Studies of South Asia, Africa and the Middle East* 20, nos. 1–2 (2000): 128–37.

San Akca, Belgin. "Supporting Non-State Armed Groups: A Resort to Illegality?" *Journal of Strategic Studies* 32, no. 4 (2009): 589–613.

Sanasarian, Eliz. *Religious Minorities in Iran*. New York: Cambridge University Press, 2000.

Saseen, Sandra M. "The Taif Accord and Lebanon's Struggle to Regain Its Sovereignty." *American University Journal of International Law & Policy* 6, no. 1 (1990): 57–75.

Sassoon, Joseph. *Saddam Hussein's Ba'th Party: Inside an Authoritarian Regime*. New York: Cambridge University Press, 2012.

Satia, Priya. "The Defense of Inhumanity: Air Control and the British Idea of Arabia." *American Historical Review* 111, no. 1 (2006): 16–51.

Sawani, Youssef M. "The February 17 Intifada in Libya: Disposing of the Regime and Issues of State-Building." In *Revolution, Revolt and Reform in North Africa*, edited by Ricardo Laremont. New York: Routledge, 2013.

Sayej, Caroleen Marji. *Patriotic Ayatollahs: Nationalism in Post-Saddam Iraq*. Ithaca, NY: Cornell University Press, 2018.

Sayigh, Yezid. *Armed Struggle and the Search for a State: The Palestinian National Movement, 1949–1993*. New York: Clarendon Press, 1997.

Sayigh, Yezid. "Inducing a Failed State in Palestine." *Survival* 49, no. 3 (2007): 7–39.

Sayigh, Yezid. "Redefining the Basics: Sovereignty and Security of the Palestinian State." *Journal of Palestine Studies* 24, no. 4 (1995): 5–19.

Sayigh, Yezid, and Avi Shlaim, eds. *The Cold War and the Middle East*. New York: Clarendon Press, 1997.

Schaller, Dominik J., and Jürgen Zimmerer, eds. *Late Ottoman Genocides: The Dissolution of the Ottoman Empire and Young Turkish Population and Extermination Policies*. New York: Routledge, 2013.

Schildkrout, Enid. "Ethnicity and Generational Differences among Urban Immigrants in Ghana." In *Urban Ethnicity*, edited by Abner Cohen. New York: Routledge, 1974.

Schulze, Kirsten E. "The 1948 War: The Battle over History." In *Routledge Handbook on the Israeli–Palestinian Conflict*, edited by Joel Peters. New York: Routledge, 2013.

Schwarz, Rolf. "Does War Make States? Rentierism and the Formation of States in the Middle East." *European Political Science Review* 3, no. 3 (2011): 419–43.

Schwedler, Jillian. "Spatial Dynamics of the Arab Uprisings." *PS: Political Science and Politics* 46, no. 2 (2013): 230–4.

Scobell, Andrew, and Alireza Nader. *China in the Middle East: The Wary Dragon*. Washington, DC: RAND Corporation, 2016.

Sela, Avraham. *The Decline of the Arab–Israeli Conflict: Middle East Politics and the Quest for Regional Order*. Albany, NY: SUNY Press, 2012.

Shaw, Stanford J. "The Ottoman Millet System: An Evaluation." In *Tolerance and Movements of Religious Dissent in Eastern Europe*, edited by Béla K. Király. New York: Columbia University Press, 1975.

Sheppard, David, and Heba Saleh. "Libyan Oil Chief Warns Renewed Fighting Threatens Production." *Financial Times*, April 11, 2019.

Sherry, Virginia. *Syria, the Silenced Kurds*. New York: Human Rights Watch, 1996. https://www.hrw.org/sites/default/files/reports/SYRIA96.pdf.

Shimko, Keith L. *The Iraq Wars and America's Military Revolution*. New York: Cambridge University Press, 2010.

Shlaim, Avi. "Britain and the Arab–Israeli War of 1948." *Journal of Palestine Studies* 16, no. 4 (1987): 50–76.

Sidaway, James Derrick. "Geopolitics, Geography, and 'Terrorism' in the Middle East." *Environment & Planning D: Society & Space* 12, no. 3 (1994): 357–72.

Siklawi, Rami. "The Dynamics of the Amal Movement in Lebanon 1975–90." *Arab Studies Quarterly* 34, no. 1 (2012): 4–26.

Singer, J. David. "The Level-of-Analysis Problem in International Relations." *World Politics* 14, no. 1 (1961): 77–92.

Sladden, James, Becca Wasser, Ben Connable, and Sarah Grand-Clement. *Russian Strategy in the Middle East.* Washington, DC: RAND Corporation, 2017.

Slater, Dan. "Violent Origins of Authoritarian Variation: Rebellion Type and Regime Type in Cold War Southeast Asia." *Government and Opposition* 55, no. 1 (2020): 21–40.

Sluglett, Peter. "An Improvement on Colonialism? The 'A' Mandates and Their Legacy in the Middle East." *International Affairs* 90, no. 2 (2014): 413–27.

Sluglett, Peter, and Andrew Payne. "The Cold War in the Middle East." In *International Relations of the Middle East*, fifth edition, edited by Louise Fawcett. New York: Oxford University Press, 2019.

Small Arms Survey. "Yemen Armed Violence Assessment." 2010, *http://www.smallarmssurvey.org/focus-projects/yemen-armed-violence-assessment.html*.

Smit, Wim A. "Military Technologies and Politics." In *The Oxford Handbook of Contextual Political Analysis*, edited by Charles Tilly and Robert E. Goodin. New York: Oxford University Press, 2009.

Smith, Benjamin B. *Hard Times in the Lands of Plenty: Oil Politics in Iran and Indonesia.* Ithaca, NY: Cornell University Press, 2007.

Smith, Simon C. *Ending Empire in the Middle East: Britain, the United States and Post-War Decolonization, 1945–1973.* New York: Routledge, 2013.

Smith, Steve. "The Increasing Insecurity of Security Studies: Conceptualizing Security in the Last Twenty Years." *Contemporary Security Policy* 20, no. 3 (1999): 72–101.

Smooha, Sammy. "Minority Status in an Ethnic Democracy: The Status of the Arab Minority in Israel." *Ethnic and Racial Studies* 13, no. 3 (1990): 389–413.

Smyth, Phillip. "The Battle for the Soul of Shi'ism." *MERIA Journal* 16, no. 3 (2012): 1–20.

Sørli, Mirjam E., Nils Petter Gleditsch, and Håvard Strand. "Why Is There So Much Conflict in the Middle East?" *Journal of Conflict Resolution* 49, no. 1 (2005): 141–65.

Spiegel, Steven L. *The Other Arab–Israeli Conflict: Making America's Middle East Policy, from Truman to Reagan.* Chicago: University of Chicago Press, 1986.

Spracklen, Karl. *Making the Moral Case for Social Sciences: Stemming the Tide.* New York: Springer, 2015.

Sprinzak, Ehud. "Extremism and Violence in Israel: The Crisis of Messianic Politics." *The Annals of the American Academy of Political and Social Science* 555, no. 1 (1998): 114–26.

Sriram, Chandra Lekha. "Beyond Transitional Justice: Peace, Governance, and Rule of Law." *International Studies Review* 19, no. 1 (2017): 53–69.

Stein, Ewan. "Beyond Arabism vs. Sovereignty: Relocating Ideas in the International Relations of the Middle East." *Review of International Studies* 38, no. 4 (2012): 881–905.

Stockholm International Peace Research Institute. *SIPRI Yearbook 2017*. New York: Oxford University Press, 2017.

Suganami, Hidemi. "Explaining War: Some Critical Observations." *International Relations* 16, no. 3 (2002): 307–26.

Suhrke, Astri, and Ingrid Samset. "What's in a Figure? Estimating Recurrence of Civil War." *International Peacekeeping* 14, no. 2 (2007): 195–203.

Suny, Ronald Grigor. *"They Can Live in the Desert but Nowhere Else": A History of the Armenian Genocide*. Princeton, NJ: Princeton University Press, 2017.

Swan, Jonathan, and Alayna Treene. "Trump to Iraqi PM: How About That Oil?" *Axios*, November 25, 2018. *https://www.axios.com/trump-to-iraqi-pm-how-about-that-oil-1a31cbfa-f20c-4767-8d18-d518ed9a6543.html*.

Tabaar, Mohammad Ayatollahi. "Factional Politics in the Iran–Iraq War." *Journal of Strategic Studies* 42, nos. 3–4 (2019): 480–506.

Tabaar, Mohammad Ayatollahi. "How Iranians Are Debating the Nuclear Deal." *Washington Post*, April 21, 2015.

Tabler, Andrew. "How Syria Came to This" *The Atlantic*, April 15, 2018. *https://www.theatlantic.com/international/archive/2018/04/syria-chemical-weapons/558065/*.

Talhamy, Yvette. "The Fatwas and the Nusayri/Alawis of Syria." *Middle Eastern Studies* 46, no. 2 (2010): 175–94.

Talmon, Stefan A. G. "Recognition of the Libyan National Transitional Council." *ASIL Insight* 15, no. 16 (2011).

Tamari, Salim. "Normalcy and Violence: The Yearning for the Ordinary in Discourse of the Palestinian–Israeli Conflict." *Journal of Palestine Studies* 42, no. 4 (2013): 48–60.

Tamari, Salim. *Year of the Locust: A Soldier's Diary and the Erasure of Palestine's Ottoman Past*. Berkeley: University of California Press, 2011.

Tamir, Yael. "A Strange Alliance: Isaiah Berlin and the Liberalism of the Fringes." *Ethical Theory & Moral Practice* 1, no. 2 (1998): 279–89.

Tankel, Stephen. *With Us and Against Us: How America's Partners Help and Hinder the War on Terror*. New York: Columbia University Press, 2018.

Tauber, Eliezer. *The Emergence of the Arab Movements*. New York: Routledge, 1993.

Taylor, William. *Military Responses to the Arab Uprisings and the Future of Civil–Military Relations in the Middle East: Analysis from Egypt, Tunisia, Libya, and Syria*. New York: Springer, 2014.

Telhami, Shibley. "Kenneth Waltz, Neorealism, and Foreign Policy." *Security Studies* 11, no. 3 (2002): 158–70.

Temby, Owen. "What Are Levels of Analysis and What Do They Contribute to

International Relations Theory?" *Cambridge Review of International Affairs* 28, no. 4 (2015): 721–42.

Tessler, Mark. *A History of the Israeli–Palestinian Conflict.* Bloomington: Indiana University Press, 2009.

Thayer, Bradley A. *Darwin and International Relations: On the Evolutionary Origins of War and Ethnic Conflict.* Lexington: University Press of Kentucky, 2009.

Thompson, Elizabeth F. *Justice Interrupted.* Cambridge, Mass.: Harvard University Press, 2013.

Tibi, Bassam. *Arab Nationalism: Between Islam and the Nation-State.* New York: St. Martin's Press, 1997.

Tibi, Bassam. *Conflict and War in the Middle East: From Interstate War to New Security.* New York: Springer, 1998.

Tilly, Charles. *Coercion, Capital, and European States, AD 990–1990.* Cambridge, Mass.: Basil Blackwell, 1990.

Tilly, Charles, and Robert E. Goodin. "It Depends." In *The Oxford Handbook of Contextual Political Analysis*, edited by Robert E. Goodin and Charles Tilly. New York: Oxford University Press 2006.

Tinti, Alessandro. "Contested Geographies of Kurdistan: Oil and Kurdish Self-Determination in Iraq." Sant'Anna Scuola Universitaria Superiore, Pisa, 2019.

Toft, Monica Duffy. "Ending Civil Wars." *International Security* 34, no. 4 (2010): 7–36.

Transfeld, Marekie, and Marie-Christine Heizne. "Understanding Peace Requirements in Yemen: Needs and Roles for Civil Soviet, Women, Youth, the Media." Center for Applied Research in Partnership with the Orient, 2019.

Tripp, Charles. "Theatres of Blood: Performative Violence in Iraq." *International Journal of Contemporary Iraqi Studies* 12, no. 2 (2018): 167–81.

Ulrichsen, Kristian Coates. *The First World War in the Middle East.* London: Hurst, 2014.

Ulrichsen, Kristian Coates. *Qatar and the Arab Spring.* New York: Oxford University Press, 2014.

Ulrichsen, Kristian Coates. "The Rationale and Implications of Qatar's Intervention in Libya." In *Political Rationale and International Consequences of the War in Libya*, edited by Dag Henriksen and Ann Karin Larsen, New York: Oxford University Press, 2016.

United Nations Development Programme. "Arab Human Development Report 2009." 2015.

United Nations Institute for Training and Research–Operational Satellite Applications Program. "Syrian Cities Damage Atlas." 2019.

United Nations Office for the Coordination of Humanitarian Affairs. "Largest Consolidated Humanitarian Appeal for Yemen to Provide a Lifeline to 13.1 Million People." 2018.

Valbjørn, Morten, and André Bank. "The New Arab Cold War: Rediscovering the Arab Dimension of Middle East Regional Politics." *Review of International Studies* 38, no. 1 (2012): 3–24.

van Dam, Nikolaos. "Middle Eastern Political Clichés: 'Takriti' and 'Sunni Rule' in Iraq; 'Alawi Rule' in Syria: A Critical Appraisal." *Orient* 21, no. 1 (1980): 42–57.

Van Evera, Stephen. *Causes of War: Power and the Roots of Conflict.* Ithaca, NY: Cornell University Press, 2013.

Vandewalle, Dirk J. *A History of Modern Libya.* New York: Cambridge University Press, 2012.

Violations Documentation Center in Syria. "Monthly Statistical Report on Casualties in Syria." April 2019. *https://vdc-sy.net/monthly-statistical-report-casu alties-syrian-april-2019/.*

Visser, Reidar. "Proto-Political Conceptions of Iraq in Late Ottoman Times." *International Journal of Contemporary Iraqi Studies* 3, no. 2 (2009): 143–54.

Vitalis, Robert. *America's Kingdom: Mythmaking on the Saudi Oil Frontier.* Stanford, Calif.: Stanford University Press, 2007.

Volgy, Thomas J., Paul Bezerra, Jacob Cramer, and J. Patrick Rhamey. "The Case for Comparative Regional Analysis in International Politics." *International Studies Review* 19, no. 3 (2017): 452–80.

Voller, Yaniv. "From Periphery to the Moderates: Israeli Identity and Foreign Policy in the Middle East." *Political Science Quarterly* 130, no. 3 (2015): 505–36.

Voller, Yaniv. "Kurdish Oil Politics in Iraq: Contested Sovereignty and Unilateralism." *Middle East Policy* 20, no. 1 (2013): 68–82.

Wallensteen, Peter. "The Origins of Contemporary Peace Research." In *Understanding Peace Research*, edited by Kristine Höglund and Magnus Öberg. New York: Taylor & Francis, 2011.

Wallensteen, Peter. *Quality Peace: Peacebuilding, Victory, and World Order.* New York: Oxford University Press, 2015.

Walter, Barbara F. "Does Conflict Beget Conflict? Explaining Recurring Civil War." *Journal of Peace Research* 41, no. 3 (2004): 371–88.

Waltz, Kenneth N. *Man, the State, and War: A Theoretical Analysis.* New York: Columbia University Press, 2001.

Watenpaugh, Keith David. *Bread from Stones: The Middle East and the Making of Modern Humanitarianism.* Berkeley: University of California Press, 2015.

Weber, Eugen. *Peasants into Frenchmen: The Modernization of Rural France, 1870-1914.* Stanford, Calif.: Stanford University Press, 1976.

Wedeen, Lisa. *Ambiguities of Domination: Politics, Rhetoric, and Symbols in Contemporary Syria.* Chicago: University of Chicago Press, 1999.

Wedeen, Lisa. *Peripheral Visions: Publics, Power, and Performance in Yemen.* Chicago: University of Chicago Press, 2008.

Wedgwood, Cicely Veronica. *The Thirty Years War.* New York: New York Review of Books, 2016 [1938].

Weeks, Jessica L. P. *Dictators at War and Peace*. Ithaca, NY: Cornell University Press, 2014.

Wehrey, Frederic. "The Authoritarian Resurgence: Saudi Arabia's Anxious Autocrats." *Journal of Democracy* 26, no. 2 (2015): 71–85.

Wehrey, Frederic. *The Forgotten Uprising in Eastern Saudi Arabia*. Washington, DC: Carnegie Endowment for International Peace, 2013.

Wehrey, Frederic. "A Minister, a General, & the Militias: Libya's Shifting Balance of Power." *New York Review of Books*, March 19, 2019.

Weidmann, Nils B. "A Closer Look at Reporting Bias in Conflict Event Data." *American Journal of Political Science* 60, no. 1 (2016): 206–18.

Weinberg, Leonard, Ami Pedahzur, and Sivan Hirsch-Hoefler. "The Challenges of Conceptualizing Terrorism." *Terrorism and Political Violence* 16, no. 4 (2004): 777–94.

Weinstein, Jeremy M. *Inside Rebellion: The Politics of Insurgent Violence*. New York: Cambridge University Press, 2006.

Weisgerber, Marcus. "US Defense Firms Eye Expansion into Saudi Arabia." *Defense One*, April 4, 2018. *https://www.defenseone.com/business/2018/04/us-defense-firms-eye-expansion-saudi-arabia/147182/*.

Weiss, Max. "The Historiography of Sectarianism in Lebanon." *History Compass* 7, no. 1 (2009): 141–54.

Weizman, Eyal. *Hollow Land: Israel's Architecture of Occupation*. New York: Verso, 2012.

Wheatcroft, Andrew. *The Enemy at the Gate: Habsburgs, Ottomans, and the Battle for Europe*. New York: Basic Books, 2009.

"White Helmets Are Terrorists, Can Choose Surrender or Death – Assad." *RT*, July 26, 2018. *https://www.rt.com/news/434368-white-helmets-surrender-death-assad/*.

Williams, Paul D. "The African Union's Peace Operations: A Comparative Analysis." *African Security* 2, nos. 2–3 (2009): 97–118.

Williams, Paul D. *War and Conflict in Africa*. Cambridge: Polity, 2016.

Williams, Paul D., with Alexander Bellamy. *Understanding Peacekeeping*. Third edition. Cambridge: Polity, 2021.

Wimmer, Andreas, Lars-Erik Cederman, and Brian Min. "Ethnic Politics and Armed Conflict: A Configurational Analysis of a New Global Data Set." *American Sociological Review* 74, no. 2 (2009): 316–37.

Wood, Elisabeth Jean. "The Ethical Challenges of Field Research in Conflict Zones." *Qualitative Sociology* 29, no. 3 (2006): 373–86.

Wright, Robin. "How the Curse of Sykes–Picot Still Haunts the Middle East." *The New Yorker*, April 30, 2016. *https://www.newyorker.com/news/news-desk/how-the-curse-of-sykes-picot-still-haunts-the-middle-east*.

Wu, Zhengyu. "Classical Geopolitics, Realism and the Balance of Power Theory." *Journal of Strategic Studies* 41, no. 6 (2018): 786–823.

Wyrtzen, Jonathan. "Colonial Legitimization–Legibility Linkages and the

Politics of Identity in Algeria and Morocco." *European Journal of Sociology* 58, no. 2 (2017): 205–35.

Wyrtzen, Jonathan. "Reimagining Political Space: Jihad, Empire, and the Interwar Making of the Modern Middle East and North Africa." UCLA African Studies Center, 2016.

Ya'ar, Ephraim. "Continuity and Change in Israeli Society: The Test of the Melting Pot." *Israel Studies* 10, no. 2 (2005): 91–128.

Yergin, Daniel. *The Prize: The Epic Quest for Oil, Money and Power.* New York: Simon & Schuster, 2011.

Yetiv, Steven A., and Katerina Oskarsson. *Challenged Hegemony: The United States, China, and Russia in the Persian Gulf.* Stanford, Calif.: Stanford University Press, 2018.

Yiftachel, Oren. *Ethnocracy: Land and Identity Politics in Israel/Palestine.* Philadelphia: University of Pennsylvania Press, 2006.

Zarif, Mohammad Javad. "Rid the World of Wahhabism." *New York Times,* September 14, 2016.

Zarqawi, Abu Musab. "February 2004 Coalition Provisional Authority English Translation of Terrorist Musab Al Zarqawi Letter Obtained by United States Government in Iraq." US Department of State, 2004.

Zenko, Micah. "Mercenaries Are the Silent Majority of Obama's Military." *Foreign Policy,* May 18, 2016. *https://foreignpolicy.com/2016/05/18/private-contractors-are-the-silent-majority-of-obamas-military-mercenaries-iraq-afghanistan/.*

Zimmerman, Katherine. "The Al Qaeda Network: A New Framework for Defining the Enemy." In *AEI Paper & Studies.* Washington, DC: The American Enterprise Institute, 2013.

Zisser, Eyal "Who's Afraid of Syrian Nationalism? National and State Identity in Syria." *Middle Eastern Studies* 42, no. 2 (2006): 179–98.

Zubaida, Sami. "Contested Nations: Iraq and the Assyrians." *Nations and Nationalism* 6, no. 3 (2000): 363–82.

Zunes, Stephen. "The United States: A Hegemon Challenged." In *The International Relations of the Contemporary Middle East,* edited by Tareq Y. Ismael and Jacqueline S. Ismael. New York: Routledge, 2013.

Zunes, Stephen. "The United States Middle East Policy: The Need for Alternatives." *Peace Research* 25, no. 3 (1993): 105–16.

Zureik, Elia. "Colonialism, Surveillance, and Population Control." In *Surveillance and Control in Israel/Palestine: Population, Territory and Power,* edited by Elia Zureik, David Lyon, and Yasmeen Abu-Laban. New York: Routledge, 2011.

Index